'This is an excellent book. It contributes significantly to our understanding of the telecommunications/internet boom and bust, and parts are ideal for teaching.'

– John Zysman, University of California, Berkeley, US

'This accomplished research monograph breaks new ground by looking at the relationship between internet entrepreneurship and public policy. The first part charts the development of the internet as the basis for a new global network economy, and the contribution to its success of government telecoms policy in the USA, while the second part examines in detail the rise; and underlying vulnerabilities – of internet entrepreneurship in Germany, examining in close detail the character of the policy relationship between the German federal government, the incumbent national telecommunications operator and the new internet ventures. It also offers a useful comparative European chapter looking at developments in France, the Netherlands and in particular Sweden. Analytically penetrating, detailed and thorough, the book shows how national institutions (such as German corporatism) and government policies for telecommunications and for national innovation have refracted the opportunities presented by global networks, causing internet businesses to develop along unique, national trajectories. Theoretically informed and grounded in careful empirical research, the book makes for compelling reading for anyone interested in public policies for the communications revolution and the new network economy.'

– Peter Humphreys, University of Manchester, UK

'The commercialization of the internet unleashed a massive wave of entrepreneurial activity around the world. In his excellent book *Internet Entrepreneurship in Europe* Niko Waesche explains the reasons for the relative lag that Europe, in general, and Germany in particular experienced in establishing firms in internet-related business areas. He presents a sophisticated analysis that recognizes that creating an entrepreneurial environment requires the creation and coordination of a wide spectrum of policies including, but not limited to telecommunications regulation, tax policies, and mechanisms for encouraging venture capital formation. This book is vital reading for all business persons and policymakers wishing to understand the reasons that Europe has had such a mixed record in creating new ventures capable to taking advantage of the internet to build entrepreneurial firms.'

– Martin Kenney, University of California, Davis, US

Internet Entrepreneurship in Europe

Internet Entrepreneurship in Europe

Venture Failure and the Timing
of Telecommunications Reform

Niko Marcel Waesche

*Principal, Communications Sector, Business Consulting
Services, IBM, Munich, Germany*

Edward Elgar
Cheltenham, UK • Northampton, MA, USA

Published by
Edward Elgar Publishing Limited
Glensanda House
Montpellier Parade
Cheltenham
Glos GL50 1UA
UK

Edward Elgar Publishing, Inc.
136 West Street
Suite 202
Northampton
Massachusetts 01060
USA

A catalogue record for this book
is available from the British Library

Library of Congress Cataloguing in Publication Data

Waesche, Niko Marcel, 1968-
    Internet entrepreneurship in Europe : venture failure and the timing of telecommunications reform / Niko Marcel Waesche.
    p. cm.
    Includes bibliographical references.
    1. Internet industry–Europe–. 2. Internet industry–United States. 3. Telecommunication policy–Europe. 4. Telecommunication policy–United States. 5. Entrepreneurship–Europe. 6. Entrepreneurship–United States. I. Title.

HD9696.8.E852 W34 2003
384.3'094–dc21

ISBN 1 84376 135 1 (cased)
                                       2002037927

Printed and bound in Great Britain by MPG Books Ltd, Bodmin, Cornwall

Contents

Figures   vii
Tables   viii
Acknowledgements   xi

1. Introduction: Uneven development and internet
    entrepreneurship in Europe   1

PART I   GLOBAL OPPORTUNITY

2. The global growth of the internet and the role of the
    United States   33

3. Unregulation and the death of distance   63

PART II   NATIONAL POLITICAL ECONOMY

4. Institutional reform and political compromise   95

5. Incumbent telecommunications operator strategy and
    internet access   133

6. Survey of internet entrepreneurship in Germany   174

7. Varieties of internet venture development in Europe: The
    Swedish case   191

8. Conclusion: The timing of policy reform and internet
    entrepreneurship in Europe   239

Appendix A: Procedure and results of the globalstartup
survey   254

Appendix B: Interviews   285

Appendix C: Selected financial figures for international
telecommunications operators   295

Appendix D: Internet advertising expenditures and the
number of internet users by country   299

Bibliography   302
Index   329

Figures

2.1	Revenue growth of SAP AG	37
2.2	Growth of internet host computers	52
2.3	Commercial versus eductional host computer growth	53
2.4	Active internet universe in a selection of countries	54
5.1	Debt of Deutsche Telekom	143
5.2	Net cashflow of Deutsche Telekom 1990 to 1998	144
6.1	The typical German internet start-up in Spring 1998	177
7.1	Country-specific top-level domain names	198
7.2	Internet cost and host density	201

Tables

1.1 Differences in network thinking and institutionalist views   16

2.1 International presence of independent internet ventures with US origins   50
2.2 Growth in venture capital investments   50

4.1 Investments by the tbg compared to total venture capital investments in technology in Germany   120

5.1 Comparison of selected internet access costs USA/Germany in 1998   142
5.2 Basic earnings per share (EPS) of selected telecommunications operators   145
5.3 Top six internet providers in 1997 and 1998   147
5.4 Percentage ISDN lines to main lines   147
5.5 Number of T-Online subscribers compared to total number of internet users   151

6.1 Forms of financing   179
6.2 Proportion of start-ups generating most of their sales from project work or product sales   180
6.3 Number of firms with given percentage of foreign sales   181

7.1 Macroeconomic indicators, end 1997   194
7.2 Internet and Minitel penetration in 1998   197
7.3 Estimated absolute number of secure web servers   197
7.4 Estimated internet advertising spending per internet user   199
7.5 The most and least expensive countries for consumer internet access   200
7.6 Hours spent online per month in 1999   202
7.7 Key dates of telecommunications IPOs and basic services competition   204
7.8 Number of new listings on Europe's growth exchanges   208
7.9 Early stage venture capital investments by amount of investment compared to total venture capital investments   210

7.10 Venture capital investments in technology 211
7.11 The largest independent web development companies 216
7.12 Prevalent structures of leading electronic commerce ventures 222
7.13 Internationalization of Swedish 'pure-play' electronic
     commerce start-ups 222
7.14 Most popular web properties in Autumn 1999 225
7.15 Examples of surviving, independent internet companies 227
7.16 Company headquarter locations in Bathwick Group
     e-League of top 100 European internet ventures 229

A.1 Breakdown of employees 261
A.2 Key characteristics of the original sample and the 30
    selected firms 261
A.3 Forms of financing 263
A.4 Financial strategies of different business areas 263
A.5 Business areas and employment 264
A.6 The largest average employers 264
A.7 The smallest average employers 264
A.8 Frequencies of software and service start-ups by business
    area 265
A.9 Business areas and proportion of international activity 266
A.10 Expected turnover and current employee growth 266
A.11 Start-up capital required by selected internet firms 267
A.12 Mean start-up capital required and months to break-even 267
A.13 Mean distribution costs 267
A.14 Geographic distribution of sales 268
A.15 Number of firms with given percentage of foreign sales 268
A.16 Importance of different international markets 269
A.17 Break-up of revenue sources from project work or
     products 269
A.18 Proportion of start-ups generating most of their sales from
     project work or product sales 269
A.19 Percentage current working capacity 270
A.20 Number of active founding managers 270
A.21 When did managing directors first encounter commercial
     value-added networks? 271
A.22 Types of university or vocational college courses completed
     by founding managers 271
A.23 Other career experiences listed by managing founders 271
A.24 Number of entries from selected firms, which recommended
     public funding 272
A.25 Recommended public funding programmes 272

A.26 Number of affirmative responses to the question whether
      the given issue affects the firm today   272
A.27 Demand for international laws and controls regulating the
      internet   273
A.28 Percentage of affirmative answers on questions regarding
      growth objective and financing   273
A.29 Break-up of revenue sources by client firm type   274
A.30 Percentage of affirmative answers on questions regarding
      partnerships   274
A.31 Existing strategic alliances with major corporations   274
A.32 Likelihood of selecting a given partnership   275
A.33 Frequency of firms with given postal code   276
A.34 Software start-ups   277
A.35 Portal sites and electronic commerce start-ups   280
A.36 Other start-ups   283

C.1   Selected financial figures for international
      telecommunications companies   296
C.2   Market capitalization of selected firms   298
C.3   Market capitalization as multiples of net revenues, and
      market capitalization growth   298

D.1   Internet advertising expenditures and users   300

Acknowledgements

Many, many people have helped me with this book, some were perhaps not even aware of this fact. I am indebted to them all. Here, I can only mention those who were involved to a great degree, even so, I have probably forgotten some.

My PhD supervisor Dr Razeen Sally of course put his mark on this effort and has always been very encouraging. Personally, his work has influenced me because it always returns to the fundamentals, whether it is in international political economy research or the history of political thought. I also want to thank past teachers who have trained me in business history and economic history, Professor Dr Toni Pierenkemper and Dr Ralf Banken, both now at Universität zu Köln, as well as Professor Volker Berghahn, now at Columbia University.

I would be very selfish indeed if I forgot to mention those employers who, by extending me part-time or project-based work during the 'New Economy', helped me finance this study. They included Matthias Graf von Krockow, Wulf Matthias, Jörg Birkelbach, Jerome H. Mol, Ives Brant, Mirko Lorenz, Eamonn Wilmott, Michael Mathews, Oliver Samwer and the rest of the Alando.de family, Pierre Morin and Yves Sisteron.

Without Jochen Rieker at *Manager Magazin* there would not have been any quantitative survey. He was of invaluable help just by believing in this project. All of the entrepreneurs and policy-makers who granted me interviews are also thanked here for their time, their valuable insight and their trust.

The book is dedicated to my father, Horst Waesche, who throughout the years did not cease to encourage me to complete it. He was never able to see the final product. He passed away unexpectedly on 13 March 2002, leaving Gisela, Josefina, Julinka, Noah and me with a void nobody can replace.

Of course, none of these people bear any responsibility for the flaws in this study. This work reflects only the personal views of the author and can in no way be seen as a statement by current or previous employers of the author.

1. Introduction: Uneven development and internet entrepreneurship in Europe

Entrepreneurship has awoken in Germany. Everywhere across the country, experienced business people, investment as well as legal professionals, are quitting their secure jobs and are starting internet ventures . . . In terms of internet entrepreneurship, Germany is, as yet, still a developing country in comparison to the United States. In America, internet companies, which started in a similarly small way, have already created 2.5 million new, attractive jobs. These companies already today generate 6 per cent of the total GDP of the United States. Germany has only begun to move down this path. But one thing is certain already now: the new entrepreneurial scene is the best thing that has happened in German business for a long time.[1]

Sweden is an ideal starting place for internet entrepreneurs. Here, we develop internet services before moving out to other countries. We have a small population of very advanced internet users. We have to convince a network of only about 30 critical, but opinion-leading journalists of our service. We have to persuade a small, tightly integrated network of private investors. Once we succeed at this, all doors are open. A well-oiled start-up engine is in operation here (Interview, Ahlvarsson, 18 October 1999).

This study explains why Europe, despite initiating a tremendous amount of change in the 1990s, failed to produce independent internet ventures of note. No independent newcomers survived which were able to seriously and in a sustained way challenge American internet ventures or established European telecommunications and media companies. Given the history of uneven development in information technology (IT), this was not surprising. Previous cycles of innovation in IT, which resulted in the development of markets such as the personal computer or data networking, were led or redefined by US ventures such as Apple Computer or Cisco. One prominent reason for the global leadership of the United States in IT innovation was the Silicon Valley region, with its 'entrepreneurial ecosystem' of entrepreneurs, venture capitalists and legal experts (Kenney, 2001, 13).

Yet, this time around, things were supposed to have been different for three reasons. Firstly, internet technology was initially not an exclusive Silicon Valley domain. Before its commercialization, it was an academic research network which spanned the globe. Its infrastructure costs were shared, making its use distance-insensitive. The World Wide Web standards, an important prerequisite for the commercialization of the internet, were not created in the United States, but by a British researcher in a Swiss particle physics facility (Berners-Lee, 1999). The international nature of the internet continued to be of importance also after its commercialization. The internet and other global data networks potentially enabled an increase in the international trade of services, giving rise to a 'weightless economy' (Welfens and Jungmittag, 2002, 59; for the term see Quah, 1997).

Secondly, internet innovations were not specific to the IT sector. The internet was a horizontal technology which could be adopted in a diverse set of economic sectors. By linking customers to services and suppliers to manufacturers in 'real time', seamless 'business webs' could be formed which had the potential to increase economic productivity by reducing transaction and inventory costs.[2] Service industries such as telecommunications and media would be affected strongly by the internet, confirming theories about the convergence of IT, telecommunications and media (Bane et al., 1998).

Finally, in terms of know-how and legal framework, and due to its architecture, barriers to entry for internet services initially were low (see Lessig, 2001). The internet was run with intellectual property, for example UNIX and the TCP/IP standard, which were either 'open' or easily accessible. The internet allowed the global sharing of program codes, enabling the spread of Linux and 'open source' software development, which bypassed software copyrights (Raymond, 1999; Lessig, 2001, 49–72). The architecture of the internet was designed as an 'end-to-end' system, or a 'stupid network', which allowed the addition of innovative applications at its periphery without the requirement of changing the way the network was run (Isenberg, 1997). In fact, every personal computer connected to the internet could host an internet service, a concept that was further developed in so-called P2P technologies (Lessig, 2001, 134–8). The international nature of the internet, horizontal applicability of the technology to numerous economic sectors and the low barriers to entry implied that, this time around, the innovation opportunity was global.

The Achilles' heel of global internet development was a national factor. This factor was telecommunications liberalization and its impact on the local telephone line, the local loop. In the early days of internet commercialization, small and medium-sized enterprises (SMEs) as well as consumers accessed the internet through the local phone line. Due to the dependence of internet access on the local loop, Welfens and Jungmittag correctly called internet access an 'indirectly regulated market' (2002, 93, 94). While multinational enterprises and financial services firms had long before the commercialization of the internet used their company-only data networks to realize lower transaction costs or to control supply chains, the particular 'disruptive' opportunity of the internet consisted in the integration of SMEs and consumers into these 'business webs'.[3] The local loop was an Achilles' heel because it was a crucial aspect of internet development, yet was not a factor which had previously been recognized as a national innovation advantage prior to the commercialization of the internet. The highly advantageous national environment in the United States surrounding the local loop and its predominantly flat-rate pricing was the inadvertent result of a specific historic trajectory of telecommunications liberalization. The fixed-line local loop will remain crucial in the future as well, due to its significance for the development of broadband services.

While the role of the local loop specifically for internet development was not known to policy-makers and regulators in the first half of the 1990s, policy experts and regulators in the US and Europe were very well aware of its importance as a point of control by the former telecommunications monopolist. The telecommunications landscape in Europe was being thoroughly reformed at the time and control of the local loop was a deeply debated issue. Infrastructure competition achieved through alternative, competing networks, such as wireless local loop (WLL) or cable TV, was regarded as advantageous. Yet, the development of alternative infrastructures would take time. An enforced opening of the local loop ('unbundling') was seen as an alternative. In the first half of the 1990s, therefore, decisions regarding telecommunications liberalization and local access were made in Europe which in some countries were detrimental and in other countries advantageous for internet entrepreneurship.

The entrepreneurs of Silicon Valley did not suffer from a 'not invented here' syndrome. The 'entrepreneurial ecosystem' managed to respond swiftly to the internet opportunity. Strong internet ventures were created in the Northern Californian region which used the international reach of the internet to their advantage and achieved global significance in a very short amount of time. Yet, Silicon Valley entrepreneurs were not the only ones which reacted to the unique global opportunity presented by the commercialization of the internet.

Internet entrepreneurship surged in Europe as well. IT growth picked up in Europe, with rates beginning to match those of the United States.[4] In Germany, the new Frankfurt stock exchange, where numerous internet ventures were listed, seemed to symbolize the birth of a new entrepreneurial culture. From the end of 1999 to the turn of the century, growth rates on the Neuer Markt were identical to those on NASDAQ. In the two months prior to the financial downturn from March 2000, the Neuer Markt had actually grown twice as fast as the booming NASDAQ.[5] By the end of 2000,

344 IT, media and telecommunications companies, including 67 internet ventures, had been listed on the new German technology exchange.[6] While it was surprising that entrepreneurship had apparently reawakened in Germany, it was noteworthy that this reawakening had occurred in telecommunications, media and IT and not in traditional German areas of leadership such as the engineering-based industries. Because of the discrepancy between the success of the Frankfurt technology stock exchange and the historic, disappointing record in IT entrepreneurship, Germany represented the most astounding turnaround story in Europe (see Lehrer, 2000). In other countries, however, entrepreneurship surged as well; 4202 seed and start-up companies received venture capital financing in Europe during the course of 1999. Of these, only 703 ventures were in Germany.[7]

The objective of this research is to explore the hypothesis of a global opportunity for technology innovation delivered via the internet and to explain Europe's entrepreneurial response.[8] During the 1990s, this promise of global opportunity was contained in a popular vision of a so-called 'New Economy' or a 'Digital Revolution', promoted with missionary fervour by technologists and writers close to technological developments. It was adopted by entrepreneurs and investors. Aspects of this vision were further developed by critical scholarship, especially by sociologists who studied technological change as part of a globalization research agenda. The vision of a New Economy, however, conflicted with contemporary research on innovation and technological development in economics and the political sciences. This research adopted an institutionalist approach and emphasized the existence of distinct local structures determining innovation capacity. Yet, for this very reason, institutionalist scholarship was sceptical *vis-à-vis* global innovation opportunities which seemed to travel rapidly across borders and eradicated differences among distinct institutional landscapes. The approach taken with this study was to understand the validity of these conflicting visions of technological change by studying actual development in a specific setting. Europe, and especially Germany, seemingly was home to a strong entrepreneurial turnaround in response to global technological opportunity. The apparent entrepreneurial turnaround refers to the number of new ventures appearing in Germany targeting the global internet opportunity. Their appearance in a country marked in previous years by a characteristic lack of entrepreneurial dynamism seemed to validate the popular vision of the New Economy.

In this introductory chapter, the most important themes of this volume will be presented and placed in a theoretical framework. Firstly, the theme of a global innovation opportunity associated with the spread of international data networks will be explored. Practitioners closely involved with IT developments as well as scholars, mostly with a sociology background, have extensively described the nature of this New Economy innovation opportunity. The second theme to be discussed is the role of national institutions in promoting or constraining innovation. The central research framework will then be described; based on a novel concept called 'refraction'. Refraction is the distorting effect national institutions have on a global innovation opportunity. The refraction framework is used here as an analytical tool to study the role of national institutions *vis-à-vis* global shift in the setting of a particular domestic economy, in this case Germany. The main domestic agents and policy arenas in Germany influencing internet development as well as the empirical basis of the study will then be presented. Before moving to the closing comments of this Introduction, the reasons for selecting Germany as the main focus for the study are reviewed. While Germany represented a particularly strong case of an apparent turnaround in response to the global internet opportunity, many of the issues applying to Germany also related to other European countries. In this study, the argument developed in the case of Germany is extended to other countries in Europe (Chapter 7).

GLOBAL OPPORTUNITY AND THE NEW ECONOMY

A body of work appeared in the 1990s which sought to explain a contemporary, far-reaching and universal shift in the global economy related to digitization and convergence. Convergence of information technology, media and telecommunications was viewed as only the beginning; eventually, convergence would encompass all industries. In some of the literature, the internet manifested this structural shift. Elsewhere, in texts written before the commercialization of the internet, the main concepts were none the less already apparent. These writings became influential guides for contemporary commentators seeking to explain the explosive growth of the internet and the strong entrepreneurial response. It is important to emphasize that this body of work pre-dated the most extreme manifestation of the stock market bubble. It was very different from money-making guides for internet business or airport bestsellers containing internet investment advice – although it probably inadvertently helped contribute to the ideas contained in these texts.

Instead of using the emotionally charged terms 'New Economy' or 'Digital Revolution', the body of work under examination is referred to here as 'network thinking'. Network thinkers were contemporary observers who had privileged access to new developments in IT. Examples of these so-called 'evangelists' were the populist futurist George Gilder (1989, 2000), the technology analyst, activist and investor Esther Dyson (1998) or the writer and *Wired* magazine editor Kevin Kelly (1994, 1998). It is precarious to place very diverse thinkers such as these together in a group, but beginning from a premise of technological change, all predicted a strong social and economic global shift. Technology was seen almost entirely as a positive, liberating force, ushering in new actors, new rules and the demise of the dinosaurs. The differentiating characteristics of the internet discussed at the beginning of this Introduction – the global diffusion of the internet, its horizontal applicability to numerous industries and the low barriers of entry – were recognized and described by these writers, each in their own style and with different emphases.

At the same time as practitioners were promoting network thinking, academics began to concern themselves with similar themes. This body of literature did not at first emerge from within those areas of scholarship which traditionally analysed innovation capacity. Much of this literature was associated with new directions in sociology, such as urban sociology (Sassen, 1996; Castells and Hall, 1994), post-structural economics (Lash and Urry, 1994; Harvey, 1990) or the analysis of the information age (Castells, 1996). As part of a detailed exploration of globalization as a contemporary social shift, sociologists early on addressed the significance of the spread of global data networks in financial services and among industrial multinational enterprises (MNEs). Here, the discussion of social effects in this body of work will remain in the background while emphasis is placed on technology and innovation aspects. Nevertheless, the theme of globalization was such a crucial element to contemporary sociological research that it had to be addressed in this study.

But not only sociologists, also researchers in business strategy concerned themselves with the New Economy. Business strategists sought to explain the rapid growth of new internet ventures. In the words of Cusumano and Yoffie:

> For companies competing in the new information economy, the internet is forcing managers and employees to experiment, invest, plan and change their ideas constantly *while* they are trying to build complex new products and technologies. The internet also requires companies to face the reality that competitive advantage can appear and disappear overnight . . . It was the electronic distribution capability of the internet that allowed Netscape to burst onto the scene in 1994 and, in only a few months, emerge as one of the most serious threats Microsoft had ever faced. This sudden rise to prominence of new companies can and will happen again. (1998, 5).

Cusumano and Yoffie emphasized that it took Netscape only three years to reach annual sales of more than half a billion US$, whereas the software giant Microsoft reached comparable revenues in 14 years (1998, 10). The basis of this rapid growth was what economists labelled 'network effects'. Network effects appear when the value of a good increases with the number of users. In this environment, users themselves recommend their good to others, leading to rapid distribution. But advantages of network externalities benefiting a single company need not be sustainable; competing companies could also benefit from these effects. Danny Tyson Quah stated this in the following way: 'Superstar successes are in turn replaced, and easily' (1998). And in attempting to benefit from network effects, companies sometimes begin to compete in ways that erode their own established competitive advantages and can lower their profitability (Porter, 2001).

Finally, economists discussed a surprising rise in US productivity and its possible connection to the diffusion of IT in the US economy, leading to lower transaction costs and lower inventory costs (DeLong, 2001; Litan and Rivlin, 2001). While contributing to the understanding of the potentially far-reaching effects of a commercialized and widely available internet, neither business strategists nor economists dwelled on the issue of the global diffusion of the network.

Network thinkers such as Esther Dyson went a step further in describing the consequences of a networked world: 'Analysts and investors wonder who will replace Microsoft the way Microsoft replaced IBM as the information industry's standard. The answer is that no one will: The model of an industry revolving around a central leader will give way to a new decentralised market' (1998, 20). Kevin Kelly stated similar thoughts differently: 'The world of the made will soon be like the world of the born: Autonomous, adaptable and creative, but consequently, out of control' (1994, 4). The sociologist Manuel Castells wrote: 'The information technology paradigm does not evolve towards its closure as a system, but towards its openness as a multi-edged network' (1996, 65). The vision was one of a fluid world marked by constant change which was hazardous to those established players who would not adjust. This vision did not accept national borders, it was by default global.

This volatile environment was deemed to lead to two possible structural consequences. First, the literature seems to suggest that a shift away from established innovation clusters such as Silicon Valley was in progress. Stated differently, a 'Silicon Valleyisation' of the world was occurring. '[The internet is] a powerful tool for integrating local economies into the global economy and for establishing their presence in the world', wrote Dyson (1998, 17). Yet, the new centres of innovation need not be greenfield projects, they could also be old cities which assumed new roles in the world economy. Castells contended that 'the largest, old metropolitan areas of the industrialized world are the main centres of innovation and production in innovation technology outside the United States' (1996, 57). Regarding the new role of global cities, disagreement existed whether they represented forces of decentralization or centralization. For example, a further influential urban sociologist, Saskia Sassen, showed that the global digital era brought with it concentration in power (2000, 104–12). One key theme of most of this work, however, was that the new regions or cities were perceived as having their own dynamics independent of the specific country they happen to be in. Sassen spoke of 'a partial denationalising of national territory' (Sassen, 1996, xii). She emphasized the partial nature of this process because: 'The state itself has been a key agent in the implementation of global processes, and it has emerged quite altered by this participation' (1996, 29).

A second consequence of technological change was perceived to be the transfer of innovation capacity away from the industrial laboratories of large enterprises and research universities, to new entities. These were new ventures but were also enterprising individuals or newly organized, decentralized large corporations (Castells, 1996, 156). New ventures did not need to stay small; they could leverage the network to become large very fast.[9] International data networks were seen as enablers of new global business processes involving new types of specialized business entities. Related to this were trends towards outsourcing in industry, the increasing value of services as well as an emphasis on cultural production. Castells stated that the economic operating unit in the new global environment was the network itself and ceased to be the firm. The name he assigned to the new organizational form was the 'network enterprise' (1996, 171).

Thus, while some work focused on new geographies, such as the appearance of new regions and cities, other work highlighted the emergence of new organizational units such as new ventures. In some of the writings discussed here, these two possible consequences were described as part of a general trend. New geographic regions appeared outside of the established clusters, and they were populated by new ventures. What was more interesting, however, were differences implied by these two perspectives. While it was still very much possible to speak about the importance of unique local determinants specific to the new regions, work that focused on new organizational units could almost completely ignore specific local factors. Kelly stated: 'People will inhabit places, but increasingly the economy inhabits a space' (1998, 95). Castells, citing a fellow sociologist, David Harvey, referred instead to a process of 'time-space compression' (Castells, 1996, 434–7; Harvey, 1990). The second organizational perspective thus represented a radicalization of thinking. It will be argued here that, while this perspective was – especially with hindsight – easily susceptible to refutation due to its naivety, it was also the most consequent description of contemporary technological shift available at that time. It provided one explanation of how technological opportunity was able to rapidly move across borders by allowing new ventures to integrate themselves in consumer networks and contribute to new types of seamless and global networked business processes.

On the whole, research within sociology was more critical of technological development and emphasized that while specific regions or new types of enterprises could potentially have immense success, others could face further marginalization (Sassen, 2000, 33–57). These concerns developed into a debate about the 'digital divide'. In contrast, network thinkers were optimistic, believing that technology could reduce global inequality on the whole and provide unique leapfrogging opportunities for new actors. To understand this stance better, it is important to emphasize that what is called network thinking here contained elements of both equality-oriented social democratic thinking as well as elitist, libertarian economic ideas. The New Economy and the Digital Revolution were American inventions, with strong influences from 1960s counterculture and not without jingoistic tendencies as evident in George Gilder's book *Microcosm* (1989, 344, 346). This set of ideas has early on been masterfully analysed and critiqued in terms of a 'Californian Ideology' (Barbrook and Cameron, 1995).[10] Cultural critic Mark Dery, moreover, attacked escapist, dangerous tendencies of the 'cyber-hippe worldview' (1996, 21–72). In a sequel to his original book Escape Velocity, he wrote:

> In the silicon social Darwinism ostensibly popular with the 33-year old, 81-k earning male who is *Wired*'s typical reader, the evolutionary race goes to the wunderkind small player enshrined in computer industry myth . . . while the unskilled and deskilled masses are stampeded in the mad rush to the millennium (Dery, 1999, 231).

It is a valuable exercise to point out the hidden currents in network thinking, the unstated text in between the lines. This was part of the agenda. Consciously or unconsciously, network thinking was functionally designed for the evangelical purpose to spread ideas of self-fulfilment in an allegedly new network era. This self-fulfilment itself, however, was not escapist in the sense of a social or economic exit. It was linked to creativity and technological innovation in business. In fact, the Digital Revolution was spread over the internet, through bestsellers and periodicals such as *Wired* magazine, and prepared the ground for the 'investment stories' preached by internet entrepreneurs and investment bankers. This effect was not limited to the United States – network thinking was adopted as a credo for innovation by entrepreneurs all over the world (Waesche, 1999a; Waesche, forthcoming). Yet, network thinking was also a set of ideas born directly out of the technological experience of the 1990s. It was an inseparable aspect of the global entrepreneurial opportunity, its 'ideological framework.' The next section will discuss why the central tenants of network thinking, the unique aspects pertaining to network technologies, have to be taken seriously by scholarship.

Network thinking ended at the beginning of the 2000s when the optimism surrounding the internet opportunity proved more and more difficult to uphold. This was due both to the financial downturn as well as to changes in the internet opportunity itself: rising barriers to entry in terms of international leapfrogging, horizontal applicability, the internet's design and legal framework. In his elegy on internet innovation, Lessig wrote:

> The story I want to tell is not about the death of innovation generally; it is about the relocation of innovation from the diverse, decentralized internet back to the institutions that policed innovation before. The story is about the bureaucratisation and capture of the innovation process – relocating it back to where it was – as a response to the structures originally enabled by the internet itself (2001, 140, 141).

The innovation opportunity associated with the internet apparently was finite not in terms of geography, but in terms of time.

STRUCTURES AND AGENTS: INSTITUTIONALIST THEORY

In the previous section, recently occurring technological changes were presented as part of a global structural shift, the so-called New Economy. The structural view of the New Economy suggested that global shift provided new opportunities for a diverse group of new entities such as regional clusters and enterprises. The role of national governments in being able to implement change was seen as severely compromised. Even the new entities favoured by global shift were merely participants; they were not agents driving the change process. Technological change was seen as a powerful, exogenous force.

In this sense, network thinking shared similarities with neo-Marxist theory, which viewed structural change as a constant, driven by very generalized forces such as the accumulation of capital (Wallerstein, 1979, 272; Cox, 1987). Underlying these approaches was an implicit belief in linear progress. A diversity of outcomes caused by the existence of individual agent choice was purposely excluded from the model. As Geoffrey Hodgson pointed out, however, the neo-Marxist approach could account for structural change but not for the simultaneous existence of different types of capitalism; in Hodgson's words, 'impurities' within capitalism (1996, 416–9).

This leads to a further explanation which could be used to explain internet development internationally, which meshes agent-induced change into a structural framework. Here, actors such as national governments were both contributors to structural shifts as well as captured within structures. Outcomes were not fixed. Therefore, change opportunities existed, but they were scattered and refracted. To emphasize the less deterministic and less universal use of the structure concept (compared to Marxist work), the term 'institution' is used. The term has been defined as: 'The rules of the game in a society or, more formally, the humanly devised constraints that shape human interaction' (North, 1990, 3).

As is evident from this definition, there is little distinction in institutionalist research between the realm of politics and economics. In fact, it is this blurring of distinctions which characterized 'new' political economy (Gamble, 1995) as well as 'new' economic history (Wischermann, 1993). Economics itself became broader and had, in the words of Mancur Olson, 'expand[ed] into the suburbs ' (Olson and Kähkönen, 2000, 1). According to Peter Hall, a political economist, institutions play a role in: 'the definition and articulation of interests, the dissemination of ideas, the construction of the market behaviour and the determination of policy' (1986, 5). In this view, the market is itself an institution, as not only Hall but also the economist Geoffrey Hodgson and the economic historian Douglass C. North would point out (Hall, 1986, 12; Ash et al., 1994, 9; Wischermann, 1993, 250). Especially, financial markets as institutions seem to play a critical role in fusing the political and the economic (Zysman, 1983, 7, 8). This approach to the role of institutions can be summarized with the phrase 'institutions do matter' and can be found in the disciplines of economics, economic history and political economy.

Broadly, two approaches of institutionalism can be differentiated. Historical institutionalism explains differences in structures through historic development (North, 1990). The key concept here is that present structures were influenced by historic development. Institutions thus follow certain trajectories; this concept is called 'path dependence' (Hill and Deeds, 1996, 435–7). Related to this, institutions tend to be 'sticky'; they define actor relationships most of the time and can preserve these over longer terms. This flavour of institutionalist scholarship is popular with scholars describing technological change because it allows insight into the origins of sustainable innovative capacity. The second approach, rational choice institutionalism, focuses on structures and information asymmetries at a specific period in time (Milner, 1997; see also Garrett and Lange, 1996, 49). Game theory is used as an analytical device to discuss rational choices among different policy options. This is only a rough categorization; institutionalist theory has been applied to a wide variety of research agendas.

The similarities of the institutionalist approaches found in these disciplines, in emphasizing the role of agents and their relationship to institutional structures, are more important for this study than their differences (discussed in Steinmo et al., 1992, 8).

In discussing actual cases, however, the reconciliation between agent choice and institutional structure is not straightforward in instituionalist scholarship. As Helen Milner has pointed out, 'new institutionalism' has often tended to emphasize institutional constraints over actor-induced innovation of institutional structures (1997, 14–17). Yet, the theory allows for the possibility of significant agent-induced structural change. In the classic object of study for technological innovation, the Industrial Revolution, a radical sea change occurred, resulting in institutional changes brought about by specific actors. Technological innovation occurred in combination with a broad set of parallel social and economic changes. Yet, even during and after the Industrial Revolution, older institutional structures continued to exist and exert influence (Landes, 1969). Thus, a tension between actor-centric and structure-centric explanations is fundamental to institutionalist thought. There is no universal outcome to this tension, which is one of the strengths of the institutionalist approach. Yet, this also necessitates a close appreciation of historic detail; the possibility of unique social and economic trajectories needs to be taken seriously by scholarship.

Major contributions to institutionalist theory originally emerged out of the detailed study of technological change by economic historians such as Douglass North. Economic historians examining the history of innovation have found technological explanations alone are insufficient as an explanatory framework and have extended the discussion to a wide variety of political and cultural factors. Economic history therefore frequently approaches technological change by identifying groups resisting innovation and those promoting it. But interaction always occurs within a given historical institutional environment market by path dependence (Olson and Kähkönen, 2000, 13). Therefore, the inventive achievements of the entrepreneur are not sufficient alone to bring about change, despite the popular prevalence of what Mancur Olson calls the 'parable of the self-made entrepreneur' (Olson, 2000, 183).[11]

The guiding premise of new institutional economic history regarding technological innovation can be summarized in the following way:

> But the market is by no means the only way of aggregating the gains and losses from adopting an innovation; a variety of regulatory or political processes can be used to determine whether an innovation is to be adopted, and each will in general aggregate the gains and losses differently and thus will often come up with different answers about whether an innovation should be adopted.[12]

Moreover, the timing of change has been studied. Economic historians such as Joel Mokyr have examined occasional, disruptive periods of intensive innovation activity which may be accompanied by significant economic and political changes. These periods are called 'punctuated equilibria', leaning on lessons from modern evolutionary biology (2000, 69–72). These periods can be triggered by events not directly related to technology, such as changes in the social environment. An example was the Glorious Revolution of 1688 in Britain, which was an important precursor to the technological breakthroughs of the eighteenth century (Mokyr, 1990, 298, 299).

A further body of work studying innovative capacity which is closely related to economic history in its approach is national innovation systems (Nelson, 1993) and sectoral innovation systems research (Mowery and Nelson, 1999a). This research approach focuses on the impact of institutional factors on the innovation capacity of contemporary economies and emphasizes, for example, differences in national educational systems. This work also highlights differences among distinct types of technologies and industrial sectors, as does economic history. Systems technologies such as electrical systems or aeronautics, for example, require a complex combination of improvements while other technologies do not (Nelson and Rosenberg, 1993, 13–15).

A related direction of innovation research can be labelled the 'resource-based' view found in management studies and within a research agenda called 'evolutionary economics'. Here, attempts are made to describe the origins of innovation within the firm and pry open the 'black box'. Firms are seen as independent agents capable of change. Their potential for innovation is limited by their internal resources – their management capabilities, for instance. These resources are mostly intangible; Nelson and Winter therefore call them 'routines' (1982). In this view, firm strategy should focus not on pursuits such as erecting entry-barriers but on nurturing, accumulating and deploying resources (Penrose, 1966; Foss, 1996, 1). Thus, routines can be compared directly to institutional linkages, the habits found in institutionalist scholarship. They exhibit path dependency but can, at times, be changed accidentally (mutations) or purposefully through individual agency.

A final, influential body of work discussing innovative capacity is not directly related to institutional scholarship. Industry organisation research and the 'industrial cluster'-based theory is closely associated with Michael E. Porter (1990).[13] While the cluster-based theory of national industrial competitive advantage does not explain the rise of a new industry or a new technology, it is an extremely instructive research tool for comparative work in innovative capacity. The objective of this research is to identify country-specific or region-specific factors that lead to international competitive success. Porter focuses on microeconomic factors such as local demand conditions, regional industry structure and the intensity of local competition. Advanced local demand structures, for example, allow enterprises to develop products and services which excel in international competition. However, the industry cluster is a mostly static framework. Porter's recent work shows how change occurs within these clusters, yet he still relates it to largely exogenous factors such as technological change, changes in demand structures and an ebbing of domestic rivalry (Foss, 1996, 4, 9–12; Porter, 1990, 166–73).

Institutionalist research has come a long way towards understanding the forces driving innovation. It is viewed not as an exogenous force, but as a capability which can be nurtured by policy-makers, entrepreneurs and managers. Yet, in different historic periods, innovation capability itself differs and industry structure evolves (Mowery and Nelson, 1999b, 370–75). Because of the possibility of significant change, the danger implicit to active, sectoral technology policy is that policy may very well be promoting the 'wrong' players. Whereas chemical-pharmaceutical and electrical innovations at the turn of the twentieth century emerged to an extent out of the industrial research laboratories of large concerns and the research university, IT innovations at the turn of the twenty-first century may instead have favoured different organizational entities.[14] Innovation opportunities need to be understood not in general, but in specific terms related to the sector and the time period, and this has deep implications for domestic policy intending to promote national innovative capacity.[15] The institutional approach, therefore, is not incompatible with concepts of change proposed by network thinkers. Institutionalist thought does not rule out the possibility of transformation wrought by technological innovation; it does, however, emphasize that this happens only rarely and that it is accompanied and influenced by political and social changes.

SUSTAINED VARIETY VERSUS GLOBAL CONVERGENCE

The previous section explained the view that 'institutions do matter'. The institutionalist approach was developed within political economy and economic history as an analytical tool to account for subtle differences in diverging paths of developments during the Industrial Revolution and the twentieth century. Network thinking emerged out of the experience with information technologies in the 1990s. Differences existed in between the two views in terms of agency. Independent agent-influenced change is possible in institutionalist analysis, although continuity is more usual (Steinmo et al., 1992, 15). Government bodies involved in a catching-up process of national competitiveness can purposefully strive to make improvements in their institutional structure; their success usually depends, however, on whether they can 'get it right' and, among other things, the participation of other agents in the financial establishment.[16] Technological change is endogenous and can be explained through the interplay between agents and structures. All this stands in strong contrast to much of network thinking, under which technological change is exogenous.[17] Change is not independent actor induced, but deterministic, thus bearing ironic similarities to neo-Marxist views of structural change.

Both views have incorporated evolutionary models. Institutionalists such as Hodgson have pointed out that evolutionary change is driven by the necessary existence of diversity among institutional arrangements (Hodgson, 1996, 417). The impurities of capitalism trigger change. In the network thinking of Kelly, evolution and diversity are also stressed. They are based, however, on what Hodgson would call a populist, Darwinian interpretation of evolution. In contrast, recent biological studies emphasize the fact that evolution does not always guarantee the 'survival of the fittest.' In fact, the criteria of fitness very much depends on the current evolutionary landscape and is continually subject to change (Hodgson, 1994a, 209, 210). A domestic institutional environment which has been successful as an export-based industrial economy does not have to be suited to perform successfully in a post-industrial world. 'Populist' interpretations of evolution, therefore, assume the world is static and a certain winner type remains a winner for all time. The approaches utilized in this study, institutionalist political economy and economics, evolutionary economics and the resource-based view in management studies, emphasize the necessity to examine not only corporate successes, but also failures (see Schendel, 1996a, 1). Firms or even whole nation states surviving for many years on the brink of bankruptcy may contain resources that lead to success in another environment.

The main concepts of network thinking are summarized in Table 1.1 where they are compared to institutionalist scholarship. The two opposing lines of network and institutionalist thinking should not be overemphasized. Their differences reflected their very distinct objectives. To a certain extent, they echoed the contrasting views on technological change found within the work of Max Weber and the early work of Joseph Schumpeter. In fact, juxtaposing the two scholars has been a popular academic activity (Hamilton, 1996; Galambos, 1996). Interestingly, the work of the German sociologist resurfaces in the technology perspective of economists, management theorists and economic historians, whereas sociologists and popular

Table 1.1.   Differences in network thinking and institutionalist views

	Networks matter	Institutions matter
Process of change	Deterministic global structural change. Schumpeterian creative destruction.	Refracted and scattered change taking place within institutional constraints. Path dependence. Stickiness.
Actors	New actors and regions are favoured by change, but they are not driving it.	Firms, national governments, lobbying groups, regions, institutions of all types.
Possibility of individual agency	None.	Difficult but possible within institutional constraints. Most probable through influence over powerful central institutions, especially financial institutions. Contest between groups resisting and groups promoting innovation.
Type of interconnections	Open computer networks. Low barriers to entry.	Historically formed institutional relationships.
Technological innovation	Exogenous.	Incremental. Path dependent. Endogenous.
Result of change	Global convergence and equality of opportunity. Less political and economic hierarchy. 'Dinosaurs' left behind. New actors emerge as winners. 'Leapfrogging' by new regions or cities.	Sustained variety. All institutions involved in incremental change. New roles for 'old' actors.

network thinkers refer to the Austrian economist. These two great thinkers will be returned to at the end of this volume.

The approach taken here is to focus on a specific, large national economy where institutional factors influencing information technology innovation initially seemed especially constraining but where, nevertheless, a significant entrepreneurial wave did seem to materialize, apparently in response to outside global developments. This economy could not be the United States, since as the originator of the internet wave, it did not contain the potential conflict between domestic institutions and a global technology opportunity arriving from the outside. And it is exactly this conflict between inside, domestic agents acting within the constraints of domestic structures, and outside, global structural change, which is the focus of the book. In Germany, this conflict seemed especially severe. Many Germans and observers in other countries had almost completely forsaken the thought that Germany could achieve prominence in IT and participate in global IT innovation when, apparently, a significant wave of entrepreneurship in IT suddenly did materialize in Germany.

This book evaluates in what specific ways global technology interacts with national institutions. To do so, a framework for the study of cross-border innovation is introduced, based on the concept of 'refraction'. Refraction is the distorting effect national institutions have on a global innovation opportunity. Change agents, for example new ventures, respond not directly to global shifts but to their refracted state. The refraction effect can either magnify or reduce opportunity for new international ventures and therefore directs the path of development of new ventures in a specific country. Other actors, for example, government bodies or established enterprises, also act within this framework. Refraction is a hypothetical framework; the assumption made is that both global structural change as well as domestic institutional constraints can co-exist. In fact, the concept inversely measures the strength of global technological change. The stronger the refraction effect is, the weaker is global shift.

The refraction framework is closely indebted to work in international political economy (IPE). IPE began as a field of international relations (IR) which can be defined through its object of research, the world economy and the role of international and domestic institutions in the world economy. IPE from the early 1970s onwards wrestled with the concept of systemic changes in the world economy (see Katzenstein et al., 1999b, 15–17). Much of the debate was focused on the role of multinational enterprises (MNEs). A debate emerged between scholars emphasizing global change and the retreat of the state (Stopford, Strange and Henley, 1991) and those pointing to the continuing role of the nation state (Krasner, 1994, 15; see also Inayatullah, 1997). In the United States, this debate has been seen as a contest between so-called liberal and realist camps. In Europe, and more recently in the US (Gilpin, 2001), the discussion was less focused on the liberal–realist contest and led to original, combinatory research approaches. Sally, for example, began with an IPE inquiry to carry out what he called a micro-political examination of 'embeddedness' (Sally, 1994; 1995). Embeddedness described the extent to which multinational enterprises (MNEs) were rooted in their home countries. The concept is similar to refraction, but the analytical emphasis is different. The objective when measuring embeddedness is understanding home country linkages of global enterprises abroad. The focus when measuring refraction is the distorting effect of national institutions on globally oriented enterprises at home. Most importantly, the refraction concept attempts to build a make-shift bridge between network thinking and institutional scholarship for analytical purposes.

Within IPE, the refraction framework reflects a current debate surround-ing the resilience of national institution *vis-à-vis* internationalization. Increases in international economic interaction in recent years have been linked to domestic political instability, 'political entrepreneurship' and domestic institutional reforms (Milner and Keohane, 1996, 16–20). However, while technology is seen as a key influence in globalization, IPE research has not explicitly explored the relationship of power and techno-logical innovation. This is why the refraction framework has borrowed from different sources: sociological studies of globalization, and what is called here 'network thinking' – contemporary popular accounts of tech-nological opportunities wrought by global networks – as well as institution-alist scholarship on the history of technology and innovation.[18]

The concept of refraction is put to active use to study the development of the internet in Europe. The interplay of global technology and specific domestic agents in specific domestic policy arenas was analysed through a close qualitative and quantitative examination of the development of new internet ventures in European countries, especially in Germany. The resource-based view on enterprise development was drawn upon to gain a better understanding of how different types of external factors influence the development of company resources at an early stage of formation. Some specific national factors examined here were local demand structures, the promotion of risk capital and the legal and regulatory framework relat-ing to entrepreneurship. Economic history and research in national indus-trial competitive advantage, especially the cluster-based theory, were consulted as well, and the determinants are linked to two policy arenas, telecommunications liberalization and research policy.

The apparent blurring here of national determinants 'external' to the firm and resources 'internal' to the firm was purposeful and reflects the con-tention that they are different perspectives of the same phenomena.[19] The new ventures themselves are, metaphorically, the vessel in which different influences make themselves felt. The measure of success is 'industrial lead-ership' of the start-ups as a group and not solely of one exceptional venture. Mowery and Nelson define the term as 'being ahead of one's competitors in production or process technology, or in production and marketing, [giving] firms an advantage in world markets' (1999b, 2). Mowery and Nelson differentiate the term industrial leadership from the term 'compet-itive advantage', which may confuse because it is often used to refer to the success of specific firms. It is important to reiterate that some network thinkers explicitly stated that leadership in a New Economy is not sustainable and this view contradicts, to a certain extent, the concept of industrial leadership which is used here as a yardstick. However, what is attempted here with the refraction framework is to find common ground in comparing two very different sets of ideas; establishing this common ground may at times be problematic.

The author is aware that the task taken on here is complex. What is attempted in the study appears here to be very abstract. This is not the case. The focus on enterprise-level quantitative and qualitative data in Europe and specifically in Germany serves as a backbone of this effort, allowing research from different sources as well as insight from different theories to be incorporated in a structured way. In addition, the study is organized around a limited number of specific domestic agents and specific policy arenas.

THREE DOMESTIC AGENTS AND TWO POLICY ARENAS

To understand how domestic institutional structures operate, it is necessary to adopt a micro-political, detailed perspective on individual agents and policy arenas (see, for example, Sally, 1995, 206, 207). Different types of agents, not simply government bodies, contribute to policy decisions. To describe the complex structure policy decisions are typically made in, Helen Milner uses the term 'polyarchy'. Polyarchy refers to power-sharing arrangements among domestic groups. The distribution of power in given historic situations is always more complex than in a simplistic hierarchy, even in what appears on the surface to be extremely hierarchical, totalitarian regimes (Milner, 1997, 11–14).

Three types of domestic agents and two policy arenas were regarded as being especially relevant for this study of Europe. The three domestic agents in the polyarchy were national government bodies, the former public telecommunications operators (PTOs) and young, innovative internet ventures. The policy arenas were telecommunications policy, which influenced internet access and demand, and national technology policy, especially the promotion of venture capital.

What were the reasons for selecting these agents and policy arenas? National government, for example, needed to be differentiated from other state actors such as regions and supranational policy bodies, both of which played an increasingly strong role in Europe. In the case of Germany, at least three regions, Baden-Württemberg, the city-state of Hamburg as well as Bavaria, were very active in subsidizing small firms in

IT and telecommunications. The European Commission was also engaged in different initiatives to support small firms in this area, some programmes were being carried out with other G7 or G8 members. National government was, therefore, not the only actor involved in competitiveness policy directed at internet ventures. National policy-makers were not even necessarily the most active; regional and supranational incentives both specifically tended to target individual firms or groups of firms with support packages including network access subsidies or free consulting services. One of the reasons why national government is central to this study, however, is because of its role in telecommunications liberalization, the Achilles' heel of global internet development. The contention made here is that this national policy arena, by influencing the demand structure for internet services, was the crucial determinant for new venture success on an international basis. It was thus a strong contributor to refraction. When we shift our emphasis away from internet development to other industries or other historic periods, however, the national perspective may be misleading (Mowery and Nelson, 1999b, 366–70; Nelson and Rosenberg, 1993, 15–18).

When speaking of national government, this study is referring to different policy bodies which did not always have compatible interests. National government policy almost always was the result of intense internal negotiation, causing policy inconsistencies and contradictions. In the case of Germany, three specific ministries were of greatest interest. These three were the Ministries of Finance, of Economics, and of Science and Education. The democratic representative bodies also played a role, as well as intermediary organizations placed in-between the private and public sectors. One such intermediary, parapublic organization was a very important public–private SME financing institution, the Deutsche Ausgleichsbank.[20] These different bodies were central in framing both telecommunications policy, and innovation and technology policy – which included a programme to promote venture capital. Scholars analysing the German policy-making process in comparative studies have classified German politics as 'corporatist'. In Chapter 4, this term will be examined for its usefulness in understanding the decision-making process among different national policy groups.

The second agent to be introduced here was closely linked to national government. However, the PTOs needed to be understood as independent economic and political agents. Their interests were shaped by a unique historical trajectory, which cannot simply be equated to a purported unified government interest. In the case of Germany, six historical themes stand out; they have shaped today's Deutsche Telekom AG (DTAG). They are the universal telephone system, the technological capabilities of DTAG, the former monopolist's involvement in the roll-out of a modern telecommunications infrastructure in the so-called New German States, the privatization and stock market listing of the company, its desired transformation from a domestic to a global player, and its response to the actions of the regulatory authority after liberalization in 1998.[21] Through its near-universal ownership of all means of consumer internet access before liberalization, it is not possible to understand the development of internet services in Germany without analysing the role of Deutsche Telekom and its historically determined interests.

The final type of agent to be introduced here is the new internet venture. While in the 1990s only a limited amount of academic research was carried out on internet start-ups, scholarly attention began in the 1980s to be focused in general on the innovative capacity of small and medium-sized enterprises (SMEs) (Rothwell and Zegveld, 1982; Curran et al. 1986; Haskins, 1986; Klandt, 1987; Bannock and Albach, 1991; Mullineux, 1994; Baker, 1996). The innovation capacity of small and medium-sized enterprises has been discussed with German cases as well (Koschatzky, 1997b; Harhoff, 1997). Scholarly efforts initially were directed at showing that small firms can indeed be innovators. Traditionally, dominant views, also in political economy, emphasized the power of Chandlerian large firms in terms of market domination and innovative potential.[22] Work on SMEs has often been accompanied by research exploring the role of regional networks for SME development. One of the best-known of these efforts is AnnaLee Saxenian's work which explores the advantages of Silicon Valley over Route 128 in Massachusetts (1994). In Europe, it was hoped that SME growth would be a solution to unemployment problems. This work has been accompanied by parallel developments in government programmes targeted at the needs of SMEs. Aspects of this body of scholarship were very helpful here, especially analysis of the symbiotic relationships between large and small firms (Rothwell, 1986) and the significance of regional networks of large and small firms. German research, specifically, was invaluable to provide insight into the effects of research policy targeting SMEs in Germany. However, the usefulness of SME research for this study is restricted, due to the focus of much of this work on older industries, not the role of new types of ventures in areas undergoing rapid technological change and supported by venture capital, such as software development or internet services. Perhaps this is the reason why a few of the SME studies cited above came to the conclusion that SMEs are well suited to primary inventions but do not have the financial resources to bring these to the market (Carnoy et al., 1993, 8; Rothwell, 1986, 134, 135).

The reason research on SMEs has not delved into the role of new ventures in IT, media and telecommunications innovation is obvious: much of

SME research predates these development. For this study, recent work examining the role of small firms in Silicon Valley was important to gain comparative insight. Serious work in business strategy on Silicon Valley firms emphasized both the equally innovative role of specialized 'pure play' small network players and the support given to them by experienced venture capitalists and private investors (for example, Cusumano and Yoffie, 1998). Steven S. Cohen and Gary Fields have re-emphasized the regional advantages of the success-driven, networked and highly diverse environment of Silicon Valley (1999). But regional differentiating factors associated with Silicon Valley were not the only reasons why a small number of US internet ventures managed to achieve a sustainable global presence.[23] As in Germany, one national policy arena was especially important for the development of the internet in the United States, namely, telecommunications policy influencing local demand structures for internet services.

Business press articles discussing the contemporary development of the internet repeatedly pointed out the importance of internet access as one crucial country-level institutional factor. As such, the identification of this factor is not unique to this study. These popular accounts, however, fail to examine in what way forward linkages from the telecommunications industry influenced internet entrepreneurship. The firm-level analysis combined with a study of institutional reform provided the right type of approach for this concern.

THE CASE FOR GERMANY

> Germany excels at, and is stuck in, mid-level technologies – great cars. But it has little of the upper-level technologies that matter today to be a frontrunner, nor the mindset or the structures to quickly become a player (Dornbusch, 2000, 74).

While the intention of this study was to describe the development of European internet ventures, the approach chosen required detailed analysis of national institutional reform and firm-level resources. It was necessary to dwell on a specific European country which seemed to display a particularly strong response to the global internet opportunity. In Chapter 7, the German case is extended to other European countries.

German history is a popular subject of study for economic backwardness. Germany caught up during the Industrial Revolution and, after the destruction due to the Second World War, again regained economic strength. Although this is a subject of particularly fervent debate, part of the success of the Federal Republic after the Second World War was due to financial initiatives targeting SMEs, the so-called *Mittelstand*.[24] In accordance with the Marshall Plan, so-called parapublic institutions extended credit for rebuilding businesses. Germany historically has a very strong small and medium-sized enterprise (SME) base.[25] Ergas described German technology policy as 'diffusion oriented', meaning that it is primarily concerned with encouraging the spread of technology throughout the economy and especially to the smaller, export-oriented firms (1987).

Yet, by the 1980s, entrepreneurial dynamism in Germany seemed to have all but disappeared, including in the key sector of information technology. For this reason, the seeming resurrection of the *Wirtschaftswunder* in the late 1990s came as a surprise and was featured in the media, for example, in two memorable cover stories in the news magazine *Der Spiegel*.[26] In no other country in Europe, including the United Kingdom, was the entrepreneurial boom surrounding the converging technologies and the internet so apparent as in Germany – in fact, it could be directly compared to what was occurring at the same time in the United States, albeit on a much smaller scale. In the year 1999 alone, German venture capital funds invested in 510 IT and communication technology companies, including 117 internet start-ups.[27] By the year 2000, dozens of internet start-ups had been listed on the Neuer Markt. The seemingly strong reappearance of entrepreneurial activity makes Germany an especially rewarding subject of inquiry.

Yet, while Germany was exceptional in the number of listed internet companies and the apparent suddenness of this entrepreneurial activity, it was not the only country where the boom was felt. The internet was generally perceived as a cross-border phenomenon, a technology which not only enabled the worldwide exchange of goods and services, but which could serve as a global entrepreneurial platform. Should the entrepreneurial turnaround in Germany be understood as a development with mostly global origins? Or was it the result of fervent domestic institutional reform in the telecommunications sector, supported by national innovation policies promoting venture capital? The objective of this book is to explore these questions using evidence gathered directly from the new ventures themselves.

COMPANY FOCUS AND EMPIRICAL RESEARCH

A close look at the firm level is necessary to fully understand the origins of entrepreneurial revival in Europe and to explain its failure after financial downturn. The delicate linkages between firms and policy-making on a micro political economy level (Sally, 1995, 206, 207), help expose the importance of specific global and domestic determinants. Without detailed analysis, US, German and other experiences can easily be conflated into one universal, worldwide structural phenomenon or, alternatively, domestic developments can be cited as sole determinants.

An awareness of timing is crucial for this study. It is important not to equate the stock market bubble with the entrepreneurial wave surrounding the internet, at least not off-hand without detailed analysis. Initial entrepreneurial activity in Europe in response to converging technologies, online services and data networks clearly began before 1995 (Waesche, 1999a). Furthermore, even the first generation of European internet entrepreneurs who founded their companies around 1995 and 1996 could not have predicted the future course of the stock markets, especially the development of the Frankfurt stock exchange Neuer Markt. The Neuer Markt started only in 1997 and its first year of activity was relatively slow. The same applies to the first generation of internet start-ups in the United States, although here stock market growth was evident much earlier. 'Irrational exuberance' on the stock markets was identified in a frequently cited speech by Alan Greenspan in 1996. First generation internet start-ups in the United States were founded in 1994 and 1995. It cannot be denied, however, that strong stock market growth until consolidation in the year 2000 greatly benefited the first generation of US internet entrepreneurs. Stock market growth provided these companies with a considerable flow of funding through secondary stock offerings as well as acquisition opportunities based on high valuations. With this advantage bestowed by the capital markets, a limited number of first generation US internet companies could pioneer new, networked business models, achieve sustainability and seriously establish their presence in international markets in Europe and Asia. In order to compare first generation internet venture activity in Europe to that of the United States and other countries, the intentional choice was made to collect empirical data early, in this case, in the Spring of 1998.

But the year 1998 was also important for another reason. It was the year in which basic telecommunications services were liberalized in many European countries including Germany. The demand structure for internet services would be considerably influenced by the actions of the new regulatory agency for telecommunications in Germany operating from 1998. By analysing the innovative capabilities of internet ventures in Germany at the beginning of this crucial year, the perspective gained is that of internet entrepreneurship before the demand effects of liberalization could unfold. Demand structures changed significantly after 1998, but by that time the competitive capabilities of the first generation of German internet ventures had already been defined. Second generation activity did not have sufficient time to develop before the downturn of the capital markets in 2000.

The challenge to this research approach was that, in 1998, there was a lack of quality information about internet ventures in Europe. At the time of research, Europe was still populated mostly by privately-held internet ventures. For this reason, the country case study of German internet ventures was supported by empirical research carried out together with a major German business publication. Data from over 120 German internet ventures was collected.

Despite the insight provided by this data, the conclusions that could be drawn from a single-country empirical study were to a certain extent limited. The trade-off between the level of detail provided by a single-country empirical study and the comparative insight of a multi-country study was apparent. To overcome the limitations of this trade-off, a brief survey of Sweden has been included in this volume, in Chapter 7.

While the key years for this study were the years from 1995 to 1998, the full time period surveyed here extends from the 1970s, when the first corporate data networks were implemented and the internet was developed as a research network, to the beginning of 2002. In 2002, the effects of the downturn of the stock markets were evident. The period of innovation and entrepreneurial activity surrounding the internet was clearly over.

CHAPTER BREAKDOWN

The chapters of this book are arranged in the following way. The study begins with an analysis of the global internet opportunity, moves to the domestic level with a detailed examination of Germany, and ends in a European comparative overview. In this overview, internet development in Sweden is dwelled upon as a special case. Initially, the study is concerned with insight emerging from sociology and network thinking. The focus is not on specifically technological aspects or the commercialization of the internet, which have been thoroughly examined by other scholars using the US case. While this literature is addressed to provide a basis for further discussion, Chapters 2 and 3 are explicitly dedicated to the global nature of the internet opportunity. How did it arise – what were the economic and political prerequisites for the internationalization of the internet? The themes of globalization and global convergence will also be explored. Globalization was a strong social shift some researchers believe was occurring; in a specific sense it played a crucial role in the worldwide diffusion of the internet.

The first, global section serves as an entry point to the detailed study of Europe, which stands at the centre of this book. While the global internet infrastructure was being built and extended, policy-makers were at home pondering national competitiveness in a new era. Policy reform was under way. But to what extent was internet entrepreneurship driven by global or domestic developments? To answer the main research question, one domestic economy was selected and analysed on a micro-political and enterprise level. The following three chapters on Germany successively discuss the three main agent types in relation to the development of the German internet: the role of national government bodies, the Deutsche Telekom and the internet ventures themselves.

Chapter 4 has a dual function. It broadly describes the policy-making process in Germany. It also discusses various reform initiatives, such as research policy, including venture capital support programmes and the promotion of the national online service BTX. It focuses on the research policy shift under Christian Democrat government from a dirigist programme to an initiative emphasizing public–private partnerships and indirect financial support. Chapter 4 also has an important introductory role. It is difficult to understand the strategy of the Deutsche Telekom as an independent agent without discussing German government policy first.

In the fifth chapter, telecommunications liberalization is analysed, especially how it impacted on the demand for internet services in Germany. The chapter concentrates on the role of the Deutsche Telekom and why it was unable to act as a catalyst for the uptake of internet services in Germany. To do so, it traces the historic transformation of former postal and telecommunications ministry to the Deutsche Telekom. When DTAG was partially privatized and listed as a public company in 1996, it needed to modernize its technological base, reduce its debt burden and internationalize. The result was a large cash requirement which was served by comparatively high basic telephony tariffs as long as possible until and after liberalization in 1998. High prices restricted demand for internet access. For the purposes of this study, the period from the stock market listing in 1996 to liberalization in 1998 is critical. During this time period, Deutsche Telekom (DTAG) has to be understood as an independent agent, despite its links to German government, especially in the Finance Ministry. The objectives of DTAG were very different from those of other policy bodies, although these differences were perhaps not even understood by the policy-makers themselves.

Chapter 6 builds upon empirical research – a survey of over 120 internet start-ups in Germany – to gain a detailed look at the enterprise level. The intention was to expose forward linkages originating from telecommunications liberalization and discuss the overall impact of different policies of competitiveness, including the promotion of venture capital. In this chapter, the refraction framework, presented in the theoretical part of this introductory chapter, is put to use. A detailed analysis of the trajectory of German internet start-ups allows us to understand the strength of the refraction effect and also how it operated.

In Chapter 7, the development of internet ventures and policy conditions is compared with that of other European countries. In particular, Sweden stands out with its distinct path of internet development. The purpose of this section is to understand better what was learned in the one-country study of Germany and to place these learnings in an international context. The international focus at the end of the book essentially returns to the theme of the first part of the book, however, under consideration of possibly unique national characteristics. The exploration of global technological shift and a specific, institutionally conditioned domestic environment can then be concluded.

WAS IT MERELY 'IRRATIONAL EXUBERANCE?'

Before beginning with the discussion on European internet entrepreneurship, it is important to recall that the period under examination here coincided with a massive bubble on the international stock markets and with unprecedented investor interest in internet companies. From the famous Alan Greenspan warning about 'irrational exuberance' in 1996 (see Schiller, 2000) to the downturn in the year 2000 and the associated emergence of stories of 'infectious greed', the stock markets were on a continual rise, with a slight dip in 1998. Investors seemed to temporarily have believed that the world was, indeed, entering a New Economy of sorts. Public preoccupation with the stock market bubble and the subsequent loss of considerable sums of money by small investors tended to overshadow some of the underlying currents of internet development. One such important underlying current was the relationship of internet entrepreneurship to telecommunications liberalization.

One of the intentions here was to expose some of these underlying currents, an activity which seemed to the author to have shared similarities with an archaeologist scraping at a slab of ancient material to isolate some fossilized bones. At times, an archaeologist may find that the fossil he worked so hard to uncover was an insignificant, common find, not particularly beautiful and not adding to his knowledge of the era. The archaeologist can even fall victim to a hoax. Considering the amount of work involved, these were, indeed, frightening thoughts. These thoughts continually accompanied this research task.

It was crucial to consider the hypothesis that the internet opportunity may actually not have been an overly significant aspect when viewed against decades of telecommunications and information technology (IT) development. An accurate portrayal of internet entrepreneurship and innovation should, perhaps, emphasize a longer-term development of telecommunications and IT technologies with a definite leading role occupied by the

United States. Development was continual, albeit uneven, because it was constrained to the US. This would have been the expected path for interpretations guided by institutionalist thinking. Given the excesses of the 'bubble', it seems very possible that the 'Internet Revolution', a glorious neo-Schumpeterian vision of discontinuity and global convergence, was exaggerated. The internet was inflated out of proportion by stock market interest in a number of new ventures which disappeared soon after the market downturn. This was one of the challenges the study faced. A further challenge was that the entities under study were in continual flux.

The rise of internet entrepreneurship clearly happened in unexpected places and was accompanied by a period of national policy experimentation. Network thinkers emphasized global policy convergence, stressing that governments were forced to liberalize their industries in response to a severe loss of control. In contrast, policy-makers saw themselves as catalysts of change; their active reforms were preparing their country for a new age of network competition. Pushing aside the hype, unravelling these global and domestic factors and understanding how they contributed to internet development in Europe were the intentions behind this study.

NOTES

1.   Holger Schmidt, 'dot.com. Zur neuen Gründergeneration im Internet,' *Frankfurter Allgemeine Zeitung*, 1 January 2000, page 17 (author's translation).
2.   For a review of macroeconomic implications of the 'New Economy', such as the reduction of inventory costs, see DeLong (2000, 2001). For the term 'business webs' see Tapscott, et al. (2000). A discussion of the real time economy including business cases can be found in *The Economist*: 'How about now? A survey of the real time economy.' 8 February 2002.
3.   For the concept of 'disruptive technologies' and the reactions of established enterprises to new, initially inferior technologies see Christensen (1997).
4.   Press release by European Information Technology Observatory (EITO), 'EITO 2001: Strong acceleration in Net Economy development expected to continue in Europe, despite present storms in capital markets. ICT market in Europe grows by 13 per cent in 2000, outdistancing US growth rate (8.2 per cent)', Brussels, 28 February 2001.
5.   Over the year 2000, NASDAQ had lost 56 per cent of its value, while the Neuer Markt index, NEMAX, lost about 80 per cent. 'Falscher Glaube an eine neue Ära. Aufstieg und Fall des Neuen Marktes: Wie die Euphorie entstand und wer sie antrieb', *Financial Times Deutschland*, 15 March 2001, 21.
6.   DG Bank Deutsche Genossenschaftsbank AG Research, 'Neuer Markt', February 2001.
7.   742 seed and start-up companies received venture capital financing in France, 354 in Sweden, 250 in the Netherlands and 123 in the United Kingdom. Figures from EVCA (2000).
8.   For a critical examination of leapfrogging opportunities provided by innovation in the telecommunications industry in developing countries see Singh (1999).
9.   See, for example, George Gilder's discussion of the fibre-optics venture Global Crossing (2000, 183–92) as well as his critique of US anti-trust policy (2000, 165–80).
10. See also the instructive German-language article on the demise of the 'New Economy'

by Peter Glotz, 'Aus der Traum', *Die Woche*, 23 March 2001, 14. Also: Nicholas Garnham (2000, 63–81) and Brian Winston (1998).

11. Douglass North also downgraded the significance of the entrepreneur and innovator (1966, 8).

12. Excerpt from an editorial introduction to an essay on resistance to technological innovation by Joel Mokyr (Olson and Kähkönen, 2000, 12).

13. For a discussion, see Hill and Deeds (1996, 429–31).

14. See the section 'The Best of Times' in Thurow (2000, 16–22). For a short discussion about industrial research laboratories: Nelson and Rosenberg (1993, 10–11).

15. Mowery and Nelson developed the term 'sectoral innovation system' to reflect this insight (1999a, 369, 370).

16. See the classic comparison between Russia and Germany during the Industrial Revolution by Alexander Gerschenkron (1962).

17. Lawrence Lessig's exceptional book strongly and correctly emphasized agent decisions; the internet was deliberately designed to encourage innovation (2001).

18. Interestingly, this echoes yet another, theoretical debate within IPE scholarship in the United States between sociological and institutionalist accounts of change in the international economy. However, this debate is broad and has not explicitly focused on technology either. Refer to Katzenstein et al., (1999b, 30–42).

19. The economists David Mowery and Richard Nelson have dedicated a section in their recent book to the difficulties of distinguishing between resource availabilities, institutions and domestic market conditions (1999b, 5–7).

20. For a discussion of parapublic institutions see Webber (1994, 156).

21. For excellent research on the origins of the universal telephone system in Germany and the unique path of development of this system, refer to the work of Frank Thomas (1995).

22. It was small firms which were seen as anachronistic elements obstructive to progress which cannot afford extensive research programmes. Business historians such as Chandler showed how large firms developed powerful efficiencies of scale and scope. The political economist J. K. Galbraith in 1957 emphasized the importance of large firms in technological innovation, made possible through the deployment of additional resources for R&D within the firm. The later Schumpeter tended to agree with this view when discussing the twentieth century (1975). Williamson used the concept of transaction costs to explain the efficiencies of large firms (see, for example, Williamson and Winter, 1992). In the global economy, the advantages of large firms were compounded. Multinational enterprises (MNEs) were linked in works on international political economy (IPE) to national governments in terms of their power and wealth. IPE has, to a great extent, been preoccupied with MNEs (Carnoy et al., 1993, 8). MNEs used their transnational structures in order to allocate their resources more effectively and cut their costs. They negotiated with governments, using their global mobility as a powerful bargaining chip. John M. Stopford, Susan Strange and John S. Henley called this 'new diplomacy' (1991). In a similar way, John H. Dunning, who has extensively studied international business and multinational firms, recognized the contributions of small firms in the global economy, but saw their activities very much as 'orchestrated' by MNEs (1993b).

23. Mowery and Nelson have argued recently that a narrow focus on industrial districts does not do justice to the variety of networks firms are linked to at different geographic levels: regional, national and global. They prefer the term 'sectoral innovation systems' (1999b, 9–10); previously, the emphasis was on national innovation systems (Nelson, 1993).

24. Werner Abelshauser disagreed that the economic foundation of Germany in terms of capital equipment and know-how was destroyed during the Second World War and therefore downplays the impact of the Marshall Plan (1983). Alan S. Milward emphasized the importance of the Marshall Plan and widened the debate to its role in having promoted European economic cooperation (1984). Christoph Buchheim discussed the role of the Marshall Plan in the development of a post-war multilateral free trade system involving Germany (1990, 99–107).

25. In 1986, SMEs, defined in Germany to be firms with under 500 employees, accounted for 46 per cent or private sector GDP, compared to 32 per cent in Britain (Bannock and Albach, 1991, 56).
26. 'Hilfe gegen Arbeitslosigkeit? Erhards Enkel. Gründungs-Boom durch junge Unternehmer', *Der Spiegel*, 3, 13 January 1997; 'Die 68er regieren – und ihre Kinder gründen Unternehmen. Generation Ich. Von der Revolte zur Rendite', *Der Spiegel*, 21, 22 May 2000.
27. Statistics from the Bundesverband Deutscher Kapitalbeteiligungsgesellschaften e.V. for 1999 (dated 31 December 1999, accessible on the web site http://www.bvk-ev.de/).

PART I

Global Opportunity

2. The global growth of the internet and the role of the United States

This study seeks to understand how, in the so-called New Economy, a global innovation opportunity related to national innovation policy. Specifically, the international diffusion of the internet in the late 1990s is examined. Then, its reception by new ventures in particular European countries, especially Germany, is studied. The entrepreneurial response was conditioned by national innovation policy, including telecommunications liberalization. In the first part of this book, comprised of Chapters 2 and 3, the worldwide diffusion of the internet and the role of the United States are examined. Then, in Part II, the European entrepreneurial response and innovation policy are addressed.

Three interrelated aspects need to be reviewed when seeking to explain the internationalization of the internet. First, the internet's infrastructure costs were shared, making its use distance-insensitive. This was due to its origins as a government-supported academic research network, but it was also dependent on the 'unregulation' of leased line data services. The issues associated with cost sharing and leased data lines will be explored in Chapter 3. Second, the internet was a horizontal technology which was applied to a broad set of sectors and industries. It offered the potential to lower transaction and inventory costs by connecting large and small enterprises to each other and to consumers in seamless business webs.[1] Due to its horizontal applicability, the internet tended to follow the interconnected international economy and connected previous company-only and country-only networks to each other. Finally, the internet was, in terms of its technology, architecture and legal framework, very different from other types of networks. It was especially distinct from the switched telephone network, but it also had advantages to other data networks which further enabled its global diffusion. The internet was characterized by its openness and initially low barriers to entry. All three factors listed here were deeply interrelated.

The internet was international almost from the very beginning of its existence. The military and research precursor network to the internet, the ARPANET, was extended outside of the United States already in 1973, when the Norwegian National Data Centre (NDC, later NORSAR) was

connected to transfer information to the United States about underground
nuclear testing activity. In the same year, the University College in London
was connected via Norway. In the 1980s, the internet was connected to a
multitude of research organizations across the world. In 1982, for example,
EUnet was established to provide internet services initially between the
Netherlands, Denmark, Sweden and the UK.[2] The World Wide Web standards were released in 1991. The WWW standards, developed by a British
researcher in a Swiss nuclear physics facility, were an important prerequisite for the commercialization of the internet (see Berners-Lee, 1999). Yet,
the commercial development of the internet was sparked in the United
States. 1995 was the 'Year of Internet'. It was the year of the stock market
listing of the inspirational internet software developer Netscape as well as
of Bill Gates's internal Pearl Harbour Day declaration that Netscape's
dominance of the internet would be challenged by Microsoft.[3] It was,
however, also the year that the internet backbone services of the govern-
ment-financed NSFNET were handed over to commercial internet providers. The Clinton Administration's Electronic Commerce Working Group
was formed in December 1995 which enshrined an initial stance of unregulation to encourage the development of electronic commerce.

While the internet experienced very rapid international diffusion as a
global network infrastructure, internet services in the late 1990s were dominated by US companies. While the whole study seeks to explain this development, this first chapter approaches this issue in terms of an analysis of
the international supply and demand for internet services. The technological underpinnings of the internet are also explored in this chapter. Chapter
3 approaches the role of international and national polity in contributing
to the global diffusion of the internet as well as US dominance of the
network.

DATA NETWORKS BEFORE 1995

The history of the take-off of the internet has been often simplistically
described as the *tabula rasa* adoption of a new networking technology
emerging from the research community. Commentators were surprised
when they compared the adoption of the internet to that of other technologies, such as television. The growth of the internet occurred as rapidly as
it did because it was a 'network of networks', a 'connective tissue', linking
different types of previously insular company-only and country-only data
networks. Financial services firms and corporations were internally using
proprietary data networking technologies. Since the 1970s, the company-
only networks linked international subsidiaries and production centres of

these firms. Consumers in the United States, Europe and elsewhere were using what to a great extent were country-only proprietary online and teletex services. In this initial section, the world before the take-off of the internet in 1995 is outlined, by describing the state of company-only and country-only networks. In the next section, the hypothesis is extended that the strong demand for internet technologies and services in most countries was linked precisely to its ability to act as a global 'connective tissue' linking previously insular company-only and country-only networks.

In the 1970s, the first network-based data services for business use were born out of necessity due to the high cost of computing. Time-sharing systems allowed several users to share computing resources. With the rapid fall of computing costs, however, computer network technologies were put to new uses because they allowed exchange of data among remote locations, including international locations. The financial industry had a pioneering role in the transnational, corporate use of network-based services. This role has been described numerous times in political economy literature; therefore, it is not necessary to dwell upon the details here. Largely as a result of financial deregulation starting with the Eurodollar market in the 1960s, the volume of transnational currency market transactions grew in the 1970s and 1980s, reaching a much-quoted figure of US$1.2 trillion daily (Dicken, 1992, 365–7; Castells, 1996, 434–7).

The role of networks within the global financial industry had two main characteristics which could be attributed to the use of transnational network-based services generally. The first was that network-based services allowed what Dicken called a 'new global division of labour' to come into existence. In the instances where this occurred, the result was increasing interdependence. The second was the arrival of a new temporal division of labour, the 'new time regime' of Castells (Castells, 1996, 429). It was the possibility for 24-hour trading which Susan Strange referred to in the title of her book *Casino Capitalism* (Chandler and Cortada, 2000b).

If financial services, especially currency markets, were a case where network-based services were put to truly transnational use, it was also a limited example. Although the negative impact on worldwide political and economic stability was emphasized by contemporary observers, this was due mostly to the deregulated environment in which international currency trades took place and not to the transformational character of network-based services. Although modern financial services involved highly sophisticated uses of computer and network technology,[4] the basic transmission of price information itself did not require more than a telegraph. In fact, the financial system can be described as being global already in the late nineteenth century. Although global financial markets were an especially spectacular example of how network-based services could be put to transnational use, the limited number of players[5] and the long communications technology tradition made it less important than the transformation brought about by the combination of low-cost computing and data networks for industrial use.

From the 1950s, industrial enterprises had mainframe computer systems installed primarily as a means to make the organization of structured data more efficient. Payroll, accounting, production scheduling and order entry were some of the first tasks these systems were put to use for. Some of these systems were networked and could already be transnational in scope; writing a paper for the *Columbia Journal of World Business*, Nanus coined the term 'multinational computer' in 1969, reflecting this development (cited in Hagström, 1991, 19). The first network-based services within industrial enterprises moved beyond the experimental stage only in the second half of the 1970s, however. At that time, SKF, the Swedish ball-bearings manufacturer, for example, integrated its production in Europe with the help of computer networks. By 1979, five computing centres in five countries – Sweden, West Germany, Italy, France and the UK – had been linked through the corporate Global Forecasting and Supply System. The internal efforts by SKF were supported by a third party, General Electric Information Services (Hagström, 1991, 221–3).

One way to map the spread of network-based controlling and production systems within international corporations is through the growth of the enterprise resource planning (ERP) applications market. The birth of the ERP market dates to the late 1970s and early 1980s, when the first standardized software replaced custom controlling or production systems in large companies. Standardized software could be applied throughout the corporation and later allowed separate systems to be linked via corporate networks. One ERP market leader, SAP, was founded in 1972 in Mannheim, Germany, and launched its mainframe ERP system in 1979. Two international clients, US-based firm John Deere and UK-based Imperial Chemical Industries, persuaded SAP to develop English and French versions of its software in the early 1980s. Growth really took off, however, when a client/server-based version of the SAP software was introduced in 1992, allowing individual units within companies with worldwide operations to be linked more effectively. A large number of Fortune 500 companies use SAP applications, including Coca-Cola, Chevron and General Motors. The growth of SAP derives from the success of its software in implementing the network-based services necessary to support globalization of large companies. Figure 2.1 shows the take-off of SAP in the 1990s; it had a 30 per cent share of an estimated US$7.2 billion market.[6]

ERP systems had one thing in common with their in-house predecessors. They were company-only systems, which until the late 1990s communicated only in rare instances with the outside world. These drawbacks led to the

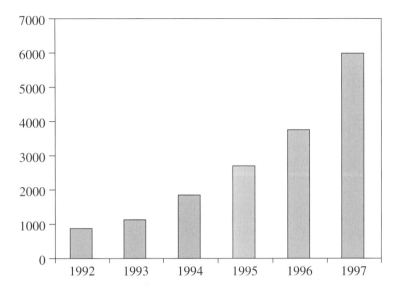

Source: From annual reports 1996 and 1997, SAP Aktiengesellschaft, Walldorf/Baden.

Figure 2.1   *Revenue growth of SAP AG, a major vendor of enterprise resource planning (ERP) applications (in DM million)*

rapid adoption of internet-based standards businesses which could be used across company borders. Internet systems, which were open and flexible, furthermore represented a means by which corporate information technology (IT) departments could regain cost control over their systems; they had become aware of strong dependence on vendors of proprietary software.[7] The shift towards internet standards within the corporation was so strong that proprietary SAP systems were made internet compatible. Before the rise of the internet, demand for transnational network-based services within industrial enterprises was linked to the increase in globally coordinated production efforts.

Rising production costs and increasing economic volatility, beginning in the 1970s, were responded to with a drive towards increased flexibility within MNEs as well as an increased appetite for experimentation.[8] In fact, researchers from different disciplines emphasize that the 1980s and 1990s were a phase of unprecedented organizational experimentation within corporations. The demand for increased foreign direct investment (FDI) as well as transnational computer networks within firms can both be attributed to this need for experimentation (see Castells, 1996, 81–6).[9] Little choice existed but to do so: either one withdrew from a global presence and its attached 'immense fixed costs' (Ohmae) or one sought to make the most of it. This resulted, among other things, in a wave of massive FDI increases: 'This new logic forces managers to amortise their fixed costs over a much larger market base and this drives them towards globalization' (Ohmae, 1994, 6, 7). The average annual growth in FDI from 1983 to 1990 was 34 per cent compared to growth in global merchandise trade of 9 per cent (Hirst and Thompson citing UNCTAD and other sources, 1996, 54, 55).[10]

In fact, the massive growth in FDI was the most noticeable change in the world economy from the 1980s onwards. It is also the main quantitative change in the world economy which can clearly be associated with the controversial term globalization.

> In the period 1945–73 the dominant factor driving the world economy was growth in international trade; from the early 1980s onwards, we argue, it has been growth in FDI (Hirst and Thompson, 1996, 51).

Management studies literature shows how increased FDI efforts were accompanied by organizational changes within enterprises. These have been described as the shift from the multinational to the global enterprise. Whereas the multinational enterprise replicated its functions to serve local markets, the global enterprise went one step further. It tried to decrease redundancy by concentrating different parts of the business process in the regions where these were best carried out. Production centres were distributed worldwide. Service activities within industrial enterprises, such as R&D and design, were distributed globally, taking advantage of the uneven global distribution of labour and know-how. The globalization of production processes has been described and discussed frequently, for example within 'global commodity chain' (GCC) research (Gereffi and Korzeniewicz, 1994).

Transnational computer networks have been installed within firms in all of the cases just described in order to coordinate and control the global division of labour. They have also been instrumental in speeding up global activities in those instances when time-based competition is critical and 24-hour processes are necessary (Cash et al., 1992, 226). Interestingly, organizational change and organizational experimentation were to a degree implemented by management via the introduction of new computer network-based services.[11] Technology has purposely been used as a catalyst for change. The 'Transformation of the IT function at British Petroleum' is just one example. Here, 'The drive for a new, global [IT] architecture confronted local and cherished technical beliefs head-on' (Cross et al., 1998, 34).

It is a controversial question how many multinational enterprises in the 1990s transformed themselves into global firms by means of a computer network. Hirst and Thompson refuted the existence of many more than a handful of such globally networked, globally oriented companies (Hirst and Thompson, 1996, 11, 76–98).[12] FDI itself is strongly concentrated and the 100 largest MNEs account for a third of total FDI stock (Hirst and Thompson citing UNCTAD, 1996, 53). Even the usually enthusiastic Dicken stated that:

> In fact, only 4 or 5 per cent of the total population of TNCs [transnational corporations] in the world can be regarded as truly global corporations (1992, 49).

It was, however, not necessary for a multinational firm to be global in order to take advantage of transnational computer networks, although the intensity of use and the dependence upon these services probably increased as the firm started integrating its worldwide activities to a greater extent. In fact, it did not even have to be the case that the firm was located in more than one country. Companies in just one location were integrated into transnational computer networks. An interesting case were smaller firms, usually suppliers for industrial enterprises that were integrated into the international networks of their clients. In the 1990s, it became evident that, although FDI boomed, ownership was not necessarily the only means by which the experimentally inclined MNE globalized its business processes; this was in the words of Dicken, 'an unsatisfactory narrow view of its geographical scope and influence ' (Dicken, 1992, 48).

Whereas corporate networks from the 1970s onwards already carried international traffic, consumer use of network-based services was for the most part domestic. This was due to the fact that the greatest number of consumers subscribed to on-line services which were initially national in focus.[13] In the US, it was mostly new entrants that began to offer on-line services to consumers. Examples were CompuServe, America Online (AOL), Prodigy or Delphi.[14] In Europe, consumer use was initiated in the late 1970s by national telephony operators, BTX in Germany, Prestel in the UK and Minitel in France. Yet, the growth of country-only networks was comparatively slow. In Germany, the service developed by the Deutsche Bundespost languished throughout the 1980s and early 1990s; it reached its target user base of one million only at year's end 1995, after it had opened itself to the internet. Only Minitel in France was a real success; by the mid-1990s, it was offering 23 000 services and 6.5 million terminals were in use. Next to the free distribution of terminals, one of the main reasons for its success was that France Telecom encouraged private providers of services, foreshadowing the openness of the internet in this regard (Castells, 1996, 343–5).[15] Many of these country-only subscriber on-line services included basic services such as communications, information and some instances of transactions already in the 1980s. On-line banking was popular in Germany, for example, Americans developed on-line discussion forums into 'communities' and the French used a telephone directory database.

TECHNOLOGICAL ASPECTS OF THE INTERNET ENABLING GLOBAL DIFFUSION

Although the internet was a computer network standard comparable to its company-only and country-only peers, it had two distinguishing characteristics: Its legal framework was 'open' and its architecture was 'stupid'. Stanford Law Professor Lawrence Lessig's important overview *The Future of Ideas* (2001) emphasizes that these distinguishing characteristics encouraged innovation and creativity. But they also allowed rapid international diffusion. Anyone, worldwide, wanting to connect her computer to the internet to offer information or new services could do so with a minimum of know-how and without needing to infringe or procure private intellectual property (IP) rights.

The technological basis for the internet actually consisted in combining two 'open' technologies, the networking computing platform UNIX and the communication protocol TCP/IP which allowed computers to exchange data over a decentralized network. TCP/IP was developed for the government-funded ARPANET (Ceruzzi, 1998, 296) and therefore originated in the public domain. The UNIX operating system for workstations, which incorporated and ran TCP/IP, was in 1969 originally developed within AT&T's Bell Labs but was basically given away for a nominal fee. AT&T had decided not to commercially exploit its operating system because, before its break-up in 1981, it had agreed, as a regulated monopoly, not to engage itself in the computing industry (Ceruzzi, 1998, 282–5).

But it was important also to insure that internet IP was kept 'open'. Improvements in internet technologies were the result of an open peer selection process based on the principle of merit, the so-called 'Request for comments' (RFC). The RFC series was introduced in 1969. In addition, an array of different boards and task forces such as the Internet Engineering Task Force (IETF) were formed by the publicly and privately funded research community to coordinate the various development activities surrounding the internet.[16] A legal framework for the internet and software IP was pioneered which enshrined public use of these technologies, an example was the GPL, or General Public Licence (Lessig, 2001, 48–72). The internet enabled the spread of Linux and allowed worldwide 'open source' software development, which bypassed software copyrights

(Raymond, 1999). The Linux platform, an offshoot of UNIX, could be used to develop advanced services on the internet.

Just as important as the IP framework was the 'end-to-end' architecture of the internet, which encouraged innovation and international diffusion. Isenberg labelled the internet a 'stupid network' to contrast it to the 'intelligent networks' which were engineered by telecommunications firms (so-called 'end-systems'). Intelligent networks required central control, stupid networks only functioned as pipes, with networking instructions coming from participating computers all along the network. This meant that it was easy for an entrepreneur to offer new services at the periphery of the network.[17] The 'end-to-end' principals were first articulated in the early 1980s and served as an architectural model through to the turn of the century (Blumenthal and Clark, 2001, 91, 92; see also Kruse et al., 2001).

At the start of the 2000s, however, the uniquely low technological barriers to entry were being challenged by three different developments. Firstly, in the late 1990s, internet business applications were starting to become very complex because they were being connected to enterprise functions such as resource or supply chain management. While this was the natural course of development to create value in business webs, advanced systems integration know-how was now required both for consultants as well as new ventures. Proprietary IP was being connected to open IP. Secondly, demand for simpler and omnipresent consumer internet applications led to the connection of the internet to proprietary systems such as interactive television, mobile or miniature internet applications. Finally, security and reliability concerns associated with the increased commercial use of the internet, as well as the aforementioned new requirements from the corporate and consumer world, led to discussions about altering the 'end-to-end' design of the internet itself (Blumenthal and Clark, 2001; Kruse et al., 2001; see also Part III in Lessig, 2001).

RISE IN TRANSNATIONAL DEMAND FOR INTERNET SERVICES

The purpose of this section is to discuss the demand-side factors driving the adoption of the internet among different companies and countries worldwide. Multinational enterprises used the internet to restructure their worldwide businesses, using it to replace different proprietary systems existing in different countries. They also used internet standards to integrate smaller firms, for example, suppliers, and thereby extended the reach of their cross-border network-based services. New internet-based linkages among firms enabled tightly integrated worldwide processes to an extent that older, proprietary networks could not. The internet came to replace company-only systems at about the same time it moved with strength into the consumer sphere. The premise to be explored here is that the two were deeply dependent upon each other. International users following researchers and students, the early adopters of the commercial internet, belonged to an elite group of mobile knowledge workers, whose work was affected by the interlocking of worldwide business processes. Because they were working within an environment which was increasingly globally integrated, they demanded a correspondingly international network standard which their peers abroad could also use. They had little use for consumer online networks which were exclusively domestic. Thus, the rising integration of global business processes was an important force explaining early adoption of the internet internationally both among firms as well as consumers. Without the rising international integration of business processes, company-wide and country-wide solutions would have gone a longer way in satisfying compatibility demands.

Before the commercialization of the internet, the data networks of large corporations were linked to the networks of external companies through a set of standards called electronic data interchange (EDI). EDI standards allowed flexible manufacturing techniques to be implemented and shifted holding costs and business risk from the manufacturer to the participating supplier (Cash et al., 1992, 71, 72). In the USA, more than 60 per cent of all firms apparently utilized some form of EDI in the mid-1990s (Wigand et al., 1997, 260).[18] Yet, EDI was no more than a set of standards to facilitate data interchange among different company networks. The connection of networks to each other still required intense system integration work and was costly to maintain. Internet standards met an acute demand for a simplified and less costly exchange of data among different company networks. The demand for data interchange among firms had grown tremendously, accelerated through outsourcing.[19] Using the internet, large concerns could be connected to hundreds of smaller suppliers; as the pioneer corporate internet user GE demonstrated convincingly.[20] By building shared network structures new enterprise structures appeared to function as a whole, yet were separate entities.[21] Management literature has referred to this as the 'boundaryless corporation'.[22] This trend climaxed in the widely publicised corporate models of Toyota, Nike and Benetton, all so-called 'hollow firms' because they largely consisted of subcontracting networks of hundreds or thousands of suppliers.[23]

But network enthusiasts did not stop here. The last bastion of the spread of corporate networks was the consumer.[24] If consumers could be integrated into the network, not only as a receiver but also as a sender of information, business processes could be further optimized. Thus, when the individual became part of the network, it was possible to create a complete 'network economy'[25] in which, for example, a computer order placed by an internet user resulted in an immediate signal being sent to the assembly plant which automatically manufactured the product according to customer specifications. These transactional services were of the 'self-service' type.[26]

Initially, these schemes were realized only in a few instances such as computers, as well as in the travel and financial industries. Customized manufacturing processes such as the so-called 'Dell system', named after a computer manufacturer, were feasible early on due to their highly modular components. It is important to note here that on the internet there was no distinction in network costs whether the networked individual was abroad, thus sparking a transnational transaction, or within the same country as the company offering the service. Some cases were known in which internet firms have provided services which have involved significant cross-border transactions. One example was Tiss, a two-person German internet start-up in Heilbronn selling flight tickets mostly to consumers in the USA and generating substantial, nine-digit DM revenues already in 1997 and 1998. In this way, the internet and other global data networks uniquely enabled an increase in the international trade of services (mention in Welfens and Jungmittag, 2002, 59).

Work in sociology researched the use of the internet by individuals. Sociology was also an avid contributor to literature about globalization. Although the amount of people actually working outside their home country was very limited and the percentage of these that were globally mobile workers even smaller,[27] sociologists attempted to show why those living in their country of origin were feeling more aware of global interdependence. The work ranged from examining how the identity of individuals may have been affected in a global environment to discussing the risks or fears people may have felt.[28] The possible effects of a parallel increase of self-employment and independent contractorship as well as increasing uncertainties regarding retirement were debated (Coyle, 1997, xiv, xv, 216).[29] Another strand of work culminated in the concept of the 'knowledge worker', or, what Robert Reich called the 'symbolic analysts' (Reich, 1991).[30] A growth in cultural production was noted in industrialized countries.[31] In the United States, the number of teleworkers working from home via a network connection was estimated to be as high as 7 million by the Department of Transportation (US Department of Commerce, 1998, 48, 61). Castells generalized these trends into a development he called the 'individualisation of work' (Castells, 1996, 201–26).

This thinking also began to inspire writers within the field of political economy, leading to alarmist as well as enthusiastic ruminations. Rosenau stressed the reflexive self-consciousness of individuals exposed to globalization (Castells, 1996, 229, 230; Rosenau, 1990, 13, 15). Stopford and Strange contended how the transnational flow of ideas and beliefs, reflected also in consumer expectations and demand, could result in pressure on governments (Stopford, Strange and Henley, 1991, 20). Ohmae stated the same even more idealistically:

> Governments can still arbitrage information or otherwise protect their markets by forcing citizens to buy high-priced beef (as is the case in Japan) or poor-quality automobiles (the case in India and Brazil), but product labels are spreading all over the world and news of product performance is harder to suppress. Information has empowered consumers (1994, 4).

Discussing the effects of globalization on the individual was, as this brief excursion into sociology shows, very much in vogue in the late 1990s. It is indeed quite possible that early consumer demand for internet services in the late 1990s was, in part, related to the global reach of the network, in contrast to older, country-only on-line services. It was also true, however, that most internet services were devised for a local audience, despite the possibilities of global reach. A study of the European Commission showed that 42 per cent of all European internet services were offered only in the local language, not in English (European Commission, 1997, 29). The key to understanding more about the history of internet uptake among consumers would be to segment users into early adopters and mass users. This is not the place to follow this lead, but the contention made here is that internet demand was initiated by early pioneers who explicitly searched for international services, academics and knowledge workers. These early adopters also were witnessing increased globalization in their careers and private lives.

It can, however, be safely said that the demand for internet services and other network-based services at home was highly dependent on cost. Cost also prevented video-on-demand or interactive television from being realized on a broad scale (Wigand et al., 1997, 277). For private consumers, the cost of internet access depended largely on the cost of telephony services, because usually they dialed into their internet service provider over a local phone line. Regulation was an important issue affecting the cost of telephony services as well as influencing the growth of internet infrastructure directly, as we will see in the next chapter.[32]

Given cost sensitivity, it is important to bear in mind, however, that internet use may still be growing, but that it is far from being ubiquitous, even in the Triad countries. In this study, therefore, the author refers to the potential for ubiquity which acted as an important incentive for entrepreneurship. The use of global computer services, among consumers as well as among firms, was largely an experiment which considerably slowed its pace after market downturn from the year 2000. Similarly, the transition to the global corporation (as opposed to the multinational enterprise) itself is on precarious grounds; the period of transition coincided with a period of strong economic growth in the USA. Some sociologists and management theorists, even political economists, can be criticized for forgetting this when extrapolating trends from the late 1990s into the future. This speculative section on the origins of demand will be concluded with a reminder that similar issues to those discussed here were already popular in international relations and political economy at an earlier point in time. The 1970s heralded the rise of the 'international society' and an increasingly interdependent world.[33]

ENTREPRENEURIAL ACTIVITY AND SUPPLY BOOM

The internet was a classic example of a 'disruptive technology', a reference to Clayton Christensen's useful concept (1997). Although large corporations were already using computer networks for several decades in company-only systems, entrepreneurs could act upon the global window of opportunity associated with potential ubiquity, especially the possible mass use of the internet by consumers. Company-only systems could now be interconnected to previously closed country-only consumer online systems. The promise of a seamless computer network linking consumers and businesses was a powerful proposition enabling wholly new ways of conducting business. Entrepreneurs recognized this opportunity of potential ubiquity early, during a phase when internet use was still limited to pioneer adopters. A stream of experiments and innovations were initiated by entrepreneurs. Some were successful, some failed in the early 2000s after the financial downturn, others, such as internet 'push technology' failed immediately (Kenney, 2001, 24). The entrepreneurs realized also that it would take time before established players would fully understand the potential of the internet. Indeed, established players at first underestimated and therefore bypassed the internet, allowing newcomers to step in and innovate.

The founder of Amazon.com, an internet electronic commerce company with one of the highest profiles in the late 1990s, described in an FT interview how he had originally perceived his chances of success:

> Yes. I find [the growth of Amazon.com] surprising. Anyone who had predicted what has actually happened would have had to be institutionalised.[34]

Growth in the demand for internet services was, therefore, met from the mid-1990s to the end of the decade by a supply boom, a period of experimentation with new services and entrepreneurship. This occurred globally, but was most pronounced in the United States. Retrospectively, this supply boom was associated with financial exuberance, the internet bubble. In fact, the years after 1995 saw an unprecedented rise in venture capital investment in internet-related companies from US$134 million to almost US$2 billion in 1997. This figure rose to almost US$20 billion in 1999 (see Table 2.2). Private investment activity by the venture capital industry was accompanied by dozens of stock market listings of internet service and software companies, a small number of which were spectacular, fuelling the imagination of the financial industry and further inciting investment. Already at the end of 1996, there were more than 20 internet companies listed on NASDAQ (Reid, 1997, xvi). The public funding opportunity was extraordinary in the United States from 1996, when Alan Greenspan held his famous speech warning of 'irrational exuberance' to the end of the internet bubble in 2000. The total public market valuation of US internet companies in May 1999 already stood at approximately US$300 billion.[35] Stock prices of internet firms were based on expected earnings, not on current earnings.[36] In anticipation of the closure of the funding opportunity, firms were hastened through the development stages at an extraordinary pace. The Silicon Valley newspaper *San Jose Mercury News* stated as early as 1998 that it was not uncommon for an IPO to occur 18 to 24 months after a company was founded.

In their book called *A Nation Transformed by Information*, business historians Chandler and Cortada examined continuities between the rise of software and the internet to that of the postal system, the telegraph, the telephone, radio and television. But they also identified discontinuities related to software and the internet: 'what occurred in the 1980s and 1990s is that the barriers to entry remained far lower than for any previous form of information technology and products' (2000b, 297). Two aspects of low entry barriers which were cited were that know-how requirements were low and capital requirements were 'virtually nonexistent' (296, 297).[37] For the development of internet services in the late 1990s, the low barriers to entry in terms of know-how have already been discussed. But how can the observation made by Chandler and Cortada be reconciled with the massive sums invested in internet ventures in the late 1990s? Venture capital investments were not a necessary requirement for internet entrepreneurship, as we will see in later chapters dedicated to European development, but they were an important aspect explaining the development of internet ventures in the United States and their path development. In addition, advanced demand conditions for internet services were absolutely necessary, for reasons which will be discussed below. US internet demand was early on marked by both high absolute user numbers, with the number of internet users in 1998 estimated at 79 million, as well as high penetration in the population, 29 per cent. Advanced demand conditions helped US ventures develop sophisticated services which could then be offered internationally in countries which were just reaching similar demand structures. Both factors were emphasized by Martin Kenney in his analysis of the development of the internet in the US (2001).

Three main types of internet start-ups will be examined here: web development companies, electronic commerce ventures as well as portal and community sites. All three types of firms contributed to the commercialization and international success of the internet, yet they had distinct revenue models. Indeed, one could extend this list much further. The internet created a great variety of companies with different business models many of which disappeared. Furthermore, the 'pure play' types presented here were later diluted. As the internet sector consolidated, portal players, for example, sought to generate electronic commerce revenues. Yet, the 'pure play' approach was crucial in the beginning, because it allowed the entrepreneur to focus his limited resources on extending a specific business model. Missing from the list of types of firms to be examined here are internet service providers (ISPs), internet software companies and so-called business-to-business (B2B) start-ups. This is because these latter three venture types were more difficult to distinguish than the former three. ISPs were competing in the telecommunications and data networking industry, most software companies extended their applications to become internet software companies and B2B firms were innovating upon older electronic data interchange (EDI) initiatives. Furthermore, the three company types discussed here, web developers, e-commerce ventures and portals, had their greatest window of opportunity where the 'disruptive' potential of the internet was the largest: In linking consumers to businesses and enabling seamless network transactions.

Of the three internet businesses discussed here, web development companies employed the most traditional revenue model: professional services. In the mid-1990s, web development companies appeared in large numbers all over the United States and the rest of the world. They helped other companies establish a presence on the internet; especially lucrative opportunities were those in which corporate systems were extended to consumers and new interfaces were formed between businesses and consumers. Here, the web developers had clear advantages over the traditional consultants working with established companies, the IT consultants and systems integrators. The top web developers, firms such as USWeb, iXL and Agency.com, grew rapidly in the USA and abroad, mostly by acquiring smaller firms in their field. In Europe, all three were active in several countries, giving them pan-European scope. Internationalization was a key growth strategy, because the most lucrative clients were multinational companies, which demanded that global accounts be executed by several worldwide offices in concert. The three players mentioned here were well financed, either through venture capital groups or, in the case of Agency.com, through a global advertising holding company. All were listed on NASDAQ. The acquired firms were often smaller companies, which were under-capitalized and focused on a local market – this was true for in Europe as well as the USA.

The second type of internet start-up to be discussed here was electronic commerce ventures. They generated revenue by selling products or services to consumers through the internet. Some of the highest profile US start-ups here were Amazon.com (books), eBay (consumer auctions) or E*TRADE (internet broker). In the beginning, these firms did not internationalize through offices abroad. From a single location, Amazon.com sold books in 160 countries; E*TRADE carried out transactions for investors in 119 countries.[38] Yet, global internet commerce from a single location reached a natural limit in most business models. In effect, these companies initially served an ex-pat community, for example, US citizens trading their US stocks from abroad. Broader commercial activity required a local presence. Firms which sold goods to foreign consumers over the internet ('e-tailers'), for example, required local merchandising and a local inventory. By early 1998, Amazon.com had expanded internationally through acquisition of existing foreign players in Germany and the UK.[39] E*TRADE launched its third international web site in France in March 1999 together with a local investment bank, CPR.[40] US electronic commerce players found that the foreign companies they bought and partnered with were well established in their local market – similar to the web development companies. But most had not built an extensive international presence themselves; they were domestic players.

The final basic type of internet start-up to be discussed here was the portal site. It obtained its revenues mainly through advertising. The most initially successful portal players from the USA, Yahoo!, Excite and Lycos, all internationalized quickly in an effort to extend their 'mindshare' and brand equity. In its internationalization strategy, Yahoo! was an innovator by first realizing it needed to enter each foreign market separately with its own presence instead of trying to use the global reach of the internet to host an internet service for several countries from a single location.[41] Lycos engaged itself in a partnership with Bertelsmann in Europe, acquired a popular Scandinavian portal, Spray networks, and carried out a separate stock market listing of its European entity. Yahoo! carried out a separate stock market listing in Japan. A significant original investor in the US Yahoo! was the Japanese software and investor group Softbank.

All three types of revenue models described here relied directly or indirectly on sophisticated internet demand structures. High penetration rates, for example, were crucial for web development companies. Their clients, such as banks or airlines, only considered an extensive internet presence and advanced internet service offerings if they could be sure that these new services would be able to reach a significant proportion of their customers. This was echoed in a *Financial Times* article on Sweden: 'Once Internet penetration reaches a certain point, the development of services such as internet banking can take off.'[42] Penetration also was important for electronic commerce companies – if internet penetration had not increased in the US and spread the internet more broadly in the population, Amazon.com would not have sold more than computer books. Established firms such as the aforementioned banks and airlines invested in internet advertising only if their advertising demonstrated adequate reach; thus, advertising expenditures were also dependent upon penetration. Portals, in turn, relied on advertising revenues. Time spent online also was crucial for some of the same reasons. For users to become acquainted with new service offerings over the internet, it was important that time spent online was not discouraged by metered pricing in the USA.

Michael Porter, who has helped popularize the concept of home demand conditions in the analysis of internationalization, argues that advanced domestic demand is crucial for the long-term competitiveness of internationally oriented companies (Porter, 1990, 86–100). US internet start-ups certainly took advantage of the sophistication of their home market, that is, strong consumer penetration, to develop innovative business models which could be exported abroad (see Table 2.1). Start-ups also benefited considerably from aggressive and buoyant capital markets – both venture capital and private investors vigorously pursued internet opportunities in the late 1990s.

Advanced demand for internet services was necessary for all types of US internet ventures. While internet entrepreneurship would also have happened in the United States also without the strong funding opportunities available to new ventures in the period from 1996 to 2000, the development of the internet in the United States would certainly have occurred very differently without these opportunities. To finance its pre-IPO growth, for example, the web developer iXL raised more than US$60 million. From its foundation in March 1996 to its public listing at NASDAQ in June 1999, iXL acquired 34 companies. It grew from 90 employees in January 1997 to approximately 1300 employees by December 1998.[43] It would have been impossible at the time to replicate the iXL story in Europe. Table 2.2 below shows the massive amount of funding poured into internet start-ups by venture capitalists in the United States in the 1990s.

Table 2.1   International presence of independent internet ventures with US origins among the top ten web properties of each country in January 2002

	Yahoo!	Amazon	Lycos Network	eBay	Google
US	2	6	7	8	9
France	5	–	2	–	10
Germany	4	–	3	5	6
Japan	1	–	–	–	–
Netherlands	6	–	5	–	9
Singapore	1	–	3	–	10
Sweden	10	–	6	–	–
United Kingdom	2	10	9	–	6

Source: Data on top ten web properties for each country was quoted from Nielsen//NetRatings Audience Measurement Service (http://www.nielsen-netratings.com), accessed on 25 February 2002.

Table 2.2   Growth in venture capital investments USA in US$ billion

	1995	1996	1997	1998	1999	Growth 1995–99 (%)
All industries	7.6	9.5	13.8	14.3	35.6	368
Technology	4.0	6.0	8.5	10.8	32.4	710
Internet-related	0.1	ca. 0.9	1.9	3.4	19.9	19800

Source: Price Waterhouse Venture Capital Surveys, now the PricewaterhouseCoopers Money Tree Survey. A measurement change occurred after 1998; the numbers before that year are cited slightly lower in subsequent surveys. The most recent data used was PricewaterhouseCoopers, 'Moneytree US Report, Full Year & Q4 1999 Results'.

But the venture capital industry also was useful beyond the financial dimension. In the US, well-known venture capitalists opened doors to partnerships and other business relationships. They provided a start-up with legitimacy. It is not the objective of this study to examine this point in detail, although some researchers still feel the process of adding value beyond capital by venture capitalists is as of yet imperfectly understood (Steier and Greenwood, 1995, 340).[44] The financial as well as other services provided by the venture capital industry were, furthermore, closely connected to other services, such as legal advisors. Together, 'entrepreneurial ecosystems' were formed in a few specific areas in the United States; the leader being Silicon Valley.[45] Indeed, Silicon Valley is such a dominant cluster that it is accurate to call venture capital in the United States a region-specific advantage. For example, close to one-third of all venture capital investments in the United States were initiated in 1998 from the Silicon Valley region.[46]

In summary, it was a combination of different national and regional factors which helped US internet start-ups grow both at home and internationally. The most important were advanced demand conditions nationally – early transition from pioneer to mass consumer use. The strong availability of venture capital and public capital for internet ventures, especially in the relatively long bubble period from 1996 to 2000, also was an crucial component for the US 'national system of innovation' as it related to internet development (see Kenney, 2001).

THE ROLE OF THE USA: MULTILATERAL OR BILATERAL FLOWS?

The original commercial drivers for the international growth of the internet were related to its ability to function as a 'connective tissue' for company-only and country-only networks. While the internet as a 'network of networks' initially connected across different previously insular data networks growth later consisted of new connections. At this point in time, network externalities began to operate which speeded up the diffusion of the technology even further.

When network externalities operate, each additional user of a given technology in a network causes the value of that piece of technology as a whole to grow.[47] Because of the linkage between value and user numbers, a technology that has become adopted by a certain critical mass of users can, at times, capture the whole market almost exclusively, leading to the exponential growth mapped in Figure 2.2. It is here that an effect called 'lock-in' sets in. It does not have to be the superior technology that succeeds; in fact, historical chance events can lead to the adoption of inferior technologies.[48] Network externalities can occur without an overt network being involved, too. It works with computer operating systems or software when compatibility issues raise the value of a program.

World demand by consumers for the internet took off in the second half of the 1990s. This is when network externalities set in. Figure 2.2 shows the growth of internet host computers – these are the main access points to the internet (located at internet service providers (ISPs) and which are usually shared by several users). UUNET, one of the largest internet backbone providers, estimated that internet traffic doubled every 100 days in the 1990s. Country-wide network efforts as well as commercial on-line services

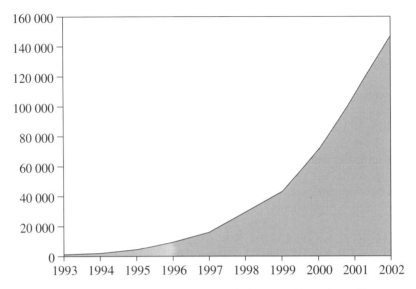

Note: An internet host is a computer connected to the internet with a unique address (Internet Protocol IP address). The number of hosts is the most accurate indication of internet growth available. Usually, several users connect through a single host.

Source: Internet Software Consortium, http://www.isc.org/. All host figures are from the months of January. The data: 1993, 1313; 1994, 2217; 1995, 4852; 1996, 9472; 1997, 16146; 1998, 29670; 1999, 43230; 2000, 72398; 2001, 109574; 2002, 147245.

Figure 2.2   Growth of internet host computers (thousands)

eventually adopted the internet model and became part of the 'network of networks'. The internet was simply 'backpacked' on their existing infrastructure. The applications that ran on the old networks were supplanted by 'superstar' internet applications; only the network infrastructure remained.

The take-off of the internet coincided with the commercialization of the research network. In 1988, the privatization of the internet began and was a carefully government-orchestrated process that ended with the defunding of the NSFNET backbone in April 1995.[49] Whereas educational traffic expanded steadily, commercial services boomed (See Figure 2.3).

Yet, was the internet in the late 1990s characterized internationally by multilateral flows with different parts of the world interchanging data in a complex pattern? Or should the early worldwide internet more aptly be described as a bilateral system wherein most data travelled to and from the United States? This question will in different guises follow us throughout

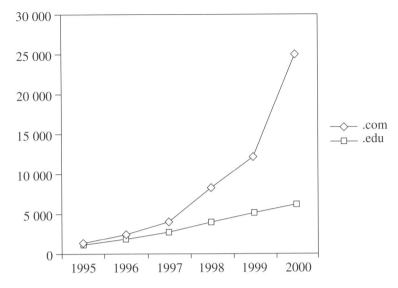

Note: This data refers to the number of hosts with the top-level domains .com (commercial) and .edu (educational) only. There are numerous other domains which are owned by commercial as well as educational organizations. A comparison between .com and .edu indicates the rapid growth of commercial hosts in contrast to the stable growth of educational hosts, however.

Source: Internet Software Consortium (http://www.isc.org/), accessed on 25 February 2002. The data (1995–2000, thousands): .com: 1317, 2431, 3965, 8202, 12141, 24863; .edu: 1134, 1793, 2654, 3945, 5022, 6085.

Figure 2.3   *The commercialization of the internet. Commercial versus educational host computer growth (thousands)*

this study. A multilateral flow would match the vision of the networkist thinkers, which believed 'their' network to be non-hierarchical and without a centre. This belief was supported by the technological underpinnings of the internet. Furthermore, the global electronic networks originally pioneered by financial services and multinational enterprises (MNEs), the predecessors to the internet, seemed to link the so-called Triad of industrialised regions in a multilateral way.

Bilateral flows would signal dominance of the US supply of internet services; multilateral flows correspond to a scenario in which different countries are equal participants in an entrepreneurial leapfrogging contest. Indeed, existing data on internet flows did reveal the strong dominance of the US at the time and was highly bilateral. Unfortunately, it was impossible to tell whether this was due only to the architecture of the network.

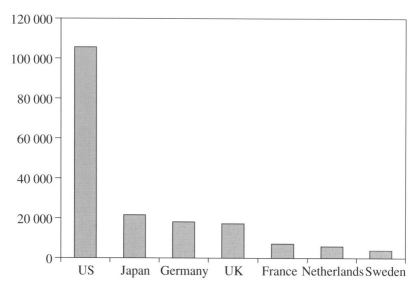

Source: Data obtained from Nielsen//NetRatings Audience Measurement Service (http://www.nielsen-netratings.com), accessed on 25 February 2002. Active internet universe is defined as all members of households with access to the internet on a personal computer who actively use the internet. The data (thousands): US 104793; Japan 21591; Germany 17901; UK 17012; France 7176; The Netherlands 5505; Sweden 3619.

Figure 2.4   Active internet universe in a selection of countries, January 2002

Data was often transported via the US while moving from one international location to the next.[50]

The United States dominated the internet not solely in terms of its architecture. After a little more than half a decade of commercialization, the largest group of internet users by far were located in the United States (Figure 2.4). It was, furthermore, very clear that the wave of entrepreneurial activity surrounding the commercialization of the internet had its centre in the United States. This activity was financed by enthusiastic capital markets including a buoyant venture capital industry.

In fact, a strong case can be made that internet flows among businesses were, in the late 1990s, multilateral, whereas consumer flows were to a large degree still bilateral. As described in this chapter, internet innovations had their greatest 'disruptive' potential in networking consumers and linking them to businesses. Most of the new services for consumers were pioneered by US entrepreneurs acting upon this opportunity. The timing in the mid- to late 1990s was perfect. Internet usage in the United States was moving rapidly from early adoption towards mainstream penetration rates. Approaching ubiquity increased the disruptive potential of the internet, a clear signal for entrepreneurs (Christensen, 1997). This was not the case in most other countries. There, early pioneers existed but the movement towards mainstream use was not apparent. The early adopters outside the United States took advantage of North American internet service offerings. Local offerings or services from other non-US countries did not seem as innovative and did not have a comparable depth.

A discussion of entrepreneurial activity outside of the USA is conspicuously absent from this chapter. Using the case of Europe, however, much of the rest of this book will be dedicated to explaining a case of development of internet entrepreneurship which was distinct from the United States. One of the objectives of the study is to understand how international growth of the internet – described in this chapter and the next – actually signified a venture opportunity in countries other than the United States.

Before this discussion shifts to Germany, however, Chapter 3 will focus on the role of governments in the internationalization of network-based services and the internet. In Chapter 3, the shifts discussed in this chapter will be linked to initial US government subsidies of the internet when it was a fledgling research network, the purposeful lack of effective direct regulation of internet services and the indirect effects of deregulation carried out by governments in financial services, telecommunications and FDI. The internationalization of the internet cannot be correctly understood without discussing government contributions – especially US government contributions.

HOW PERMANENT IS US LEADERSHIP IN THE GLOBAL MARKET FOR INTERNET SERVICES?

When network externalities were a subject of academic and practitioner debate in the late 1990s, the economist Danny Quah disagreed with some of the conclusions of network externality research. He stated he did not believe products or services that have won the game of network externalities have captured the market indefinitely. They could be toppled by a new standard just as fast as it took them to lock in. Because of this, he reintroduced the term 'superstar economics' as a substitute for network externalities. The basis of superstar economics was the infinite expansibility of a commodity which can be secured by reproducing digital content, for example. In fact, Quah believed that trade will increasingly involve reproduction and not exchange.[51] Quah described the consequences of superstar economics in this quote:

A weightless-economy industry cannot erect entry barriers in the form of set-up costs to protect its established successes. Rather, ongoing success has to come from continual innovation and perpetual paranoia . . . The upshot is the economics of superstars, where the top few supply the entire market, and are rewarded far beyond what would have been initially expected of them. But the picture is dynamic. Superstar successes are in turn replaced, and easily (Quah, 1998).[52]

Some internet business models were characterized by lower network effects and switching costs than others. While the internet as a data network standard, after its take-off, enjoyed high switching costs and network effects, specific internet services, such as electronic commerce sites, benefited less from network effects and were more susceptible to attack by newcomers. Pure search functions, while a very popular internet service, were characterized very low switching costs and no network externalities (Gandal, 2001, 365). Search newcomer Google, which entered the market only in 1999, demonstrated this convincingly. The fact that Google became a rapid international success also showed to what extent the internet even after consolidation and increasing localization could serve as a global network (see Table 2.1). Internet companies seem to need to continually innovate in order to remain successful in the long term.

This having been said, the opportunity for global internet entrepreneurship in the late 1990s had unique characteristics. Internet technologies were open to innovation, globally. The funding environment from 1996 to 2000 was favourable, which was rare in economic history. The next chapter will focus on how government contributed to this window of opportunity. There was, after all, only one successful independent venture latecomer, only one Google, at the turn of the decade.

NOTES

1. For a review of macroeconomic implications of the 'New Economy,' such as the reduction of inventory costs, see DeLong (2000 and 2001). For the term 'business webs' see Tapscott, et al. (2000). A discussion of the 'real time economy' including business cases can be found in *The Economist*, 'How about now? A survey of the real time economy', 8 February 2002.
2. See Hobbes' Internet Timeline, accessible at http://www.zakon.org/robert/internet/time-line/.
3. David Bank discusses the Microsoft strategy respective to the internet in his book, based on internal Microsoft correspondence (2001, for Pearl Harbour Day, see p. 61). 'The Internet Tidal Wave' memo by Bill Gates from May 1995 is mentioned by Martin Kenney. Kenney also describes the timing of internet development in the United States (2001, 20–22).
4. See the survey 'The Frontiers of Finance' (*The Economist* Newspaper Ltd., 1996, 265–97).

5. Castells quotes François Chesnais with an estimate of 50 major players in world financial markets (Castells, 1996, 435).

6. SAP is present in 40 countries, the software is avaliable in 24 standard language versions and first-level system support can be called upon 24 hours via four centres in Germany, the USA, Singapore and Japan. Information was obtained from the 1996 annual report of SAP AG as well as 'SAP's Worldview', *Red Herring*, November 1988, GG6–GG10 and 'Baan's Voyage,' *Red Herring*, August 1998, 66–8.

7. The advantages of the deployment of internet technologies within corporations can be illustrated with the case of Reuters. In the late 1990s, Reuters expanded its supply of industry information to global industrial enterprises. This new, lucrative client base had been made possible through the proliferation of internet standards. For the first time, Reuters did not have to worry about the underlying network infrastructure because it simply provided its information on top of internet standards. In the 1980s, when Reuters intended to provide the financial services industry with a similar network-based service, it had to finance the network infrastructure itself. Reuters, then the largest international news agency with an annual income in 1984 of £313 million and a profit of £74 million had to undergo public flotation in order to finance its proprietary news network for the financial industry (Boyd-Barrett, 1989, 108, 125).

8. From the Second World War until the 1970s, multinational enterprises (MNEs) enjoyed average profit margins above 20 per cent. Corporate profits dropped precariously in the 1970s to levels between 10 and 20 per cent. The G7 average rate of return in the manufacturing sector fell from 25 per cent in 1965 to 12 per cent in 1980. This resulted in what was labelled by some as the 'Crisis of the Large Corporation' and by others as 'The Great Profits Squeeze' (Castells, 1996, 152–68; Harrison, 1994, 125–7). Falling profits were due to rising overhead costs and rising volatility in the international economy. Two events can serve as markers, one was the so-called oil shock, the other the collapse of the Bretton Woods system and the ensuing uncertainty in the foreign exchange system.

9. For an investigative and critical account of MNE experimentation see Harrison (1994). Explicit references to experimentation and management information systems can be found on p. 9, 10. See also Beck (1986), 345–57. On p. 345, Beck writes (in the 1980s): 'Wir befinden uns am Beginn einer organizationskonzeptuellen Experimentierphase, die dem Zwang der Privatsphäre, neue Lebensformen zu erproben, keineswegs nachsteht' (italics removed) ('We are at the beginning of an experimental phase focusing on organizational concepts, which is in no way less profound than the experiments occurring in the private sphere', my translation). The management theorists Bartlett and Ghoshal cite 'traditional' and 'emerging' motivations for globalizing tendencies in MNEs. The first group includes: secure key supplies, market-seeking and access to low-cost factors of production. The second group includes: increasing scale economies, ballooning R&D investment costs, shortening of product life cycles, global scanning and learning capability (Bartlett and Ghoshal, 1995, 5–9; Hirst and Thompson, 1996, 62).

10. Measured in relation to domestic investment worldwide, FDI in the 1980s eclipsed the previous period of FDI growth in the 1960s by a factor of two (Julius cited in Dicken, 1992, 51). Of global merchandise trade, approximately one-third is conduced within MNEs on an intra-firm basis. Outward FDI stock stood in 1992 at US$2.6 trillion. Global sales by foreign affiliates stood in 1992 at US$5.2 trillion, compared to the worldwide export of goods and (non-factor) services of US$4.9 trillion – again, including intra-firm trade (UNCTAD, 1995, xx, xxi, 3, 4; the approximation of intra-firm trade levels was derived from US data; intra-firm trade is also mentioned by Hirst and Thompson, 1996, 53).

11. Computer networks carrying corporate services were not always installed from above within the firm. Even before the rise of internet technology, research into the global networks of the Swedish multinational ball-bearings producer SKF revealed that the worldwide corporate network was being used by employees to form their own 'rebellious' *ad hoc* network-based services. These led to examples of 'spontaneous coordination' among organizational units which were hierarchically not directly linked (Hagström, 1991, 107,

108, 123, 124). Hagström called this 'revealed demand' (Hagström, 1991, 110). Noticing this, the management of MNEs in some instances introduced network systems explicitly to break up traditional hierarchies within firms. Although the rationale for introducing network systems has shifted with time, and the emphasis on control has declined, it has to be stated that even decentralized intranet-type approaches can be used for the purposes of control as well as for empowering non-hierarchical project groups. Hagström elegantly views control as just one among a diverse set of types of services that can be carried by corporate networks (Hagström, 1991, 58, 98, 106). It has been emphasized that networked IT systems are being viewed in corporations both as a means to achieve more central control and as a means to limit the control of the centre (Cash et al., 1992, 82). (For the classification into three eras of corporate computing see Cash et al., 1992, 10). Both strategies of control and decentralization were empirically found to exist side by side within one MNE, the Swedish roller-bearing producer SKF (Hagström, 1991, 100).This tendency increased when cheap software for information-sharing with open standards proliferated due to the rise of the internet. By 1997, most of the largest MNEs had so-called 'intranet islands' that had been initiated 'parasitically' on top of corporate networks through *ad hoc* initiatives without central control. The following articles refer to the adoption of internet standards within German multinational corporations. Claudia E. Petrik, 'Intranet krempelt hierarchische Strukturen um. Außer Kontrolle', *Gateway Magazin für Daten-und Telekommunikation*, Heise Verlag, September 1996, 44–46; 'Chemie-und Pharmakonzern experimentiert mit internem Web. Hoechst: Intranet-Guerillas unterwandern Infokultur', *Computerwoche*, 27, 5 July 1996, 69, 70; Niko Waesche und L. Nikolaus Guntrum, Hoechst AG Frankfurt am Main, 'Realisation einer Intranet Kultur – Am Beispiel des Hoechst Wide Web', *Industrie Management*, 6, December 1996, 39–42; 'Intranet/ Die elektronischen Medien befinden sich auf dem Vormarsch, Der PC dient als Informationsmittel und Arbeitsinstrument', *Handelsblatt*, 25 November 1996, 28.

12. The World Investment Report cites a total of 40000 parent MNEs with 250000 foreign affiliates for 1992 (UNCTAD, 1995, xx, xxi); it is obvious that the great majority of these corporations are not installing computer networks to conduct global business strategies. In fact, the same report labels 40 MNEs as being very transnational, measuring over 50 per cent on the UNCTAD's composite index of transnationality (UNCTAD, 1995, xxvi, xxvii). UNCTAD has published an index of global corporations by using estimates of the proportion of foreign employees and foreign turnover. Only the largest companies are included in the list. Through these statistics, it is evident that only a small proportion of today's large multinational firms are becoming truly global. It has been pointed out that although foreign direct investment is growing rapidly, much of this is generated by firms with a single location abroad.

13. With the exception of CompuServe. CompuServe was the first on-line service to venture abroad, and therefore to offer a transnational service; the first countries it expanded into included the UK and Germany in 1991. By Autumn 1995, CompuServe provided access to users in more than 140 countries.

14. Among established players, the telephone operator AT&T planned a service called Interchange, Microsoft launched Microsoft Network and Apple started eWorld, but these services did not meet expectations as on-line services. At the high point for on-line services with their proprietary business model, Autumn 1995, the following subscriber numbers were available (in millions): AOL 3.8, CompuServe 3.5, Prodigy 1.7, Microsoft Network 0.2, Delphi 0.1, eWorld 0.1 (listed in OECD, 1996a).

15. Sex services accounted for more than half of Mintel use in 1990, this dwindled later with the commercialization of the internet. Up to 60 to 70 per cent of internet traffic may be sex-related. Sex services seem to be a major force driving the use of commercial network-based services. See Susanna Glaser, 'Sex Drive. Pornography is pushing the pace of technology', *i-D Magazine*, December 1998, 62.

16. For these developments, see the section 'Formation of the broad community', in: Leiner et al. (1998).

17. In an article, David Isenberg summarizes how the 'stupid network' encourages innova-

tion: 'Stupid Networks make no assumptions about voice or other content. Users can put bits in one end, and the same bits come out in the other. Unlike the Intelligent Network model, the Stupid Network features abundant infrastructure, not carefully engineered scarcity. Addressing, features and class of service are specified in the user's terminal, at the edge of the network. Furthermore, the Stupid Network's simple interface makes underlying network complexities irrelevant to the user. This creates an environment that fosters wild-eyed innovation, in which users can try out harebrained ideas without asking permission of a big bureaucracy. This unimpeded ability to innovate is most crucial. Think of the cost to humanity had Mosaic, the first internet browser, not been invented. The 'Next Big Thing' is more likely to come from a hacker's terminal than from an engineer at a central switching office, or a telephone company marketing department' (1997). Further information is contained in a series of three articles, in which Isenberg debates with an Ericsson executive: Isenberg (1998a and 1998b) as well as Jomer (1998). See also Niko Waesche, 'Clever Servers Hold the Key to Dumb Networks', *Communications Week International*, 18 January 1999, page 9. Thanks go to Kenneth Niel Cukier of *Communications Week International* for pointing me towards this debate and allowing me to join the discussion.

18. An externalization of risks and costs can take place in subcontracting relationships between large and small firms also without EDI services, of course. Although subcontracting has existed since the beginnings of industrialization ('putting-out'), network technologies have allowed the development of 'just-in-time' systems which intensify the externalization of risks and costs. (Dicken, 1992, 216–20; Rabach and Kim, 1994, 128; Cash et al., 1992, 71, 72).

19. For an in-depth overview of outsourcing, see 'Outsourcing: The new IT strategy', Chapter 6 of Currie (1995), 130–53.

20. The GE business case can be found in *The Economist*: 'How About Now? A Survey of the Real Time Economy'. 8 February 2002.

21. Given this background of EDI and internet-based data exchange, demand for network-based services can be divided into 'purposive' and 'passive' adopters. The first group are early adopters, users who want to be on the forefront of technology or firms seeking competitive advantage. The second group are users who adopt a technology only when has become widespread or who are asked to adopt network-based services by their industry, by either dominant customers or suppliers. Firms leading in the adoption of inter-organizational computer networks can also be labelled 'facilitator' or 'electronic market maker' in contrast to the 'participant.' For a concise discussion of reasons for adoption and a classification of adopters into 'purposive' and 'passive' see DTI (1987), 'Executive Summary' and 49, 50; for inter-organizational systems initiatives see Cash et al. (1992, p. 74); for the term 'electronic market maker' see Wigand et al. (1997, 275, 276).

22. Seen another way, computer networks make transaction costs affordable for certain less hierarchically organized tasks even in inter-organizational exchanges (for a discussion of transaction costs in the light of IT systems, see Wigand et al., 1997, 37–42).

23. The Toyota, Nike and Benetton examples can be found in Dicken (1992, 221, diagrams 222, 251, 281). These subcontracting networks were primarily organizational and not necessarily supported by IT networks.

24. Consider the quote from the back cover of an American bestseller: 'The individual will become more of an entrepreneur, a private contractor, in complete control of his or her finances, with easy access to enormous computing power – in fact the sovereign individual' (Davidson and Rees-Mogg, 1997).

25. For an ode to demand power updated to the age of the internet see McKenna (1997). Like so many other books in the popular management literature segment, it is based almost entirely on anecdotal evidence.

26. From the view of the economy as a whole, the proliferation of these services partially results in a transfer of labour from paid, employee jobs to unpaid labour carried out by the client herself. This has been pointed out by Beck (1986, 352), who, however, does not consider new jobs created by computer network maintenance.

27. The group of truly globally mobile can be reduced to a small group of highly skilled, highly paid professionals, the so-called 'club class' (Hirst and Thompson, 1996, 22–31) or 'transnational kernel' (Sunkel quoted in Stopford and Strange, 1991, 21). Only 1.5 per cent of the global labour force worked outside their country in 1993. In the EU, despite the existence of only a few restrictions of labour mobility, this figure was only 2 per cent (Castells, 1996, 232, 234).

28. Regarding the question of identity in a global age, it was Akio Morita of Sony who coined the phrase 'global localization' (See Ohmae, 1994, 8, 9). Globalization is viewed by sociologists as a force that redefines what is meant by the 'local'. Globalization and deglobalization thus go hand in hand (Robertson, 1992, 8, 10). Whereas in traditional societies the local was simply what was commonplace and usual, the local now is something that constantly interacts with the 'global.' The local thus is not what it used to be, but instead is a 'tricky version of the local which operates within, and has been thoroughly reshaped by the global and operates largely within its logic' (Wilson and Dissanayake, 1996, 5). The local covers a diverse range of phenomena from food to forms of communal resistance such as religious fundamentalism (Castells, 1997, 11,12). Global risks and uncertainty play a role in the global–local nexus as well. In the case of Ulrick Beck, this is fuelled by fear; in the case of Giddens, by an increasing need to understand identity in a global context (Beck, 1986). Within international relations writing, James Rosenau has called this the 'emergence of global issues' citing AIDS and atmospheric pollution (Rosenau, 1990, 12, 13). World society thus becomes a 'community of danger' (Waters, 1995, 62). Others argue that there is a trend for more people to be involved in cultural production itself and that this type of production is inherently globally oriented. With the real or perceived changes of the information society came new insecurities and the need for experimentation, felt by businesses as well as individuals. Kenichi Ohmae points out that 'Nothing is "overseas" any longer' (Ohmae, 1994, viii).

29. Part-time and temporary work has increased by about 30 per cent in industrialized countries to about 50 million workers (Castells, 1996, 266).

30. Michael S. Scott Morton defines the 'knowledge worker' as a fraction of the workforce working with information and adding value to it. Morton believes that in the manufacturing industries 40 per cent of employees, and in the service industry 80 per cent of employees are knowledge workers or information workers (who process information without significant modification) (1991, p. 10).

31. Harvey discusses the growth of cultural production citing the rising numbers of artists as an example, 'and this is only the tip of an iceberg of cultural production'. Harvey then names local entertainers and graphic designers, 'as well as those who are the "culture transmitters"', in publishing, magazines, broadcast media. Paris apparently boasted only 2000 artists in the nineteenth century, whereas New York City in the 1980s was the home for 150,000 artists exhibiting in 680 galleries (Harvey, 1990, 290). The cultural or design services are, furthermore, becoming increasingly international in scope. King cites the importance of international contracts for US architectural firms as an example of this trend (King, 1990, 398–400). It could be added that, due among other things to changes caused by the internationalization of media, firms are aware of the need to communicate on a political and moral level; one of the contentions of some sociologists is, therefore, that corporations are becoming more like cultural institutions and are in increasing need of cultural-type services. Beck describes how business is acquiring a new moral and political dimension (Beck, 1986, 304, 305, 356).

32. In some countries, internet access is restricted, for example in Vietnam, where an internet user requires a police permit. In India, a monopoly for internet service existed until Autumn 1998.

33. There were important differences, however. Whereas the growing interdependency of the world was in the 1970s seen as strengthening international organizations such as the UN, it is today viewed more ambivalently. Interdependency means new opportunities as well as new risks. Computer networks allow 'minority' forms of personal and collective identification – some sociologists refer to a rise of 'sub politics' (for example, Beck, 1986, 304,

238, 329) – to be established worldwide. Globalization thus involves complexity and density, not homogeneity. In fact, heterogeneity is a response to globalization (Robertson, 1992, 98–105, 188; Featherstone, 1990, 1, 2, 10). Despite the apparent proliferation of American television programmes and other aspects of US culture, an 'Americanization,' or 'Coca-Colonization' as a form of homogenization is not taking place; the response to global or American culture is varied (Featherstone, 1990, 10).

34. 'Billionaire Nerd on his Own Bandwidth', *Financial Times*, 13 November 1998, 13.

35. European public internet companies at that time had a total valuation of less than US$ 10 billion. Morgan Stanley Dean Witter, Equity Research Europe, 'The European Internet Report,' June 1999, 167.

36. The stocks of the so-called Internet portal services which offer Internet search enjoyed especially high valuations. In Autumn 1988, for example, the stock prices of Yahoo and Excite were 184 and 88 times (P/E) that of their 1999 expected earnings per share (EPS). The share of Lycos, a similar service, was priced 107 times that of their year 2000 EPS. Internet professional services companies did not enjoy multiples that high. CKS Group, for example, achieved a P/E of 15 times before its acquisition by USWeb Corp. (then named Reinvent).

37. Chandler and Cortada do mention venture capital briefly in the passage, but emphasize capital requirement differences between entry in the software market to 'computer hardware or complex radio and TV transmission equipment' (2000b, 296).

38. According to company web sites accessed on 28 November 1999.

39. In Germany, Amazon acquired Telebuch ABC Bücherdienst and in the UK, Bookpages. Amazon.com press release, 'Amazon.com Acquires Three Leading Internet Companies, Acquisitions Extend Company's Ability to Serve International Customers', Seattle, 27 April 1998.

40. Previous international launches were in Canada and Australia.

41. This was the initial European strategy for France and Germany followed by Excite from its London office. See Niko Waesche, 'Building a Global Brand Name that the Locals Can't Spell, Excite Takes on American and Indigenous Portals in Europe', *Tornado-Insider.com Magazine*, 1, April 1999, 67–70, 103.

42. Nicholas George, 'Chilly Regions of North Warm to the Net', *Financial Times*, 13 October 1999, 16.

43. Filing of iXL Enterprises, Inc. with US Securities and Exchange Commission (http://www.sec.gov/), S-1, 8 February 1999. See also Waesche (1999b), 201, 202.

44. For a discussion of some of these value-added services beyond capital, please refer to MacMillan et al., (1988) and Timmons and Bygrave (1986).

45. For the term 'entrepreneurial ecosystem' as well as for a concise discussion of internet development in the United States, see Kenney (2001, 13).

46. PricewaterhouseCoopers Money Tree Survey, 'Full-year 2000 & Q1 2001 Results'. This survey included revised historic figures for the years since 1996, yet without a separate mention of internet investments.

47. As has been pointed out numerous times in other work, a fax machine is the classic example of network externalities. A single fax in the world linked up to the telephone system is not worth anything. But the value of that one fax machine is increased with each additional facsimile hooked up to a telephone line.

48. Realizing how network externalities operate, users, when given a choice between incompatible standards, try to use the information they have to select the technology that will be successful in the future – meaning the technology does not have to be superior today. Michael L. Katz and Carl Shapiro have studied the formation of standards and cases under which inferior technologies capture markets (Katz and Shapiro, 1996). See also Arthur (1989).

49. Initially, NSFNET encouraged the use of its networks by commercial organizations on a local and regional level, while prohibiting commercial usage of the backbone. The idea was to stimulate the emergence of commercial backbone services such as PSI and UUNET (Leiner et al., 1998).

50. See the useful article by Kenneth Neil Cukier, 'Global Telecom Rout', *Red Herring*, February 1999, 60–64.
51. The concept of superstar economics was introduced in 1981 by Sherwin Rosen. Superstar economics and weightless economics has been popularized by Danny Quah and also by Diane Coyle (1997) with her book *The Weightless World*.
52. For the concept of infinite extensibility see also Quah (1997).

3. Unregulation and the death of distance[1]

As described in the previous chapter, in the second half of the 1990s, the internet represented a global window of opportunity for new ventures and other small firms. For the cost of setting up an internet site, a small firm could instantaneously achieve a worldwide presence and sell products or services to customers or businesses. Distance-insensitivity was unique at the time, because it stood in strong contrast to the pricing regime associated with basic telecommunication services, in which transnational connections were both distance-sensitive and costly.[2]

Drawing on a diverse set of literature, including practitioner thinking, economics and sociology, the previous chapter described the formation of two different types of globally connected data networks. One type were the private networks of industrial multinationals and their data-sharing partner companies. These networks served to coordinate worldwide business processes. They replaced the company-only networks of the past. The second type was an emerging, transnational consumer network; the country-only online services of the past were left behind. Both types of networks shared some common characteristics including embracing internet technologies as a worldwide standard. The most innovative internet start-ups dedicated themselves to connecting the two to create seamless business webs (Tapscott et al., 2000). But the business and consumer networks described here shared a further characteristic, which was not discussed in Chapter 2: they were both run over leased lines. By doing so, they bypassed the regulation regimes of basic telecommunication services. This impacted on the pricing of both, and allowed them to be generally distance-insensitive.

Distance-insensitivity is commonly associated with technological factors such as the decentralized 'end-to-end' architecture of the internet and the co-operative peering system; technological factors were discussed in the previous chapter. A further enabler, is, however, often overlooked: government unregulation. This chapter serves to describe the various roles of government policy in creating a global network opportunity for internet ventures. The main political driver was US government.[3] It is simplistic to view the role of US government regarding the development of the internet as either hands-on or hands-off. The US government was active in financing the initial development of the internet, for example the NSFNET backbone. It was also active in purposeful unregulation, in terms of telecommunications policy, electronic commerce legislation and standards specification.

Telecommunications policy was a crucial determinant. Firms using data networks such as the internet ran over leased lines and benefited from asymmetric regulation. The way international data networks were regulated was very different from the way basic telecommunication services were regulated. Worldwide demand for the internet by both business users and consumers was deeply indebted to this regulatory asymmetry and the pricing regime it encouraged. It was even possible to argue that, to an extent, users of basic telecommunication services subsidized the use of the internet.

Next to distance insensitivity, a further – yet not uncontroversial – factor, which may have benefited start-ups, was the intentional lack of regulation in the areas of trade tariffs and cross-border consumer protection on the internet. It is argued here that the *laissez-faire* approach adopted by US negotiators pre-empted international agreements. These agreements could have stunted small firm innovation and experimentation with new, internet-enabled business models on an international scale. Most important, perhaps, was the abstinence of government intervention in the demand-driven process of developing 'open' worldwide internet technological standards. The recent history of internet standards has shown that top-down government intervention in some cases was unnecessary and that unaided pressure by business users and consumers could lead to interoperability, at least through 'open but owned' standards. Given the conditions of massive investment in the late 1990s, there was no evidence that large software developers and network owners were able to use their market power to prevent interoperability. Although the largest and most influential software developer, Microsoft, at a certain point in time attempted to embrace the internet with its own proprietary standards, it failed. And this not because of the trial waged against it by the US justice system, but because of pressure by business and consumer users of the internet. Again, innovative small firms seem to have benefited.

In discussing this international window of opportunity for start-ups, it is impossible to ignore the role of the Clinton administration. An Electronic Commerce Working Group was formed in December 1995, and Bill Clinton was proclaimed by his own officials as: 'The first world leader to give the internet and electronic commerce a central role in his policy agenda' (US Government Working Group on Electronic Commerce, 1998, 5). The US stance was mapped out a central policy document, 'A Framework for Global Electronic Commerce' dated July 1997 (Clinton and Gore, 1997). It was endorsed by Bill Clinton and Al Gore. Although the principles behind this document were not new and had characterized US negotiations in the IT area for some time, they were clearly articulated here. Negotiation was focused on creating optimal conditions for worldwide electronic commerce for US firms, according to the rule: 'What is good for US internet ventures is good for the world.' In the words of Al Gore: 'we are . . . helping to ensure that commerce goes digital, that business goes global and that innovation goes wild' (US Government Working Group on Electronic Commerce, 1998, i).

The first part of this chapter will describe how data networks bypassed international telecommunications regulation. They were purposely left unregulated. In the second part, a 'telegeography' of the internet will be presented. This section relies on research carried out by the TeleGeography research group; it showed that the global internet infrastructure was heavily dependent upon United States infrastructure acting as a worldwide hub and data centre. The reason for this could be traced back to US domestic policy which endorsed an important cross-subsidy privileging the internet, leading to both growth in use as well as massive infrastructure investment. The importance of this cross-subsidy shows that it was not just unregulation which was critical for the development of the internet in the US, but also the way the regulated telecommunications network supported the unregulated data network. Due to the primacy of the United States in data networking, US pricing of leased lines and its excellent infrastructure had an important impact on the worldwide direction of flows and usage. Infrastructure has also had a profound effect on the comparative size of national electronic commerce markets. It followed that for the purposes of many international start-ups, the world market was the US market. Also for this reason, internationally coordinated attempts at government intervention were difficult to carry out without the participation of the United States. The third part of this chapter describes the intentional lack of regulation that existed in areas other than infrastructure, including the complex issue of technological standards. Then, an important and problematic question will be briefly considered, that is, a lack of international policy and regulation overall beneficial to small and innovative firms? There is no easy answer to this question. It seemed certain, however, that mainstream success for an emerging worldwide consumer internet would eventually require government framework intervention, such as that suggested by the EU Directive on Electronic Commerce. The last part of this chapter examines an alternative to international coordinated policy – spontaneous occurrence of an internationally converging policy framework through regulatory competition among national governments. The key to institutional convergence is transnational transactions and flows. The history of financial services is instructive here.

DIFFERENCES IN THE REGULATION OF INTERNATIONAL DATA AND TELECOMMUNICATIONS NETWORKS

A presence on the internet was automatically a global presence, at no additional cost. This was not only crucial for ventures which wanted to reach a worldwide consumer market but also for small companies that used the internet to share data with other businesses. Much has been written by network thinkers about the technological underpinnings of this instantaneous worldwide reach and the rise of a global standard associated with the internet. Less credit has been given to the role of asymmetric regulation.

Internet messages could traverse interconnected, separate worldwide data networks at zero marginal cost (Mason, 1998, 937, 938). As explained in the previous chapter, there were a number of technological and organizational reasons for this. The 'end-to-end' architecture of the internet meant that the internet could be extended through 'stupid' pipes. This reduced costs and increased the simplicity of adding new network segments. Historically, internet networks passed data along in a cooperative fashion, relying on so called 'peering' agreements. Usually, data lines were leased, and were charged according to the capacity of the line and not usage. Once the network infrastructure was in place, it could be used to carry vast amounts of messages simultaneously. In contrast, basic, switched-circuit analogue telecommunications had defined capacity limits. Furthermore, analogue signals had to be reinforced across long distances. Basic telecommunication services were more sensitive to distance and were often charged accordingly.[4]

But technology alone could not explain the price differences between international data and telecommunications services and the distance insensitivity of the internet. Up to 75 per cent of the price of an international phone call was related to the costs of international settlements (Mason, 1998, 937). The international accounting rate system, which fixes the settlement rate, was firmly re-established after the Second World War and essentially was a set of bilateral pricing arrangements between national telephony monopolies. These bilateral arrangements were supported by an international organization, the International Telecommunications Union (ITU).[5] This international system traditionally functioned remarkably well. According to two policy experts: 'The international telecommunications system is among the most successful examples of multilateral co-operation. The standards, rules, and regulations elaborated by the ITU and its subbodies have been widely respected by telecommunications common carriers, and the institutions themselves have avoided the crisis of legitimacy that has more generally affected the

United Nations and its specialised agencies.'[6] This cosy club system contributed to an elevated price regime.

However, private leased lines lay outside the international accounting rate regime; and the internet used leased lines. This position was confirmed in the agreements for services within the Uruguay Round (1993).[7] In many developed countries, leased line data networks were liberalized before the GATS negotiations were completed. In Germany, for example, the PTO lost its monopoly on selling value-added network-based services (VANs) in 1989.[8] In the United States, leased lines were from the very beginning unregulated. The Federal Communications Commission (FCC) made this decision in 1971, after closely examining data networking services in its first Computer Inquiry. The Commission distinguished between basic services and enhanced services, which would not be subject to regulation (Cannon, 2001, 5, 6). While the FCC noted that the data processing industry 'has become a major force in the American economy' it also pledged abstinence by concluding that there were 'no natural or economic barriers to free entry into the market for these services' (quoted in Oxman, 1999, 9).

Thus, the process of liberalization of basic telecommunication services on a worldwide level was always a step behind data lines, which were never regulated to the same extent. It should be noted that a WTO agreement on basic telecommunication services was achieved four years after the completion of the Uruguay Round, in 1997.[9] Yet, the international accounting rate system remained untouched due to a gentlemen's agreement between the signatory governments (see Cave and Waverman, 1998, 888, 889).

Regulatory asymmetry and competition led to massive investment in data networking infrastructure throughout the world. In the 1980s and early 1990s, the largest providers of VAN network services in Europe for business-to-business use were American firms; at that time they already were generating considerable revenues with data services.[10] During the 1990s, rising worldwide demand further accelerated investment decisions. In addition to investments by traditional telecommunications companies which wanted to benefit from offering international data services, new companies began to build extensive worldwide networks. One example was the CTR Group, New Jersey, whose project Oxygen was an unbroken, undersea fibre-optic network connecting 175 countries. Its estimated cost was US$14 billion.[11] These additional capacities were intended to be leased to internet service providers as well as other resellers of data services. In the late 1990s, investors thus expected that the demand for data lines would increase even more in the future. In the end, their prospects were destroyed by overinvestment, but they were also deeply linked to government unregulation. In several OECD countries some types of value-added data services were illegal.[12] Furthermore, governments could, theoretically, have intervened to break the asymmetry in regulation between international telecommunications and data network regimes.

Because of its technological design, the internet was decentralized and this would make it difficult for governments or corporations to impose distance pricing even if they wanted to. But it was not impossible. Despite its technologically rooted decentralized nature, the internet internationally was (and still is) subject to a high degree of ownership concentration as well as high traffic concentration in certain key points. In the late 1990s, one company, MCI WorldCom, owned a significant proportion of all worldwide internet lines, despite a ruling by the European Commission which forced it to sell part of its internet holdings. Furthermore, intercontinental internet traffic between Europe and the United States travelled mostly through a few, highly concentrated paths, mainly between Amsterdam and New York and London and New York. Both the largest owners as well as the data hubs represented possible loci for intervention. Other potential points of control were specific, centralized technological functions which insured the smooth operation of the internet, especially the Domain Name System (DNS).[13] It would not have been impossible in the late 1990s to meter intercontinental traffic and to charge distance-sensitive fees. In fact, a volume-based charge for incoming transcontinental internet traffic was levied on academic users of the UK JANET network as of August 1998.[14]

Although the positioning of data networks outside the basic telecommunications regime seemed an established fact in the late 1990s, this was not always the case. Historically, there was tension between the two worlds. Incumbent telecommunications carriers tried to bring data networks back into the comfortable fold of telecommunications, resorting to both political and technological means. One example was the push for ISDN in Germany. ISDN was originally introduced as a data networking alternative to leased lines and the data networking standards of IBM, IBM-SNA. Although this undertaking probably was chimerical from the onset, it shows that the data network regime was perceived as a real challenge to PTO-style telecommunications already in the early 1980s. An account by Jill Hills described this conflict from the perspective of a contemporary, passionate observer (Hills, 1986, see especially the 'Introduction', 1–23).

THE SUBSIDIZED US INTERNET ACTS AS A GLOBAL HUB

The US in the late 1990s was the network hub and data centre of the world, both for business and in consumer use. In the late 1970s, the French Nora-Minc Report noted the preponderance of US data centres.[15] This was related to the fact that a large proportion of multinational industrial as well as financial corporations were American. The competitive advantage in data centres for business use was extended in the late 1990s to the commercial internet. During the 1998 football World Cup, for example, internet coverage of the French event was served mostly out of the United States for a mostly European audience. Hosting the service in Europe would have been less economical and less efficient. Disney's web sites for the European market were formerly hosted by AT&T in Amsterdam – they were moved to Hawaii in 1999 to benefit from its better network infrastructure.[16] Sixty per cent of all users of the internet were located within the United States. An estimated 80 per cent of all electronic commerce transactions occurred within the USA.

The research group TeleGeography analysed the global data network at length in 1998. Not only did most of the data originate from the United States; often, data flows between different countries, for example Germany and France, were channelled across the US as well. One statistic was especially instructive. In Europe, no two nations were connected to each other through more than 700 mbps, whereas total bandwidth to the US amounted to 4 gbps.[17] There were two related reasons for this. One was that the internet backbone network in most countries outside the United States was not centrally planned. Most internet service providers, noting that much of the flow was between their users and servers located in the United States, leased a network connection to the USA and did not bother with domestic connections. The few domestic or intra-European requests could be routed across the USA. The second reason for the global hub function of the USA was that the network infrastructure within the States was excellent. New ventures such as Level 3, Qwest, IXC and Williams invested large sums in building a long-distance domestic data infrastructure which could be put to use for both corporate as well as consumer data networks (Pospischil, 1998, 747, 748).

The excellence of the domestic US internet infrastructure was in part due to direct and indirect subsidies which promoted usage growth and acted as an incentive to investment. The internet backbone network was originally constructed as a research network connecting several universities scattered across the United States. This centrally planned and federally financed research network was the foundation for the later, privatized internet.

Even more influential for user demand and private infrastructure investment, however, was the indirect subsidy of the internet in the United States. This indirect subsidy began as an unintentional consequence of evolving regulation in the aftermath of the AT&T break-up and was later supported by the federal government in order to encourage growth of the internet. Low local call fees in the United States were a result of vicious competition between AT&T and local telephone competitors (Kenney, 2001, 9). US regulation supported the packaging of local telephony service monthly fees with the capacity to make local calls. In much of the USA, therefore, a flat fee was charged for unlimited local service. In the interests of universal service, local calls were cross-subsidized through a charge on long-distance service, which represented about 40 per cent of long-distance carriers' costs and was levied by local telecommunications carriers. This charge, however, did not apply to enhanced service providers (ESPs), including internet service providers (ISPs).[18] The emerging commercial internet thus profited in two ways from this regulatory structure. Firstly, local access to an internet service provider was part of the flat local fee and thus appeared free to the user. Secondly, internet service providers did not have to contribute to the upkeep of this cross-subsidization because they were a data and not a voice service. It could be argued that this regime effectively meant that long-distance telephony users subsidized internet use through their payments (see the excellent discussion by Pospischil, 1998, 750, 751). With the growth of internet use, this imbalance was bound to upset local telephony carriers. The FCC considered in April 1998 to amend this asymmetrical regime, but postponed a decision in this sensitive area (Pospischil, 1998, 752, 753). Throughout the 1990s, federal policy emphasized the protection of the emerging internet industry.

The dominance of US networking infrastructure in the global system of flows is one example of how domestic policies spill over into the international realm. The advantages for companies that chose to host their international services from a location within the United States were very apparent. From the dominant US position in data networking followed some critical realities for both business and government. Start-ups from countries outside the US adjusted to US standards and usage patterns. The world market was the US market. Attempts at international cooperation between governments would probably have failed without participation of the US. For this reason, US policy-makers could act in a strategic and pre-emptive way, blocking any possible international agreements which could be based on the strong, international and cooperative regulatory traditions in telecommunications.

INTENTIONAL LACK OF REGULATION IN OTHER AREAS

. . . The Administration wants the internet to provide an open and stable environment with a minimum of government regulation for trade and commerce.[19]

For all the rhetoric of an internet free trade zone, will the United States readily accept an internet that includes Thai child pornographers, Albanian tele-doctors, Cayman Island tax dodgers, Monaco gambling, Nigerian blue sky schemes, Cuban mail-order catalogues? Or, for that matter, American violators of privacy, purveyors of junk E-mail or 'self-regulating' price-fixers? Unlikely. And that other countries will feel the same on matters they care about (Eli Noam quoted in Magaziner, 1998, 534).

The international reach and pricing structure of the internet and other data networks would in itself have been sufficient to amount to a massive window of opportunity for small firms with global ambitions. It is possible to contend that the international manoeuvrability of firms was further increased by an intentional lack of regulation in other areas, this applies especially to the lack of international technical standard-setting through governments. But what appeared to some as a welcome recess from government intervention seemed to others an uncertain, volatile environment. And the debate needs to be clearly differentiated according to specific issues; in some areas, government intervention may seem more necessary than in others.

In this section it will be shown that, if it wanted to, the US government could have, alone or in cooperation with partners, intervened and significantly have changed the course of development of the internet.[20] In various issues and in various multilateral and bilateral fora, however, US government negotiators argued for a temporary hands-off stance. *Laissez-faire* was the cornerstone stance of US policy towards the internet, heralded on 1 July 1997, when Bill Clinton and Al Gore released the 'Framework for Global Electronic Commerce'.[21] The document contained the key foreign policy stance of the US and was designed by Ira Magaziner, who was Senior Advisor to the President until November 1998.[22]

In May 1998, 132 WTO member countries signed a one-year moratorium on any form of internet tariffs.[23] US negotiators claimed it would be difficult to retract on this concession and viewed this agreement as one of their greatest successes in 1998.[24] At that time, the easiest to implement form of tariff on internet transactions and services would have been a 'bit tax' on traffic volume. Luc Soete, Professor of International Economics at Maastricht University, was its most vocal advocate. As Chairman of the European Commission's High Level Group of Experts on Social and Societal Aspects of the Information Society (formed in 1995), he proposed that the idea of a 'bit tax' should be further studied as a redistributive mechanism in a world moving from tangible to intangible goods and as a substitute for European VAT and US state sales taxes. It was also suggested as a means of combating 'information pollution' on the internet (Soete and Kamp, undated).[25] Soete's call for study was misunderstood as a policy recommendation and was quickly rejected by both the European Commission (EC, 1997-157, 19) as well as by Ira Magaziner, who took credit for preventing a 'bit tax' from materializing. Nevertheless, the concept refused to die, especially among those constituencies that stood to lose the most from eroding VAT and sales taxes.[26] Jörg Tauss, a German parliament member from the Socialist Democratic Party, joked in an interview that one-fourth of Bill Gates's wealth stems from unpaid German value-added sales taxes.[27] Serious studies of tax effects of internet transfers are thus far not known to the author, however. They would have to take into consideration the economic effects of greater cross-border trade including lower input prices of digital goods and services purchased and accessed over the internet.

Next to a 'bit tax,' other modes of imposing tariffs on international electronic transfers would also have been possible. Points of data flow concentration were not the only bottleneck points of government intervention. The international payments system was also a very promising target.[28] The majority of payments over the internet were carried out with credit cards, and credit card transactions were controlled by a limited number of players.[29] There were further examples of centralized financial choke points. Ninety-five per cent of all international dollar transactions moved through a central clearing point, the CHIPS network in New York (set up in 1970). It is important to note, however, that the most potent financial control points were located in the United States and to a lesser degree the United Kingdom, giving policy-makers in those countries greater power to intervene in worldwide financial flows. This was demonstrated when the US threatened to cut off access to CHIPS to encourage international cooperation in combating money laundering initiatives (Helleiner, 1998, 394–6).

Most of the literature discussing internet policy issues in the late 1990s argued that government intervention on the internet in any form would have been very difficult. Common statements ran like this: 'The generic properties of the new networks render them inherently unfriendly to monopolies, hierarchies and centralised control' (from Neuman et al., 1997, xvii). Examples such as Singapore were cited; governments were unable to control unwanted information flows into the country. What was often unmentioned was that Asian states such as Singapore or even China viewed the internet as a means of modernization and access to a global electronic market. If they had wanted to reduce access massively they could have. In other countries, the internet naming system (Domain Name System, DNS) was used to impose payments on content or service firms who want to register themselves with a native address.[30] Japan was a prime example here; in order to qualify for a .jp-address, companies had to have a business location within the island country and pay relatively high fees.

The most direct way governments could have intervened was by directly approaching key firms developing internet services or software. Both the US and French governments, for example, negotiated with Netscape on the issue of encryption policy. Building on a very useful metaphor proposed by Peter Swire and Robert Litan, 'elephants' were difficult to hide – even on the internet – whereas 'mice' could easily escape government control (Swire and Litan, 1998, 200–204). An international start-up company with expectations to become a major, high-growth public company had to act like an 'elephant' and not like a 'mouse'. The *laissez-faire* choice the US government made and endorsed internationally could therefore not be fully explained with the impotence of governments in internet issues; rather, it was an intentional choice. As Magaziner remarked in an interview when asked to look into the future: 'I think there are possibilities for establishing agreements for international tax standards' (Magaziner, 1998, 532).

The United States, however, argued that trade tariffs at an early stage would have inhibited the development of electronic commerce: 'We . . . think there should be no discriminatory taxes on the internet, no bit taxes, no internet access taxes and no internet telephony taxes that would stifle the development of the medium' (Magaziner, 1998, 530). Indeed, the non-imposition of tariffs was a benefit to firms selling goods and services over the internet. Mostly, these were American companies, however. It would be amusing to imagine a counter-factual scenario of US trade policy within a reversed situation where most electronic commerce would have originated from Europe.

Regarding tariffs, US negotiators maintained that they were acting in the interests of an emerging industry. This was consonant with US policy on consumer protection issues. Here, US federal officials endorsed self-regulation and technological solutions.[31] Self-regulation was the central policy concept of the White House; it was viewed as a natural means of governance for the internet. This was argued also by lobbying groups from the internet, hardware and software industries, as well as some non-profit associations that were associated with internet self-governance.

In an interview Ira Magaziner explained the US stance in the following way:

> As we discussed [industry self-regulation] . . . with others around the globe, governments that tend to be more regulatory by instinct, we tried to explain it as a matter of practicality rather than ideology. Its not that we don't care about privacy; we do care very much, but we think this is a more effective way to enforce it (Magaziner, 1998, 529).

He continued:

> Part of what we see as a paradigm shift in the Digital Age versus the Industrial Age is that, increasingly, government's role will be to empower people to protect themselves rather than having them rely on their government for protection (Magaziner, 1998, 535).

However, just as it was unrealistic to believe that governments could not have enforced trade tariffs if they had wanted to, it was equally unrealistic to state that governments could not have acted directly to protect consumers on the internet from fraud or misuse of private data if they had wanted to. Sixty-eight per cent of internet fraud, for example, occurred on popular and well-known internet auction sites such as eBay.[32] This was because the well-known internet brands were also what most consumers were attracted to and trusted. These firms were 'elephants,' not 'mice'. Self-regulation in the USA resulted in insufficient consumer protection on the internet, as US trade authorities noted in an extensive survey of electronic commerce sites.[33] A spokesperson from a US consumer group stated that 'self-regulation has been a lot of smoke and mirrors'.[34] The first annual report by the federal government admonished private industry that progress was required in self-regulation in 1999. The status quo at the end of the 1990s thus benefited firms and emerging internet business models, but not necessarily consumers. But also here, benefits for consumers in terms of lower prices, especially of digitally accessible goods and services, need to be taken into consideration. Most importantly, the long-term benefits for consumers from innovation in business processes catalysed by the new ventures should not be ignored.

US negotiators extended the argument for self-regulation into the international arena whenever different types of key issues were raised. Thus, they opposed the imposition of what they called non-tariff barriers in three main areas: cultural safeguards, digital signatures and privacy protection laws. In the cultural realm, the US secured bilateral agreements with Japan and France in May and June 1998 that internet content should be exchanged openly and not be subject to cultural or language quota provisions of any sort (US Government Working Group on Electronic Commerce, 1998, iv). The latter two areas, digital signatures and privacy protection, were more controversial, because they involved not only a means by which government could block imports but also promote exports. They also involved technical standards. US negotiators were suspicious of all European attempts that aimed at standard setting, the general US opinion being that: 'Concerns about the American communications infrastructure are deepened by the realisation that extraordinary well-financed, coordinated plans for system enhancement are being undertaken in Europe and Asia' (Neuman et al., 1997, 14–18). These types of fears were strongest in the 1980s and early 1990s, when US economic ascent was not yet apparent. Nevertheless, they still lingered on in the 1990s and could be encountered in policy statements and academic literature.

Although fraught with internal contradictions,[35] a Europe-wide law for data protection was passed in 1995 and came into effect in October 1998.

The main goal of the law was to remove significant differences within the European Union regarding data laws, which made it difficult to operate across borders. Although an issue apparently restricted to the internal market, the law also forbade the export of personal data into countries which had data protection laws that the European Union regarded as insufficient, including the United States.[36] In this way, the law threatened US-based data centres, including those run by internet services, which contained information on citizens of European countries. As in other examples, the transnational nature of data networks operated to export essentially domestic laws into other countries. Again, US negotiators viewed European data protection laws as non-tariff barriers and instead argued for self-regulation. In doing so, they elevated the goal of nurturing a new business sector over consumer privacy concerns.[37]

There were two major areas in which US government principles were not in line with the overarching goal of encouraging entrepreneurship and innovation, however. These were legislation on encryption and intellectual property. In both areas, the emphasis on self-regulation was reduced and government intervention was advocated. To support domestic law enforcement efforts, the White House continually attempted to enact so-called 'key-escrow' legislation. Key escrow legislation would have made it obligatory for companies offering encryption products to include a 'back door' for policing efforts. Lobbying by industry and consumer privacy groups prevented federal government from progressing on the law's introduction (Magaziner, 1998, 532, 533; US Government Working Group on Electronic Commerce, 1998, 22, 23). It was ironic that such a law, if passed, would have been regarded as a non-tariff trade barrier – just like European digital signature or personal data privacy legislation. Furthermore, non-US politicians pointed out that US government control over encryption keys in electronic commerce had the ability to enable US industrial espionage activities on foreign firms.

A parallel and related issue to key-escrow was barriers preventing the export of strong encryption outside of the United States.[38] The export barriers were opposed by internet start-ups such as Netscape who would have liked to develop and export strong mass-consumer encryption products. The export barriers allowed several non-US companies, such as the German firm Brokat, to sell encryption products to the worldwide market.[39]

The US policy emphasis on self-regulation was not applied in the area of intellectual property rights either. It was frequently argued that strong intellectual property rights encouraged innovation and investment by allowing companies to cash in on their achievements. Some researchers pointed out, however, that intellectual property protection could stifle innovation if it is too rigidly defined. Discouraging reverse engineering of software products had the potential, for example, to limit the possibility for incremental innovation of existing products. The relationship between intellectual property and contract laws in the information age was also unresolved. Some argued that the ease of digital replication mandated an extension of contract law, that is, previously non-licensable products such as information should be licensable. Others believed that this would inhibit innovation by further increasing possibilities for protection. In the United States, this debate was waged around the proposed model law Article 2B of the Uniform Commercial Code (Samuelson, 1998, 809–26). The model law seemed to serve not only as a model for state legislation, but was also meant to inspire globally recognized commercial law rules.

The complex issues raised in the late 1990s have not been resolved and it is certain this political process – especially at an international level – will continue to unfold, albeit at a slower pace than during the bubble. In the meantime, innovation and investment continue despite regulatory uncertainty.[40]

THE ISSUE OF TECHNOLOGICAL STANDARDS

> The benefits of electronic commerce will only be achieved if interoperability is ensured at a global level. The European Community and its member states have consistently been committed to international standards, and expect its major trading partners to act likewise (EC, 1997-157, 11).

The issue of technological standard-setting is a difficult one and it was a major issue of contention between the United States and the European Union.[41] The European Commission, as well as specific countries such as Germany, formulated policy 'ensuring interoperability in a competitive environment' (EC, 1997-157, 5, 6), one example was the further support of standardization projects.[42] This emphasis on standardization as a policy tool dated back at least to the 1978 Nora-Minc report to the French President.

A good example was the issue of digital signatures. The digital signature was an encryption technology used to authenticate messages sent over a network. Using digital signature technology, for example, signed contracts could have been exchanged electronically. Widespread use of this technology would have been beneficial for diverse business-to-business uses as well as government procurement initiatives. The emphasis, however, was on the word 'widespread'. As with any other network technology, digital signatures are subject to network effects, meaning that the technology becomes more valuable and useful the more users put it to use.

Two different policy approaches were followed regarding digital signatures: Germany domestically introduced a legislative foundation for the use of digital signatures; the Clinton administration heavily opposed any government intervention, arguing that industry had to develop the technology further – although several US states went ahead regardless and introduced their own digital signatures legislation in the late 1990s. German legislation only dictated procedures such as the setting up of 'trust centres' which would distribute signature IDs. It also contained some technological remarks, pertaining to the use of smart-card hardware systems. At the time the law was introduced, German policy-makers stressed the model character the law could have on EU and other supranational rule-making. At the time, the European Commission also supported a 'necessary regulatory and institutional framework supporting such technologies', (EC, 1997-157, 13) and recommended that worldwide agreements on digital signatures be adopted (EC, 1997-157, 18).[43] The result was an EU directive based on the German precursor. US federal government seemed to fear any initiatives in the realm of digital signatures, especially those which were directed at introducing international standards. Despite the non-technological framework character of the German law it was understood as an international standard-setting initiative much like other technological standard-setting efforts.[44]

This was not the first time US policy has been suspicious of international technological standard-setting initiatives. The role of standards as a tool for competition policy was described in the following words by American telecommunications specialist Alfred Thimm:

> National governments have employed various aspects of industrial policies to help their national telematics champions obtain the global market share necessary for survival. In this context international telecommunications standards have not only become a device to assure network interconnection, compatibility and interoperability but a complex policy system to attain strategic enterprise objectives (Thimm, 1992, 221).

For example, in the early 1980s, the US held the view that it was too early to implement an international standard for videotex systems.[45] The debate surrounding ISDN and the international CCITT-ISO standard was similar; only AT&T expressed its support.[46] The US Department of Commerce officials viewed all European standard-setting initiatives and the telecommunication monopolies that proposed them, especially the German Post and Telephone Administration, as 'mercantilistic enemies of free trade', according to Thimm (1992, 225).

In these two instances, however, US worries were misplaced and the international standards initiatives failed to achieve the business breakthrough its advocates from the telecommunications industry expected.[47] Digital signatures did not achieve the level of importance in facilitating electronic commerce its proponents had supposed. In another case, however, European standard-setting was highly successful in an economic sense. This is the oft-cited example of the European digital mobile telephony standard GSM (Général système mobile). GSM created a unified, European mobile telephony space and contributed to the success of European players Nokia and Ericsson on the world market. GSM was a typical, European-type standard which closely defined technological specifications. Thimm has described it thus: 'A tightly written book of technical specifications the size of a medium city's telephone book' (Thimm, 1992, 102). Two UK network operators, Vodaphone and Cellnet, adopted the standard even before it was fully approved by the newly founded European Technical Standards Institute (ETSI) and launched GSM services in 1992 (Thimm, 1992, 172). The recent history of GSM has served as a justification for standard-setting policy in other areas. German businesses were very competitive when it came to encryption and digital signatures, and a successful international agreement at this time would have supported their export activities – thus German policy-makers argued.[48]

But the discussion surrounding technical standards culminated in the final years of the 1990s in the debate surrounding the next generation mobile telephony standard, UMTS. Given the success of GSM, the United States felt that this time it needed to participate in the definition of a world-wide standard. The agreement between the major telecommunication equipment vendors surrounding UMTS was heralded as a victory for European telecommunications. The delays required in bringing about this standard were, however, detrimental to start-ups in Europe which wanted to introduce innovative new services based on next-generation packet-based mobile telephony. The Japanese operator DoCoMo, on the other hand, did not wait for UMTS to materialize, and introduced its own standard, 'i-mode', early.

The European approach is deeply influenced by traditions from the telecommunications world and can be labelled 'engineer-driven'. The policy on UMTS is but the most recent example in a history of public standard-setting digital signatures, ISDN and GSM. PTOs have used standard-setting as a means to introduce greater flexibility in their purchasing decisions and thereby reduce their dependence upon equipment suppliers – which would have more to gain by implementing proprietary standards. The same conflict existed in the internet world; open standards were advocated by service firms that demanded interconnecting software and hardware. Despite their touting of open standards in the age of the internet and their desire to gain more users through interoperability, firms that were overwhelmingly software-based still viewed proprietary standards as the 'breadwinners of last resort'.[49] In their perceptive commentary on software business models, Michael Borrus and John Zysman introduced the concept 'open but owned'. 'Open but owned' systems were open systems meant to be interconnected while their core functionality remained proprietary (Borrus and Zysman, 1997, 151). 'Market-driven' US policymaking sided with the software industry and denounced international standard-setting initiatives as premature and elements of European industrial policy. Arguably, the US approach amounted to industrial policy as well. The hidden agenda to US negotiation was to delay rule-making while the dominant players in the internet field, mostly US firms, established themselves and their 'open but owned' standards. The benefits of engineer-driven versus market-driven technological standards are not clear-cut, and vary according to the specific historical moment.

THE DEBATE ON SMALL FIRM INNOVATION AND REGULATION

In their book on privacy and data protection, Swire and Litan briefly summarized the debate on innovation and regulation. On the one hand, the existence of rules and regulations seem to dampen innovation, especially on the part of small start-up companies. Start-ups focus on change and often do not have in-house legal resources to direct at legislation. On the other hand, it is argued, for example, that lack of data protection has not benefited firms because privacy concerns have prevented more consumers from using the internet. The authors conclude that privacy protection rules would have a beneficial impact on the development of the internet over time, but the lack of rules on an international level has not had much of an impact on rapid, pioneer growth. Thus far, user growth has been strong and most users seem to be more concerned about security than about privacy issues (Swire and Litan, 1998, 76–89).

Start-up firms frequently do not have the necessary legal resources required for competition in environments with significant regulation. This was confirmed by the experience of internet companies which were addressing divergent legislation in different European countries.[50] The same problem existed in the United States as well, as the country has 30000 tax jurisdictions.[51] As a result, specific national laws of other countries on the whole were being ignored by internationalizing internet start-ups, and this even applied to firms operating in subnational entities when faced by considerable regulatory and taxation differences within a country (as is the case within the United States). Start-ups were concerned that their disregard for national and state laws would one day be used against them – but it was impossible to take into consideration every myriad country law a global service might have infringed upon.[52]

Ambiguity on issues such as the taxation of cross-border sales as well as in trademark protection, consumer protection or commercial codes may, over time, hurt companies as they and the markets they operate in become more mature. It is important to note that there was an essential difference between international business-to-business electronic transactions – which existed for a long time and reached stages of maturity early on – and business-to-consumer transactions, which raised new, unresolved issues when they were conduced electronically across borders.

Internationally operating rules or a correspondence of national rules will be necessary over time. Parts of an international rules framework are already in place. The WTO Agreement on Trade-Related Intellectual Property Rights (TRIPS) seeks to protect copyrights through an international dispute settlement mechanism. The WTO General Agreement on Trade and Services (GATS) has – at an early date – addressed some of the unique issues arising from the electronic trade of services, including the division of services into four modes of supply, one of which includes electronic cross-border transmission (previously, services were considered non-tradable).[53] The WTO Declaration on Global Electronic Commerce, which was announced at the May 1998 Ministerial Conference, included a one-year customs duty moratorium on internet transactions and was complemented by the mandated formation of a WTO work programme to study electronic commerce policy. The goal of the work programme was to 'confirm the rules on electronic commerce that already exist in the WTO [such as TRIPS and GATS] – to avoid undermining existing rights and obligations by treating electronic commerce as if it were outside the normal trade regime'. A further intention was to 'identify any weaknesses in the existing legal structures that need to strengthened or clarified'.[54]

In addition to the WTO, the issues surrounding electronic commerce attracted the formation of committees and work groups in a wide array of different international organizations at a very early stage. Within the OECD, a 'neutral, fair and simple' framework for electronic taxation was worked on, similar issues were being discussed in the Asia-Pacific Economic Cooperation (APEC) forum and within the Free Trade Area of the Americas (FTAA). A government–private sector Committee of Experts on Electronic Commerce has also been established. A G-10 Working Party on Electronic Money has been established. The Basle Committee on Banking Supervision issued a 'Risk Management for Electronic Banking and Electronic Money Activities' report on 20 March 1998 which outlined key issues relating to electronic money and financial services technologies for banking supervisors. In 1996, the United Nations Commission on International Trade Law (UNCITRAL) had already developed a Model Law on Electronic Commerce which suggested some guidelines for migrating from paper to digital contracts. In 1997, UNICTRAL proposed to examine the issue of uniform rules on digital signatures.[55] Finally, further international treaties relating to intellectual property protection and electronic transmission were forwarded through the World Intellectual Property Organization (WIPO).[56]

However, neither the existing framework nor some of the newer initiatives effectively address some of the more subtle, yet profound challenges that global electronic commerce poses for the first time. A good example of some of these issues is trademark law and the internet domain name system (DNS). It is clear here that the trademark system, which has thus far operated territorially, is ill-equipped for an a-territorial system such as the internet. US attempts to solve the problem on an international scale have been highly controversial. One central question always recurs: Who supervises what? This question relates to a wide range of issues such as taxation and consumer protection. The difficulties of addressing the questions raised by electronic commerce on an international level become clear when one examines the attempts by the European Commission at building a coherent legal framework in Europe by the year 2000 (EC, 1998-586). It achieved some of its objectives. For example, the European Commission instituted a country of origin principle in determining jurisdiction (EC, 1998-586, 13, 14). In the United States, the opposite stance was taken in targeting the jurisdiction of destination (Magaziner, 1998, 531; Electronic Commerce Advisory Council, 1998, B-1).

The tasks ahead are complex. The issue here is the creation of a efficient and fair worldwide market mechanism, including consumer protection, for goods and services exchanged over the internet. This market mechanism would replace the currently operational myriad domestic markets. There are two possible ways through which rules could internationally converge. International cooperative agreement is only one of these. Competition and the convergence of national, unilateral policy-making can have definite cross-border cumulative effects as well. The subsequent section will discuss how the latter process has already set in. The history of national policy convergence in the financial services and telecommunications, even environmental regulation, is instructive.

INTERNATIONAL POLICY CONVERGENCE: THE LESSON FROM FINANCIAL SERVICES

The lack of specific, international laws in the electronic commerce area could be contrasted to the considerable array of domestic laws that affect electronic commerce. In theory, a firm exporting its services through a global network needed to be concerned about legislation in every country in which it may have a client. Especially in the consumer area, this would have been a very difficult task, as is pointed out in the previous section. Considerable legal costs would have to be borne in order to operate in several countries at once. It is in this instance that the global logic of the internet seemed at first glance to make national lawmaking redundant at best and obstructive at worst. Writing about the privacy protection rules of the European Union, Swire and Litan concluded that enforcing the rules unilaterally in Europe would have required severe enforcement efforts:

> If, however, the Directive is primarily hortatory . . . crash efforts to comply will seem expensive and unnecessary. Many businesspersons have expressed the view that 'they just can't do that' – the European Union will simply not be willing or able to enforce the directive as written (Swire and Litan, 1998, 156).

The overall effect of the US negotiation stance endorsing non-intervention and self-regulation was that firms could proceed with international expansion and a development of their innovative online business models without being obstructed by globally coordinated policy efforts. US policy was mainly pre-emptive and tactical. It was designed to prevent coordinated supranational efforts that could have seriously harmed international electronic commerce development of US firms – at the time.

While the 'mice' were perhaps unconcerned, the 'elephants' were worried. Those firms that did worry about legislation in the late 1990s were significant ventures which were establishing foreign subsidiaries in the main electronic commerce markets. Some American internet companies based in Germany, for example Yahoo!, were at pains to adhere to local data protection laws. Before they were removed early in 1999, French laws prohibiting the use of encryption were a major block to the development of on-line business models in France. The export barriers on encryption technologies had a similar impact on internet firms based in the United States.

It is obvious that, in some cases, it is advantageous to operate from a location with the least domestic legislative burdens. A tendency for countries to compete for entrepreneurs could, therefore, lead to a so-called 'race to the bottom'. This has been called the 'Delaware Effect' after the US state that adopted relatively lax incorporation laws. It is the Delaware Effect which the European Commission wanted to avoid by initiating its harmonization project targeting electronic commerce-relevant laws in Europe. But there are also well-documented cases in which local policy-makers adopted the laws of a strict legislative entity. One of the cases is environmental standards on automotive emissions. It made sense for multinational automotive manufacturers to adhere to the toughest local laws for reasons of corporate image and uniformity on production. The toughest laws were found in California. The state had a broad impact on laws in other states and countries. David Vogel, studying the worldwide impact of Californian emission regulation, has termed this the 'California Effect' (Vogel, David, 1995).

The lessons from the worldwide financial services industry are very important in this discussion. They show that industries that are intensely globally connected do not necessarily tend to 'race to the bottom'. Instead of the Delaware Effect, the California Effect in many cases more aptly describes regulatory trends in financial services. The basic argument runs thus; the more globally interconnected an industry becomes, the more important it becomes to establish rigid business standards and transparent, codified rules. This spells an end to the cosy clubs of the past (Cerny, 1996, 92). In an article on regulatory competition, Henry Laurence describes how financial services players themselves proposed to be regulated more strictly for two reasons; they wanted to enter foreign markets which they wanted to be as transparent as their own and they wanted foreign, mobile investors to have confidence in their own services (Laurence, 1996). Within a very short amount of time, both Britain and Japan – joined later by Germany – enacted strict rules devised to prevent insider trading. In Germany, bankers were very aware of the fact that transparency would be the price for participation in the global game (Lütz, 1996, 10). Another author discussing financial sector reform, Andrew Sobel, uses the term 'inside-out' to explain change initiated by domestic groups which strategically use international pressures to overcome domestic opposition (Sobel, 1994, 1–20). This is not the place to discuss the considerable differences the approaches and conclusions of the aforementioned authors (Sobel emphasizes domestic actors, Laurence focuses on the role of mobile consumers of financial services), but they all describe how domestic shifts can lead to an overall, worldwide policy convergence and more transparent, codified systems, without the involvement of internationally coordinated public policy initiatives.

Researching the telecommunications industry, Steven Vogel has arrived at a comparable conclusion in his book *Freer Markets, More Rules*: 'Hence we have wound up with freer markets and *more* rules. In fact, there is even a logical link: liberalization requires reregulation' (Vogel, 1996, 3, emphasis added). The European telecommunications industry has moved from informal, opaque regulation to a more transparent, rules-based regime.

Deregulation of telecommunications has gone hand-in-hand with the establishment of new regulatory agencies. This is an American model that was adopted first in the UK in 1984 in the guise of OFTEL. Again, a global logic of international convergence of regulatory regimes seems to be at work, the common explanation being that global market players demand transparency and similar market conditions in the different countries they operate in. In an important essay, Eli Noam asks if instability in the form of either regulation or liberalization in an interconnected system does not work globally like a contagious process (Noam, 1994). Echoing the roles taken by the London Stock Exchange and by Japanese banks, Siemens itself was instrumental in tearing down the 'court supplier' system it has most befited from historically (Humphreys and Simpson, 1996, 114).

In studying the California Effect, however, David Vogel hastens to point out that one of the main reasons why California's strict standards triumphed was that its automobile market was substantial; it was especially important for German exporters, who had a major influence on the EU (Vogel, David, 1995, 261–3, 268–70). It comes as no surprise, therefore that, according to some researchers, global convergence in different industries is leading not only to greater transparency and more formal rules, but also to specific types of governmental roles which most closely approximate the current US approach.[57] A further example is the increasingly important role competition policy plays in the European Union, a role again foreshadowed by competition policy in the USA.[58] In his essay, 'The Rise of the Regulatory State in Europe', Giandomenico Majone summarizes this trend:

> In sum, neither privatization nor deregulation have meant a return to laissez-faire or an end to all regulation . . . Thus neither American deregulations nor European privatizations can be interpreted as a retreat of the state, but rather as a redefinition of functions. What is observed in practice is a redrawing of the borders of the public sphere in a way that excludes certain fields better left to private activity, while at the same time strengthening and even expanding the state's regulatory capacity in other fields like competition or environmental and consumer protection (Majone, 1998, 195).

Despite policy convergence and the trend towards independent regulatory agencies and an emphasis on competition policy, the permanent differences between the United States and Europe are worth emphasizing. One of the primary differences that remain despite some movement towards each other is in the area of technological standard-setting. From about 1998 there have been indications that on the level of the European Commission, on the one hand, a convergence in legislative approaches with the US approach favouring industry-led interoperatability initiatives is occurring.[59] In the United States, on the other hand, there seems to be the realization that government can have a limited role in standard-setting with industry; the definition of the UMTS standard is the example here.

CONCLUSION

The internet – both the consumer internet and corporate internet-based data networks – were distance-insensitive. The 'death of distance' as well as the horizontal applicability of internet innovations and the low barriers to entry provided new ventures with unique opportunities – globally. This chapter was dedicated to describing how distance-insensitivity was not just related to much-touted technological aspects of the internet and the unique cooperative peering arrangements that characterized it throughout much of the 1990s, but also to government unregulation. Government regulation was asymmetrical; the internet enjoyed a favoured position outside international telecommunications arrangements. Regulatory asymmetry was a critical factor without which demand for worldwide standards and data services cannot be properly explained.

The notion of global networks should not be misunderstood, however. To a large extent, the worldwide network was the US network. The United States was the world's network hub. It also was the location where the most value was added to network services, were the majority of electronic commerce services and data centres were hosted. And the majority of internet users and consumers were located there. This was a result of many factors, but prominent among those was domestic telecommunications deregulation, which privileged internet services and thus encouraged network investment and use. Politically, the network topography of the US also put the Clinton administration in a privileged position in international electronic commerce framework negotiations.

The low barriers of entry associated with the internet were due, in part, to an 'openness' which was insured not simply because of its technological design but because of government abstinence and unregulation in this area as well. One of the main objectives of the Clinton Administration was to keep the development of internet standards market-driven. The critical role of standards was obvious to all policy-makers involved in international negotiations. Without a minimum degree of international interoperability, the worldwide network would fragment into different isolated parts. A global network exists only as long as there are global networking standards.

Standards can range from minimum-level basic networking protocols to complex digital signature systems, which establish authenticity. The latter include both technological specifications as well as organizational arrangements. In the previous chapter, the point was made that global demand, generated by businesses as well as consumers, led to the widespread use of internet standards in both corporate and consumer networks. Corporate users sought independence from software companies such as IBM and abandoned company-only standards. This led to the rise of intranets and extranets. Consumers forced change upon traditional proprietary online services such as AOL and Microsoft Network and on country-only online services such as Germany's BTX or France's Minitel. Nevertheless, the balance that existed regarding internet standards during the late 1990s was delicate; the largest software companies tried vigorously to introduce proprietary elements. The standards balance was actually being propped up by a massive investment bubble, which sped up development of open systems, privileging user numbers over company revenue generation. Without the investment bubble, internet commercialization would have taken a far more proprietary course. This is a point which was not mentioned by the critics of the excesses of the New Economy of the late 1990s (Perkins and Perkins, 1999). And the openness of the system could in the future be reversed, as one scholar has argued (Lessig, 1999).

The global window of opportunity created by distance-insensitivity, horizontal applicability and low barriers to entry needs to be put into perspective, however. Local laws and politics did matter as well, affecting the extent to which small firms could take advantage of the window. Although start-up firms largely ignored the domestic legal and taxation frameworks of the numerous countries they were exporting their services into, they were affected by the laws of the country they operated in. And the legal framework was only one aspect among many influencing the domestic conditions for entrepreneurship which also included investment patterns and the quality of investment, management and IT know-how. The most important factor, the Achilles' heel, for entrepreneurs probably was national as well, namely telecommunications liberalization. National governments played prominent roles in influencing many of these factors. In fact, the role of US government in developing a national marketplace for internet services domestically was also discussed in this and the previous chapter.

In non-US countries, government policy acted to 'refract' the opportunities posed by global networks, causing small firms to develop along unique, national trajectories. The effects of government actions are explored in the subsequent chapters, which focus on the German case. Yet, the degree of refraction may be decreasing as governments outside of the US have become aware of the effects of domestic policy on internationally competing local companies. Although major differences in policy approaches persist (main examples are standard-setting initiatives and

SME policy), policy competition has already led to policy convergence. The worldwide harmonization effects of unilateral, domestic efforts in areas of strong international flows have already been observed in the case of the reform of financial markets and telecommunications. There are few alternatives to convergence if flows are to remain global. In the longer term, convergence caused by competition will be combined with some form of international policy coordination as the electronic commerce market matures.

Policy convergence does, however, raise new questions, which will be explored in the next chapters. One of these questions is the distinct timing of policy convergence in different countries. Policy convergence often does not happen simultaneously in different countries. Even in moments of simultaneous convergence, the involved institutions can remain distinct. This has been demonstrated by Mark Thatcher using the example of telecommunications policy in France and the United Kingdom (1999). For these reasons, it seems crucial to study the timing of policy convergence and the institutional landscape in detail, that is, the specific, national pattern of policy convergence. One of the main objectives of such an effort would be to understand the economic effects of such specific patterns of convergence. In this study, dedicated to policy convergence in the internet era, the specific economic effect studied is the impact on entrepreneurial innovation. If the internet did represent a global innovation opportunity in a Schumpeterian sense, policy convergence may simply have come too late in some countries to be of help to ventures addressing this unique opportunity. To arrive at answers, a detailed country-level examination seems to be necessary; this is offered in the subsequent Part II of this book.

NOTES

1. The term 'unregulation' stems from Jason Oxman's working paper: 'The FCC and the Unregulation of the Internet' (1999). 'The Death of Distance' was the title of an *Economist* survey dedicated to developments in telecommunications and the internet. Frances Cairncross, 'The Death of Distance', *The Economist*, 30 September 1995.
2. This general statement was not true in all cases. The price of cross-border basic voice services depended on bilateral agreements within an international accounting rate system. Pricing depended on the degree of competition allowed and the exact nature of the settlement. For this reason, the price of a telephone call between London and Paris could be higher than between London and New York.
3. 'US government' has been used as a general category and the internal political process is not discussed, save occasional references to the roles of the Federal Trade Commission, the Federal Communications Commission, Department of Commerce, individual states and the Clinton administration.
4. Analogue technologies are being improved and these statements may be invalidated in the near future.

5. For a discussion on the 'Future of International Settlements', see Cave and Waverman (1998).

6. Ergas and Pogorel continue: 'Compared with areas such as trade, finance or development assistance, international cooperation in telecommunications has been distinguished by the resilience of the institutional mechanisms on which it is based, the widespread acceptance and observance of multilateral rules and regulations, and a relative lack of conflict between the technical function of solving immediate problems and the claims of contrasting ideologies and interests' (Ergas and Pogorel, 1994, 17–19). Among the reasons for this stability, the authors cite the necessity that international linkages between two domestic monopolies had to be provided jointly as well as 'the small total number of participants and the high degree of control exercised by each over its environment, by the dominance of an engineering/public service culture and by a technological context whenever change was evolutionary' (Ergas and Pogorel, 1994, 18).

7. In the GATS Annex on Telecommunications, special considerations in the national schedules were made for private leased line data networks (Feketekuty, 1998, 82, 85).

8. Previously, the 1987 European Commission 'Green Paper on the Development of a Common Market for Telecommunications Services and Equipment' proposed a fully open competitive environment for new, data-based services. The Green Paper influenced proposals for reform on a national level in two key markets with a strong public service telecommunications tradition: Germany (the Witte Report, September 1988) and France (Thimm, 1992, 191).

9. The General Agreement on Basic Telecommunications Services (GBT) entered into force on February 1998 and included 69 signatory countries. Liberalization of basic telecommunications in the EU was secured in accordance with the WTO schedule and went into effect in January 1998.

10. Noam lists the largest firms in the European VAN market in 1991: GTE Telenet (US$500 million), IBM (US$500 million) and GE Information Services (US$450 million). The top markets were the UK (US$918 million), France (US$665 million) and Germany (US$428 million) (Noam, 1992, 372, 373).

11. Jonathan Burke, 'Submarine Attack', *Red Herring*, November 1997, 104, 106.

12. Such as voice-over data services ('internet telephony') which was banned in one-third of OECD countries if it involved a telephone on at least one end of the line (Mason, 1998, 937).

13. The US administration of the DNS was internationally criticized, leading in October 1998 to the formation of a more international non-profit governance body, The Internet Corporation for Assigned Names and Numbers (ICANN). The formation of ICANN was initiated by the US Department of Commerce through a White Paper released in June 1998. The step to increase international participation in a privatized DNS was initially directed through the Clinton Administration's 1997 'Framework for Global Electronic Commerce'. See http://www.icann.org/

14. The 'Announcement of the Start of Usage Charging for Transatlantic Traffic' from 31 July 1998 can be found on the web page http://www.ja.net/press_release/charging.html.

15. Eli Noam mentioned the US head start in on-line databases in his book on telecommunications in Europe. He cites an OECD report that listed 1983 sales of on-line data services in Western Europe as amounting to less than 10 per cent of sales in the United States (Noam, 1992, 402).

16. Kenneth Neil Cukier, 'Global Telecom Rout', *Red Herring*, February 1999, 60–64.

17. Kenneth Neil Cukier, 'Global Telecom Rout', *Red Herring*, February 1999, 61.

18. Rachelle Chong, 'Controlling Tendencies', *Red Herring*, January 1999, 116. See also Jason Oxman's comments on the effect of universal service and the ESP exemption (1999, 15–18).

19. Testimony of John McPhee, Director, Office of Computers and Business Equipment, International Trade Administration, US Department of Commerce, before the Senate Committee on Finance, United States Senate, 16 July 1998.

20. In a thought-provoking article, Eric Helleiner described the many ways in which governments could cooperate to control monetary transactions in the age of the internet. Some

of the examples he cited were the 1988 Basle Accord on capital adequacy standards as well as the OECD Financial Action Task Force (FATF), designed to combat international money laundering (Helleiner, 1998, 392).

21. The 'Framework' represented a departure from previous National Information Infrastructure policy. Announced on 15 September 1993, as 'The National Information Infrastructure: Agenda for Action', this initiative emphasized a greater government role in promoting private sector investment via tax and regulatory policies as well as 'universal service' goals. Essentially, it was a domestically oriented document (Neuman et al., 1997, 20–23).

22. Magaziner was the key person in pushing the US stance in international fora as well as the main contact for the US internet industry, the 'evangelist for the internet industry in a global marketplace'. Jeri Clausing, 'Magaziner, Head of US Internet Policy, Plan to Resign', *New York Times*, Cybertimes, 6 November 1998.

23. In addition to this agreement, passed on May 1998 as a 'Declaration on Global Electronic Commerce', 44 WTO members in March 1997 signed an agreement to eliminate tariffs on computer and telecommunications equipment trade from the year 2000 (Information Technology Agreement, ITA). This should boost US exports and contribute to a growing data networking infrastructure throughout the world.

24. According to an IDG News Service story from 29 May 1998, 'Magaziner Outlines US Internet Policy, White Paper Expected Soon', by Nancy Weil.

25. One redistributive use that was recommended by the High Level Group was financing the European social security system. A detailed information archive on the 'bit tax' issue can be found on the 'Taxing Cyberspace' home page of the Maastricht Economic Research Institute on Innovation and Technology (MERIT): http://meritbbs.unimaas.nl /cybertax/caybertax.html. On that site one can also access Soete and Kamp, undated.

26. The size of internet-based transactions was significant already in 1998. That year, internet consumer sales amounted to US$8 billion. In the United States, all but five states collect sales taxes, and they derive half their total revenue from them. John Simons, 'States Chafe as Web Shoppers Ignore Sales Taxes', *Wall Street Journal*, 26 January 1999. Many countries outside of the US also fear loss of value added taxes. It was estimated that Germany forfeited about DM 5 billion alone in 1999 in lost VAT due to goods and services sold directly to German customers over the internet instead of from a German location. Ulrike Wirtz, 'Steuerkick im Internet,' *impulse Das Unternehmermagazin*, 3:99, 164–8, estimate p. 168.

27. Meeting with Jörg Tauss, MdB, 25 March 1999, Bundeshaus, Bonn.

28. A further strategic site that Saskia Sassen identified was the digital production process, involving the multimedia industry. It was located in the world's largest cities and was very concentrated in terms of infrastructure, talent and buildings (Sassen, 1998, 178).

29. Even if electronic cash as a more anonymous transaction form would have been popular in the 1990s – which it was not – it would been linked to institutions transparent to government, such as banks or other financial services corporations. The reason for this was that most consumers would have not trusted electronic cash distributed by organizations unknown to them. This argument regarding electronic cash can be found in Helleiner (1998, 400–403).

30. Mueller argues that national entities as top-level domains (TLDs) such as .de for Germany provide national authorities with welcome points of control (Mueller, 1998, 103).

31. One technological solution was the PICS rating system for content advocated by the private internet standards body World Wide Web Consortium (W3C).

32. Louise Kehoe, 'Microsoft and eBay in "Piracy" Row', *Financial Times*, 26 February 1999, 21.

33. The report, dated June 1998 and titled 'Privacy Online: A Report to Congress', can be accessed on the US Federal Trade Commission web site http://www.ftc.gov/. According to the report, 85 per cent of commercial sites collect personal information, but only 14 per cent notify consumers of the company's data practices.

34. Jeri Clausing, 'Internet Commerce Study Stresses Self-Regulation', *New York Times*, Cybertimes, 30 November 1998.

35. Especially when applied to client-server systems, intranets, extranets and laptops. The inconsistencies were pointed out in the timely book by Peter P. Swire and Robert E. Litan (1998, 58–75).
36. United States data protection laws were not uniform. In some specific instances, for example, academic records and video rental facilities, it was very strict, in others, almost non-existent (Swire and Litan, 1998, 170–72; Noam, 1992, 398).
37. One study commissioned by the industry privacy group TRUSTe tried to show that electronic commerce would double if websites widely adopted privacy programs. This argument tried to support the contention that consumer protection would have been good for internet business. The conclusion was partially invalidated by another result from the same research, which showed that up to 40 per cent of consumers do not distinguish privacy from security issues.
38. An update on export guidelines in 1998 enabled the export of encryption products in some areas and to some countries (US Government Working Group on Electronic Commerce, 1998, 23).
39. In a California state report, drafted by state and industry groups, addressed the issue is explicitly: 'Therefore, while US policies are not keeping strong encryption technology out of international markets, they are keeping out US encryption technology' (Electronic Commerce Advisory Council, 1998, III-9).
40. Most recently, for example, in the music industry in the case surrounding the venture capital-financed internet start-up Napster.
41. US negotiators viewed it as a major achievement that they were able to convert a worldwide conference in Brussels on standards 'Building the Global Information Society for the 21st Century' in October 1997 into a business-dominated affair, although the original plans called for a forum directed by governments and international organizations (US Government Working Group on Electronic Commerce, 1998, iv, 20).
42. Despite its emphasis on interoperability throughout its central policy document 'A European Initiative in Electronic Commerce', the possibility of *de facto* interoperability achieved through industry collaboration was recognized (a US document would call this self-regulation). But this is not without pointing to the role of the European standards bodies CEN, CENELEC and ETSI. (EC, 1997-157, 10, 11).
43. The Commission from the mid-1990s began to move towards a more US-style self-regulatory approach (see EC, 1998-586, 3).
44. 'The United States believes it is not wise at this time to attempt to identify a single model that these transactions will use or to develop a legal environment using a single model. Indeed, such an approach would prevent the market from testing different possible approaches and prematurely impose a particular model on all electronic commerce, inevitably limiting its growth . . . A few governments . . . are establishing detailed rules for electronic authentication which the United States considers to be premature, burdensome, or unnecessary' (US Government Working Group on Electronic Commerce, 1998, 14, 15).
45. A videotex standard was promoted through the international standards body Consultative Committee on International Telephone and Telegraph (CCITT). It was supported by European and Canadian telecommunications carriers as well as AT&T, but not by the US computer industry (Noam, 1992, 382, 383).
46. Again, European telecommunications companies accepted an open, international standard for digital networking as an alternative to private standards used by the computer industry. Firm European standards for ISDN were established by the European Telecommunications Standards Institute (ETSI) in July 1990. The international standard forwarded by the Consultative Committee for International Telephony, Telegraph-International Standards Organization (CCITT-ISO) was used as a basis for the European standard. Contemporary analysts, such as Thimm (1992), praised European policy on ISDN standards and the resulting uniform telecommunications landscape in contrast to heterogeneous US implementations. Already, however, Thimm warned that 'The rate of technological innovations, however, has made the ISDN copper cable 64 kbits networks obsolete almost before they will have become operational' (Thimm, 1992,

192–204, quote p. 193, AT&T note p. 226). And: 'The PTTs, especially the DBP, empha-sised investments in ISDN network transmission systems and switches, and failed to encourage the equipment manufacturer to develop attractively priced business or resi-dential terminal ISDN equipment until the physical network was almost completed.' Thimm calls ISDN an 'engineering-driven innovation' and mobile telephony a 'market-driven innovation' (Thimm, 1992, 235–6, quote p. 236). Compare with Noam (1992, 360–68).

47. On a domestic level, however, ISDN was a platform that was used to justify massive modernization investments on the part of the German PTO and Siemens. It can also be linked to the efforts of the German Bundespost to introduce usage-based pricing for data lines (Noam, 1992, 355, see discussion 360–368). The ISDN roll-out did provide national market opportunities for some German family-owned enterprises such as Hagenuck and ANT (Thimm, 1992, 232, 233).

48. In Germany, at least four different start-ups were competing in this space: Brokat Infosystems, Utimaco, Netlife and Me-Technology. Brokat and Me-Technology announced a merger in March 1999 ('Die Softwareanbieter Brokat und Me-Technology fusionieren', *Frankfurter Allgemeine Zeitung*, 18 March 1999, 23). Already in the late 1990s, Germany had a 15-year tradition in online banking and businesses had managed to gather substantial experience in the related technological issues: secure transactions, encryption and authentication.

49. Sun's strategy with Java software is instructive here (see: Luc Hatlestad, 'Briefing Java', *Red Herring*, June 1998, 84–140). See also Saskia Sassen's insightful discussion on standard-setting and business objectives in the age of the internet: 'The issue today, it seems, is once again to set standards, and to do this by providing the software for free, eventually, to control access and browsing standards and thus be able to charge' (Sassen, 1998, 185–8).

50. A survey undertaken within the European Commission in which 80 responses by inter-net firms were studied revealed that legal costs for cross-Europe services already were considerable in the late 1990s. One figure cited was DM 70000/year (EC, 1998-586, 8, 9). In the study of German internet start-ups presented in subsequent chapters, 77 per cent of selected firms called for internationally harmonized laws and controls (Appendix A, Main Survey Results, Table 27).

51. John Simons, 'States Chafe as Web Shoppers Ignore Sales Taxes', *The Wall Street Journal*, 26 January 1999.

52. Research in the field of management studies and entepreneurialism has shown that inter-nationally oriented start-up companies are very concerned about regulation. The research is inconclusive, however, in establishing whether internationalization occurs in a quest to actively seek out areas with the least amount of regulation or whether the regulation problem simply increases when firms internationalize (McDougall, 1989, 388, 398).

53. Services transmitted transnationally across data networks are labelled as 'cross-border services' and are defined in the following way: 'Services supplied from the territory of one member to the territory of another' (Altinger and Enders, 1996, 307, 308). Jagdish Bhagwati pointed out in 1984 that in extending GATT to services, the 'disembodiment' of services through technologies should be taken into consideration (Bhagwati, 1984). For a discussion of trade in services and the WTO see Feketekuty (1998).

54. See 'A Borderless World', a speech by Renato Ruggiero, Director-General, World Trade Organization, to the OECD Ministerial Conference, Ottawa, 7 October 1998. Other speeches by Ruggerio are relevant as well and can be accessed over the WTO web site.

55. 'Planning of Future Work on E-Commerce: Digital Signatures, Certification Authorities and Related Legal Issues', from February 1997.

56. The WIPO Copyright Treaty and the WIPO Performances and Phonograms Treaty of December 1996.

57. But even US policy has been attracted to 'ill-advised attempt[s] to micromanage' (Neuman et al. 1997), one example was the US Telecommunications Act of 1996 with its '100 pages of detailed legal mandates' and '90 bureaucratic inquiries' (Neuman et al., 1997, xiv). Another example, possibly, is intellectual property protection.

58. Anyone discussing the hands-off policy US federal government adopted to promote the growth of the nascent internet industry must also mention how it simultaneously has acted to curtail the powers of firms that have achieved considerable size and influence, Microsoft and Intel. In both the hands-off approach as well as the anti-trust action, the US government arguably acted to protect start-up interests.
59. A communication by the European Commission emphasized 'a light, enabling and flexible approach' and self-regulation (EC, 1998-586, 3). The 'US–EU Joint Statement on Electronic Commerce' released in the US–European Union Summit in Washington on 5 December 1997 stated: That industry self-regulation is important. 'Within the legal framework set by government, public interest objectives can, as appropriate, be served by international or mutually compatible codes of conduct, model contracts, guidelines, etcetera, agreed upon between industry and other private sector bodies' (see http://www.useu.be/).

PART II

National Political Economy

4. Institutional reform and political compromise

The division of this book into two parts, the first international, and the second national, is deceiving. The objective of the first part was to show in what ways the two realms have been fused into one. Formerly separate marketspaces have become enmeshed by technology to such an extent that domestic agents such as small firms could, in theory, become 'instant internationalizers'. But it is also the objective of this book to discuss ways in which the international and the national remain distinct despite the opportunities presented by the internet, hence the division of the volume into two parts. To show distinctiveness, we will depart from the worldwide perspective and zoom into one geographic segment of the global network: Europe, and here, specifically, the German economy.

As outlined in the Introduction, Germany is interesting because of the apparent reversal of entrepreneurial dynamism towards the end of the 1990s. While small German firms have been at home in the world market for decades, the economy seemed to have become rigid and unentrepreneurial in recent times. In terms of telecommunications policy, Germany embarked much more slowly on liberalization than the first-tier reformers, the USA, the UK, Japan and Scandinavia. Enterprises in the IT industry were regarded as domestic adopters and not global leaders, with the exception of a single company, SAP. This seemed to suddenly have changed in the last years of the 1990s, as numerous internet ventures were founded and listed on the stock exchange. The new Frankfurt stock exchange symbolized the birth of a new entrepreneurial culture. Venture capital surged, transforming itself from a trickle to a glut. The telecommunications landscape was thoroughly reformed; decades of stagnation seemed to have been left behind in a few years. A new economic miracle appeared to be in the making.

To understand how the national economy is both part of and yet distinct from the international network economy, the concept of 'refraction' was discussed in the first chapter. Why not just use the term 'distortion' used by neoclassical economists for decades? Whereas distortion is negative, refraction is a neutral term, that emphasizes how government policy may have positive as well as negative effects. Another quality of the term 'refraction' is that it emphasizes the fact that government policy is not simply a one-way effect on firms. 'Refraction' is not a direct relationship, it is distributed. It is the combined result of the activity of several different players embedded in an institutionally conditioned domestic environment.

Using the example of Europe, the effect of refraction on internationally oriented New Economy start-ups will be examined in depth. To do this, the roles of three different types of actors need to be discussed: national government, the incumbent national telecommunications operator and new ventures. This chapter focuses on relevant national government policy but is sensitive to how different types of firms participate in the policy-making process. Most instructive is the policy relationship between government and the dominant national telecommunications operator. This chapter and the next will focus on this relationship and examine it from the perspective first of government and then of the operator. In both chapters, the involvement of the small players, the new ventures themselves, will be analysed as well. In the end, an integrated picture can be presented in which interconnections between the actors are emphasized. To start, however, the focus is on policy-making on a national level. Two specific policy arenas were especially relevant for internet start-ups: telecommunications liberalization and national innovation policy. National innovation policy included programmes supporting venture capital.

Policy changes in both arenas were initiated during the Kohl era. The ruling coalition from 1982 to 1998 consisted of the conservative people's parties CDU and CSU as well as the liberals, the FDP. When they assumed power, this constellation emphasized that they stood for change, a *Wende*. In both policy arenas discussed here, policy reform actually took place. In telecommunications as well as in national innovation policy, government sought to increase the role of the private sector. In telecommunications liberalization, the outcome was delayed considerably due to an imbalance between a progressive regulatory framework and problematic ownership structures.

In the first part of this book, the choices made in the USA regarding telecommunications liberalization were described. These choices had an impact on the pricing of internet access for consumers and firms. This was because, during the commercialization of the internet, basic telecommunication services still provided the main access route to the internet. Since the liberalization of basic telecommunications followed different paths in different countries, the impact of liberalization cannot be generalized and equated to the US experience. In the 1980s, when liberalization of basic services was under way in the USA, the UK, Japan and the Scandinavian countries, German policy-makers initially thought this step to be unnecessary. The focus was on global competition in telecommunications equipment, mobile telephony and value-added services; these were the primary candidates for liberalization. Only some policy-makers and advisors saw the importance of basic services competition in sparking consumer and firm uptake of 'Information Society' services.[1] The backers of full liberalization gained ground only in the 1990s, after a more than a decade of CDU-led government. And, although competition in basic services was decided upon in 1996, the results of corporatist policy compromise as well as the specific liberalization schedule contributed to a continuing regime of high and metered internet access prices well into 1999.

Whereas German economic policy-makers were laggards regarding basic telecommunications liberalization, they were among the first in the world on the level of national government to institute new framework legislation for the New Economy. Already 1997, a so-called 'Multimedia Law' was designed by the Ministry of Research and Technology (BMFT, actually the BMBF)[2] and passed by parliament. The law enshrined a basic stance towards Information Society issues, which was held by the BMFT as well as the Ministry of Economics (BMWi) in the Kohl era. The Multimedia Law pre-empted policy by the Interior Ministry and the federal states (*Länder*) which both for different reasons were regarded as potentially able to stifle the development of the Information Society in Germany. Although it was developed in consultation with individual start-ups in multimedia and internet fields, the law was a state-led initiative in national innovation, the objectives of which had been defined by policy-makers and reflected their perceptions of the needs of entrepreneurs.

For well over 30 years, the German federal government has sought to close the technology gap between Germany and the USA.[3] From the beginning, policy-makers had sensed that their dual approach to catching up was insufficient. This approach consisted of combining industrial policy focused on subsidizing research and development in a few privileged electrotechnical firms with a broad, diffusion-oriented programme emphasizing technological uptake of the SME sector. What was missing was specific policy targeting young, high-growth technology companies. US leadership in IT and biotechnology was clearly attributable to young companies. To emulate this development at home and enable the formation of innovative start-ups, German policy-makers experimented with different types of programmes from the late 1970s. By 1989, the Ministry of Research and Technology had veered away from credits and subsidies in this area and launched two successful schemes promoting private venture capital investments. The best known of these was developed in close consultation with individual entrepreneurs in a formal, specialist forum supported by the work of the independent Fraunhofer research institutes.[4] It was carried out by a public–private body, the Technologie-Beteiligungs-Gesellschaft (tbg) of the

German Equalization Bank (Deutsche Ausgleichsbank, DtA), an institution founded in 1950 and very firmly rooted in the German tradition of promoting SMEs.

Before looking at these three policy areas individually, however, the chapter will begin by reviewing literature on the Germany model of capitalism, especially the role of corporatism. This cannot be the place to examine the interesting question to what extent, if any, the German model as such was diluted in the late twentieth century and was subject to institutional convergence through external as well as internal influences. Here, the discussion regarding the German model is drawn upon to understand variations to the course of telecommunications liberalization and to the development of national innovation programmes in other countries.

THE GERMAN ECONOMY: IMPACT OF UNIFICATION AND SOCIAL PROGRAMMES

Key policy decisions which have had an effect on internet entrepreneurship in Germany were made against a backdrop of macroeconomic and fiscal developments. In contrast to the long boom of the New Economy in the second half of the 1990s in the USA, Germany faced increasing hardships, which began to recede only in 1999.[5] Among these were the costs of unification, the social programme crisis, high structural unemployment and a net outward FDI balance. The first three factors contributed to a continual budget deficit, which lingered in the background of all policy-making. Although the budget deficit was smaller in 1998 compared to 1997, this was in large part attributable to singular income flows such as privatization income and investment reductions (Sachverständigenrat, 1998, 10, 127–41). The privatization and sale of shares of the telecommunications incumbent, Deutsche Telekom, was one of these singular income flow sources. Under the Kohl administration, therefore, telecommunications policy was influenced by two contradictory policy objectives: maximizing the value of the incumbent and introducing competition into the industry. Selling shares of the former monopolist carrier offered only short-term financial gains. A German panel of economists concluded that achieving longer-term financial sustainability would mean cutting subsidies dramatically and a thorough reform of social programmes – challenging objectives that were not achieved in the Kohl era (Sachverständigenrat, 1998, 10).[6]

Although it faced high unification costs, the Kohl administration was unwilling or unable to radically cut government spending in subsidies and social programmes. The emphasis was on compromise. This section will focus on three related economic policy issues especially important to the entrepreneur: taxes, labour market regulation and labour costs. An examination of these factors affecting small, New Economy firms comes to a more or less balanced combination of negative and positive factors. Economic policy certainly left much room for improvement, but in itself did not represent a severe handicap for entrepreneurs based in Germany relative to other, more specific pressing issues such as telecommunications liberalization.

There was disagreement in Kohl's Germany about the actual gravity of the problems the economy and its enterprises faced as a whole. Left-leaning press and politicians – then in opposition – often argued at the time that the problems were not as bad as they seemed. Their agenda was to keep some of the social market policies in place and modernize others to create a new version of a flexible yet socially acceptable social market economy, a participatory society (*Teilhabegesellschaft*) (Kleinert and Mosdorf, 1998, 173). Instead of a conflict between the state and the market, synergies between market, state and society were emphasized (Kleinert and Mosdorf, 1998, 182). At the time, it was not evident that this agenda would under the first SPD mandate be used to initiate cost cutting and reform to a greater degree than attempted under Kohl's Germany. Cost cutting and reform were actually strongly advocated at the time only by the conservative and liberal press in Germany, which was joined by Anglo-American publications in painting a 'sick man in Europe' image.[7] The main problems raised were high government spending levels and inflexibility and over-regulation in many areas of the economy, especially the labour market. Both the right and the modern left were united in one belief, however: 'Germany needs a new entrepreneurial wave.'[8] In fact, the new Social Democrat-led coalition that assumed power in the Autumn of 1998 identified the internet with entrepreneurship and job-creation. One statement does not require translation into English: 'Internet-Business ist Jobmaschine.'[9]

Despite this pessimistic view from commentators more or less sharing a similar ideological platform, Helmut Kohl's coalition government did not conclusively address the symptoms of the 'sick man'. Although a *Wende*, a change, was announced when the Kohl coalition replaced the Social-Liberal government in 1982, significant changes were not realized in those economic policy areas where it would be most controversial, such as simplification of the corporate tax system and reduction of the personal income tax burden.[10] Some singular initiatives, which were important to entrepreneurs and their financiers, were successful, such as the removal of wealth taxes in 1997. In general, many entrepreneurs were dissatisfied with policy-making. Their dissatisfaction had its origin in widespread disillusion with the scope of reforms and a pragmatic forecast of where Germany would be heading if it further travelled down the road of 'rotten compromise'.[11] Indeed, this dissatisfaction was one of the reasons leading to entrepreneurship in the first place (Lehrer, 2000, 20, 21). The actual conditions New Economy entrepreneurs faced regarding taxation levels and the labour market were surprisingly positive, although they could certainly have been improved as well.

The largest tax disincentive entrepreneurs faced in Germany were in the form of high personal income taxes. These were aggravated by the so-called 'solidarity tax' instituted to cover part of the costs of unification.[12] High personal income taxes were a barrier to hiring skilled knowledge employees from other parts of the world. One entrepreneur based close to the Swiss border, for example, had little success is attracting Swiss physicists to complement his team as programmers.[13] The success of Silicon Valley was to a great extent based on highly skilled employees arriving from all over the world and a rapid demographic turnover (Cohen and Fields, 1999, 109, 126–7). Yet, one of Silicon Valley's barriers to further growth was quotas on visas imposed by US government. Therefore, whereas the problems were of a different nature in the US and Germany, the constrained flow of immigrants seemed a growth barrier in both countries. Although entrepreneurs could easily have employed more highly skilled people and the study carried out in this project suggested that most ventures were chronically understaffed, the labour market was apparently not worse than in other highly industrialized countries.

In one respect, however, the labour market for knowledge workers such as programmers or consultants seemed better in Germany than in California. Anecdotal evidence suggested that in contrast to the high workplace mobility in California, highly skilled employees were both more loyal as well as cheaper in Germany. The German internet software start-ups Intershop, Brokat and Poet, for example, had sales offices in the USA but carried out most of their programming in Germany.

Were corporate taxes high or low in Germany? It depended on whom you asked. On an international scale, corporate taxes were not among the highest in the world.[14] They were to a great part tied to the profits of the company (with the sole exception of property taxes), and a start-up without profits was hardly subject to taxation. To an extent, the same conditions existed in the USA, the UK and the Netherlands but not in France (Licht et al., 1998, 26, 27; see also Sachverständigenrat, 1998, 193). A big plus for German entrepreneurs, however, was the capital gains tax structure, which served as a start-up incentive. In fact, shareholdings under 25 per cent which were held for a certain minimum period were not subject to a capital gains tax (Licht et al., 1998, 27).

Assessing the balance of benefits and obstacles faced by firms in Germany became the national sport of almost all publications in the 1990s

– the *Standortdebatte*. One recurring aspect of this debate was the attempt to gauge the overall state of the German economy by examining foreign direct investment (FDI). From the mid-1970s to the late 1990s, the net balance of FDI for the past years in Germany was negative, suggesting to some observers that Germany was steadily losing comparative locational advantage. Outward stock increased from DM 100 to DM 223 billion when the period from 1983 to 1989 is compared to 1990 to 1996. Inward stock also increased, however, from DM 23 to DM 47 billion (Tüselmann, 1998, 296, 297).[15] While more recent figures show a strong increase in FDI inward stock in 1999, it is still dwarfed by outward flow. Much of the rise in inward stock reflects the global trend of consolidation and merger activity in specific industries.[16]

The world of multimedia and internet ventures also saw increased cross-border merger activity. Here, however, the balance between outward and inward FDI seemed reversed. New technology players were interested in a German location because of its large absolute number of internet users, the corporate market, its favourable know-how base and its position in Europe. In 1998 and 1999, at least five German internet and multimedia start-ups were acquired by US or Swedish firms.[17] German internet start-ups, on the other hand, only began to acquire US companies in mid-1999.[18] If there was a net FDI inflow when looking exclusively at technology start-ups, this would not only suggest the importance of the German location but also the handicap of German small firms in embarking upon international expansion. This is the question that will be examined in the following chapters.

POLICY-MAKING IN GERMANY

Most legislation in Germany is a joint effort of parliament and the responsible ministry. In both policy-making arenas, specialists are often charged with working on legislation proposals and drafts. This is especially the case with technical issues.[19] Ministry bureaucrats, for example, are able to work in their areas of proficiency with a minimum of interference from other ministries. They have been described as 'experts with specialized knowledge for problem solving' (Mayntz and Derlien, 1989, 295). The German parliament (*Bundestag*) combines responsibilities of public, partisan debate with legislative output. It is, therefore, a mixture of the British debating parliament and the US style working parliament (Sontheimer and Bleek, 1998, 278). Much of the legislative work in the Bundestag is carried out in working committees staffed by specialized parliamentarians of different parties.[20] It is said that cross-partisan consensus is enhanced by these committees, where the opposition works together with the coalition government in an environment which is removed somewhat from public scrutiny and thus also party politics. They are also sites for corporatist compromise, because representatives of interest groups can participate either as members or invited speakers.[21] In summary, specialization in policy-making is reinforced by political institutions. Specialization also synchronises nicely with two important aspects of German policy-making: the Rule of Law and corporatism. It also needs to be seen in conjunction with the distributed nature of executive power in Germany.

Instead of a pyramid, the German system spreads executive power into the separate ministries in the shape of a 'focused network' (Mayntz, 1980, 144). Katzenstein has used the term 'Departmentalisation' (Katzenstein, 1978, 319, 320). In fact, the term 'Chancellor democracy', introduced to describe the powerful institution of the Chancellor during the times of Adenauer, cannot really be applied to the contemporary system. Helmut Kohl, for example, is regarded as having acted more as a manager and mediator, a guardian of the status quo and not a strong executive force (with the exception of his role during unification).[22] Individual ministers are autonomous and powerful. A chancellor can usually reshuffle them only after an election. The Chancellor is constrained by party politics since the party is his prime vehicle through which he can carry decisions into the ministries, the parliament (Bundestag) and the federal states (*Länder*).[23] For all of these reasons, chancellors 'will actively set policy goals and directives in only one or very few selected fields, limiting themselves to managing the process of collective decision making' (Mayntz, 1980, 139, 146). Telecommunications policy was not one of Helmut Kohl's highest priorities; it was not on 'the agenda of the boss' (*Chefsache*).[24] Instead, it was a steady, continuous process which conformed to German policy-making.

German economic policy-making has been equated with two very different traditions: the *Rechtsstaat* (the Rule of Law) and a reliance on corporatist methods and institutions to carry out certain programmes and solve deadlock. The Rule of Law describes the state as the originator of a legally defined order and leads to what Dyson has called a 'juridification of policy' (1992, 9, 10). It reflects the Hegelian vision of an independent, enlightened state that guides its people (Smith, 1976, 398, 400, 401). This idea transcends party differences in the Federal Republic. Both 1950s Ordoliberal free-market thought as well as the German interpretation of Keynesian supply-led economics in the late 1960s were enshrined in what were meant to be landmark laws. When Ludwig Erhard was Minister of Economics, the so-called 'Cartel Law' of 1957, the Law on Restrictions on Competition, was enacted.[25] It was the first important German competition law, a previous effort in the interwar period was largely ineffective.[26] A decade later, in 1967, the Social Democrat Economics Minister Karl Schiller contained his countercyclical policy in the Law for the Promotion of Stability and Economic Growth. This was accompanied with prescriptions for economic and technological progress, which contradicted Erhard's previous emphasis on fair competition (Küster, 1974, 78). The limited practical success of both laws, however, illustrates that although much of the political process sees its objective in law-making, other forces are at work.

Embodied in the institutional landscape is the reliance on corporatism in responding to challenges and change, which in specific instances had the effect of diluting German judicialism. Although the Cartel Law was meant to break the power of large corporations in Germany whose market powers had begun to limit competition, the law in its four decades of existence was not wielded as was intended. To a certain extent, large enterprises managed to retain the dominant hold they had in their home economy (Vernon, 1974, 6) and played political roles within a corporatist system. Similarly, despite Schiller's attempt to contain Keynesian economic policy in a law, this policy was not followed through in Germany as it was in other countries (Kreile, 1978, 199; see also Sally, 1995, 88–93). In the late 1990s, specific effects of a progressive law prescribing telecommunications competition were delayed.

There are two interrelated uses for the term 'corporatism' in political science. The first refers to a theoretical framework for analysing the politics of interest groups.[27] A second use of the term occurs when it is applied to actual structures and methods in policy-making. It is in this comparative sense that the term is used here. A triangular relationship between the state, peak industry associations and trade unions is being referred to. Another important force is the banks, which have historically maintained close linkages to top industrial concerns via board membership and shareholdings. The economic historian Werner Abelshauser calls corporatism a 'triangular pattern of wheeling and dealing' (Abelshauser, 1984, 286). Although found in most countries during the twentieth century, including Europe, Asia and South America, formal corporatist structures are often identified with Germany, especially during the interwar period. Corporatism arose out of a desperate attempt by the bourgeoisie to retain political and economic control in the light of imminent anarchy – as described by Charles S. Maier in his classic book on the subject (1975). For many years, corporatism was exclusively identified with this undemocratic alliance between the three main economic groups. It has often been noted how, until 1992, the *International Encyclopaedia of the Social Sciences* defined the term 'corporatism' as: 'See fascism' (Czada, 1994, 39).

Pre-war 'authoritarian corporatism' mutates into 'neo-corporatism', 'liberal corporatism, 'democratic corporatism' or, also, a 'coordinated market economy' (Streeck, 1994, 11; see also the useful table in Lehrer,

1998).[28] Although he was forced to revive corporatist administration of the economy temporarily during the Korean Crisis, Erhard tried to cleanse German government from the stigma of corporatism.[29] Similarly, the classic industry peak association, the Bundesverband der Deutschen Industrie (the Federation of German Industry, BDI), dominated by the largest German corporations, saw itself as an independent entity after the war. Its own perception of its mission was to respond in strength to the 'corporatist stranglehold of the state' (Czada, 1994, 58, 59). This reflected the fact that industry structures gradually opened up with ongoing Americanization after the war (Berghahn, 1985, 324–30). Further erosion of the power of the main institutions of corporatism can be observed today. Key corporate players in significant industries, such as Deutsche Bank, Allianz and Hoechst, towards the turn of the century changed their own governance structures and thereby their role in the national political economy. The third corporatist partner, the unions, also started to become more independent-minded. In the 1970s, critical currents appeared, which attacked the cooperative stance the German unions traditionally occupied. These critical currents were responses to increased competition and privatization.[30]

Despite the historic burden, it is important to emphasize that corporatism as applied to actual cases of policy-making has been regarded both negatively as well as positively in terms of its effect on German competitiveness. Abelshauser, for example, has emphasized the positive aspects of corporatist policy-making in post-war Germany, although he stated that these aspects were ideal for an export-led economy focused on established technologies and diversified quality products, not for an economy pioneering high-technology product markets (Abelshauser, 2001, 139). For years, the German model for conciliating the interests of capital and labour was admired internationally. In this study, the term 'corporatism' is used comparatively, mainly to distinguish the German political economy from the American. The tendency for government, industry and the unions to cooperate on policy formation was prominent during the course of telecommunications liberalization in Germany. But other aspects of Germany policy institutions also reappear in this chapter. The promotion of venture capital was carried out very effectively in a 'departmentalised', specialist forum. Rule of Law concepts are evident in the need felt by German policy-makers to design a general legal framework for the New Economy, a need which, interestingly, was at the time not shared to the same extent by entrepreneurs. Before these specific policy instances can be discussed, however, two important preambles to the discussion taken from the history of German policy-making in the field need to be briefly highlighted.

PREAMBLE ONE: THE NATIONAL VIDEOTEX DEBACLE

The development of the videotex system in Germany in the 1970s and 1980s was an example of state-led technology policy. It was also, incidentally, a showcase for corporatism at work in post-war Germany. The story is told in detail by Volker Schneider (1989, 69–167). A British public telecommunications engineer invented the videotex system in 1972. The invention consisted of the clever combination of different, already existing technical systems. It immediately caught the attention of the German Postal and Telecommunications Ministry, the BPM. An independent commission dedicated to the German communication system, the KtK,[31] also identified it as an important issue for examination. After videotex, called Bildschirmtext (Btx) in Germany, was demonstrated at the 1977 broadcasting trade fair in Berlin, the BPM invited all important industry associations to discuss the development of the system. Three key industry sectors saw it as a chance to either corner a new market (the banks and retail industry) or as a potential threat (the newspapers). As groups that supplied the services for a public teletex network, they formed their own industry organization in 1982, the Btx-Anbietervereinigung (Btx-AV). It had approximately 100 founding members. Btx-AV was dominated by larger businesses; only one out of 40 seats in the Kuratorium was reserved for small service firms. This association acted as the main spokesperson for business groups and was a negotiation partner for the BPM, which developed the system together with IBM. In addition, the association was instrumental in convincing state governments to find a political compromise over jurisdiction of the new system. Lastly, the unions were also involved in the development of Btx. Together with the Social Democrats and the state governments they demanded that the system be heavily regulated: service suppliers had to register themselves, there were certain consumer protection and data security features. The SPD also successfully defeated a proposal for self-regulation by the industry groups.

The German approach to videotex was secured in a state law, the Staatsvertrag for Btx, which was signed in early 1983. Of the three countries developing videotex as a public system, Germany was the only one which regulated it through legislation (see Schneider, 1989, 127, 128). This law allowed significant jurisdiction by state governments. One and a half decades later, the architects from the BMFT of the 1997 'Multimedia Law' sought to avoid that state governments would hold a similar gateway function in the commercialization of the internet.

It is astounding in what short time period a successful corporatist system unique to videotex developed. This system comprised technological development, roll-out, supply of services and a legal and political framework.

When Btx was officially launched at the Berlin broadcast fair in 1983, all major elements were in place. Despite this effort, videotex itself was not successful. In contrast to France, the German government did not heavily subsidize the use of the system. Government involvement was focused only on building the infrastructure and acting as an instigating partner in a corporatist alliance. Little effort was spent on reducing the price for using the system to be borne by consumers. Large firms, not small, and hungry services companies dominated the initial supply of services.

PREAMBLE TWO: THE RESEARCH NETWORK DEBACLE

It has often been pointed out that German policy-makers tend to shy away from direct involvement in the economy (Katzenstein, 1978, 305; Vernon, 1974, 7). In fact, corporatism can sometimes provide a means to (co-)manage the economy without direct control or ownership.[32] But there have also been numerous instances of *dirigiste* intervention historically.[33] In recent times, the government ran or financed economic activities or was involved directly in major technological decisions, mostly via what Juergen Donges has disapprovingly called the 'sectoral ministries' (1998, 202). Examples were the BPM or BMBF. These direct efforts were so widespread that another economist, Joachim Starbatty, labelled them: 'The reality of daily mercantilism' (Starbatty, 1999, 170, 171). One such story has just been told; the development of a public videotex system. Although government adopted a corporatist approach to secure the supply of services and reach political compromise with the states, it set up and ran the infrastructure. Through the Bundespost, it was also involved in technological decisions such as making the system compatible to IBM mainframe computers. The second milestone in the development of a communications infrastructure in Germany was the construction of an academic and research network in the 1980s and 1990s, the Deutsches Forschungsnetz (DFN). DFN was a debacle as well.

The fact that the DFN was a child of the Kohl era would lead one to assume that the public sector would take care not to involve itself directly or would, alternatively, plan for a withdrawal as soon as the system stood. As in other countries, the deployment of a network linking universities and research institutions was subsidized by government, in this case the BMFT. Unlike other countries, however, the network was not run in a way that would prepare it for privatization, nor did it encourage spin-offs to industry. In fact, as described by a well-known German internet expert Werner Zorn in a short and precise paper (1998), the German research network organization was antagonistic to private business.

Interestingly, the German research network (Deutsches Forschungsnetz, DFN) was founded in 1984 under the auspices of BMBF Minister Heinz Riesenhuber. In his Ministry, Riesenhuber emphasized a reduction of subsidy programmes. He also intended the DFN to be a catalyst for 'entrepreneurial spirit' (*Unternehmensgeist*). This is why the DFN was founded as an association (*Verein*), which was officially independent of the BMFT. But the DFN promptly veered off in a different direction than intended, partially because it was dependent upon government funding. From 1984 to 1990 it exclusively promoted the use of the ISO open networking standard OSI and not any other alternatives, such as the internet protocol TCP/IP. In Europe, the UK and the Scandinavian countries had a more open and experimental approach, which also allowed the implementation of the US research networking standard. Furthermore, the DFN realized its network not in cooperation with private enterprises, but with the government-owned Bundespost. The Bundespost ran its service to the DFN using the ISO/OSI affiliated standard X.25 CCITT/ISO.[34] Furthermore, the DFN even after 1990 fought to keep its domain of universities and research institutions a monopoly by refusing access to its network by private internet providers. It was, therefore, very difficult to establish private internet access providers in Germany; as in other countries, most of the initial content was to be found on academic servers linked to the DFN (Zorn, 1998, 203, 204). Zorn concludes his paper by writing: 'Today we know that the internet established itself in Germany not because of BMFT subsidies but despite them' (1998, 198). In fact, internet ventures established themselves in a space that was, albeit strongly dependent upon telecommunications infrastructure and other political conditions, and not a direct result of German policy-making. This was in contrast to the US experience.

TAKING THE LONG ROAD TO TELECOMMUNICATIONS LIBERALIZATION[35]

In the late 1990s, Germany was frequently described as one of the most liberal telecommunication regimes in the world. This was due to a very progressive telecommunications law, the TKG, passed in 1996. This law insured, for example, that foreign telecommunications firms could enter the market on the same terms as domestic players. An independent regulatory body, the RegTP, was instituted to watch over an *ex ante* asymmetrical regulatory regime, which was able to impose price controls on the incumbent operator, Deutsche Telekom AG (DTAG). It ascertained 'fair' prices derived from data obtained from outside and from within the DTAG. In fact, the prices for interconnection fees charged to competitors were considered low even by the competition itself. As a result, national and national long-distance prices fell rapidly. The complaints about the RegTP and its President, Klaus-Dieter Scheurle, by DTAG executives could be seen as a further sign that the regulatory body was doing its stipulated task well. Initially, the market share of the incumbent in international and national telephony actually fell more rapidly than in other countries that underwent liberalization. These observations seemed even more surprising given the fact that ten years earlier, Germany was universally seen as one of the more closed markets in the world, dominated by a monopoly and a clientist purchasing system favouring a handful of domestic 'court suppliers' (Lehmbruch, 1992, 40). Germany was criticized as being the 'Fortress on the Rhine', as cited by Humphreys (1992, 111).

In telecommunications, Germany moved from public to private ownership and from direct steering to regulated competition. Rolling back the state in telecommunications was not easy. It was only possible with significant compromise involving what essentially were the three corporatist partners, because major institutional hurdles had to be overcome. One of these was changing the German Basic Law, and this required a parliamentary majority of two-thirds. Another was dismantling the public ownership system with its thousands of employees, some of whom had the status of public servants. Given this constellation, corporatism mattered. In the United States, interest group resistance was much weaker and institutional barriers preventing change were low.[36]

For these reasons, liberalization was a long drawn-out, three-step process. The first postal reform of 1989 divided the Bundespost into three separate services, the postal (Post), banking (Postbank) and telecommunication services (Telekom). The second postal reform was passed in 1992 and came into effect Summer of 1994. At this stage, the DBP Telekom and the other services were privatized. No liberalization occurred at this stage in the fixed-line market of basic telephony services. Finally, the telecommunications law ('elekommunikationsgesetz, TKG) of 1996 instituted asymmetric regulation and unrestricted competition in basic services. A new regulator, the Regulierungsbehörde für Telekommunikation und Post (RegTP) was set up under the auspices of the Economics Ministry to ensure and maintain a competitive landscape. Competition was finally initiated in 1998.

In analysing the three steps, it is important to describe the lines of the debate at the time. In fact, there were modernization proponents and staunch advocates of the status quo on both the side of the ruling coalition as well as their partisan opposition. It was the modernizers on each side which contributed to the eventual success of liberalization. But the modernizers themselves had significantly different visions of the future. In general, the ruling coalition parties were opposed to state involvement in technology policy and had earlier criticized the Bundespost's involvement in technological decision-making. The opposition, with some exceptions, advocated technological innovation under the auspices of the state.[37]

This difference in emphasis had longer heritage; it previously surfaced in the debates surrounding the liberalization of media in Germany. Media jurisdiction lay with the federal states, not with the national government. Yet, after the CDU and CSU assumed power in 1982 together with the FDP, Postal and Telecommunications Minister Christian Schwarz-Schilling used his control over the federal telecommunications system to build a nationwide coaxial cable network which enabled the launch of private media programmes (Hoffmann-Riem, 1990, 182). It was at this point that modernizers among the SPD advocated the instalment of a nationwide broadband fibre-optic cable integrated services network (Hoffmann-Riem, 1990, 181). This was a technology that still had to be developed instead of the widely available, standard, relatively low-cost coaxial system.[38] The difference between the two views of national innovation continues to be relevant today. The concept of state-led innovation has been recast as policy for support of a 'national champion'. It is, therefore, not correct that traditions of state-led innovation were exclusively a French phenomenon.

The process of telecommunications deregulation can be described in terms of a battle between a coalition for change and its opponents. And it was only in the 1990s that the coalition for change began to gain ground. From 1985 to 1987, the telecommunications policy commission, the so-called Witte Commission, named after its chairman Professor Eberhard Witte, which included the broad scope of concerned interest groups, was marked by heavily dissenting positions (Schmidt, 1991, 214–15). Its corporatistic mission resulted in the moderate first postal reform of 1989, the Bill to Restructure the Post and Telecommunications of the German Bundespost (Poststrukturgesetz). To describe how difficult it was to pass the reform bill, Humphreys cites Schneider and Werle that 50 different organizations participated in bitter hearings by the Bundestag committee. In the end, however, the bill was passed more easily than was expected – thanks to the corporatist process it had been through (Humphreys, 1992, 118, 121–4).

The first proponents of change were the computer industry, especially the German company Nixdorf and, to a lesser extent, IBM, who attacked the purchasing policies of the state-owned carrier.[39] They were backed by the rising frustration which was felt among the German Chamber of Commerce, the BDI and the Bundespost adversary, the Association of Bundespost Users ('Verband der Postbenutzer,' VPB) (Humphreys, 1992, 115).[40] Another critical player in the late 1980s was the BPM, the

Bundespost Ministry itself. It was convinced reform was necessary to address the 'technology gap.'[41] In fact, the BPM was generally perceived by other participants as the central policy actor advocating reform (Humphreys, 1992, 124).[42] Lastly, the EC also played an important role. The European Commission's influential telecommunication Green Paper of 1987 called for liberalization.[43]

The opposition included the Postal Union, the Deutsche Postgewerkschaft (DPG), and parts of the SPD. The opposition also included representatives of rural areas, especially in the CSU, who were against liberalization because they believed that the concept of universal service would be compromised. The most fiercely fought battle between the advocates and opponents of reform was that of privatization. The main fear by the Postal Union was that the shift in status of their members would result in a loss of jobs and of privileges. At one point, the loss of 60 000 jobs was forecast.[44] All sides were aware that the achievement of privatization was a crucial step which almost automatically would result in liberalization and the initiation of competition. After the battle for privatization, however, the new privatized company was left with significant assets. Only afterwards did it become obvious how misbalanced the ownership structure was and what effect this would have on the competitive environment.

The new privatized entity owned not just the complete fixed-line telephony network, it also owned significant parts of an alternative network, the cable TV infrastructure. In other countries, policy-makers had mandated separation of this alternative network infrastructure. In the US Telecommunications Act of 1996, the so-called 'Baby Bells' or local phone services were not allowed to own more than a 10 per cent share of cable companies. In the UK, the dominant PTO was barred from providing broadcast entertainment over its networks. Competitors were from 1991 onwards allowed to offer telephony services over cable TV and bypass the local loop of the dominant PTO. In 1995, one million customers in the UK already used telephony services provided by cable TV operators (OECD, 1996b, 7, 10; Gerpott, 1998, 283; Freytag and Jäger, 1996, 231).

Despite their victory in the privatization measure, it was obvious to the proponents of change in Germany that the lack of infrastructure competition would be problematic. Some believed in an alternative means of access by which competitors could bypass Deutsche Telekom's local phone lines. This was wireless local loop (WLL) technology. One of these wireless systems, DECT, was a standard defined by the European standards body ETSI in 1992.[45] According to Dr Martin Mayer, a CSU parliamentarian who was active in a number of relevant commissions: 'At that time, we all believed that competition would come through the wireless local loop. Everybody spoke about DECT. Cable telephony, on the other hand, seemed an experiment. I must note, however, that the association of private telephony carriers (VATM) did argue for a separation [of the cable TV network]' (Interview 23 April 1999).[46] But although DECT may have looked promising in 1996, it was a technological chimera, at least in the medium term.

Others, such as Arne Börnsen, one of the main advocates for moderniza- tion within the SPD and later Vice-President of the national regulator, were more pessimistic about the WLL option. When asked why he did not engage himself for a separation of the cable TV network, Börnsen blamed the bad state of German cable and pointed out the fact that the value of cable TV was not recognizable before the privatization measure of 1994. He emphasized that a separation post-privatization would have infringed upon the property of a private enterprise.[47] In addition to the cable TV network, however, Deutsche Telekom was left with a further strategic asset, the teletex service Btx. Also here, the value of the asset was questionable. At the time of its launch in the late 1970s, it was hailed as a breakthrough. But by 1994, Deutsche Telekom had all but given up on the service and out- sourced much of the marketing effort associated with it.

Since infrastructure competition was not possible to achieve in the medium term, an alternative was pursued. Section 35 (1) of the telecommu- nications law, the TKG, provided for the access to single customer lines by the competition. This was only one of the progressive aspects of the TKG, but it seemed promising for those concerned about competition in the local loop, such as Börnsen. After the start of fixed-line competition, the tele- communications regulator RegTP used this option, and Germany was the first European country to mandate complete unbundling of the customer line for a fixed monthly fee.

For the participants in the telecommunications reform process in Germany, the ownership concessions made to Deutsche Telekom seemed necessary. In fact, they emphasized that the value of neither the cable TV network nor Btx were recognizable at the time. This was indeed the case in 1994, at the time of privatization. One needs to ask a further question, however. Was the property structure of Deutsche Telekom indeed unchangeable in 1996, at the time the TKG was passed? As the independent telecommunications expert and long-standing critic of the course of liber- alization, Dr Bernd Jäger, points out, government was a full owner of the joint stock company and property could have been disposed of at any point in time by invoking a general assembly (Interview, 19 February 2002). Together with an economist, Jäger in 1996 had carefully analysed the TKG and addressed the misbalanced ownership of the cable TV network and the old videotex system. Andreas Freytag and Jäger furthermore argued that there were no economic reasons justifying a grace period and that the competition should have been allowed to enter the market right away (1996, 219, 237). In fact, the incumbent was granted a period of almost two years from Summer 1996 to the end of 1997 during which it could prepare for competition. The TKG mandated the start of competition only for January 1998, conforming to the final EU deadline.

What was the reason for the grace period? To cite the dry commentary of Dr Martin Mayer, a CSU Bundestag Committee member: 'The SPD wanted to prevent liberalization; this is why there were concessions such as the grace period' (interview 23 April 1999). This explanation was subjective; there were strong factions among the SPD in favour of liberalization just as there were CSU members opposed. It was conceivable that the effect of the grace period was simply underestimated by the advocates of competition. It was more likely, however, that a logic began to operate for the first time here which would reappear later. The stock market listing of DTAG was carried out as rapidly as possible after the passing of the telecommunications law. Both German government as well as the former PTO required the funds which would be obtained through a listing. The state, which would transform itself through the IPO from an infrastructure provider into a shareholder, was highly interested in a smooth listing. The grace period would guarantee this; there would be no disturbances by the competition.[48]

The battles surrounding telecommunications competition did not end in January 1998. The new conflict was a contest between the regulatory authority, equipped with a progressive telecommunications law, and a mixture of liberalization critics, animated by short-term financial interests as well as a 'national champion' vision of innovation. DTAG was seen by the liberalization critics as the main German global competitor in telecommunications, chief employer and sacrosanct contributor to the coffers of the Finance Ministry.[49] As Markus Müller pointed out in his analysis of 1990s regulation initiatives in Germany, telecommunications regulation was so recent that a distinct culture had not yet developed between the regulator and the regulated, the incumbent operator. One result was a lawsuit on average every other day during the first two years of RegTP's existence (Müller, 2001, 58). Even after liberalization, the DTAG retained 'excellent networks' in Bonn 'dating back to the days of public ownership', according to an article in the newspaper *Handelsblatt*. For this reason, the article continues, 'political attacks at the regulatory agency mirror almost verbatim statements of the Deutsche Telekom'.[50] After election of the SPD–Greens coalition in late 1998, the new Economics Minister Werner Müller publicly announced that he was the 'agent for the people and the employees of the Deutsche Telekom'.[51] The SPD Minister of Economics of the State of North-Rhine Westphalia, Wolfgang Clement, as well as the Chairman of the Postal Workers Union (DPG), Kurt van Haaren, recommended changing the telecommunications law to the benefit of the incumbent operator.[52] The Finance Ministry also complained to the chief regulator and warned him not to attack the DTAG too much. Even Mosdorf, a self-professed champion of entrepreneurship and the top New Economy expert of the SPD, subscribed to this view: 'We want the DTAG as largest player in her field to be in the global top league. We have no interest to break it up and sell it off cheaply' (Interview 10 May 1999). In contrast to the SPD view, the Managing Director of a competitor to the DTAG viewed 'the obvious mingling of regulatory and finance policy as standing in complete contrast to international rules and can be compared to market behaviour in the Third World'.[53] These conflicts as well as the misbalance in ownership by the incumbent caused delays in the effect of liberalization; this will be discussed in the next chapter.

MULTIMEDIA LEGISLATION: THE *RECHTSSTAAT* OFFERS ITS SERVICES

As was pointed out in the beginning of this chapter, German economic policy-makers see themselves primarily as law-framers. This corresponds to the vision of a *Rechtsstaat*. The German approach has often (but not always) been characterized by the attempt to create a legal framework without getting directly involved in an industry through ownership or mandate. The framework does, however, contain extensive security and quality considerations. Government involvement in traditional German industry sectors such as machine tools is typical of this approach: government combined non sector-specific general market rules as well as sector-specific encouragement of standards and certification schemes. The objectives of these sector-specific initiatives were to provide a secure and high-quality work process and work environment with a maximum of industry self-regulation. Certified occupational categories are one example.

The arrival of the New Economy put German policy-makers once again into the perceived position of having to define a general legal framework to increase business certainty and introduce quality certification schemes. The implicit objective was to use such initiatives to bolster the international competitive advantage of small and medium-sized German firms and start-ups. Standard-setting attempts were extended as offers to firms, not as mandatory, market-restricting obligations.

The Information and Communication Services Act (Informations-und Kommunikationsdienste-Gesetz, IuKDG), in short, the so-called Multimedia Law, was passed by the Bundestag in July 1997 and came into effect on 1 August 1997. Its main intention was to pre-empt the possibility at a federal level that state jurisdictions enact licensing obligations for providers of 'individual communication services' such as online and internet services (Gerpott, 1998, 329). Whether this would have been a real threat at that point in time is debatable, as will be discussed below. The law also contained other elements, such as defining responsibility over content and reducing the scope for overzealous policing efforts. It offered a certification and standards scheme for digital signatures as well as data protection legislation. Here, the main aspects of the law will be discussed briefly together with its intended objectives. Overall, this legislative initiative did not harm the entrepreneur in Germany but it is also not clear whether it thus far has been of great advantage.[54] It seems to have arisen more out of a need perceived by policy-makers than out of acute entrepreneurial issues.

The German digital signatures law which was passed together with the Multimedia Law was to a great extent misrepresented in the international press. It was also the implicit target of criticism by the Clinton Administration Working Group on Global Electronic Commerce. It was viewed as an initiative of the German government designed to create a mandatory global digital signatures standard for the benefit of its own growing encryption and smart card sector. When asked about this perception on the part of press and the US Working Group, a parliamentarian involved in the legislation stated: 'If the Americans really think this, that is fine. This is precisely what we want to do, to challenge them' (Dr Michael Meister, Interview 22 March 1999). The objective of the law was indeed to improve the competitive advantage of domestic industry. But it addressed this task by providing an institutional, legal framework typical of other efforts in German industry. It was not designed in the market-closing way in which it has been internationally represented, but as a non-mandatory offer. Its main elements were the establishment of standard recommended guidelines and a certification scheme.[55] Certification schemes have been used in German industry for decades to insure a high standard of industrial production. German policy-makers had hoped that voluntary standards and a certification scheme would encourage internet users to conduct more transactions such as the 'signing' of legally binding documents over the internet and to carry out these tasks using German software and hardware products. It could be argued that these ideas were too early for the market; consumers were just becoming acquainted with the internet and the services policy-makers had in mind did not exist yet. Although entrepreneurs at the time regarded digital signatures and encryption in principle to be important issues, especially in an international context, they did not believe the law had any impact on their business.[56]

The Multimedia Law contained data protection and privacy stipulations in the Teleservices Data Protection Act (Teledienstdatenschutzgesetz,

TDDSG).[57] This Act mandated how private data could be collected, how it was to be stored and how it should be sold. There was also an identification obligation for service and information providers. The stipulations in most cases were straightforward to apply and did not extend the scope of European Data Privacy legislation. Like its European counterpart, however, the data protection law was generally viewed as necessary by most internet firms to establish consumer trust, even if they would theoretically rather do without laws.[58] Unlike European privacy law, however, the TDDSG did not contain export clauses, which could be viewed as an electronic trade barrier.[59]

The Multimedia Law was also driven by another objective, which was political. In 1992, Kenneth Dyson wrote about 'a new contest for power within German regulation' (Dyson, 1992, xiv, xv). Especially intense was the battle in Germany between federal government and the states (*Länder*) over control of what was widely seen as the next leading economic sectors. As the political scientist Fritz Scharpf pointed out, the advantages of federalism were often emphasized in the post-war period as a device to prevent the abuse of state power. In the 1990s, however, it seemed to be fashionable to criticize federalism as a system that reduced the ability of federal government to act flexibly and decisively in an environment marked by change. Although Scharpf framed his analysis on the European Union and on the system of interlocking federalism – in which legislative and fiscal powers are wielded by the federal government and implementation is the responsibility of the individual states – it can easily be generalized (Scharpf, 1994, 221).[60] This led to an even more intensive criticism of the federal system, under the label 'particularism' (*Kleinstaaterei*), where state power was seen almost universally as blocking effective new media policy.

In contrast to this prevailing view, it could be hypothetically argued that the needs of entrepreneurs could be met by less centralized responsibility and more flexibility on a state (*Länder*) level. In the 1980s, inter-state competition insured that even SPD-led states staunchly opposed to media liberalization would soon jump on the bandwagon and encourage the formation of private broadcasters, led by Hamburg and North-Rhine Westphalia (Hoffmann-Riem, 1990, 190; Humphreys, 1988, 205–6).[61]

The possible lesson to be learned is that state-level competition can lead to overall convergence of policy without the need for centralised authority. 'Spontaneous harmony' can come about through policy competition, as discussed in the previous chapter. Local resistance to convergence and the establishment of an isolated 'fortress' could cause electronic flows to be diverted and could cause harm to the local economy. In the 1990s local state governments were intent on attracting internet entrepreneurs and multimedia firms. Some of their policy, such as some ill-constructed technology parks and wrongly staffed and positioned venture capital companies under state control (MGBs), was misguided and at best contributed to learning.[62] This will be discussed in more detail in the following section on the promotion of entrepreneurship in Germany. Newer efforts tend to head in a different direction by emphasizing network access as well as urban small-firm clustering. But although the regional policy goals were largely the same, a diversity of approaches existed at the end of the 1990s. North-Rhine Westphalia (NRW) and Bavaria both emphasized internet access. Through its municipal energy companies, NRW was an indirect owner of NetCologne, a privately operating regional full-service carrier. Bavaria directly launched its own online service which generated much enthusiasm for the internet in rural areas. A plethora of other regional initiatives existed across the country. The California/ Bavaria Business Forum, for example, was an attempt to help Munich-based start-ups in their internationalization strategy. The most active state governments were NRW, Bavaria as well as Hamburg and Berlin which combined to form a 'Multimedia Corridor.'

Although regional policy competition can be viewed as positive, and differences are reduced over the longer term in areas in which successful policies establish themselves, the federal government tried to centralize jurisdiction of the internet and multimedia services by arguing that while regional policy was laudable in principle, specific responsibility of the states over internet issues would lead to fragmentation and inefficiencies. This view could be found both in the Bundestag, the former Ministry of Research and Technology (BMFT) as well as among other contemporary observers.[63] This issue was what the so-called Multimedia Law was about. Its intention was to stipulate responsibility over content ownership and, by doing so, explicitly removed most state control in new media issues. One parliamentarian involved in multimedia legislation asked: 'What if local states would ask for licences modelled on radio licences from firms that run large web sites? The imagination of state leaders goes wild if they are provided with too much power.' Officials in the Economics Ministry rightly pointed out that individual states had rights over the Btx videotex system and that this was a barrier to development. With the Multimedia Law the BMFT succeeded to a great extent in limiting state power, although, even here, a Media Services State Contract (*Mediendienste-Staatsvertrag*, MDstV) was necessary and the compromise solution required allowing states power over broadcast-like media services, *Mediendienste* (in contrast to 'tele-services' targeting the individual user).[64] This was probably the greatest weakness of the law, since firms offering video services for individuals seem to be in an overlapping, uncertain legal space. One lawyer therefore called this compromise the Achilles' Heel of internet development in

Germany (BMBF, 1997, 27). This interpretation was probably exaggerated, however. In designing the Multimedia Law, the BMFT actually minimized the power of the states and in this regard, it was much more successful than others before them in meeting this objective. The Media Services State Contract was seen as the lesser evil necessary for compromise.

Next to a policy battle with the states, however, stood another objective; reducing the possibility for overzealous policing efforts in on-line content. These efforts were pronounced in the Interior Ministry as well as among local prosecutors for different reasons. The content ownership issue was an important one for all firms offering content or internet access.[65] The law reduced the amount of responsibility that network providers had over the third-party content they carried. A criminal law and computer law expert praised the Multimedia Law as a very clear and liberal law. His only worry was precisely that local policing efforts misunderstand the implications of the law (BMBF, 1997, 94).

It needs to be noted, however, that the German federal government responded quickly to the early stage of internet commercialization by using the law as an non-intrusive means to experiment with new policy frameworks. Exactly this learning, experimental approach to regulation is what the German internet and media expert Axel Zerdick from the Freie Universität Berlin recommended and believed was suited to 'the internet economy' (Zerdick et al., 1999, 260). Specific law-making on a federal level in the multimedia and internet sector did not harm electronic commerce and did not stunt entrepreneurship in a major way. Perhaps it has also prevented some counter-productive legislation on a state level, and also stifled possible initiatives by the Interior Ministry.[66] However, policy-makers on a federal level looked down upon the ability of state-level policy-makers to design regional initiatives to encourage internet uptake and start-up activity. Actually, policy experimentation on a state level was vibrant and led to some successes – the best example probably was the aforementioned initiative NetCologne with its flat-rate internet offerings.

The entrepreneur community was only dimly aware of the Multimedia Law, however. The law has to be characterized as a government-initiated project, which arose out of the perceived needs of entrepreneurs as envisioned by federal specialists. It failed to address many of the real issues faced by internet entrepreneurs which existed in the areas of regulation, taxation, financing and internet access. Although the designers of the law had actively sought out the advice of entrepreneurs, the general feeling among policy-makers on a federal level in general was that entrepreneurs were themselves not politically active enough. One member of staff on the Enquete-Kommission, for example, was a little hurt by the lack of desire on the part of entrepreneurs for a strongly proactive government: 'And those start-up firms that we did talk to gave us very little to work with. They do not have a lobby and do not frame political demands. They only kept repeating they wanted lower telecommunication prices' (Lutz Reulecke, Interview 25 March 1999). In fact, until July 2000, there was no political lobby group for internet entrepreneurs.[67]

PROMOTING THE 'GARAGE ENTREPRENEUR'

A vast number of programmes existed at the EU, national and regional level directed at small and medium-sized enterprises (SMEs) in the 1990s.[68] Germany was, in fact, known for its innovative, diffusion-oriented programmes encouraging technological uptake among a broad range of SMEs (Ergas, 1987). These programmes targeted at SMEs generally need, however, to be differentiated from more focused support schemes for high-growth technology ventures. Whereas the SME support schemes were focused on the needs of SMEs in more traditional sectors of the economy such as machine tools or medical research, newer programmes such as BioRegio,[69] InnoNet, Business Angels Netzwerk Deutschland (BAND) e.V. were tailored specifically to the needs of new technology ventures. Others, such as MEDIA@Komm, sought to encourage the use of digital signatures by the public administration. All these initiatives intended to promote the formation of new, high-technology ecosystems in Germany involving entrepreneurs, private financiers and regional and national policy-makers.

Yet, is important to emphasize that there were links between traditional programmes for SMEs and the institutions charged with carrying these out and the newer, high-growth schemes. Some already have been discussed, such as the certification programme for digital signatures. This section will focus on the promotion of venture capital in Germany. Two institutions oversaw the effort, the Technologie-Beteiligungs-Gesellschaft (tbg) of the German Equalization Bank (Deutsche Ausgleichsbank, DtA) and the German Development Bank (Kreditanstalt für Wiederaufbau, KfW). The DtA was founded in 1950 and extended credit to manufacturers and craftsmen. The KfW started in 1948 with the objective to finance the reconstruction of Germany. Both public and private institutions drew upon funding originally provided by the US Marshall Plan.

None of the diverse range of programmes targeting high-growth firms mentioned at the beginning of this section such as InnoNet or BAND, were as important as the schemes promoting venture capital in Germany. While the KfW programme provided a refinancing programme to venture capital funds and extended guarantees, the tbg directly invested in start-ups, side-by-side with a venture capitalist or a private investor. For this reason, the tbg was the better known of the two schemes.[70] The BMFT must be credited for developing these programmes without which venture capital funding would have dried up in Germany in the decade from 1989 to 1998. The mechanism used was a 'co-venturing' concept in which the tbg doubled investments of venture capital firms and private investors without diluting their stake. This greatly reduced the risk that venture capitalists faced. The scheme, like that of the KfW, left the investment decisions to the market, meaning that private know-how could be exploited and governments did not have to make technology decisions.[71] The tbg and KfW programmes could not be combined in a single investment.

tbg and KfW support was essential for the survival of the German VC sector until the Neue Markt had fully emerged as a viable exit option during the course of 1998. Without these programmes, early internet software start-ups such as Brokat and Intershop would not have been funded out of Germany. In interviews carried out in 1998, all venture capitalists that were consulted credited these programmes with helping venture capital survive in Germany in the 1990s. One high-level official in the Ministry of Economics characterized the benefits of the programme in this way: 'In this program, we show that the state can allow the market to handle important decisions. By the way, one cannot learn how to manage technology start-ups in a seminar. One has to do it oneself' (Interview 11 May 1999).

Three different developments had led to the creation of these equity investment support programmes in Germany.[72] One was the emphasis of the Minister of Science and Technology Heinz Riesenhuber on cost savings and a reduction of what was called *Zuschussfinanzierung*, subsidy financing. *Zuschussfinanzierung* was to become a word to be avoided in the Ministry. Indirect support of the enterprise was emphasized over direct subsidy of specific research projects. It was thought that government should not involve itself in making technology decisions on behalf of private businesses. Another factor was the ongoing positive experience in the Netherlands with publicly supported start-up venture capital equity programmes. The success of the self-sustaining venture capital industry also was apparent in the USA.[73] Another decisive factor was an analysis of experimental predecessor programmes targeting young technology companies on a federal level by the Ministry. The new equity-based BTU programme was merely the last in a series of federal programmes targeting young technology-oriented companies, albeit with a credit and subsidy emphasis. These programmes had been examined in detail by an independent think-tank, which was part of the association of Fraunhofer Institutes. The Fraunhofer Institutes also researched the effectiveness of other programmes at a state level, such as technology parks and MBGs.

In fact, the various Fraunhofer Institutes served as an intermediary, linking entrepreneurs to the public bodies. Researchers from the Institutes were in contact with entrepreneurs, collecting feedback, aggregating it and making concrete design recommendations. The forum of policy discussion therefore consisted in this case entirely of specialists, of Ministry experts from the BMFT, of the programme administrators at the tbg as well as the researchers from the Fraunhofer Institutes.

The total volume of investment in young, technology-based firms by the tbg was significant. When one compares it with the total amount of technology venture volume in a given year in Germany at the time, however, its importance relative to private investments becomes even more apparent (See Table 4.1). The amounts invested through the tbg in 1997 represented a third of total technology investments in Germany.

Table 4.1   Investments by the tbg compared to total venture capital investments in technology in Germany (in EUR millions)

	tbg	Total technology investments in Germany	tbg proportion of total (%)
1996	44	182	24
1997	109	331	33
1998	198	664	30
1999	388	1 317	29

Source: Technology investment data from: EVCA, *Yearbook 1998*, *Yearbook 1999* and *Yearbook 2000*. Technology investments in Germany were defined as the sum of investments in the following sectors: communications, computer related, other electronics related, biotechnology, and Medical/health related. Constant exchange rates were used for all three years: 1 EUR equals 2.0 DM. tbg data from tbg internet site. http://www.tbgbonn.de/, data was dated 10 May 2000. Accessed on 20 August 2000.

The BMFT must also be credited for having shied away from national technology park schemes, with the exception of a series of parks in Eastern Germany. Technology parks were favourites of regional policy-makers.[74] Interest in setting up these parks peaked in 1985 and 1986, with 43 new centres set up in those two years alone (Kulicke, 1997b, 119). Regions also extended special subsidies to entrepreneurs, but these were mainly focused on structurally weak areas.[75] Lastly, regional promoters also sought to address the financing of high-growth enterprises. Entrepreneurs – especially in IT and biotechnology – were complaining that bank officials were unwilling to extend credit to them without solid securities. Realizing that bank credits were an unsatisfactory means of promoting young software and biotechnology firms, promoters were inspired by the equity financing model of the US venture capital (VC) community and especially also the US programme surrounding the Small Business Investment Corporation (SBIC). The result was the creation of regional investment vehicles, the Mittelständische Beteiligungsgesellschaften (MBGs). These were founded in many states. They were, however, unable to operate like real VCs. Firstly and most importantly, their public nature dampened incentives to maximize profits. Secondly, investment managers had little know-how in software and biotechnology. As a result, companies financed by MGBs generally did not do as well as those that were financed by private venture capital firms (Kulicke and Wupperfeld, 1996, 220, 221). Nevertheless, in 1995, these investment firms accounted for 60 per cent of all investments in SMEs (Kulicke, 1997c, 140–42).

In summary, it was the separate learning experiences on a federal and state level as well as the desire to move away from subsidy financing which resulted in the initiation of two very successful equity support schemes administered by the tbg and the KfW. The salient point was that they both involved the venture capital community as private partners. The redirection of funds from direct credit subsidies to indirect support of private investors was not accomplished without resistance. In fact, a high-level Ministry official remembers that the press as well as entrepreneurs had strongly criticized the departure from the previous subsidy scheme: 'There was great lamentation by entrepreneurs, industry associations and journalists. They cried out: "A great program will be destroyed." At that time, the Ministry displayed a great amount of courage' (Interview 11 May 1999). This meant that German entrepreneurs in the early 1990s were still unaware of the benefits of venture capital investment and of the culture of Silicon Valley-style rapid growth. This was confirmed by other studies, but was changed considerably in the late 1990s, as will be shown in the subsequent chapters. What was also apparent through the episode was that the Ministry of Research and Technology (BMBF) had the ability to initiate unpopular programmes and could steer away from consensus if the issue was deemed sufficiently technical and uncontroversial. The difference to telecommunications policy was considerable. This technical policy-making process was highly formalized including the previously mentioned 'experts with specialized knowledge' and a public private intermediary in the form of a research institute. Technology policy was in this instance highly effective in reaching its target of supporting venture capital investments in Germany at a time when public markets in Germany were still not receptive to listings of young technology start-ups.

CONCLUSION: THE TIMING SACRIFICE

German policy-makers have for 30 years tried to close the so-called technology gap with the United States. Policy mistakes in national innovation policy were made and government in the Kohl era tried to learn from them. And, in fact, some mistakes were not repeated. From the 1980s, a partial shift occurred in technology policy. Instead of subsidizing specific projects directly, government officials in the Ministry of Research and Technology (BMFT) tried to redirect funds at the corporate level, letting private business decide how to use the money most effectively. The most successful of these programmes were the venture capital support schemes realized through the public–private organizations Technologie-Beteiligungs-Gesellschaft (tbg) and the KfW. The funds channelled towards start-ups and the guarantees extended to venture capitalists kept the German venture capital market alive until the alternative stock market Neue Markt invigorated the industry. Without the tbg and the KfW, there probably would have been no German internet software start-ups backed by venture capital firms in Germany in 1996 and 1997 (such as Intershop and Brokat) and know-how regarding high-growth entrepreneurship would neither have been cultivated in start-ups nor in venture capital firms. Key policy-makers in the Kohl coalition such as Riesenhuber did not believe government should be involved in downstream technology decisions; he was responsible for sending the signal which resulted in the development of these public–private promotion schemes. Interestingly, the success of these schemes also seems to have been dependent on the fact that the issue was not of interest to the general public. Policy was designed in an isolated forum by specialists, which introduced the new programmes despite resistance by some entrepreneurs who favoured direct state credits and the corresponding retention of complete control.

Institutions and traditions of German policy-making emphasize the idea of the Rule of Law, or *Rechtsstaat*. Although there are numerous contemporary and historical examples of German government intervention, emphasis – in both popular political camps – is placed on creating a framework for the development of market and society. Framework legislation is viewed as superior to direct intervention in achieving the objective of a vibrant market economy. The Multimedia Law of 1997 sought to provide a straightforward legislative framework for the development of the New Economy in its early stages. It was designed as a temporary law, set for re-evaluation. For example, it initiated a digital signature certification scheme. The law's main purpose was to insure that providers of online and internet services could offer these services freely without licensing or similar obligations. It was feared that state governments would have imposed these, as they did in the case of Btx videotex. Yet, the law was a largely state-led initiative, sparked by the German Rule of Law tradition, in areas where entrepreneurs did not perceive an obvious legislative need.

Direct, state-led technology initiatives existed in Germany. The tradition was not exclusive to France. One example of a state-led initiative gone wrong in Germany in the online arena was Btx, the German public videotex project of the 1980s. Again, it arose out of a perceived need by government. Initiated before the Kohl era but continued throughout it until privatization in 1994, millions of DM were spent on Btx. Btx never proved popular because it stood awkwardly between the US and French models of on-line development. US government, on the one hand, built a public internet infrastructure but commercialized it later, removing its own presence almost completely. Cross-subsidization of internet access was not paid for by government. Telephone users subsidized their own flat rate local access to the internet via their telephone long-distance connections. French government, on the other hand, incorporated Minitel into its universal service obligation and insured that the system was rolled out to a great number of households. In effect, in both the USA and France, access was subsidized. In the USA access was subsidized by telephone users in an intense competitive landscape and an asymmetric telecommunications regime favouring internet access providers over local telephony companies. In France, Minitel access was a government target and was publicly realized, for example, by giving away terminals. In Germany, Btx was jump-started by government initiative, but the access pricing issue was ignored. It was assumed that even though the service was prohibitively expensive, it would be used. In addition, it was a closed, country-only system which offered only selected services and no international choice. The tradition of state-led technology innovation in telecommunications did not die with the privatization of the former PTO, however, it was recast as enthusiasm for a 'national champion'.

The privatization of the former PTO and the initiation of competition in basic telecommunications services were two of the most significant institutional reform projects in Germany in the 1990s. Regarding the liberalization of basic telecommunications services, advocates of competition were concerned about the control the incumbent provider had on the local loop. Competition in the local loop would, among other benefits, have had a favourable impact on internet access prices, which were prohibitive due to the relatively high price of local calls. Yet, one possible alternative network infrastructure to the household and small firm was temporarily barred from use through ownership by the incumbent, the coaxial cable TV network. Alternative Wireless Local Loop (WLL) technologies were still in their pilot phase. Already in 1996 wireless technology seem to have been used merely as an excuse to justify the compromised course of liberalization. In order to promote competition in the local loop, competition advocates enshrined possibilities for access by the completion of the incumbent's network in the TKG telecommunications law. Yet, the effect of unbundling had to wait until the start of competition in 1998. Thereafter, arbitrage between the regulator and the incumbent further delayed the roll-out of alternative services in the local loop. Delays were already a characteristic of telecommunications liberalization before the TKG. Liberalization itself was a three-step process, lasting almost a decade. Delays were a necessary result of negotiation and compromise with different stakeholders. Later, delay was instrumentalized by government agencies such as the Finance Ministry, which was interested in an unobstructed stock market listing of the incumbent.

It is instructive to contrast policy in the telecommunications area with that in the financing of high-growth technology ventures. In the specialist, departmentalized forum charged with the promotion of venture capital a highly effective public–private programme was designed and executed. Government gave support, but it did not take full ownership. Telecommunications policy, however, was highly controversial and corporatist compromise was the only way forward.

The story of high, metered internet access costs well into 1999 cannot be told by focusing on government alone; the involvement of Deutsche Telekom is crucial as well. The next chapter will concentrate on explaining the rationale behind its actions. A crucial question emerges out of the fact that Deutsche Telekom was both a telecommunications operator as well as an internet provider, through T-Online. Why did the 'national champion' not promote the use of its internet service among consumers and small firms more if it recognized the internet as one of its own strategic areas of business? In other words, why was the Deutsche Telekom on its own accord unable to act as a force for innovation in Germany – a role that some policymakers in Germany, especially some among the SPD, had trusted it with.

NOTES

1. One of these was Wernhard Möschel, who fittingly described Germany's first step towards telecommunication liberalization in the late 1980s as 'nibbling on the edge of a monopoly', ('Knabbern am Rande eines Monopols'). Quoted by Susanne Schmidt in footnote 35 (1991, 216). Möschel is a professor of economic law and a member of the liberal Kronberger Kreis (Lehmbruch, 1992, 38).
2. Depending on the emphasis of the ruling coalition, the focus of the Ministry of Research and Technology (BMFT) has changed. Under Kohl, the scope of the Ministry was extended and it was called the Bundesministerium für Bildung, Wissenschaft, Forschung und Technologie (BMBF) the 'Federal Ministry for Education, Science, Research and Technology'. Journalists usually referred to it simply as the 'Future Ministry.' To avoid confusion, the old term will be used here and the ministry will be consistently called the Ministry of Research and Technology (BMFT).

3. Peter Humphreys has described how the technology gap was thematized by the ruling Social Democrats in the early 1970s, leading, among other things, to the founding of the Ministry of Research and Technology (BMFT) in 1972. Furthermore, the first commission was put together at this time to examine the 'expansion of the technical communication system', the KtK (Humphreys, 1988, 187–9).

4. For a history of the Fraunhofer research institutes, see Trischler and vom Bruch (1999).

5. Average estimates for the period 1996–98. USA: GDP growth 3.6, unemployment 5 per cent; Germany: GDP growth 2.1, unemployment 10 per cent (Sachverständigenrat, 1998, 29, 32, 33).

6. The Kohl era will be remembered also as one in which, despite its liberal leanings, extended support to the ailing coal industry up to the year 2000, in response to massive coal worker demonstrations joined in by leading SPD politicians (Donges, 1998, 208). Agriculture and other areas were special cases which were subsidized already under Erhard and were excluded from the 'Cartel Law' (Donges, 1998, 203). For an overview of subsidies see OECD (1998d, 124).

7. The title of a study by Merrill Lynch from March 1999 described Germany as the 'sick man of Europe'. Cited in Tony Barber, 'German Economy: Structural Weaknesses are Seen as Bar to Recovery', *Financial Times*, Survey, 'The Pink Book, The European Economy', 28 May 1999, 8.

8. The quote comes from the Social Democrat and Green politicians Hubert Kleinert and Siegmar Mosdorf (1998, 214). See also the section 'Innovator und Firmengründer: Die Säulen eines Standortes' ('Innovators and Entrepreneurs: The Pillars of the Economy') in a book co-authored by Lothar Späth, a former leading CDU politician who now is in industry (Henzler and Späth, 1997, 153–6).

9. Part of the title of a press release by the Economics Ministry. The complete title reads 'Internet World '99 in Berlin. Mosdorf: Innovation partnership between the State and the Economy Marks Germany's Path into the Information Society – Internet-business is a Job Machine.' Press release number 74/99, Bundesministerium für Wirtschaft und Technologie BMWi, Dienstbereich Berlin, 18 May 1999.

10. Germany was known for the Byzantine complexity of its corporate tax system. Speed was lost as entrepreneurs adjusted their operations to the tax system. Several proposals were made during the Kohl administration to simplify the tax structure across the board and thereby also make it more palpable for entrepreneurs. One example was the Ulldahl model, preferred by many entrepreneurs. Under Helmut Kohl, however, tax reform was severely compromised. Gerhard Schröder managed to address these issues more effectively.

11. One entrepreneur equated the Kohl coalition with the politics of 'rotten compromises' (Interview, Living Systems AG, 18 April 1999).

12. Due to unification tax, Germany is the only OECD country which saw its peak income tax rate rise overall in the past decade, to 57 per cent. This rise was only 1 per cent if viewed over the whole period, but this must be compared to falling rates in most other OECD countries by over 10 per cent (Sachverständigenrat, 1998, 192).

13. Interview with Living Systems AG (18 April 1999).

14. This point is emphasized by Stefan Welzk in an instructive but emotionally charged paper (1998).

15. Heinz-Josef Tüselmann has contributed to the location debate by compiling different studies on the motivations for FDI by German firms. He argues that FDI is motivated by the lure of foreign markets and not the pressure of rising locational costs. Rising FDI is a global, not a German trend. Furthermore, he demonstrates that capital investments abroad contribute to job creation at home, negating the common argument that jobs are exported. As a consequence, what worries the scholar is not outflow of capital but rather the relatively meagre trickle of funds being invested in Germany by outsiders. This indeed seems to indicate the unattractiveness of the German location in a world that is becoming more interdependent (Tüselmann, 1998).

16. Birgit Marschall, 'Großfusionen treiben Direktinvestitionen in Deutschland auf Rekordhöhe. Finanz-Engagements von Ausländern 1999 nahezu verdreifacht. Deutsche

Unternehmen sehen Auslandsinvestition als Standortsicherung', *Financial Times Deutschland*, 15 August 1999, 11.

17. In 1998, three German internet and multimedia start-ups were bought by US players, InnoMate (by USWeb), Lava (by iXL), ABC Bücherdienst (by Amazon.com). Another small German multimedia start-up was acquired by the Swedish player Spray. On 4 January 1999, Adobe Systems Incorporated acquired internet software start-up GoLive Systems, which had a sales office in Menlo Park, California, but carried out its software development in Hamburg.

18. The first purchase abroad was a small New York-based firm, Fountainhead Management, which was bought by Intershop. Two weeks later, Brokat Infosystems AG bought Transaction Software Systems (TST), Norcross, Georgia. Purchases by large German firms in the internet sector such as Bertelsmann's acquisition of a share in Barnesandnoble.com date back to 1998. 'Intershop kauft sich in New York ein,' HighText Verlag, 3 May 1999; 'Brokat übernimmt Softwarehaus TST', *Frankfurter Allgemeine Zeitung*, 11 May 1999, 24.

19. According to Ziegler, technological issues require long-standing specialist relationships between scientists, engineers, technicians and skilled workers (Ziegler, 1997, vii–ix). 'Age-old political tasks' include those of 'exercising power, brokering interests and negotiating compromise'. Technology issues, however, involve 'establishing technical parameters, exercising expertise and fulfilling performance standards' (Ziegler, 1997, 9). In the German case, it seems very relevant to describe the specialist orientation of both parliamentarians and ministry officials as relating to technology issues and labelling them with Ziegler's term 'politics of competence' (Ziegler, 1997, 2).

20. Other factors further reinforce the specialization of parliamentarians. A contest of specialized proficiency takes place during the negotiations between parliamentarians and ministry officials. Parliamentarians need to be able to stand up to the arguments of ministry bureaucrats (Sontheimer and Bleek, 1998, 293). In contrast to some other countries, a large proportion of parliamentarians in Germany are politicians who have made politics their exclusive career (Sontheimer and Bleek, 1998, 296–8).

21. In media and telecommunications policy, commissions are a preferred policy instrument, starting with the Commission for the Development of the Technical Communication System (Kommission für den Ausbau des technischen Kommunikationssystems, KtK), established by the ruling Social Democrats in 1974. Hoffmann-Riem discusses the role of commissions explicitly in relation to media policy (1990, 174).

22. See the paper by Clay Clemens, 'The Chancellor as Manager' (1994). For a well-written popular account of Helmut Kohl, read Johannes Gross's chapter on the Chancellor (1995).

23. Yet, parties are also under pressure in some issues to bow to the fundamental obligations of consensus. In opposition, the SPD was very much conscious of this and tried not to appear as a policy-blocker. In a different context, Gordon Smith has called this phenomenon of German party politics 'Yes-But' opposition (Smith, 1976, 392; see also Sontheimer and Bleek, 1998, 287).

24. Johannes Gross describes how Kohl ignored his obligation to set a key policy orientation (*Richtlinienkompetenz*) and instead used the more flexible propagandistic device of the *Chefsache* (1995, 82, 83).

25. Walter Eucken, one of the founders of the Freiburg School and influential Ordoliberal thinker in Germany immediately after the Second World War, thought one of the most important obligations of a *Rechtsstaat* was to prevent the distortion of markets through monopolies and oligopolies (Sally, 1998, 109).

26. In the USA, the Sherman Act dates back to 1890 and the Clayton Act to 1914. For a brief comparison, see Herdzina (1993, 133).

27. Corporatist analysis can be contrasted to institutionalist and pluralist approaches, if the former is seen as focusing on the structure of particular public agencies and the latter as discussing the formation and power of interest groups. While pluralist approaches emphasize the bottom-up formation of interest groups, corporatist literature investigates

the top-down involvement of different interest groups by the state (Streeck, 1994, 9–11). The role of government as instigator is critically important. Corporatist literature has in the last decade been combined successfully with institutionalist approaches to emphasize diversity in capitalist systems (Streeck, 1994, 8, 9, 19–21). As noted by Razeen Sally, however, all these approaches share a preference for analysis in aggregate units, such as national government, industry associations and trade unions (Sally, 1995, 2).

28. Social science sometimes can be short-sighted, as Czada's analysis of the career of the term 'corporatism' shows. Just a few years ago, the term was almost exclusively equated with what we would today call pre-war, authoritarian coporatism. Today, a very broad interpretation of the term is used so frequently that it almost becomes meaningless. 'As a theory, corporatism did not so much gain depth as breath', Czada writes. Nevertheless, the scholar believes the diversity of the term is one of its strengths (1994, 39–41). With this blessing, corporatism is also in this volume used to refer broadly to a process of a negotiated, distributed decision-making supported by government between key interest groups. It fits very well with an institutional analysis of Germany, which is part of a general research agenda emphasizing the diversity of capitalist systems. The broad definition of corporatism resembles what other commentators have called the typical stakeholder model of German capitalism and what yet others label a consensual system. It corresponds to John Zysman's 'negotiated' power system in a taxonomy relating to financial systems, which also includes 'state-led' and 'market-led' (Zysman, 1983, 7, 233). Using Arend Lijphart's model of 'majoritarian' and 'consensual' democracies, Humphreys states that Germany is marked by a complex mix of the two, but emphasizes the consensus elements, which lead to slow change and incremental policy-making (1992, 105–7). Katzenstein emphasizes the stability of the German system as well, but notes how it was combined with 'widespread experimentation' from the 1980s (1989, 6). Much of this analysis goes back to Andrew Shonfield, who emphasized the unique aspects of German capitalism. Shonfield prefers, however, to use the term 'organized private enterprise' (Shonfield, 1969, 239–64).

29. See Abelshauser (1984) for a brilliant and succinct analysis of this historical development. In Germany, the corporatist system received its severest blows in the first few years after the Second World War, when US occupation forces delegated a dismantling of industry concentration. This policy was supported by the post-World War mood as well as by Erhard's disdain of industry associations (Lehmbruch, 1992, 39). The industry associations persisted, however, and already in the 1950s, Erhard was forced to cooperate with them. During the Korean Crisis, Erhard was faced with the task of implementing a partially planned economy with explicit orders from the USA. Instead of embarking upon a *dirigiste* course, however, he took recourse to what he saw as the lesser evil by allowing high-level joint economic administration of peak associations and government. But the form of cooperation was very different from the period before the Second World War, and became increasingly different after the Korean Crisis.

30. Humphreys cites the heavy industry union's slogan 'Microchip = Jobkiller'. Another trade union slogan was: 'Defend against the dangers of the new media' (1988, 197). During the liberalization of telecommunications, the German Postal Union stated the campaign: 'Save the postal service, defend the public operator' (cited in Glotz, 2001, 64) (author's translation).

31. The Kommission für den Ausbau des technischen Kommunikationssystems, KtK, was instituted by the Ministry of Research and Technology, BMFT, to discuss how technological progress in communication systems could be promoted in Germany. It began its work in 1974 and submitted a report in 1975 (Schneider, 1989, 83–6). See Humphreys (1988, 187–99) for an English-language description of the role of KtK and the development of videotex in Germany.

32. A specific example can be found in Abelshauser (1984, 308) and a general mention in Czada (1994, 42, 43).

33. In early nineteenth-century industrializing Prussia, liberal policy-makers had to engage in long drawn-out conflicts to dismantle many mercantilist state initiatives intended to promote industry and innovation. Through its mining corps, Prussia directly owned

several mines. The glamorous historical accounts of industrialization written in the nineteenth century by Heinrich von Treitschke and Gustav Schmoller emphasized and
greatly exaggerated the pioneering and direct role of the Prussian state. For an excellent
description of the battle between liberals and mercantilists in Prussia's early industrialization, read Eric Dorn Brose's account (1993). Today, some economic historians believe
Prussia's direct involvement was counter-productive. In a later phase of industrialization, during the construction of the railroads, the Prussian state was initially not
involved in any way. The railroads were privately financed and built (Fremdling, 1975,
129). But the historical debate continues today. The founding myth of the Federal
Republic and its *Wirtschaftswunder* is universally attributed to the Marshall Plan, a substantial transfer of funds to jump-start the economy. The Marshall Plan has had an
impact on policy-making ever since its inception. A similar jump-start based in some
ways on the experience of the Marshall Plan was attempted in the new, East German
states. The actual effect of the Marshall Plan on the German economy, however, is object
of a highly contested debate. For example, the prominent economic historian Werner
Abelshauser tried to show very early that it was not the Marshall Plan that was responsible for the 'Economic Miracle', but rather the largely intact capital base of Germany
in terms of machines and know-how (Abelshauser, 1983). A further interpretation of
economic revival emphasizes the Erhard's liberal free-trade stance of the young nation
after the Second World War (Buchheim, 1990).

34. X.25 CCITT/ISO was a hierarchical packet-based service and was very different to the
decentralized networks that TCP/IP systems enabled. In a research project at the Max
Planck Institute for the Study of Societies, Dr Raymund Werle and his colleagues are
analysing the development of research networks under technological and political
aspects. Werle emphasizes the open, decentralized capabilities of TCP/IP. In fact,
TCP/IP was used to replace the Network Control Program of the US research network
Arpanet in January 1983 precisely because it did not require a centralized network architecture. Werle contrasts TCP/IP to the hierarchical approach of ISO/OSI and X.25,
which was used by the Bundespost. At that time, every X.25 switch needed to be told the
route it should send its packages on by a (central) computer. This approach was both
more costly and required a centralized watchdog authority such as the Bundespost. With
technological advance over time, the difference between TCP/IP and ISO/OSI became
less relevant.

35. Susanne Schmidt used this phrase to describe German telecommunications liberalization in the title of one of her papers: 'Taking the Long Road to liberalisation' (Schmidt,
1991).

36. In his book on comparative telecommunications policy, Volker Schneider depicts this
contrast in a very useful chart (1999, 257).

37. This point is made by Herbert Kubicek, basing himself in part on a dissertation by
Dieter Klumpp (Kubicek, 1998, 1094).

38. SPD modernizers also were responsible for launching the nationwide public teletex Btx
service. For a good overview of the media policy battle, see the chapter 'The Controversy
over the Introduction of New Media' in Humphreys (1994, 193–238).

39. To reduce pressure, the state-owned carrier included these companies in its circle of
equipment suppliers (Schmidt, 1991, 212–15). In the 1990s, however, the position of the
proponents of change was considerably strengthened through Siemens, the former 'court
supplier' now intent on entering the US market and thus favouring liberalization at
home. Siemens had an important role to play in the corporatist system of telecommunications policy; this role was institutionalized by its being a member of the Administrative
Council (Verwaltungsrat) of the Bundespost (Humphreys, 1992, 110). The important
shift was first signalled during the CeBIT computer trade fair in Hanover early in 1987,
when a Siemens Vice-President expressed approval of greater liberalization of the
Bundespost (Junne, 1989, 272–3). Siemens was crucial in tipping the balance also
because of its direct and indirect links with large industrial companies and banks as well
as its regional importance to Bavaria, home of the ruling coalition partner CSU (Junne,
1989, 271–2). An exogenous factor was the unification of Germany and the accompany-

ing budget deficit. Building up a new telecommunications infrastructure was very costly: an estimated DM 60 billion was estimated to be spent from 1990 to 1997. It was argued that part of these sums would be shifted to the private sector through telecommunications reform (Thatcher, 1996, 193, 194).

40. It is important not to overemphasize the role of the group of corporate users. However, Schmidt has included them in the 'telematics coalition'. In the UK, the telematics coalition, also consisting of suppliers of value-added services and data-processing companies, were a powerful force for change. In Germany, the Bundespost was one of the main suppliers of some of these telematics services for businesses and made sure its most important clients, such as the banks, were given special concessions (Schmidt, 1991, 213–4).

41. German policy-makers were not alone. Indeed, scholars have observed this development all over the world and have characterized it as a 'complex interweaving of liberalism with mercantilism' (Dyson and Humphreys, 1990, 2).

42. This matches Steven Vogel's observation of privatization worldwide that it was the state, and not interest groups, that were decisive for reform. Vogel mentions that interest groups were hopelessly divided; Knudsen adds that most beneficiaries of reform were new market entrants that did not yet exist when the reform was first embarked upon (Vogel, 1996, 'Introduction'; Knudsen, 1998, 29, 30).

43. On indirect effects of EC measures, see Mark Thatcher's paper on the subject (1996, 179, 185, 195). Schmidt examines the underlying conditions that favoured a progressive stance of the EC in telecommunications in comparison with the difficulties the Commission encountered in the energy sector (Schmidt, 1998, 180–1). Knudsen describes how the EU level contributed to a breaking of the German 'joint-decision trap' (1998, 35–7).

44. In contrast, the telecommunication industry as a whole grew by 102 000 from the passing of the Telecommunications Law in 1996 to 1998. In 1999 another 91 000 were estimated to be employed by the new telecommunications competition. Frank Dohmen, 'Telekommunikation: An der falschen Stelle. Ist die Telekom für den rauhen Wettbewerb noch nicht stark genug? Die rot-grüne Regierung in Bonn will nachhelfen – Zum Nachteil der Kunden', *Der Spiegel*, 46, 9 November 1998; see also a newspaper article from 1996: Gerhard Hennemann, 'Wirtschaft: Serie: Eine Behörde auf dem Weg zum Weltunternehmen: Die Konkurrenz der Telekom ist auf Draht: Nicht nur am lukrativen deutschen Markt formieren sich potente Wettbewerber', *Süddeutsche Zeitung*, 17 October 1996, 30.

45. For a short discussion of DECT as it pertains to Germany, see Gerpott (1998, 38–54). Gerpott lists 11 different wireless local loop pilots in Europe in December 1997 (1998, 48).

46. This view about the viability of DECT was confirmed in interview 31 May 1999 with Green parliamentarian Dr Manuel Kiper. He added, however, that the access solution over cable TV already at that time was considered more readily available and less costly to develop. Arne Börnsen, a parliamentarian who is currently the Vice-President of the RegTP, also believed in DECT in late 1996. In a newspaper article, he emphasized that a greater allotment of frequencies for the wireless local loop. Arne Boernsen, 'Wirtschaft: Serie: Mit dem Ende des Telekom-Monopols ist es nicht getan: Wettbewerb erfordert Marktregulierung: Plädoyer für eine Liberalisierung mit Augenmaß', *Süddeutsche Zeitung*, 07 November 1996, 36.

47. The original quote in German language reads: 'Das Kabelnetz hätte von der Deutschen Bundespost nur vor der Privatisierung 1994 und der Entstehung der DBP Telekom getrennt werden können. Später wäre eine Trennung ein Eingriff in das Privateigentum einer Aktiengesellschaft gewesen. Und vor 1994 war der spätere Wert des Kabelnetzes als alternative Netzwerkinfrastruktur nicht erkennbar. Schwarz-Schilling hatte sich bei dem Bau des Kabelnetzes für eine veraltete, kostengünstige Technologie entschieden. Man hätte mit dem Kabelnetz unnötigen Ballast aufgenommen' (interview, 19 February 2002).

48. In fact, Arne Börnsen criticized the widespread arguments heard within the SPD that

competition would hurt the IPO of the Deutsche Telekom. Arne Boernsen, 'Wirtschaft: Serie: Mit dem Ende des Telekom-Monopols ist es nicht getan: Wettbewerb erfordert Marktregulierung: Plädoyer für eine Liberalisierung mit Augenmaß', *Süddeutsche Zeitung*, 7 November 1996, 36.

49. 'Scheurle: Telekom-Aufsicht muß politisch unabhängig entscheiden. 'Regulierungsbehörde trägt nicht nur die Verantwortung für den größten Anbieter', *Frankfurter Allgemeine Zeitung*, 4 May 1998.

50. Donata Riedel, 'Meinung und Analyse: Regulierungsbehörde für Telekommunikation gerät unter Druck der Partien. Politiker mißtrauen dem Wettbewerb', *Handelsblatt*, 129, 9 July 1998, 2.

51. Frank Dohmen, 'Telekommunikation: An der falschen Stelle. Ist die Telekom für den rauhen Wettbewerb noch nicht stark genug? Die rot-grüne Regierung in Bonn will nachhelfen – Zum Nachteil der Kunden', *Der Spiegel*, 46, 9 November 1998; 'Regulierung: Bericht des Wirtschaftsministers. Kabinett stellt sich hinter Telekom', *Handelsblatt*, 214, 5 November 1998, 1.

52. Heinz Stuewe, 'Leitartikel Wirtschaft. Die Telekom und die Wahlen', *Frankfurter Allgemeine Zeitung*, 10 September 1998; 'Boernsen warnt SPD vor Änderung des TKG', *Süddeutsche Zeitung*, 11 September 1998, 24; 'Postgewerkschaft attackiert den Regulierer. Kurt van Haaren: Bonner Behörde setzt nur auf Preissenkungen, 'Rexrodt ohne Sachverstand', *Süddeutsche Zeitung*, 15 September 1998, 17.

53. Frank Dohmen, 'Telekommunikation: An der falschen Stelle. Ist die Telekom für den rauhen Wettbewerb noch nicht stark genug? Die rot-grüne Regierung in Bonn will nachhelfen – Zum Nachteil der Kunden', *Der Spiegel*, 46, 9 November 1998; Donata Riedel, 'Meinung und Analyse: Finanzstaatssekretär Jürgen Stark kritisiert die Regulierungsbehörde. Telekom baut Druck auf Scheurle auf', *Handelsblatt*, 27 April 1998, 2.

54. Except in the niche sector of encryption services, where German firms profited immensely from a lack of export, import and domestic use prohibition.

55. It purposely did not contain any barriers to entry by foreign firms and no import restrictions. It cannot be seen as 'engineer-driven' since it did not contain any technological stipulations (in contrast to the GSM standard, for example). 'Technical openness' was one of the main concepts of the bill (Engel-Flechsig et al., 1998, 30). Furthermore, it was compatible with other digital signature schemes and companies are free to choose which systems to use. The setting up of trust centres, necessary for signature certification, was devised as a third-party initiative controlled by the telecommunications regulatory body RegTP. The RegTP merely issued 'root' rights. What the law did do, however, was set high obligatory requirements which a digital signature must adhere to if it was to be used as a legally binding, non-reputable confirmation of identity. Given these standards, it was necessary to use devices such as smart cards and special hardware to make the signature secure. Nevertheless, the law remained an offer. The same principle was in 1999 adopted in EU advanced electronic signatures legislation, where two different digital standards levels were introduced as offers from which industry can choose. It was conceivable that for 'signing' a tax form, a high German-type standard would be used, but for purchasing a book over the internet a lower security level would be sufficient.

56. According to the globalstartup survey, only half of the entrepreneurs thought the Multimedia Law was relevant to their business. Appendix A, Table A.26. For international laws, see Table 27.

57. For detailed analysis of the TDDSG see the overview by Engel-Flechsig et al., (1998, 22–8).

58. An excellent discussion of the TDDSG from the viewpoint of firms is contained in a report by the BMBF (1997, 41–62).

59. The EU privacy law stipulates that personal data of EU citizens cannot be exported into or stored in countries in which a similar standard of privacy legislation does not exist.

60. Although Germany has a system of interlocking federalism, this is not the case specifically in media policy, where the individual states have powers that transcend mere rights of implementation. Scharpf notes this on p. 225 (1994).

61. Interestingly, a similar phenomenon occurred over a century earlier during the industrialization of Germany. It is commonly argued that the splintered and fragmented nature of the German territories into many small states has hindered the development of the railroad network. The economic historian Rainer Fremdling has argued that quite the opposite was true, namely, that inter-state competition led to rapid growth of the railway system (Fremdling, 1975, 132).

62. There are, however, examples of successful technology parks as well as successful MGBs.

63. 'Medien: Rechtsexperte plädiert für Grundgesetzänderung und einheitliche Rahmenbedingungen. Ein Mister Internet für Investoren in den Multimediastandort Deutschland', *Handelsblatt*, 143, 29 July 1998, 6.

64. For detailed description see Engel-Flechsig et al. (1998).

65. The seriousness of this issue for firms became evident in two issues involving local courts: XS4All as well as the Felix Somm case in Bavaria. One well-known internet expert in Germany has apparently commented that the one active contribution Germany had for the development of the internet is the criminal indictment of internet access providers (BMBF, 1997, 114). XS4All: this case involved radical left-wing content located on a server in the Netherlands. German authorities tried to stop German web site owners from linking to this content. Felix Somm: The former managing director of CompuServe in Germany was charged by a local Bavarian court for hosting pornographic content which members of his service had privately placed on their home pages.

66. The Interior Ministry sought to enforce strict encryption laws.

67. Internet entrepreneurs did not feel well represented in other groups that existed historically, such as the German Multimedia Association (dmmv), formed in August 1995. As a result, the European Net Economy Forum (ENEF), was founded as a political lobby group by 15 German internet start-ups on 24 July 2000. The speaker of the ENEF, Kilian Lenard, explained his reasons for helping launch a new association: 'To build our own representation within an existing association would have been much more difficult than starting an association of our own. The dmmv, for example, still has not formed a division concerned with the issues faced by internet entrepreneurs.' The first issues the ENEF addressed were immigration laws for IT specialists (the German Green Card debate) as well as capital gains taxation for private equity investments by private investors and venture capital groups.

68. The efforts by German government directed at SMEs need to be seen in conjunction with the European Union 4th and 5th Framework programmes. Although the initial EU Framework Programmes in the early 1980s focused on the 'technology gap' and benefited the so-called 'Big 12 Roundtable' companies in the information technologies sector, newer programmes have a strong SME focus and their primary goal has been cooperation between SMEs of different European countries. The EU have promoted the G7, now G8, programme on Global SMEs in which essentially the same emphasis on small firm cross-border exchange is lifted from a European to a global scale. Furthermore, it has to be pointed out that domestic support for SMEs did not wane while EU support was on the rise. On the 'Big 12 Roundtable' and a concise comparison of EC and national R&R expenditures see John Peterson's research (1996).

69. More praise for BioRegio: 'Deutschland 2000: 'Es gilt, einen Schatz zu heben', *Der Spiegel*, 35, 24 August 1998.

70. Actually, there were two important tbg programmes, the BTJU and the BTU. Business Investment Capital for Small Technology-Based Firms (BTU) lasted from 1995 to 1999 but was recently extended into the next century. Its predecessor, Business Investment Capital for New Technology-Based Firms (BJTU) ran from 1989 to 1994. Both schemes were varieties of the 'co-investment' concept. Including the investment activated by the refinancing scheme, the total investment through BJTU amounted to DM 314 million over six years. A total of 336 firms benefited (Kulicke, 1997b). The BJTU programme prided itself on the low failure rates of its firms. The low failure rate of 17 per cent may also have reflected an overly cautious approach by the programme administrators, however (OECD, 1997a, p. 24).

71. A further positive aspect of the tbg programme was the speed of its investment decisions.

The wait was reduced from 12 months to three weeks. The institution could afford to be fast because it mainly relied on the investment decisions of its co-investors from the private venture capital market. In addition, the paperwork required also matched that normally required for private investments; the business plan was the norm.

72. A similar programme emphasizing equity investment had already existed in the late 1970s and early 1980s. Instead of declaring private equity investors as partners as in the later BTU scheme, the earlier equity programme was launched in cooperation with 36 banks. The inspiration for the programme had come from the Netherlands, which began very early to support the growth of equity start-up investment to promote innovation and entrepreneurship. The programme was discontinued in Germany, however, probably because the involved financial institutions, being banks, were the wrong partners. For several years, Germany had no equity support scheme. The Ministry of Research and Technology reverted back to credit support schemes. One of these was called Promotion of New Technology-Based Firms (TOU) and was comprised of non-repayable subsidies, credit guarantees and consulting services. From 1983 to 1988, a total of 319 firms received DM 240 million in subsidies for development work and 258 potential firm founders received subsidies totalling DM 8 million for perfection of their business plans (Kulicke, 1997b, 107, 112–14). This direct government support programme was not continued, however, after it ran out in December 1988. It was revived with some alterations for the new federal states as New Technology-Based Firms in the new Länder (TOU/NBL) in May 1990 to December 1995 and Promotion and support of New Technology-Based Firms in Selected Regions (FUTOUR) in January 1997 (Kulicke, 1997b, 114). Until the end of 1999, FUTOUR was expected to support the foundation of 250 firms in the new federal states (BMBF and BMWi, 1998, 71).

73. US government passed legislation in 1958, which created the Small Business Investment Corporation (SBIC) programme. This programme included loan guarantees permitting participants to leverage their private funds. The programme must be credited as an important early step towards the creation of formalized, independent venture capital industry in the United States (Kenney, 2000a, 5).

74. The model for the technology park was the original technology park around Stanford University. In the 1980s, German local state governments wanted to promote entrepreneurship and believed the needs of start-ups were concentrated in two areas, lack of funds for infrastructure and office facilities and a need for specialized consulting services. The schemes were only moderately successful; many high-potential companies avoided the parks altogether. A problem that can be equated with some, but not all parks, was that the policy objective of promoting start-ups was combined with the objective of promoting slow-growth regions, mostly in insignificant cities or rural areas. Instead of moving away, most high-growth firms wanted to be in a city, which provided them with quality service facilities as well as easy access to other players in telecommunications, software and media.

75. Here, objectives of promotion of structurally weak geographic areas overlapped with support objectives for small and medium-sized firms, especially if they drew on European Commission funds. Hessia, for example, offered a programme to support hiring of additional personnel (called Programm zur Förderung der Humankapitalbildung durch Innovationsassistenten oder -assistentinnen). They only applied to selected regions such as parts of Fulda, Hersfeld-Rotenburg, parts of Kassel. Growth areas were excluded. One managing founder described the support programme schemes with the following words: 'Being in Düsseldorf, you always lose. On the EU level, the money goes to Spain. The federal government targets former East Germany. And in Northrhine Westphalia, funds go to "structurally weak" areas, but not to Düsseldorf. We considered opening an office in former East Germany, but it would not have been worth it' (Lars Heiden Jörg Füllenbach Realisationen interview).

5.   Incumbent telecommunications operator strategy and internet access

This study has already highlighted how growing home use of the internet and small business access had the potential to transform business in a wide range of industries. Through ubiquitous internet access, consumers and small firms could be integrated into electronic business networks, so-called business webs, connecting service firms, manufacturers and suppliers. In the previous chapter, diverse government activity to promote innovation and growth in data networking was discussed, from telecommunications liberalization, teletex, the promotion of research networks and financing initiatives. Yet, as the example of the German research network DFN showed, it is insufficient to study government intentions alone.

Paradoxically, the direct role of government in the development of the nascent internet in Europe was far less significant than in the United States. The backbone service of the US research network NSFNET, for example, was in 1995 handed over to private enterprises, speeding up the commercialization of the internet and promoting competition for data service provision. As discussed in the previous chapter, government action taken in Germany to encourage the growth of commercial data networking through the research network DFN was ineffective and misguided. The DFN, although founded by the responsible government ministry as a separate entity, resisted commercialization and veered towards the sphere of influence of the public telecommunications operator (PTO). Rapid commercialization of the DFN, which would have enabled competition to the PTO, would have been resisted.

This chapter, which delves into internet uptake in Germany, is based on the premise that the interaction between government and the dominant telecommunications player, the German public telecommunications operator (DBP Telekom) and later Deutsche Telekom AG (DTAG), was a more important influence on internet access than any direct government initiatives. It is this relationship which impacted upon the mass uptake of internet services more than any other factor, because DTAG owned almost all of the infrastructure necessary to bring internet access into homes and small firms. It is important to note that DTAG legally became a private company in 1994 and in 1996 a minority share was floated on the stock exchange. But even before these events, the actions of the dominant telecommunications player cannot be understood merely as a straightforward consequence of government action, however. It is crucial to understand the specific interests and strategy of the postal ministry and the later DTAG company. Much of the focus here is on the activity of a single firm, and most of the chapter will be dedicated to understanding what caused Deutsche Telekom to act in the way it did. At the end of the chapter, however, the competition of DTAG will also be discussed briefly because of their role in introducing cheaper internet access after liberalization in 1998.

The formerly public telecommunications operator had a say not just in the running of the DFN network, it owned almost all of network infrastructure enabling access to the internet. In 2001, after four years of competition, DTAG still fully controlled over 97 per cent of all access lines (VATM, 2001, 14). Despite sales of single stakes in regional entities from February 2000, DTAG still in 2001 retained significant shares of several cable TV broadband access networks across Germany with a total of 18 million active subscribers. It also owned a majority share in the largest internet access provider in Europe, T-Online, with 11 million subscribers in late 2001.[1] T-Online was spun off Deutsche Telekom in April 2000. In the last chapter, the political trajectory was described which resulted in the liberalization of the German telecommunications market with the dominant player retaining control over these key assets. Here, the emphasis will shift to how DTAG used these assets from the year of the Telecommunications Law's passing and the public listing of Deutsche Telekom in 1996 through to liberalization in January 1998 and the immediate period thereafter.

Policy-makers concerned about the uptake of internet services in Germany among consumers and small firms were aware of the importance of local call prices in the 'last mile', since the local telephone line was the main means of accessing the internet. But even before full awareness of the significance of the internet from 1995 onwards, policy-makers were concerned about the local loop as a point of control of the incumbent. As described in the last chapter, the preferred option, infrastructure competition through alternative networks, was obstructed by the incumbent's retention of the cable TV network. Wireless local loop (WLL) technologies were only being tested at the time. This is why unbundling was pursued as a temporary alternative to network infrastructure competition. Section 35 (1) of the telecommunications law, the TKG, provided for the access to single customer lines by the competition. The telecommunications regulator, RegTP, used this option and Germany was the first European country to mandate complete unbundling of the customer line for a fixed monthly fee. The power of this option was that it freed the competition from the underlying metered pricing regime of the incumbent and therefore had the potential to pave the way for flat-rate internet access offers. However, unbundling, as progressive as it was, initially did not yield the intended results of increasing competition in the local loop. While it engaged in a price battle in the international and national call segments, Deutsche Telekom used all available means to delay effective competition in the local loop. It engaged in extensive arbitrage with the regulator and courts concerning the pricing of the unbundled access line. Competitors, furthermore, dependent as they were on the service of DTAG, faced long delays in the instalment of their network connections. The first significant price reductions in internet access in Germany were in the Spring of 1999, due not to unbundled access of the local loop, but to an interconnection arrangement (Internet-by-Call) implemented on a metered basis defined by DTAG.

Before 1999, internet access prices in Germany were prohibitively high, restricting usage. In fact, Germany consistently ranked among the most expensive countries among the OECD for internet access. Most policymakers and observers acknowledged that the pricing of local calls had a prohibitive effect on internet usage.[2] It is important to note that before 1982, local calls in Germany were charged according to a flat rate of 0.23 DM per call. Even after this time, however, local calls continued to be cheap: one minute for 0.03 DM. It was only in preparation for competition that prices were raised by the former PTO 400 per cent to 0.12 DM per minute (Kubicek, 1998, 1098). Dieter Wolf, the President of the German federal cartel office, stated in early 1998: 'The cartel fortress of the Deutsche Telekom are local calls.'[3] Even some politicians of the former opposition, the SPD, acknowledged this. In an interview, Jörg Tauss, Social Democrat Member of Bundestag, succinctly stated: 'Prices for long-distance calls have fallen, the problem is with local calls' (Interview 25 March 1999). Siegmar Mosdorf was clearer: 'Obviously, the Deutsche Telekom will use her traditional advantages derived from the former monopoly structure as long as possible' (Interview 10 May 1999).

Especially important for this analysis was the period from 1996 to 1998, from the public listing of Deutsche Telekom and the passing of the TKG to the actual start of fixed-line competition in 1998. This period coincided with the take-off of the internet in the United States and in a few other countries. For this period, the key question asked here is why DATG did not use its attractive timing window to capture and expand the strategically important internet access market before the arrival of competition. After January 1998, competition begun and the national telecommunications regulator, RegTP, was given the ability to control the prices of Deutsche Telekom. While RegTP oversaw unexpectedly strong price decreases in the international and national call segments, it resisted to grant the low unbundled access line price desired by the competition. This delayed the appearance of attractive flat-rate internet access offers, with the exception of those offered by the Deutsche Telekom itself. Therefore, the second question asked in this chapter is what prevented the national regulator from addressing the local loop as aggressively as it addressed price reductions in the international and local call segments.

The route taken by Deutsche Telekom from 1996 to 1998 was by no means self-evident. It cannot be extrapolated solely by analysing government actions and viewing the actions of the dominant carrier as a direct response. A publicly listed company striving to increase shareholder value is expected to maximise profits. As a company involved in the rapidly changing network economy, however, DTAG was also expected to justify higher valuations by positioning itself for future earnings. The internet and broadband internet access were after 1995 clearly viewed as one of the most promising future growth segments. It is not clear, therefore, why DTAG did not embrace this young market. Deutsche Telekom was not just the dominant telecommunications operator, it also owned the main German internet service provider, T-Online. Arguably, DTAG could actually have selectively introduced lower internet access rates while keeping general local call rates high. This would have expanded the market. This strategy was actually embarked upon in April 1999. Yet, Deutsche Telekom retained a high price for all local phone calls from privatization in 1994 through its stock market listing in 1996 until liberalization and several months thereafter. Next to the possibility that the management of the Deutsche Telekom simply underestimated the 'disruptive technology' of the internet (see Christensen, 1997) there may also have been technical reasons why Deutsche Telekom could not have followed this course earlier. This theme will also be explored here. But what about the cable TV network? DTAG could also have used its cable TV network to introduce broadband internet access services to millions of households and small businesses. In this case, DTAG's defensive strategy ruled out such a move.

This chapter will focus on the issues which prevented Deutsche Telekom from acting as a catalyst for widespread internet access in Germany. DTAG's own objectives simply did not correspond to those of an ideal 'national champion', which some politicians believed it was. It needs to be noted, however, that the same question applies also to the competition, which, although it was able to prepare for January 1998 well in advance, took so long to effectively address internet access and broadband internet access.

THE GLOBAL COST CHALLENGE AND THE TELECOMMUNICATIONS INDUSTRY

Throughout the 1990s, traditional telecommunications carriers were battered by the advances of new entrants. The new players waged what one could describe as a 'cost challenge'. The cost challenge first began in the United States but quickly moved to world markets, in the wake of telecommunications liberalization. The challenge came in two varieties, which were very much interrelated: one was in terms of market strategy. New entrants engaged in 'raisin-picking' and focused on the most lucrative clients: multinational companies and financial services firms. These new entrants, among them the so-called metropolitan carriers, shied away from the high costs of a mass access network.[4] The second cost challenge came in the form of technological change and the fact that new internet-based networks were cheaper to install and maintain than conventional circuit-switched networks. The incumbent carriers had to react by cutting their own costs with aggressive infrastructure modernization schemes and lay-offs while at the same time developing new strategies which would leverage their broad reach and well-known brand names. This was a difficult position to be in and Deutsche Telekom faced the challenge together with most other incumbents.

New entrants worked with a much lower cost structure than traditional carriers because they used internet-based data technologies instead of circuit-switched technologies.[5] When internet-based technologies (called 'packet-switched networks') were used by the first new entrants in the mid-1990s, they were largely regarded as technologically inferior to the circuit-switched networks of the main carriers. Packet-based networks were viewed as especially inferior for the transfer of so-called 'streams' such as voice, the bread and butter of telephone carriers. Obviously, circuit-switched networks, which were first developed in the nineteenth century, had been undergoing constant improvement. During the 1990s, for example, switches were digitized to offer intelligent services such as call waiting or call forwarding. To the incumbent carriers, it seemed impossible that internet technologies would be able to catch up. This type of error of judgement on part of dominant enterprises is not uncommon in the history of technology, as Clayton Christensen shows in his book: *The Innovator's Dilemma* (1997). Christensen argues that incumbents often underestimate the cost-cutting potential of initially inferior technologies. Inferior technologies thrive first in market niches, niches that are too small to warrant action by large firms. But although they are first used in low-price niches, inferior technologies can potentially threaten the incumbent's business by 'suddenly' appearing in a much-improved guise.

During the second half of the 1990s, packet-based network contenders grew up, confirming Christensen's research.[6] The maintenance of these new networks was much cheaper than that of traditional telecommunications networks, perhaps even 1/27th.[7] In the United States, new challengers such as Qwest, Level3 and IXC used internet-based architecture to offer low-cost long-distance connections to businesses and consumers. Project Oxygen ambitiously intended to embrace the world with a global, packet-based 320 000 km ring. The rise of the internet came as a complete surprise to almost all incumbent carriers.

In Germany, internet-based telecommunications contenders also thrived. Some emerged as independent internet providers in the early 1980s and are now owned by major US or European data communications challengers.[8] Although Deutsche Telekom generated more revenue from data networking than its main contenders, competition was severe and the incumbent was only able to achieve its lead in the year 1998 (see Table 5.3). Deutsche Telekom therefore faced pressures from metropolitan carriers, data networks as well as from other strong contenders.

But Deutsche Telekom was not alone; most incumbents were confronted with the same challenges. At first, they addressed the strategic issue of cherry-picking. Global alliances such as Global One, WorldPartners and Concert were formed among most large telecommunications incumbents in the first half of the 1990s.[9] The concept that fuelled these alliances was that lucrative multinational business clients desired a worldwide 'one-stop-shop.'[10] These alliances of two, three or more operators did not fare well, however, because members viewed themselves as competitors and governance structures had not been agreed upon. Traditional telcos realized that only full network ownership allowed them to offer valuable global services to multinational clients. Furthermore, money could be made by keeping the client 'on the own network' as long as possible. By this time, new contenders, especially WorldCom, had already started to build their global network through an acquisitions spree aided by capital markets. WorldCom showed the established carriers how to build a 'real' global network through acquisitions based on its high valuation (the company's shares trading at the time at 40 times the subsequent year's estimated earnings). Worldwide acquisitions were forthwith viewed as the main means to achieving a true global presence using integrated data networks.[11]

Yet the battle for multinational clients was a difficult one, and not necessarily one that the established incumbents were very well prepared to fight. Firstly, their businesses were much broader than those of the specialized challengers. Secondly, their technological base was more costly and older than that of the new entrants. Acquisition was viewed as one key to success, especially the purchase of international mobile phone networks. Yet, there were only a few good properties available. A new 'story '(to use a term borrowed from financial analysts) was needed to invigorate the share values of the incumbent carriers, which were slipping compared to those of their much younger challengers. Just in time, a welcome solution for the incumbent carriers appeared on the horizon. They would be the providers of broadband mass internet access to homes and small businesses.

Incumbent carriers had three key assets: they owned well-recognized brand names, had customer relationships with millions of people and were centres of expertise in mass broadband market businesses. These assets were viewed as important factors in building a service for mass internet access. Some incumbents, such the European telecommunications operators and the US regional bell operating companies (RBOCs), supplied local telephone access to households and small businesses. These fixed lines could be upgraded to enable broadband internet services via ADSL or other technologies. Other telecommunications firms gained access by buying into cable TV networks. Starting from 1998, broadband mass internet access became the magic formula for almost all competition-plagued incumbents.[12] By discovering internet broadband, incumbents could start developing a young market using its own assets and expertise. As long-distance revenues shrink further, internet broadband will compensate – so it was hoped. But broadband internet access made sense only in combination with alternative pricing mechanisms, such as a flat fee or volume-based fees. Metered fees, even low metered fees, served as a disincentive to internet usage, especially for using the types of video or audio services which broadband access could have enabled.[13] Deutsche Telekom pursued the vision of flat-rate broadband later than other telecommunications firms. It tried to position ISDN internet access as a broadband solution until it rolled out T-DSL broadly in 2000. ISDN could not fulfil the capacity demands for broadband internet use. And, until that year, all of its services were metered offerings. Furthermore, Deutsche Telekom succeeded for a long time in preventing cable TV to be used for broadband internet access.

DEUTSCHE TELEKOM IN THE COST TRAP

> The problem for telcos is that voice is falling in its profitability, and their revenues are coming under attack from all sides . . . The temptation therefore to see internet calls as a 'cash cow' to be milked while good times last is a strong one. The first provider that has the confidence to offer a cheap, fast internet service will quickly take market share. Only time will tell whether they can make money.[14]

> Carriers are reluctant to cannibalise existing revenues, although this should be done as quickly as possible. Cannibalisation is an investment in growth, which

the computer industry understands. With forward-pricing of high bandwidth connections, the telcos could build the growth markets of the future, right in their own backyards.[15]

In his ongoing research, the telecommunications consultant Thorsten J. Gerpott analysed the transformation of the Deutsche Telekom from a public operator to a private telecommunications group engaged in global competition. In his updated book on the telecommunications landscape of Germany from 1998 – one of the few comprehensive overviews available thus far on recent developments – Gerpott presented a grim picture of DTAG's transformation process (1998, 2–3, 163–235). This was confirmed by other research (Zerdick et al., 1999, 69). Gerpott believed that Deutsche Telekom was faced with a cost trap out of which it extricated itself only very slowly. This cost trap was not only detrimental for the firm and its shareholders but also for the cause of mass internet access in Germany. This was because Deutsche Telekom, as Gerpott claimed, was using full proceeds from local phone calls to cross-subsidize its other operations, and above all to disguise its efficiency figures. Indeed, data from 1995 showed that Deutsche Telekom scored extremely low in terms of employee efficiency, compared to other telecommunications incumbents.[16]

However, since that time, DTAG achieved impressive progress. In fact, the years from 1995 to 1998 were marked by a massive catching-up effort. The former monopoly carrier lowered its employee base from 1995 to 1998 by about 50000 people, mostly through schemes such as early retirement and by not filling vacant positions.[17] Further cuts were complicated by the fact that 47 per cent of Deutsche Telekom's employees were still classified as public servants at the end of 1998, a privilege for life that granted special status.[18] Nevertheless, through the reduction of employees from 1995, Deutsche Telekom managed to improve both its revenues per employee as well the number of phone connections per employee.[19] Despite these ongoing efficiency gains, Deutsche Telekom did not lower its prices for internet access, however, in the period from 1996 to 1998.

That DTAG kept its prices high is evident through international comparisons. Some researchers in Germany challenged the legitimacy of carrying out international price comparisons (Albach and Knieps, 1997). In an interview with a news magazine, DTAG Chairman Ron Sommer has also questioned the validity of international price comparisons by citing structural differences in the world telecommunications industry. One example he used was the fact that German fixed telecommunications lines are required to be placed underground, whereas in the US or France, masts can be used.[20] These arguments were difficult to prove or to disprove. True cost structures would only become apparent with strong competition in local access.

One detailed international price comparison of 1996, which was commissioned by the association of DTAG's competitors, VATM, concluded that prices paid by large business users in Germany were in line with international standards, but that local call prices were very high. This finding was confirmed by OECD estimates reported in 1997 and again in 1999 in *Communications Outlook*, a useful study which actually compared internet access prices. In this study, internet access prices were split up into local call charges and internet access charges. Although independent German internet access providers (ISPs) seem to have charged very little relative to international rates, this advantage was erased by the extremely high local call prices German users were charged by Deutsche Telekom.[21] In the 1997 survey, Germany was on rank 20 of the 25-country survey, the cheapest countries occupying the first positions. Countries such as the USA, Sweden, France and the Netherlands offered cheaper access than Germany. In the 1999 survey, Germany had slipped even further, to position 29 out of 30 countries.[22]

A German telecommunications activist, Karl-Heinz Dittberner, examined internet access pricing on an individual company basis in 1998. In his comparison, standard internet user costs (20 hours/month) were included as well as costs faced by 'power users' and small firms (100 hours/month). The more the internet was accessed by a single user, the more prohibitive German costs became compared to US costs (see Table 5.1). This was a direct result of Deutsche Telekom's metered pricing policy in the local loop until 1999, which did not differentiate if the local line was used for a phone call or for an internet connection. Other sources, which were less systematic, also indicated that the German 'power user' and small firm faced phone bills of around DM500 / month due to internet use in 1997.[23] On 1 November 1998, internet user groups carried out a national strike in Germany in which they stopped using the internet and 'blackened' their home pages.[24]

To summarize these findings: internet access prices were high in Germany due to the metered price of the local phone call. In 1996, local call prices were raised by Deutsche Telekom and remained at this high level until liberalization.[25] The revenue stream DTAG derived from internet users through its local call lines was not insignificant, but according to the author's estimates accounted only for 1 per cent to 4 per cent of total revenues and between 6 per cent and 21 per cent of local call revenues (they could lie somewhere between DM 698 million and DM 2557 million in 1998).[26] The contribution of local calls to net income was unknown; overall, the fixed-line telephone business generated the overwhelming amount of profits for DTAG. Deutsche Telekom used the income stream generated by its local call fees to reduce its debts.

Table 5.1 Comparison of selected internet access costs USA/Germany in
1998 in DM. Normal home usage of 20 hours/month and 'power
use' by homes and small businesses.

	20 hours/month			100 hours/month		
	Local call rate	Internet provision	Total	Local call rate	Internet provision	Total
USA						
AT&T	_[a]	35.90	35.90	–	35.90	35.90
Southwestern Bell	–	35.90	35.90	–	35.90	35.90
@Home (TV Cable)	–	53.90	53.90	–	53.90	53.90
Germany, night-time rates						
T-Online	36.32	62.00	98.32	181.57	302.00	483.57
Nacamar	36.32	39.00	75.32	181.57	39.00	220.57
Mannesmann Arcor (Internet-by-call)	145.80		145.80	721.80		721.80
Germany, business hours						
T-Online	96.84	62.00	158.84	484.18	302.00	786.18
Nacamar	96.84	39.00	135.84	484.18	39.00	523.18
Mannesmann Arcor	193.80		193.80	961.80		961.80
NetCologne	_[b]	39.00	74.00	–	159.00	194.00

Notes:
[a] One-time monthly flat-rate for the local phone service was required, but was not included in this listing. All local calls were inclusive with this monthly payment. This applied to most US regions, but not all.
[b] NetCologne charged a one-time monthly flat-rate of DM 35 for local dial-in. This service was only available in the Cologne area. There was no difference between night rates and use during business hours. These prices were the initial prices in January 1998.

Source: Internet Site: 't-off: Fakten zum Internet' compiled by Karl-Heinz Dittberner, Freie Universität Berlin. http://userpage.fu-berlin.de/~dittbern/Telekom/Internet_ Facts.html. Accessed on 6 October 1998.

The debt of DTAG was large by international comparisons.[27] In part, the debts were caused by modernization of Eastern Germany's phone system after unification in 1989.[28] Unification investments started impacting upon the accounts of DTAG from the year 1991 onwards (see Figure 5.1). But research shows that DTAG's debt was high already previous to 1991 (Gerpott, 1998, 175, 176), indicating that investments were already prior to unification financed in part not by cashflow but by debt. This is confirmed by Figure 5.2 below, which shows that cashflow used for investments outweighed cashflow from operations in 1990, a year that did not include uni-

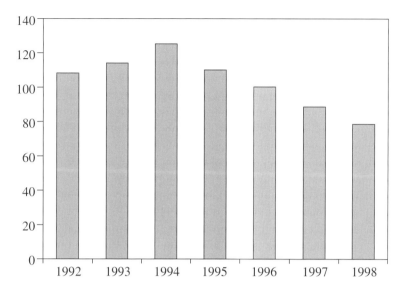

Source: Debt figures from 1994 to 1998 were obtained from the Annual Reports of Deutsche Telekom after privatization. Debts in the years 1992 and 1993 were obtained from Annual Reports prior to privatization.

Figure 5.1   Debt of Deutsche Telekom in millions of DM

fication investments. This unsustainable situation continued up to the year 1994. From 1995, Deutsche Telekom's Chairman Ron Sommer focused on reducing his firm's debt burden – in part by cutting investment.

Debt was only one of the financial worries of Ron Sommer; the other was earnings. But whereas debt was lowered mainly by reducing investment levels, it is probable that high earnings from local calls were necessary to boost profits. For its earnings, Deutsche Telekom was to an extremely high degree (94 per cent) dependent on its fixed-line business, a significant part of which was the local calls service.[29] The financial industry often compares earnings per share (EPS), an indicator with which Deutsche Telekom did not compare well with respect to its competitiveness (see Table 5.2).

The pressure to improve DTAG's balance sheet was high due to the planned tapping of capital markets in 1996 and 1999. These were the years in which the original listing and the secondary placement of Deutsche Telekom were accomplished. After the secondary placement, the path was clear for a fresh, future-oriented strategy. On 1 April 1999, significant price cuts for internet access through Deutsche Telekom's ISP, T-Online, came into effect.[30] There was a further reason other than the financial ones, however, why a strategy focusing on the young internet access market may

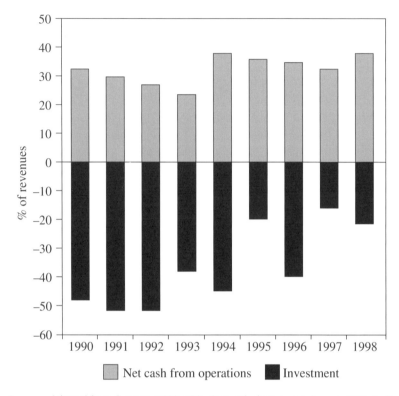

Source: Adapted from Gerpott, (1998, 176). Gerpott's chart runs only up to 1994. In its 1996 Annual Report, Deutsche Telekom applied new accounting principals in line with its privatization and adjusted its figures retroactively up to 1993. In this chart, the adjusted figures are used from 1993 to 1998; for the previous years, figures corresponding to the old accounting principles are used. Net cashflows are calculated in percentage to total net revenues for that year.

Figure 5.2   Net cashflow of Deutsche Telekom 1990 to 1998 as a percentage of revenues

not have been feasible before liberalization. This was the outdated network infrastructure of Deutsche Telekom.

INFRASTRUCTURE CHALLENGES FACED BY DEUTSCHE TELEKOM

As described in the previous chapter, Deutsche Telekom was highly regarded as a force for technological innovation in Germany. This image

Table 5.2   *Basic earnings per share (EPS) of selected telecommunications operators in US$ and return on equity for the year 1998 (calculated from annual net income and year-end share price [a])*

	EPS	Return on equity (%)
AT&T	3.59	25
France Télécom	2.49	14
Sprint	1.98	7
Mannesmann	1.79	10
Royal KPN	1.61	12
Deutsche Telekom	0.91	9

Note [a] Some Annual Reports simply list EPS without explaining how it was derived and not differentiating among different types of EPS calculations. Here, basic earnings per share are being referred to which is calculated using net income.

Source: Annual Reports. For details on these figures, please refer to Appendix C.

was remarkably persistent among German politicians of all parties, although it was probably most widespread among the Social Democrats, where it has a long history. Peter Glotz, a communications expert who for a decade was a member of the Supervisory Board of DTAG, stated that the network infrastructure of DTAG was 'one of the most advanced in the world', adding that 'it is, of course, an inheritance from the past, but an intelligently administered inheritance that has been multiplied'.[31]

This image was surprising given the low level of service the public carrier confronted ordinary Germans with for decades. Most Germans would probably have explained this by differentiating between the service quality of the Deutsche Telekom and the actual technological quality of its network infrastructure. Thorsten Gerpott drew together different indicators of the state of DTAGs network infrastructure before privatization in 1995 to show that at the time the technology was apparently not much better than the service (1998, 200). Deutsche Telekom vigorously modernized its infrastructure from 1995. Infrastructure investments were consistently high in international comparison (OECD, 1999a, 69–84). Germany, for example, achieved 100 per cent digitization of its access lines in 1997 up from 56 per cent in 1995 (OECD, 1999a, 77).[32] Yet experts, such as the Bonn-based internet consultant Harald Lux, emphasized that the modernization of DTAG's infrastructure was a difficult and lengthy process. The modernization initiative was massive, and priorities had to be set.

As has been described in the previous chapter, Deutsche Bundespost

relied on its X.25 network for its data services. X.25 needed to be administered in a much more centralized fashion than internet-based IP networks.
It was also not very efficient as a backbone network for internet access.
When Deutsche Telekom began to offer indirect internet access through a
gateway to its T-Online members in October 1995, it ran the internet service
over X.25. It was not able to cope with the ensuing demand for internet
traffic. Traffic moved slowly and the service was not reliable. According to
Harald Lux, DTAG engineers were at the time scrambling to add network
bypasses (Interview, 10 July 1999). In contrast, other internet providers in
Germany had from 1995 already build up IP-networks and were vigorously
competing among each other.[33] Deutsche Telekom began building its IP
trunk network in Summer 1996 and seriously expanded it only in 1997. T-
Online became a full internet service only in 1997 (Lux and Heinen, 1997,
34, 62; Schneider, 1997, 152). Whereas in 1997, Deutsche Telekom still
trailed other internet providers in Germany in revenue, it was able to
assume the number one position in 1998 (Table 5.3).

One technology has been purposely left out of the discussion thus far:
ISDN. When Deutsche Telekom's network infrastructure was spoken of in
a positive light, usually it was ISDN which was being referred to. The ISDN
initiative of DTAG was indeed remarkable. In the beginning of the 1990s,
ISDN uptake in Germany was far behind that of France. By the end of that
decade, Germany sported the highest ISDN penetration in the world (see
Table 5.4). In absolute numbers also, Deutsche Telekom reigned over
more ISDN connections than any other carrier (Gerpott, 1998, 201).
Nevertheless, the value of an ISDN network was debatable.

Two benefits of ISDN were cited: intelligence and bandwidth; the real
advantages of both are ambivalent. In Chapter 2, part of the discussion of
global network developments focused on the 'intelligent network', of which
ISDN was the ultimate manifestation. The 'intelligent network' approach
was coveted by many traditional telecommunications carriers because it put
them in control of new, value-added services. It required a centralized
approach to offering these services and therefore allowed little leeway for
independent service offerings or innovations. Most services that could be
offered over ISDN, such as call waiting, could be realized more cheaply over
conventional networks. Other services that were possible by combining a
'stupid network' approach such as an internet-based network with computers on the periphery of the network could not be offered by ISDN alone at
all. A further advantage of ISDN, its broadband ability to carry a large
volume of data, was being overshadowed by newer technologies, especially
xDSL, which allowed far more data to flow over a conventional copper line.[34]
By ambitiously adopting a single technology, ISDN, Deutsche Telekom may
have manoeuvred itself into its own version of a German 'Sonderweg.'[35]

Table 5.3   Top six internet providers in 1997 and 1998 and their turnover in DM millions

	1997		1998
Xlink	49	Deutsche Telekom[a]	100
Uunet	45	Uunet	87
Deutsche Telekom[a]	40	Mediaways	70
DPN	39	Nacamar	60
Mediaways	30	DPN	56
Nacamar	30	Xlink	53

Note: [a] Estimate without T-Online sales.

Source: Lux and Heinen, 1999, 9, 13.

Table 5.4   Percentage ISDN lines to main lines

	1997	1998
Germany	16	24
France	6	11
United Kingdom	8	12
USA	3	4
Japan	8	10

Source: European Information Technology Observatory, 1999, 404, 405.

For several years, Deutsche Telekom touted ISDN as its broadband solution. As will be discussed in the next section, it purposely ignored possibilities for developing the broadband capacities of its cable TV network. It also started late on offering broadband xDSL – announcing business service by April 1999 and home service from late Summer 1999. The mainstream roll-out of 'T-DSL,' as Deutsche Telekom called its service, was initiated with a flat-rate offering from September 2000. Competitors such as Nacamar already offered xDSL services to its clients in the Spring of 1998 (Interview, 12 July 1999). At the beginning, DTAG wanted to market xDSL together with ISDN. DTAG wrapped ISDN with xDSL into a combined T-DSL–ISDN package as part of an overall strategy to, in the words of Ron Sommer, 'transform Germany into the greatest online nation' (author's translation).[36] It gave up on this strategy with the roll-out of flat-rate T-DSL in Autumn 2000; the new service could be subscribed to over analogue lines as well. If it had adhered to its ISDN-only strategy longer, Deutsche Telekom would have found itself technologically isolated and dependent upon a technology that may not be developed further as vigorously as other, more widely used options. Retrospectively, the ISDN effort may seem a massive and costly investment which completely bypassed market needs at a time when it would have made more sense to build a powerful internet backbone and roll out cheap mass internet access. Deutsche Telekom would have won over a user base which later would have subscribed to high-bandwidth access services over other technologies – such as xDSL or cable TV.

GERMAN CABLE TV: LEFT TO STAGNATE?

Compared with other countries, Germany is generously endowed with coaxial cable TV connections. Over 18 million households are receiving cable TV services and another 7 million are connected to the network and are potential subscribers. This means that a full two-thirds of all German private households can be potentially reached by cable TV. The German cable network is the largest cable TV network in Europe in absolute numbers (RegTP, 1999b, 19; Gerpott, 1998, 8–9). Until 2000, this network was controlled by a single company, which put this enterprise in the enviable position of being able to roll out broadband internet access, cable telephony and media services directly into millions of homes and small businesses. If DTAG had addressed the challenges of an expensive upgrade of the outdated cable TV system and of the peculiar, historic system of local media service firms administering customer access, it would have had a unique opportunity – if only to achieve a high sales price.[37] But Deutsche Telekom's vision for the German cable future was quite distinct from the mass broadband internet access initiative just described.

In several countries, such as the US or broadband leader Korea, cable modems became an important means of broadband access for consumers at the start of the 2000s. In 1999, cable TV modems had a share of 84 per cent of the broadband market, although the share of ADSL services grew strongly in 2000 (OECD, 2001b, 5). Even before the advent of broadband internet access, however, cable TV companies offered access to telephone and narrowband internet services. In the UK, competitors were allowed to offer telephony services and bypass the local loop of BT. This policy was initiated in 1991. In that year, the duopoly approach to telecommunications competition was ended in the UK and network competition was encouraged over the cable TV network and other alternative infrastructures. Furthermore, the dominant PTO was barred from providing broadcast entertainment over its networks. In 1995, already one million customers in the UK used telephony services provided by cable TV operators (OECD, 1996b, 7, 10).

In Germany, the cable TV network was controlled until 2000 by the incumbent carrier, Deutsche Telekom. As described in the last chapter, this was the result of the specific historic trajectory surrounding liberalization. That the public predecessor organization to Deutsche Telekom was originally in 1982 put in control of the cable TV network and oversaw its construction was the result of political action, as well. The running of the network was also politically controlled, with the responsibility over broadcasting assumed in part by the local state governments. Deutsche Telekom was charged with carrying private and public broadcasting over its networks and was paid around DM 3 million annually for this service.[38] Although this is not a sum that was able to cover the costs of the coaxial network, Deutsche Telekom was allowed to exploit the additional capacity largely as it pleased. From 1995/96, for example, DTAG set aside two channels for digital television – a project that was conceived as a joint venture between the telecommunications carrier and the two German media giants Bertelsmann and Kirch. The joint venture was not realized, a matter which is discussed below. What Deutsche Telekom explicitly avoided, however, was cannibalizing its ISDN plans by offering broadband internet access or telephony services. Deutsche Telekom separated the realms telephony, internet access and media broadcasting clearly by running parallel networks.

The investment sum required to update the German cable TV network was very high. In part, this is due to original government policy; in part, however, to an intentional strategy of neglect by Deutsche Telekom. In order to swiftly provide a broadcast medium for private television, the original cable TV network was built using low-cost coaxial standard technologies available at the time. As a result, cable TV in some German regions runs over old lines that are costly to upgrade to allow for the two-way transfer required for internet access (Gerpott, 1998, 36–8). On the other hand, some housing blocks in the new Eastern German states were connected recently and offer easy upgrade opportunities. Then there is the added difficulty that two-thirds of all customers do not receive their service directly from Deutsche Telekom, but through one of 6000 local, small media service firms (RegTP, 1999b, 20). Some of these companies are represented in the cable TV service firm association ANGA, and the association has spoken favourably of an upgrade of the cable TV network and welcomes the offering of new services such as internet over the network. In fact, ANGA is antagonistic towards the DTAG as network owner and argues that the telecommunications carrier has purposely limited cable-carrying capacity.[39] In

late 1996, parts of the cable TV network were modernized but the capacity
was upgraded to allow for only two additional digital TV programmes,
although more would have been technically feasible.[40] Six pilot projects, in
which DTAG purportedly tested new, interactive cable services, were run at
'a pace rather below average compared to US commercialization efforts',
to use Gerpott's carefully worded phrase (author's translation, Gerpott,
1998, 218, 219).

Cable TV was a loss-making operation for Deutsche Telekom from the
very beginning. The service was loss-making because it was reduced to carrying media programming and was not expanded to include potentially
lucrative income sources, especially telephony and internet access.
Deutsche Telekom viewed these services as competing with its most important money-maker, the local loop. Cannibalization was not an option for
the telecommunications carrier. In fact, there has only been one attempt on
the part of DTAG to generate a positive income flow from its cable TV
holdings. In 1994, a joint venture for digital pay-television services over
cable was announced by Deutsche Telekom, Bertelsmann and the Kirch
Group. The joint venture was not realized for several reasons.[41] The most
obvious reason was that EU competition authorities indicated that year
and again in May 1998 that they would not tolerate the alliance, if it
remained exclusive.[42] Also, as was just described, Germany's federal states
had a say in the development of broadcast media and their involvement
added an unknown dimension to any deal.

In addition, however, Deutsche Telekom was asking a high price for its
network service, an annual payment of at least DM 12 million as well as a
share of sales.[43] DTAG also charged households for its access to the cable
TV network. As one editorial in a well-known German business daily
stated in 1997, using a well-known German metaphor: 'Like a sausage, TV
cables have two ends. On both ends Deutsche Telekom cashes in . . . And
both ends will be expensive for Telekom's clients.'[44] In order to have made
cable TV access an attractive mass market proposition, different revenue
streams would have to have been combined, as has just been pointed out.
If media broadcasting alone is required to pay for the network, individual
subscribers to the service would have to have paid considerable fees. This
was clearly stated by Herbert Ungerer, head of telecommunications at the
competition unit in the European Commission, DGIV: 'The cable network
cannot thrive only on television distribution, not even on additional digital
television distribution, or on attempts to monopolise programme rights to
increase pay-TV rates.'[45]

Since Deutsche Telekom was the only major European telecommunications incumbent with control over cable TV, the EU competition authorities were long critical of the situation. Deutsche Telekom was very aware

of this and sought to delay a forced sale of its assets. It did so by publicly announcing that it intended sell the network. The actual sale began only in 2000, initially under optimal conditions for Deutsche Telekom. Firstly, the cable TV network was sold not as a whole, but split up into regional units.[46] Secondly, the right to supply programmes and services was secured in contracts that were transferred to the 100 per cent Deutsche Telekom subsidiary MediaServices GmbH.[47] Thirdly, DTAG retained significant stakes in the units, which allowed it certain blocking powers. The *Financial Times* quoted a London-based analyst stating: 'Telekom's whole intention is to make it very difficult [for the new entrants] to compete with them.'[48] But, in the end, the delay strategy would backfire as the sale of the cable networks missed the opportunity created by the investment bubble.

THE RENAISSANCE OF T-ONLINE[49]

The history of T-Online in its previous incarnation as the teletex service Btx has been described in the last chapter. Thereafter, T-Online was referred to by the Deutsche Telekom as an internet access service. As such, it was the second-largest worldwide, although it trailed AOL/CompServe's worldwide figures by a large amount. T-Online was Europe's leader with its 11 million subscribers (as of December 2001). The true significance of T-Online at the time only becomes fully apparent if one compares its subscriber base to the total number of internet users in Germany (see Table 5.5). Although the

Table 5.5   Number of T-Online subscribers compared with total number of internet users

	T-Online subscribers	Internet users	Proportion (%)
1997	1.9	4.9	39
1998	2.7	6.9	39
1999	3.3	9.9	33
2000	5.5	18.0	31

Note: The year 2000 figure of total T-Online users in Europe was 6 million, because 500 000 users in France of the T-Online subsidiary Club Internet need to be included. For T-Online data: RegTP (1999b, 14). See also Deutsche Telekom Annual Report 1998 in English language, p. 51. For 1999 and 2000, press releases of T-Online were used instead of RegTP data because T-Online's figures represented mid-year estimates and RegTP's numbers were year-end. The GfK statisticts, which attempted to capture the number of internet users in Germany were also mid-year figures for 1998, 1999, 2000 and an end-year figure for 1997. The GfK-Online-Monitor was carried out by GfK Nuremberg together with G + J Electronic Media Service (EMS). The statistics used were from the first, second, fourth and sixth waves respectively. These were accessed on the web site http://www.ems.guj.de/.

two numbers cannot be directly compared, the number of T-Online subscribers amounted to about one third of total internet users in Germany
from 1997 to 2000. However, T-Online use was historically, in international
comparisons, extremely expensive. This was due especially to the metered
cost of the local telephone connection, but also due to a prohibitively high
original cost of using T-Online, which was itself metered.

How can this paradoxical situation be explained, namely that an expensive service such as T-Online gained such popularity since its relaunch in
late 1995? There were two reasons. Firstly, T-Online benefited from its past
life as Btx and its links to the incumbent telephone company. Secondly,
DTAG made sure that T-Online was expensive, but not much more so than
other internet services, which also had to rely on access via local phone
calls. In contrast to the stable (high) price of a local phone call until 1999,
the price for using T-Online was lowered several times, reflecting a defensive pricing policy, following the market.

Compared with the expectations surrounding the launch of Btx in the late
1970s, the German postal service's videotex system was a failure. Btx was
heralded as a service that would revolutionize the German home. In fact, the
estimated number of one million users by 1985 was not reached until early
1996 (Schneider, 1989, 119–25).[50] By 1994, the Deutsche Telekom had all
but given up on the service and outsourced much of the effort associated
with it. It let a small Karlsruhe-based software developer devise a more user-
friendly graphic interface called KIT. Another small company, 1&1, was
charged with the marketing the service (Schneider, 1997, 151). To outside
observers, the final symbol of sinking confidence was the signing of a letter
of intent with Bertelsmann's brand new AOL Europe service, announced in
November 1995. Deutsche Telekom would give up its objective of being the
main electronic link to the home – the goal of the original Btx. The agreement stipulated that AOL would be focused on an entertainment-based
home service, whereas T-Online was relegated to transaction-oriented uses
such as home banking.[51] The alliance eventually was forgotten as concerns
were raised by EU competition authorities and the apparently imminent
threat of the Microsoft Network (MSN) waned (Microsoft had cannibal-
ized MSN in favour of its new internet strategy).[52] Nevertheless, the service
that was renamed T-Online had arrived at its nadir.

Btx could claim one resounding success. During the first half of the
1990s, it had managed to establish itself securely in one industry, if sex services are ignored. Whereas the other range of retail services offered over
Btx stagnated, online banking flourished and became the 'killer app' of
Btx. Online banking met a demand that was perhaps created in part by
limited bank opening times in Germany. After Btx had reached its low
point in 1994/95, the downward trend was reversed, however. In October

1995, the service was given a new name, T-Online, and was equipped with a gateway to the internet (Schneider, 1997, 151, 152). User numbers went steeply upwards, as is evident from Table 5.5; yet, importantly, growth did not outpace the trend of general internet adoption in Germany.

The companies charged with software development and marketing of Btx/ T-Online had proven that the service could be saved and that new users could be won over. In fact, most observers claim that the marketing expertise and drive of 1&1 were the main reasons behind the revitalized service; 1&1 would continue to work for the service and became one of the foremost online marketing firms in Germany. It carried out a public listing on the Neue Markt in 1998.[53] But another important factor behind the success of T-Online was that it continued to offer the core Btx service of online banking. Almost all German retail banks offered a Btx service. Thus, T-Online was the only German online service from 1996 allowing both internet access and banking. In fact, the presence of German banks on Btx and the security problems associated with the internet were disincentives for many German institutions for developing pure internet banking. Many banks only began to offer pure internet-based services independent of T-Online in 1999.

A further advantage of T-Online over other online services was its link to the telephone service. Small payments for T-Online services, such as the business information database GENIOS, were charged over the public telephone bill. Again, the insecurity associated with the internet and the reluctance of many new internet users to offer credit card information over the internet meant that the combination T-Online and phone bill was a strong one. 'This advantage of T-Online in offering a micropayments mechanism very early on should not be underestimated', emphasized Stefan Kühler of the rival on-line service Callisto Germany.net (Interview, 13 July 1999). Germany.net tried to launch its own micropayments mechanism over the internet but the option could not compete with the ease of phone bill invoicing.[54]

Consistently from 1997 up to 2000, T-Online's lead was so great, that other online and internet services were competing only among themselves. For the press speaker of Germany.net, the third-largest online service, the objective was clear: 'Our goal is to overtake AOL in Germany. AOL has 800000 members, we have 660000. We believe we can do it . . . T-Online we cannot reach. It is just impossible' (Interview, 13 July 1999). Yet, the price for using T-Online was high.[55] When T-Online was first relaunched in 1995, a user accessing the internet was required to pay three metered fees simultaneously: a metered fee for the local phone call, a metered fee for using T-Online (6 pfennigs per minute during business hours) and a third metered fee for internet use via the T-Online gateway (of 10 pfennigs per minute).[56] Over the years, T-Online became cheaper in order to remain competitive with services such as AOL, CompuServe, MSN and independent internet providers. Although competitive prices existed on the level of the services itself, however, Deutsche Telekom was able to extract a toll from all internet users regardless of which service they were using – the local phone call. It was this price tag on internet access which remained essentially unchanged from 1996 to 1999; it was discussed at length in a previous section.

Finally, on 1 April 1999, Deutsche Telekom reduced the overall price for accessing the internet in Germany. Internet access was forthwith available from T-Online for 6 pfennigs a minute (circa US$ 2.12/hour), a combined price which included the local access call. For the first time, therefore, Deutsche Telekom differentiated the price of the local phone call from the price of internet access, paving the way to further price cuts for internet users. It is crucial to emphasize the importance of this development for Germany. A new era began, one in which access prices continued to fall. Pricing reflected both cost savings through technological advances as well as access competition. An old era ended, in which the demand for internet services and time spent online was restricted by high and unchanging access tolls. This also led to a flood of new users for T-Online. A press release by Deutsche Telekom stated: 'Now it's clear: the new pricing model increases the usage of the internet in Germany.'[57] This discovery came quite late: why in April 1999, 15 months after liberalization and three years after the passing of the Telecommunications Law? The same discovery process seemed to have occurred with the introduction of flat-rate internet access through T-Online in Spring of 2000. Here, the relevant press release declared that 200000 new clients could be won over through the flat rate in two months 'even without a special advertising campaign' (author's translation).[58]

German internet consultant Harald Lux emphasized that the 1 April pricing move of the Deutsche Telekom was, like those made previously with T-Online, a defensive strategy (Interview, 10 July 1999). It was a response to pricing initiatives made by newer competitors offering an internet-by-call service.[59] The reaction by the Deutsche Telekom was to introduce a package of combined local access and T-Online fees. The new fee structure resembled internet-by-call fees.[60] Although April 1, 1999 heralded the arrival of a new era in internet pricing, it still did not amount to a revolution. Both the call-by-call internet services as well as the T-Online service were still metered offerings, meaning that the user was penalised for the time he remained online. As has been pointed out previously, this discouraged intensive use of the internet. Yet, metered interconnection prices reflected the switched network infrastructure of Deutsche Telekom's local phone service. Deutsche Telekom initially wanted to retain metered pricing also for its broadband xDSL offering, although xDSL is a pure packet-based network, 'because our clients would not understand volume-based pricing plans' (Lux, Interview, 10 July 1999).[61] In Autumn 2000, T-Online actually announced flat rate pricing for T-DSL. It supplemented a flat-rate ISDN-based internet offer introduced half a year earlier. When the flat rate ISDN offer was terminated again for tactical and economic reasons in the subsequent year, the xDSL offer remained in place. In 2000, therefore, the revolution of flat-rate pricing finally came.

DEUTSCHE TELEKOM: 'A BAD LOSER?'[62]

The main immediate worries of Deutsche Telekom in the first year of the liberalized market were its shareholders and the regulator. The shareholder's view was especially important because DTAG intended to raise fresh funds through a second public offering, realized in July 1999. The debt situation needed to be improved, the balance sheet needed to look good. The regulator also was crucial because, more than the competing entrants themselves, its moves impacted directly on the ability of DTAG to make money. Low interconnection prices, for example, made it possible that the incumbent lost around a third of total long-distance minutes in the first year. National long-distance telephony prices fell by more than 70 per cent (RegTP, 1999a, 8). The local loop remained an important generator of income. It was, therefore, not surprising that Deutsche Telekom's strategy in the first year of the liberalized market was not marked by major initiatives in the local loop internet access. It is also not surprising that DTAG needed to demonstrate its savvy in two regards: in corporate strategy and in its political manoeuvres. The battle that ensued in 1998 between the regulator and Deutsche Telekom was an intense conflict in which the incumbent carrier pulled all possible levers, including its good connections with the newly elected Social Democratic Party. One of the main issues of arbitrage with the regulator and the competition was the pricing of unbundled access.

Through its arbitrage efforts, Deutsche Telekom was able to create uncertainty over the crucial issue of unbundled access to its subscriber lines.[63] In May 1997, the Postal Ministry had decided that Deutsche Telekom had to offer this powerful service option, a decision that DTAG pleaded against. Full certainty in this decision was delayed as described in the previous section. Court proceedings were still under way throughout 1999.[64] Some of the public manoeuvres of Deutsche Telekom were criticized by the press as 'bad loser behaviour'. Deutsche Telekom executives did not shy away from publicly attacking the regulator's decisions by appealing to the share value of DTAG. Indeed, the DTAG share was owned by 'an army of 2m ordinary Germans, the vanguard of popular capitalism in the country' (*The Economist*).[65] The CEO of DTAG also appealed to national sentiments concerning the entry of foreign companies into the German market (see quote in Glotz, 2001, 102). Political lobbying was to be expected in any competitive situation. However, due to the fact that the government still was a majority shareholder, this strategy carried particular weight with the German financial ministry and not only the German shareholding population.

Deutsche Telekom also tried to sabotage the competition's efforts by other means. The city carrier NetCologne, for example, was dependent upon the goodwill of Deutsche Telekom to switch new clients over from its own to the NetCologne network. Initially, this goodwill was lacking and DTAG only switched 'a handful' of customers over each day, stating this was their capacity limit (VATM, Interview, 14 July 1999). Only in 2002 was an enforcement mechanism implemented by the regulator so it could charge the incumbent fees when it delayed the connection of competitors to its network.[66] Similar complaints were filed with the regulator by new entrants, ranging from technological issues such as placed resistances into xDSL line connections to billing problems. These issues were not universal, however – they were concentrated on the local loop. In one example, Deutsche Telekom's service for its competitors proved remarkably reliable, namely, in enabling call-by-call and pre-selection telephony punctually on 1 January 1998 (Gerpott, 1998, 89; Glotz, 2001, 103). The most important lesson of these local sabotage efforts was that DTAG would fight for its control over the local loop with all means available.

Many of the future-oriented strategies that were missing before 1999 were embarked upon in that and the subsequent year. DTAG management had recognized the strategic value of the local loop for the internet and broadband markets. With this recognition, DTAG's approach shifted to using all means available to price its own services more competitively than those of the competition. In 1999, DTAG successfully negotiated for a high price for its unbundled local loop. In fact, the price the incumbent was able to charge the competition, DM 25.40, was higher than the monthly subscription fee the incumbent charged its own consumers, which amounted to DM 21.39. The competition had demanded a price between DM 15 and 20. This made the introduction of attractive alternative offers difficult for the competition (Monopolkommission, 2001, 39, 121–3, 152).[67] A spokesperson for the telecommunications operator VIAG stated: 'The rental of an unbundled access line from the Deutsche Telekom is dead.'[68]

The behaviour of DTAG was predictable; it had identified a strategic market and it was using all possible means at its disposal to capture this market. Instead, the regulator's actions require explanation, especially given the body's eager embrace of its task to support competition in January 1998. Two points are made here. Firstly, unbundling itself was only a second-best option fraught with inherent problems. These problems became apparent in the months after the start of competition in Germany. Yet, the US Federal Communications Commission (FCC) had recognized these inherent problems already in 1966, at the time of its first Computer Inquiry. At the time, the FCC outlined the realistic scenario that a telecommunications operator offering its own network services to data networking competitors would use their control of the network to disadvantage its competitors and privilege its own data services. The FCC also was concerned about cross-subsidies (Cannon, 2001, 4; Oxman, 1999, 10). Given the nature of unbundling, pricing conflicts, delays and technical sabotage, all were possible, even certain.

Secondly, RegTP purposely chose not to offer an unbundled access price below cost, whereby it calculated costs according to the data supplied by DTAG in terms of the replacement costs of the whole national network. In the words of the former Vice-President of RegTP, Arne Börnsen:

> The unbundling of the local loop was for us only the second-best alternative. But because we did not have alternative network infrastructures available, we decided on unbundling. In accordance with the telecommunications law, we calculated the price for unbundled local loop access in terms of the replacement cost. We considered the replacement cost for the whole national network. I would have liked to have followed the option of three separate pricing segments for metropolitan areas, smaller cities and the countryside. But such a scheme would not have been accepted politically, since it would have meant a disadvantage for households in the country. I was strictly opposed to a price below cost, because this would have endangered sustainable competition and infrastructure investments (Interview, 19 February 2002, author's translation).

The emphasis on replacement costs and infrastructure investments highlights a problem which is even more difficult to resolve than the issues associated with the incumbent's control and ownership. When does an offer of unbundled access restrict infrastructure competition? After analysing investment behaviour in numerous countries where unbundled access was available, the OECD stated that the alleged trade-off between unbundled access and infrastructure investment was unproven. Apparently, infrastructure investments were also significant in countries with unbundled access (OECD, 2001b, 15).

A description of the course of telecommunications liberalization in Germany would not be complete without an analysis of the competition. The regulator set the price of the unbundled local loop high as not to act as a disincentive to infrastructure investment. How realistic was infrastructure competition in the local loop? To what extent would the unbundling option be taken? The CEO of DTAG, Ron Sommer, repeatedly stated that his competition, being industrial and utility players, were anything but 'delicate plants' which had to be protected (Glotz, 2001, 102). An analysis of the competition reveals that they indeed were not delicate, yet they faced serious handicaps.

TELECOMMUNICATIONS INFRASTRUCTURE INVESTMENT AND CAPITAL MARKETS

As was discussed in previous sections, RegTP allowed the rental of unbundled subscriber lines from Deutsche Telekom for a monthly flat fee. The long delays associated with this option as DTAG engaged in arbitrage regarding unbundling and its pricing delayed the impact this option could have on the German telecommunications landscape for several years. But here, as elsewhere, government policy and the actions of the national regulator do not tell the whole story. Despite strong uncertainties, a limited number of city carriers, majority-owned by municipal utility companies, offered unmetered 'capped' internet access already early 1998 via this route. Cologne became known as 'surfer's paradise'.[69] Yet, the surprising fact that municipal utility companies were the pioneers of access infrastructure and unmetered fees in Germany came with strings attached: The city carriers financed their growth through earnings derived from other businesses and did not tap the potential of capital markets. Furthermore, management quality among the different city carriers varied considerably throughout Germany; in not all cases did the municipal utility, unaccustomed as it was to market competition, select an ideal management. Despite their early start, the progress of the city carriers was slower than it could have been.

Two different types of utility players were involved in offering telecommunications services in Germany. On the one hand, large utility conglomerates, mostly private, control the national supply and therefore owned backbone routes throughout the country which they used to build up national trunk telecommunications networks. On the other hand, local utility firms, usually owned by the municipality, owned rights of way crisscrossing the city. Municipal utility players founded the city carriers for the explicitly to take advantage of these rights. Yet, the actual infrastructure investments – which were costly and risky – proceeded slowly. To some degree, investment was trapped in these companies. Since they were municipally owned, they were unable or unwilling to tap capital markets, for example through a spin-off, in order to embark upon an aggressive investment strategy. Instead, they financed growth through returns from their monopoly businesses. In contrast, a further type of competitor, the younger telecommunications start-ups (which were listed on the alternative stock market Neuer Markt), did not inherit the privilege of their own rights-of-way. These were the companies that could potentially have financed a high-risk and high-cost investment strategy focused on local access. The result of this paradoxical situation was that, although local access infrastructure investment proceeded, it moved at a slower pace and was more risk-adverse than would potentially have been possible if it were capital markets financed.

Here, three types of competitors to Deutsche Telekom in the period immediately following liberalization will be discussed and their investment behaviour described. In part, the classification relies on that used by Gerpott in his book on telecommunications competition in Germany (1998, 261–75). The first competitors to be discussed here were the national carriers, the second the city carriers and the third the telecommunications start-ups. The first group could be described succinctly with the phrase: 'National energy conglomerates plus two.' The national energy conglomerates included RWE, Veba and VIAG. The 'plus two' were the German railway, which owned extensive rights-of-way throughout Germany along its rail tracks, as well as Mannesmann AG, an industry conglomerate which initially entered the telecommunications business without any sizeable rights-of-way. Mannesmann earned its reputation in Germany as the first challenger to Deutsche Telekom by running an alternative mobile phone network. From January 1997, Mannesmann engaged in a partnership with the German railways telecommunication arm, the DBKom, forming Mannesmann Arcor. Through DBKom, Mannesmann achieved rights-of-way and became a fixed-line telephony competitor in addition to being a mobile phones operator.[70] Between the national carriers, a consolidation battle raged long before liberalization in 1998. One national player emerged more powerful than the rest: Mannesmann.[71]

Like its large competitors from the utilities industry, Mannesmann financed the growth of its fixed-line telecommunications services through earnings generated from other businesses, in this case, to a large degree through its lucrative mobile phone business. The rest of the industrial conglomerate Mannesmann was quite distinct from telecommunications and carried a different risk and rewards potential. Why didn't Mannesmann spin off its telecommunications holdings to tap capital markets and embark upon a more aggressive expansion strategy? In this way, Mannesmann could have matched the speed of US-listed new entrants such as WorldCom and Qwest. But, whereas Anglo-American entrants financed their expansion worldwide through capital markets, European firms were slow to do so.[72] The key to understanding this discrepancy was that a spin-off was risky since the spun-off company could be easily swallowed by a competitor, especially an Anglo-American competitor enjoying high valuations. How risky this was, was proven by the later acquisition of Mannesmann through Vodafone.

In terms of market capitalisation compared with revenue, and in terms of market capitalization growth, European telecommunications companies actually compared favourably to traditional US telecommunications companies (see Appendix C). In fact, the largest European telecommunications companies were doing better than their other European blue-chip counterparts which may have experienced comparable growth over the past months but still had lower valuations compared to their US counterparts.[73] It was only when selected new Anglo-American entrants at the time were compared to European telecommunications operators, that multiples were very different.[74] The gap increased in 1999 – this was the effect of the so-called 'internet bubble'. If one considers that in October 1997, the entrant WorldCom (1996 revenues US$4.5 billion) successfully bid for MCI (1996 revenues US$18.5 billion), European telecommunications players indeed looked very vulnerable and could have been threatened through a number of new entrants, not just Vodafone. Only in the year 2000 did this discrepancy in valuations begin to collapse with the downturn of the capital markets. A large number of US telecommunications start-ups subsequently went bankrupt as easy access to capital disappeared.[75]

Like Mannesmann, the second group of telecommunications competitors to be discussed here financed their growth through earnings obtained from other businesses. Unlike Mannesman, they were small and regionally oriented. Furthermore, they owned valuable rights-of-way. These were the city carriers, telecommunications carriers founded by municipal utilities companies (Gerpott, 1998, 270–75). It is difficult to generalize upon their strategies, because these were very heterogeneous. The differences could be accounted for by the distinctions inherent in the local markets themselves as well as the particular strategies of their management teams.

Upon liberalization in January 1998, only two city carriers had significant services in place, based on renting of unbundled subscriber lines: NetCologne and ISIS in Düsseldorf (Gerpott, 1998, 305). Of these two, only NetCologne offered a very innovative service package which included internet access.[76] Later, throughout 1998 and 1999, other city carriers began to offer similar services. As has been pointed out already in previous sections, these services were introduced before regulatory certainty. The risk, however, of starting early was low because this group of telecommunications competitors intended to take advantage of their own, already existing rights-of-way. The investments in expensive billing systems and service teams, which had to be put in place for offering local service, could therefore be justified. Nevertheless, the municipal players were not quick enough to seriously compete with Deutsche Telekom in their respective regions until late 1999, perhaps even beyond. The speed of NetCologne was exceptional and did not represent the majority of its city carrier peers.

It was argued that city carriers could have represented powerful local competitors to Deutsche Telekom because they knew their region very well, had a recognized brand name and a well-established customer base (thanks to their parent companies). There was another aspect to the story, however. Werhard Möschel, one of the few vocal advocates of rigorous market liberalization in Germany, criticized the fact that funds generated by local monopolies were being invested in the recently liberalized market (with the notable exception of the city of Frankfurt which early on chose not to involve itself directly, but instead allowed private firms such as MFS and COLT to compete).[77] Möschel warned that the municipal owners of city carriers made life for other, independent new entrants in those cities difficult. Pointing to the public ownership of city carriers competing in a liberalized market, Möschel warned that privatization should not only be formal but also material. He concluded: 'The future cannot be won in this way.'[78] A further important perspective could be added to Möschel's argument, however, which he did not explicitly state. The municipal players were unable or unwilling to tap public capital markets for funding their undertaking. As a result, their initiatives did not exhibit the rapid pace they could potentially have acquired. The cautious pace of investment saved them from bankruptcy later, but also stalled the introduction of access competition.

The third and final group of telecommunications competitors to be discussed here were genuine telecommunications start-ups listed on the Neuer Markt. MobilCom, Debitel, TelDaFax and Drillisch achieved valuations ranging from about DM 400 million (Drillisch) to DM 7000 million (MobilCom) in 1999.[79] Investors expected them to be major players in the future telecommunications landscape in Germany. They were in a difficult position, however. As of 1999, all local rights-of-way were blocked by a former monopolist, Deutsche Telekom, or by the municipal carriers. In light of this fact, early local access investments based on the option of renting subscriber lines would have been risky before regulatory certainty. Instead, the telco start-ups focused initially on long-distance telephony and on securing access to national trunk lines.[80] Thus, the stars of the Neue Markt which have benefited from stock market euphoria and the internet bubble had a difficult time to enter the market of local internet access – despite the unique possibility offered by the national regulator in renting subscriber lines.

MobilCom began to offer direct subscriber lines in 26 cities at the end of 1999, entering this market two years after the municipal city carriers

(Interview, 13 September 1999). This timing was similar to that of the national carrier Mannesmann Arcor, which launched its subscriber line service in ten densely populated German cities from 1 September 1999.[81] Like the telecommunication start-ups, Mannesmann Arcor waited for regulatory certainty before considering starting an innovative local internet access service. Therefore, up to 1999, Deutsche Telekom controlled almost all local access to the internet by homes and small firms and could impose its metered pricing scheme.

CONCLUSION

The critical question that ran through this chapter, therefore, was why the 'national champion' did not act as a force for innovation in Germany, which policy-makers, especially those close to the SPD, believed it to be. This chapter explored the possibility that Deutsche Telekom was in part unable and in part unwilling to follow an innovative strategy pursuing the young internet access market in Germany in the years from 1996 to 1998. A closer look was therefore necessary. The material permitted three explanations why DTAG was unable to pursue a future-oriented course. Firstly, the management of Deutsche Telekom may simply have underestimated the 'disruptive techology' of the internet (see Christensen, 1997). Secondly, Deutsche Telekom was under steep cost pressure in the whole period under examination. It also had to reduce its large debt. Thirdly, its network infrastructure was unprepared to meet steep demand for internet access and the company lacked know-how in the internet field. Most traditional telecommunications firms were facing similar problems in that period. The two latter problems were strongly aggravated by DTAG's history as a monopoly carrier before privatization in 1994. The management of Deutsche Telekom emphasized this correctly. Yet, an argument could also be made that DTAG could in some cases have acted less defensively in the years 1996, 1997, 1998 and beyond, especially given the capital market's exuberant enthusiasm for a bold, network economy strategy in this period.

It is ironic given the politician's trust in Deutsche Telekom that while the carrier potentially was in the best position to act as a main force for innovation in Germany it actually hindered the uptake of mass internet use by imposing high metered fees. Throughout 1999, there were only three main modes by which private individuals and small firms could access the internet in Germany.[82] In all three cases, Deutsche Telekom was able to control the underlying fee structure. Until the end of 1999, private users and small businesses were confronted in Germany by metered fees and not flat rates

– a result of Deutsche Telekom's policy.[83] The US internet evangelist Nicholas Negroponte stated: 'Make local calls a flat fee and you would change Germany's economy more than any president could' (quoted in Zerdick et al., 1999, 77).

The national regulator, which acted as a strong champion of competition from the very beginning of its mandate in January 1998, was unable to rapidly inject competition into the local loop. While specific flat-rate internet access offers were introduced in some local areas in 1998, the terms of competition were set by the incumbent as soon as it entered the market in 2000. After months of delay and arbitrage, the incumbent used a high price for unbundled access to its advantage while offering its own competitive flat-rate internet access rates. Competing internet providers who alternatively attempted to offer flat-rate access over DTAG's metered lines without renting the whole unbundled line soon found out to their own detriment that the service was uneconomical. The saga continued when the regulator in November 2000 announced that DTAG would have to offer its competitors a wholesale internet flat rate, which it offered its own ISP, T-Online.[84] In the UK, the same arrangement, Flat Rate Internet Access Call Origination (FRIACO), had been mandated by the national regulator, Oftel, in May 2000. RegTP's move to launch FRIACO in Germany intelligently separated flat-rate internet offers from the burden of renting a whole unbundled subscriber line, which was economical only in certain regions and required substantial investments in billing systems. Again, Deutsche Telekom promptly opposed this decision vehemently. In March 2001, it tactically terminated its own ISDN flat-rate offer for T-Online. Proceedings continued well into 2002.[85]

The problems encountered by RegTP in the local loop and concerning flat-rate access after the advent of competition can be traced back to the trajectory of liberalization in Germany itself and to ownership structures. Most importantly, infrastructure competition was difficult to realize in Germany while the cable TV network remained in control of the incumbent and alternative technologies were still emerging. The most likely source for early infrastructure competition were the municipal networks owned by local utilities. Indeed, it was from these municipal networks that broadband competition, so-called 'property networks', emerged in Swedish cities like Stockholm.[86] Yet, in Germany, municipal utility competitors were successful only in particular cases, for example in Cologne. While Swedish municipal entities offered their own dark-fibre backbones and rights-of-way to commercial competitors on a 5, 10, 15 or 20-year basis (without competing against them), German municipal utilities started their own competitive city carriers, sometimes together with local savings banks. The German city carriers were handicapped by their own public ownership which prevented access to capital markets. Differences in competitor's strategy regarding capital markets financing was, apart from telecommunications liberalization policy itself, the single most significant factor explaining differences in the development of network infrastructures in Germany, Sweden and the United States.

An additional handicap for the regulator on top of the lack of infrastructure competition in Germany was that the largest ISP in Germany was in control of the incumbent. DTAG could price its ISP services at exactly the right level to undermine the competition, to whom it was offering an unbundled local loop or wholesale flat-rate access. Only action on the part of the regulator in changing the ownership structure of the Deutsche Telekom and a prompt separation of the cable TV network and the ISP would have fundamentally altered the competitive landscape. But the regulator had no mandate to change the ownership structure of DTAG. Alternative ownership structures would have been possible before the privatization of the Deutsche Telekom in 1994 or, with strong government support, thereafter. It was not helpful that government was a major shareholder of DTAG stock. The German case shows that a progressive regulatory framework can only go so far if ownership structures are not optimized for competition.

The initiatives of two types of domestic actors, national government and the incumbent telecommunications operator, have been discussed thus far in Part II. Attention in the next chapter will be turned to the third type of actor under examination, the new internet ventures themselves. The activities of this third type of actor are especially important for this study. The ability of German internet ventures to participate in a global innovation opportunity essentially was a measurement of the strength of the refraction effect discussed in Chapter 1. Could the development of the new ventures in the global New Economy be regarded as largely independent of the influence of powerful domestic actors such national government and the incumbent operator or not?

NOTES

1. This number included 1.9 million subscribers in France and other countries, which were added through acquisitions.
2. 'We desperately need competition in the last mile to the user', said the CSU parliamentarian Dr Martin Mayer in an interview (23 April 1999). The same view could be found in the statement by the FDP party in the Enquete-Kommission. The FDP called for: 'A reduction in internet access tariffs through regulation, because new competitors will not be active in reducing local call prices in the near future' (Enquete-Kommission, 1998, 149). This was echoed by the statement of the SPD and Bündnis 90/ Die Grünen (Enquete-Kommission, 1998, 141–4).

3. 'Telekom weist die Vorwürfe des Kartellamts zurück. Wolf: Die Telefonpreise sind rechtswidrig genehmigt worden. Rexrodt will vermitteln', *Frankfurter Allgemeine Zeitung*, 9 February 1998.
4. 'Raisin-picking' allowed specialized telecommunications newcomers to prosper. They managed to reduce the market share of the incumbent carriers in the lucrative segment of multinational clients with large volumes of data flow. Up to one-quarter of total expenditures of internationally operating financial institutions went to telecommunications services (Welfens and Graack, 1996, 29). In this case, scale weighed against the incumbent carriers, while new, specialized challengers built only where necessary. One of the best known entrants was Metropolitan Fibre Systems (MFS). Started in 1987, the company built fibre rings in major financial centres including New York, London and Frankfurt. It was allowed to operate in Frankfurt even before liberalization from September 1995 due to a special agreement with the City of Frankfurt (Gerpott, 1998, 276). MFS has since been acquired by WorldCom for US$14 billion (in August 1996), whose ambition it was to become the leading communications provider for multinational enterprises. Others followed the lead of MFS, such as COLT, City of London Telecommunications. Refer to the excellent interview with Paul Chisholm, CEO of COLT in the trade publication *Global Telecoms Business*. 'COLT: Building its Capital in Europe's Business Centres,' *Global Telecoms Business*, July/August 1998, 14–20. See also Beth Gage and Christine Heckart, 'Telecoms Players Go Down Evolutionary Path', *Global Telecoms Business*, April 1998, 36–8. The barriers to entry were low in this market segment and the new challengers vigorously competed among themselves.
5. MacKie-Mason and Varian explained the cost advantage of packet-switched networks compared to circuit-switched networks masterfully: '[With circuit-switching,] a fixed share of network resources is reserved for the call, and no other call can use those resources until the original connection is closed. This means that a long silence between two teenagers uses the same resources as an active negotiation between two fast-talking lawyers' (MacKie-Mason and Varian, 1998, 33).
6. Andy Zimmerman examined how Christensen's arguments applied to the telecommunications industry in the late 1990s, faced by internet technologies. Andy Zimmerman, 'The Innovator's Dilemma: Will "Bad" Technologies Win?' *Global Telecoms Business*, November/December 1998, 44–7. See also: Tony Jackson, 'Book Review: Bad Ideas That Win Markets', *Financial Times*, 14 November 1997, 12.
7. A Level3 executive cited in Oliver Roberts and Robert Samuelson, 'How Refrigerators Will Surf the Net', *Global Telecoms Business*, May 1999, 44.
8. Xlink was acquired by KPNQwest, a joint venture between Qwest and Royal KPN, Uunet by MCI WorldCom, DPN by the US venture capital-financed company Via Net Works and Nacamar by Netherlands-based World Online (whose investors included the Sandoz Family and Intel). World Online was later subject to an insider trading scandal. The German concerns Bertelsmann and Debis co-owned the data networking specialist Mediaways over which AOL Germany was run (for the most comprehensive summary, see Lux and Heinen, 1999).
9. During the first half of the 1990s, the initial response by the largest telecommunications firms to liberalization and the arrival of new competitors were global alliances. For example, WorldPartners, formed in 1993, comprised of AT&T, KDD (Japan) and Singapore Telecom. That same year, British Telecom (BT) and MCI agreed to ally as Concert. Deutsche Telekom's group, first called Phoenix, then Global One, was an alliance between France Télécom and Sprint, the third-largest US long-distance carrier. Neither of the carriers was allowed to enter the home market of the others. This restricted the possibilities for Deutsche Telekom to expand into the largest telecommunications market, the USA. Moreover, Global One was not a success. Deutsche Telekom sold its stake to France Telekom in January 2000. Nicole Harris, 'Partner's Rift Spurs Concerns for Global One', *Wall Street Journal Europe*, 10–11 September 1999, 3. For details on Global One see Gerpott (1998, 225–9). Other alliances, such as WorldPartners, fared a little better, but did not reach expectations. WorldPartners was also unravelled. Cooperation between BT and AT&T was being explored from the Summer of 1998.

Although BT and AT&T stated then that they did not plan to merge, BT's Concert would be integrated into the new cooperation and the partners would base their new alliance on common design standards and tighter network integration. Alan Cane, 'WorldPartners and Unisource to be Unravelled', *Financial Times*, 27 July 1999, 27. See also on the same page: Tracy Corrigan, 'Deal with BT Completes Reformation of Once-lagging AT&T' and Alan Cane, 'Seeds Sown Over Dinner Table'.

10. For a study in the German language on globalization and telecommunications focusing on Deutsche Telekom, see Paterna (1996).

11. MCI owned internet backbone providers previous to the acquisition by WorldCom. WorldCom had also bought IP-based networking businesses, especially important was that of CompuServe, which it acquired for US$1.2 billion in September 1997. See Richard Waters, 'A Bid Aimed at Domination', *Financial Times*, 3 October 1997, 26; Tony Jackson, 'Internet takes on the Phone', *Financial Times*, 2 October 1997, 21; Daniel Bögler and William Lewis, 'Bid Backed up by Strong Share Price', *Financial Times*, 2 October 1997, 28. The hold MCI-WorldCom had over the worldwide data network structure triggered a response by the European Union, which asked the carrier to divest part of its internet holdings.

12. AT&T, which was excluded from local access in 1982 ('Modification of Final Judgement'), could again engage itself locally thanks to the Telecommunications Act of 1996. It did so by buying cable TV networks, such as TCI in 1998 (for US$59.4 billion). See the background article by Richard Waters and Alan Cane on Telecommunications mergers and acquisitions: 'Making Connections,' *Financial Times*, 26 April 1999, 21. Its long-distance competitor Sprint also provided local broadband access. Sprint began piloting a new broadband internet service called ION in mid-1998 (with the actual roll-out occurring throughout 1999). ION was paid for by volume (by bit), not by time metering. Furthermore, Sprint claimed that ION, which essentially meshed traditional with internet technologies, reduced its network costs by over 70 per cent. See Sprint 1998 Summary Annual Report, pages 20–25. Also see: Oliver Roberts and Robert Samuelson, 'How Refrigerators Will Surf the Net', *Global Telecoms Business*, May 1999, 43, 44; Randall Hancock and Charles Gerlach, 'IP Revolution Transforming the Global Telecoms Industry', *Global Telecoms Business*, June 1998, 42. For a general discussion of Sprint see Gerpott (1998, 145–7).

13. Phil Dwyer, a consultant with the research firm Jupiter Communications, stated in May 1999: 'Telephone usage is metered and that alone will continue to hold back the growth of online advertising, content and commerce ventures in Europe by inhibiting internet usage'. 'European Online Households Triple by 2003, But Usage Will Remain Low', Press Release, Jupiter Communications, London, 18 May 1999.

14. Chris Cherrington and Sapna Capoor, 'E-commerce and the Opportunities for Telcos', *Global Telecoms Business*, May 1999, 51.

15. Francis McInerney and Sean White, 'Are Telecoms Giants Suffering from Tunnel Vision?' *Global Telecoms Business*, December 1998/January 1999, 45.

16. For a summary of Gerpott's argument see Gerpott (1998, p. 189, especially also p. 211, for price comparisons see pp. 191–7). Also: 'Böses Erwachen', *Der Spiegel*, 8, 1999, 112–14.

17. English language Deutsche Telekom Annual Report 1998, p. 23 as well as Gerpott (1998, 187).

18. English language Deutsche Telekom Annual Report 1998, p. 23. See also Gerpott (1998, 102). The reduced employee base of Deutsche Telekom in 1998 was completely compensated for in the overall telecommunications industry by the hiring activity of new entrants (RegTP, 1999b, 5).

19. Deutsche Telekom's net revenue per employee in 1998: DM 390000 (in 1995: DM 305000), household connections per employee: 260 (in 1995: 183). In the number of household connections per employee (including ISDN connections) in 1998, it scored better than two very well-run incumbent operators: Royal KPN (258) and Telia (207). Source: Annual Reports. In net revenues per employee, DTAG lay in-between the positions of Royal KPN (DM 446000) and Telia (DM 356000). For 1995 estimates see Gerpott (1998, 188).

20. 'Interview: Das nenne ich Enteignung', *Focus*, 28, 1997, 202–4.
21. Vigorous competition existed in Germany among internet providers. This was documented by the two excellent overview books to the German internet provider market, Lux (1995) and Lux and Heinen (1997).
22. The OECD survey cited compared off-peak access prices based on 20 hours internet use in 1998. OECD (1999a, 187, for calculations details please see pp. 175–6).
23. For an excellent summary article which discussed many of the points mentioned in this chapter, refer to Michael Wilde, 'Überdreht, Wegezoll auf deutschen Infobahnen', *c't*, 12, 97, 86.
24. James Glave, 'Germans Plan Internet Strike', Wired News, http://www.wired.com/, 1 October 1998; Tilman Baumgärtel, 'Internet-Streikwelle in Deutschland baut sich auf', Telepolis, http://www.heise.de/tp/, 2 October 1998.
25. It was unusual for local call prices to rise before liberalization of a telecommunications market. Local call prices rose in Britain, for example (Gerpott, 1998, 113). The incumbent usually wanted to reap the rewards in an area which would be addressed last by the competition. It also wanted to be able to start lowering its prices from a higher level rather than from an already low level. To defend this move, the incumbent usually argued that local call prices were subsidized to realize political objectives during the period of public ownership. In Germany, unification costs for a new phone system in East Germany made the issue more complex. In April 1991, a debate ensued whether a long-planned rise in local phone call rates should be increased further to compensate for these investments. Public opposition prevented this further rise and only the scheduled tariff changes came into effect (Robischon, 1999, 213–20). Finally, in 1996, in preparation for competition, Deutsche Telekom raised its local call prices substantially as part of a comprehensive tariff change. After an outcry that then already included internet users, Deutsche Telekom introduced CityPlus, a local call rebate, in January 1997 (which was improved slightly in May 1998). The relief for small firms and 'power' private users was minimal, however. The rebate could be acquired by paying a given fixed amount of money monthly, but a peak 50 per cent savings was achievable only at a usage of ten hours a month. Thereafter, the savings rate quickly fell; at 100 hours it amounted to only 5 per cent. Internet Site: 't-off Fakten zum Internet' compiled by Karl-Heinz Dittberner, Freie Universität Berlin. http://userpage.fu-berlin.de/~dittbern/Telekom/Internet_Facts.html. Accessed on 6 October 1998. In effect, local call prices were raised in 1996 in Germany and not lowered until 1999. For a useful table summarizing pricing developments in different tariff zones see Deutsche Telekom AG 20-F Form filed with the Securities and Exchange Commission, 15 April 1999, p. 28. See also p. 32.
26. In 1998, there were an estimated 3.2 million internet users in Germany who accessed the net an average of 19 hours a month (the rest of an estimated 6.9 million total users accessed the internet less frequently). This was the result of a representative survey carried out by G+J EMS in August 1998 ('3,2 Millionen Menschen täglich im Internet anzutreffen', G+J EMS, Press Release, 8 September 1998). EMS estimated that the most popular access times were between 09:00 and 12:00 and between 18:00 and 22:00 hours. For the first time slot, business rates would apply, for the second evening rates. For calculation purposes, I have assumed that every one of the 3.2 million users spent half of his time accessing the internet from his office computer during work hours and half at home in the evening. I assumed average use of 20 hours a month, ten from the office and ten from home. Some offices were connected to the internet via a local dial-up phone line provided by Deutsche Telekom, but others had a leased line connection. All home use, on the other hand, occurred over the local line of DTAG. If all internet access during office hours was made over leased lines and none over local phone lines, sales could be estimated to be DM 698 million (revenues would be generated only through home use). If all office calls were dial-up, DTAG would receive a total of DM 2557 million in revenues (including home use). Rates for business hour and evening use are obtained from the calculations of Karl-Heinz Dittberner (see Table 5.1). These estimates between DM 698 million and DM 2557 million applied only to internet access revenues generated for DTAG by local calls, not by internet provision via T-Online or selling leased line services.

Total sales associated with internet access therefore were probably much greater. Local call revenues through internet access solo would have accounted for somewhere in the range of 6 per cent to 21 per cent of total local call revenues and between 1 per cent and 4 per cent of the total net revenues of Deutsche Telekom (according to Annual Report 1999 of Deutsche Telekom in English language, pp. 15, 37, 112). T-Online calls accounted for about 6.5 per cent of all local call traffic, this figure can be found in the F-20 Form of Deutsche Telekom filed with the Securities and Exchange Commission 15 April 1999 on p. 54.

27. In 1995, Deutsche Telekom's debt-to-equity ratio of 15.4 per cent was below that of most international carriers (Gerpott, 1998, 180). To reduce debt, investments were cut from a level of around 40 per cent to 50 per cent of revenues to around 20 per cent of revenues. Only in 1996 did the investment level rise to 40 per cent of net revenues, before being lowered again the next year. 1996 was the year when proceeds from the initial share offering were realized, investments were paid for by the listing proceeds, not by resorting to further debts. By 1999, the debt problem was less severe than before, as shown in Figure 5.1.

28. Annual Report 1998 in English language: 'Networking Visions. Globalizing Action', p. 100.

29. Fixed-line revenues made up a 57 per cent of DTAG's total revenues 1998. Almost a third of fixed-line revenues were generated by local phone line service. But the fixed-line business was even more important for DTAG's profits. In 1998, an income of DM 9.4 million was generated in this business area compared to total income before taxes of DM 10.0 million. Although DTAG was successful in developing mobile telephony in Germany despite early competition (8.6 per cent of revenues), it did not fare well in its international acquisition strategy (3.7 per cent of revenues). Until its purchase of One-2-One mobile phone network in the UK enabled by a second offering in 1999, DTAG's only substantial investment of real value was in the Hungarian operator MATÁV. The MATÁV group included a mobile phone operator Westel 900. Global One was loss-making. Overall until 1999, DTAG was unsuccessful at developing new revenue streams; it was highly dependent upon its fixed-line business. English-language Annual Report 1998, pp. 60–62. See also the comment on Deutsche Telekom's international strategy in *The Economist*: 'European Telecoms in a Tangle', *The Economist*, 24 April 1999, 83.

30. Earnings in the first two quarters of 1999 slipped considerably due to reductions in long-distance prices and loss of market share. These results were announced in August 1999, the secondary placement was carried out earlier, in July 1999. Reductions in internet access prices through T-Online carried out in April 1999 had only a minimal effect on earnings reports for the first two quarters of 1999.

31. Author's translation from Glotz (2001, 226, 227, see also 230, 231).

32. Germany moved to a digitally switched network much slower than other European countries, for example, United Kingdom, France, Netherlands and Sweden (Welfens and Graak, 1996. See also Gerpott, 1998, 183). Digitization did not automatically mean better network quality; what it did mean, however, was that telecommunications carriers running a digitized network were gaining expertise in computer-based systems. Deutsche Telekom was late at acquiring this know-how. The organizational structure of Deutsche Telekom was partly responsible for the fact that the carrier adhered to its traditional electromechanical technology base as long as possible. Compared with France Télécom and BT, the public predecessor to Deutsche Telekom, Deutsche Bundespost, was more decentralized and more process-oriented (Pospischil, 1993, 610, 611). Deutsche Bundespost was very late in moving towards an objective-led management structure and strong client focus. Client focus still seemed amiss in the new organizational structure of 1999, where a single board member was responsible for sales and no separation was made between business and private clients, as was commonplace in most other telecommunications carriers. This marked a return to DTAG's original universal sales approach of the beginning of the 1990s (Gerpott, 1998, 202, 203, 207). See also 'Telekom: Zaudern und Zögern', *Manager Magazin*, December 1997, 43–7. Deutsche Bundespost therefore

was described as a 'machine organization' (Mintzberg quoted by Pospischil, 1993, 610). It worked as a whole by standardizing its work processes, which were linked to a historical technological base. It is not surprising, therefore, that the Deutsche Telekom was late in building an internet-based data network backbone.

33. Nacamar began offering internet service in early 1995 with a leased line to the USA (Interview, 12 July 1999). Next to MAZ, Hamburg (provider since 1994), and Contrib.net, Berlin (started 1994), Nacamar was one of the first internet providers without links to the German DFN university network. The oldest German providers, which emerged out of DFN, were EUnet Deutschland and Xlink. The German EUnet was started in 1985 in the University of Dortmund. EUnet became part of Uunet. Xlink began offering internet provider services out of the University of Karlsruhe since the early 1980s. EUnet and Xlink were privatized in 1992 and 1993. These providers all owned backbone access in 1995, which they resold to dozens of internet presence providers (Lux, 1995, 24–6, 57–61; Lux and Heinen, 1997, 33).

34. 'x' is a variable denoting various types of DSL technologies, such as ADSL.

35. 'The adoption of ISDN may lock the system in to a distinct path of development favouring the centralized network, since future investments must also be compatible with interrelated components in the chosen system' (Davies, 1996, 1171).

36. Dr Ron Sommer, Vorstandsvorsitzender Deutsche Telekom, 'Auf den Weg ins online-Zeitalter. Tendenzen, Entwicklungen, Strategien aus Sicht der Deutschen Telekom', 'Redemanuskript anläßlich des Internationalen Presse Kolloquiums am 27. Januar 1999 in Frankfurt', could be found in the press release section of Deutsche Telekom's web site. Accessed 2 February 1999. The original read: 'Unser Ziel ist ehrgeizig: Wir wollen Deutschland zu der Online-Nation überhaupt machen.'

37. A large initial investment would be required to upgrade the coaxial network for two-way communication. Various estimates for the upgrade investment exist, the highest being DM 5 billion over five years. 'German cable: Telekomplicated', *The Economist*, 21 August 1999, 63. See also Glotz (2001, 191–202).

38. 'Neue Goldgrube', *Manager Magazin*, December 1997, 47.

39. '20 Milliarden-Preis für Telekom-Kabelnetz utopisch. Unabhängige Produktgestaltung der Käufer nicht sicher', Press Release, ANGA, 11 March 1999. Was accessed on http://www.anga.de/

40. Dusan Zivadinovic, 'Auf der Bremse: Telekom verzögert den Ausbau ihres TV-Kabelnetzes', *c't*, Heft 8, 1997, 115.

41. By 1999, Bertelsmann decided to move away from pay-television altogether by selling a large part of its stake in the pay-TV company Premiere. One Bertelsmann executive stated: 'The television world in Germany is really complicated. We will have more freedom and more flexibility on the internet'. 'Bertelsmann's Big Leap', *The Economist*, 24 August 1999, 90.

42. 'German Television: Karel's Service', *The Economist*, 30 May 1998, 88.

43. 'Interview: Das nenne ich Enteignung', *Focus*, 28, 1997, 202–4.

44. Lukas Weber, 'Im Netz verfangen. Digitale Kabelträume der Telekom', *Frankfurter Allgemeine Zeitung*, 22 May 1997, 17.

45. Ungerer was explaining why telecommunications operators with cable stakes (that is, Deutsche Telekom) would themselves feel the need to divest their cable TV holdings: 'A telco with cable in his portfolio finds it incredibly difficult to cannibalise his own operations in the telephone network. At the same time he cannot justify investments for developing rapidly the broadband capabilities of the telephone network, since he has a cable network for broadband distribution. This is a very unsatisfactory situation'. 'Ungerer: Levelling the Playing Field in Europe', *Global Telecoms Business*, December 1998/January 1999, 34.

46. The first regional unit sold (in February 2000) was Northrhine-Westphalia; here, DTAG retained a 45 per cent stake. Then, the Hessian network was sold in March 2000; DTAG retained 35 per cent ownership. Baden-Württemberg was sold in May 2000; DTAG retained 45 per cent.

47. '20 Milliarden-Preis für Telekom-Kabelnetz utopisch. Unabhängige Produktgestaltung

der Käufer nicht sicher', Press Release, ANGA, 11 March 1999. Was accessed on http://www.anga.de/

48. Jeremy Grant, 'Deutsche Telekom Keeps its Foot in the Door', *Financial Times*, 16 August 1999, 19.

49. Refer also to an article in *Tornado-Insider.com*. Niko Waesche, 'Germany Goes T-Online. The T-Online Renaissance Grips the German Internet', *Tornado-Insider.com*, 5, September 1999, 27, 28.

50. At year-end 1995, there were 965400 members in T-Online. Deutsche Telekom, Annual Report 1996, German language, pp. 30–31.

51. 'Der Markt für Online-Dienste Wird Neu Geordnet', *Frankfurter Allgemeine Zeitung*, 22 November 1995, page 23; 'EU-Kommission prüft Online-Kooperation', *Frankfurter Allgemeine Zeitung*, 7 December 1995, 18. A statement on the intended partnership between AOL and T-Online could be found in the English language Annual Report 1995 of Deutsche Telekom on a central spread labelled 'The Forum.' Here, Bertelsmann executive Thomas Middelhoff was quoted referring to AOL as 'experience-oriented' and T-Online as 'benefit oriented'.

52. Only a few months after Microsoft had launched the proprietary online service Microsoft Network (MSN), the software giant decided to cannibalize its own service in favour of its free software product, Internet Explorer. For commentary see Yoffie and Cusumano (1999, 76, 80).

53. 1&1 was renamed United Internet.

54. As of 31 December 1999, the microbilling option of T-Online over the telephone invoice was discontinued by T-Online itself. Why stop a service that proved to be a competitive advantage? Jürgen Grützner, a press speaker for the association of Deutsche Telekom's competitors, VATM, speculated that this termination was a pre-emptive move designed to prevent the German regulator from stipulating that DTAG would have to offer the same service to its competitors – as it did, for example, with the rebate offered T-Online for the use of its new internet backbone (Interview, 14 July 1999). With 3.2 million users in 1999 and rising, T-Online seemed to be strong enough to do without its link to the phone service.

55. In a trade publication, a telecommunications consultant noted that the true expertise of a telecommunications operator was in finding prices for new services which reflected the value a customer placed on it and not the cost of offering it. For many years, US telephone companies were able to charge an additional fee for touch-tone dialling although the service actually meant net savings for the companies that offered it. Andy Zimmerman, 'The Innovator's Dilemma: Will "Bad" Technologies Win?' *Global Telecoms Business*, November/December 1998, 44.

56. 'T-Online und drei große Konkurrenten', Table in *Frankfurter Allgemeine Zeitung*, 20 January 1996, T2.

57. 'T-Online jetzt mit über 3.3 Millionen Kunden', Press Release, Deutsche Telekom, 7 July 1999.

58. 'T-Online jetzt mehr als 6 Millionen Kunden', Press Release, T-Online, 27 July 2000.

59. Because it intended to give as many new competitors as possible entry to the market for telecommunication services, the German regulator was set relatively low interconnection prices to allow call-by-call competition. Call-by-call service was when a user selected to use a different telephony provider than the Deutsche Telekom by dialling an initial code before each call. Obviously, telecommunications competitors still argued that some interconnection prices were high. Yet, the regulators undercut the proposals made by Deutsche Telekom and also allowed a large number of new competitors to start offering their services. Competition first focused on the long-distance market, because it sported high margins. In long-distance telephony, Deutsche Telekom purportedly lost around 30 per cent of its market share within the first year of liberalization, a statistic that was unmatched by previous liberalization efforts in the US and the United Kingdom. But interconnection could be used not only to offer long-distance telephony, but also internet access. Because prices tumbled steadily in the long-distance segment, the first call-by-call internet services were introduced in Autumn 1998. These new pricing schemes undercut

the prices that Deutsche Telekom charged subscribers of its own T-Online service. The interconnection fee was metered fee – this was important because it effectively prevented companies providing internet-by-call services from offering other fee structures. This fee represented an effective 'bottom line', below which prices could not sink unless the service company is to face constant losses. For interconnection pricing policy, see Gerpott (1998, 84, 85).

60. The German regulator, which had to sanction all new pricing schemes of the incumbent, allowed the new offering, provided Deutsche Telekom announce it as '3 plus 3 Pfennige' representing the local call and T-Online use. Although this seemed to represent a step backwards by returning to a separate local call fee structure, this was not the case, because 3 pfennigs as a constant rate vastly undercut a local call price made during business hours. This move by RegTPs was intended as a transparency obligation on the incumbent. It was combined with the obligation that Deutsche Telekom hand the same rebate it offered T-Online for the use of it internet backbone to internet service providers renting the backbone from DTAG.

61. See also the editorial in the *Frankfurter Allgemeine Zeitung*: 'Schlagaustausch Online', *Frankfurter Allgemeine Zeitung*, 27 August 1999, 22.

62. The trade publication *Global Telecoms Business* stated that Deutsche Telekom was increasingly being perceived as a bad loser due to the 'alacrity with which it has turned to litigation', *Global Telecoms Business*, 'Yearbook 1998/1999,' p. 49.

63. Gerpott (1998, 78–80, for issue location of interconnection nodes see 86–7, overview chart 66).

64. In January and February 1999, RegTP accepted some of DTAGs arguments and stipulated a rental price of DM 25.40 a month, which represented a rise from a provisional price of DM 20.65 set in March 1998. Deutsche Telekom demanded DM 37.30 a month, whereas competitors desired a price between DM 15 and 16. In addition, Deutsche Telekom charged one-time switching costs of between DM 200 to 340 per client. Germany was the first European country that allowed entrants the right to unbundled access. Deutsche Telekom AG F-20 Form filed with the Securities and Exchange Commission,15 April 1999. pp. 18, 19. See also pages 32 to 34, containing summaries of legal proceedings. Compare to Gerpott (1998, 78, 79, 86); and 'Druck der Politik zeigt Wirkung: Anschlußmiete für Telekom-Mitbewerber auf 25,40 Markt heraufgesetzt', Press Release, VATM, 8 February 1999.

65. 'A Bad Telecoms Merger', *The Economist*, 24 April 1999, 19. See also: 'Launching Deutsche Telekom', *The Economist*, 26 October 1996, 105–6.

66. 'Telekom soll bei Verzug Entschädigung zahlen', *Süddeutsche Zeitung*, 13 February 2002, 21.

67. As a result, apart from local exceptions, first flat-rate offers were introduced in Germany through DTAG's competitors only slowly from the end of 1999 onwards. The number of providers making flat-rate offerings increased from one in October 1999 to ten in June 2000 and the lowest monthly all-inclusive rental price fell from DM 249 to DM 77 (RegTP, 2000, 32). And, in Spring 2000, Deutsche Telekom itself distanced itself from its metered regime and also offered flat-rate access to T-Online. As a consequence, 200000 new subscribers joined the service. 'T-Online jetzt mit mehr als 6 Millionen Kunden', Press Release, T-Online, 27 July 2000. Several of the new flat-rate offers by the competition had to be withdrawn because they were uneconomical, however. The flat-rate of DTAG from Spring 2000 was attacked by the competition as a 'dumping price' and withdrawn a year later when RegTP stipulated that the same flat-rate wholesale offer DTAG made its own ISP for its network would have to be offered to the competition as well. A flat rate was then reintroduced for the DTAG's own DSL broadband service (see also Welfens and Jungmittag, 2002, 32, 64, 69).

68. Author's translation. Susanne Kerschner, 'Ortsnetz-Wettbewerb ausgebremst', *Funkschau*, June 1999, 67.

69. 'Köln Traumstadt für Surfer', *c't*, Heft 1 January 1998, 36.

70. Other investors in Mannesmann Arcor were AT&T, Unisource, Deutsche Bank and AirTouch. The Mannesmann group held the majority stake of this national carrier,

however (Gerpott, 1998, 269). It is important to note that the Postal Ministry granted the national energy conglomerates and the Bundesbahn the right to begin to market their trunk capacities already from July 1996, a privilege which provided these companies with a competitive head-start (Gerpott, 1998, 64, 65).

71. Between the national carriers, consolidation set in early. In fact, it began as soon as market liberalization was expected in Germany, around 1995, before the actual passing of the Telecommunications Law. The reasons for early consolidation were numerous (see also Gerpott, 1998, 286). Essentially, all of the energy conglomerates 'plus two' vied for the same asset: a national backbone network which could offer fixed-line telephony initially to large businesses and then to homes and small businesses. The second step was originally viewed as being dependent upon the promise of the 'wireless local loop', a technology that took longer to develop for commercial use than expected. When the promise of the wireless local loop moved further and further into the future, the market possibilities shrunk. In addition, all national players financed their investments from earnings derived from other sectors and not through spin-offs onto capital markets. This reinforced risk-averse behaviour. Ambitious returns on investments were expected at an early stage (in the case of Mannesmann, the return on assets was expected to be 15 per cent in the year 2000. Ralph Atkins, 'Muscular Manager of Tubes and Telecoms', *Financial Times*, 26 July 1999, 10.) In the beginning, RWE Telliance and Veba Telecom got together to form o.tel.o Communications, a telecommunications joint venture. Mannesmann managed to form a partnership with DBKom, the railways subsidiary, launching Mannesmann Arcor. VIAG Interkom remained solo and focused on developing the wireless local loop and mobile communications, but not after a series of unsuccessful partnerships with international and domestic players. In the first year of liberalization, o.tel.o encountered problems (aggravated by a late start) and was bought by Mannesmann in April 1999 for US$ 1.24 billion. On late start: Gabriele Kalt, 'Bisher funktionieren meist nur die Servicenummern', *Frankfurter Allgemeine Zeitung*, 17 January 1998, page 13. On o.tel.o acquisition: Ralph Atkins, 'Mannesmann to keep o.tel.o Brand Separate', *Financial Times*, 7 April 1999, 28.

72. In 1999, this already started to change, however. A listing of KPNQwest, a joint venture between Royal KPN and Qwest was announced in August 1999. Proceeds from the issue were to finance an expansion of its internet-based fibre-optic network across 39 European cities. Gordon Cramb, 'KPN Plans Mobile Phone and Data IPOs,' *Financial Times*, 31 August 1999, 19.

73. Since the share price low-point in Autumn 1998 up to Autumn of 1999, continental European and German industrial blue chips have matched the growth of US blue chips. The Dow rose about 45 per cent from its low point and the Dow Jones Euro Stoxx 50 Index rose about 58 per cent (from 2986 on 8 October 1998 to 4714 on 31 August 1998). Euro Stoxx 50 tracked 50 major shares in the European Union. The rise of the German DAX approximately matched that of the Dow. Out of synch was the UK FTSE 100, which rose only 26 per cent in the period under examination. Yet, all European markets started on overall lower price levels compared to the USA. The price–earnings multiple of the Dow was 34 times, compared to 28 times of the FTSE and 25 times of Euro Stoxx 50 (in August 1999). See Peter John, 'Internet Explosion Leaves Footsie Out of Step With Surging Dow', *Financial Times*, 24 August 1999, 8 and Jörg Schreiweis, 'Noch Stehen die Börsenampeln auf Grün', *Frankfurter Allgemeine Zeitung*, 27 August 1999, 24. Euro Stoxx 50 historical data was obtained from the Stoxx web site: http://www.stoxx.com/ on 1 September 1999.

74. The reason cannot be examined in detail here. Part of the overall trend was to approach valuation of companies using future earnings estimates. Since current earnings and revenue of most New Economy companies was negative and negligible, future earnings and revenue estimates were calculated – based in large part on the number of users of the service ('customer ownership'). At the time, a debate ensued between New Economy advocates embracing future-oriented valuations and those who pointed out the dangers of doing so. In most of 1990s Germany, this debate was much less pronounced, with many firms being valued according to current revenues and earnings and not according

to 'customer ownership.' This changed with the boom of the Neue Markt from 1998/1999 (Nacamar, Interview, 12 July 1999; Lux, Interview, 10 July 1999; DeTeCSM, Interview, 09 July 1999).

75.   'Wrong Numbers', *The Wall Street Journal*, 11 May 2001, 1, A6.
76.   NetCologne, founded in October 1994, was owned by the municipal utility company, but local savings banks (Sparkassen) had minority stakes.
77.   For a background article on Frankfurt and its efforts to compete as a financial centre against London see: 'Telekommunikation, ein wichtiger Standortfaktor für die Finanzplätze', *Frankfurter Allgemeine Zeitung*, 22 February 1996, 15.
78.   Wernhard Möschel, 'Der Staat auf dem Rückzug', *Frankfurter Allgemeine Zeitung*, 30 May 1998, 15.
79.   'Telefon-Markt: Preisbrecher in Panik', *Focus*, 26, 1999, 200–204.
80.   Competition raged over national trunk lines, with MobilCom bidding for the o.tel.o network early in 1999 but loosing out to Mannesmann. MobilCom was prepared to spend about DM 300 million to DM 500 million on a fixed fibre-optical backbone network. Ralph Atkins and Alan Cane, 'MobilCom Plans to Add Fibre to Low-Cost Diet', *Financial Times*, 28 April 1999, 40. In July 1999, MobilCom was able to secure a long-term exclusive lease of the national trunk network of GasLINE, a telco subsidiary of a gas supplier based in Essen. This put MobilCom in a much better position to offer innovative internet services in Germany. 'Huge Cost Savings Via Optic-Fibre Network/ Significant Capacity Increases/ Large Reduction in Interconnection Costs', MobilCom Press Release, 15 July 1999 (from the web site http://www.mobilcom.de/).
81.   'Arcor steigt in das Geschäft mit ISDN-Anschlüssen ein', *Frankfurter Allgemeine Zeitung*, 27 August 1999, 16.
82.   (1) Over Deutsche Telekom's own internet service provider T-Online, (2) over internet-by-call offers based on interconnection agreements with Deutsche Telekom, or (3) through a phone call to a local dial-in point.
83.   Deutsche Telekom's ability to impose metered access in Germany and the detrimental effect this had on the development of the economy was the theme of a short editorial in a German business daily: 'Schlagaustausch online', *Frankfurter Allgemeine Zeitung*, 27 August 1999, 22.
84.   Press release of Regulierungsbehörde für Telekommunikation und Post (RegTP), 'Deutsche Telekom muss ab 1. February 2001 Flatrate als Vorprodukt anbieten', Bonn, 16 November 2000.
85.   Arbitrage between the regulator, DTAG and the competition then focused on a technical issue, namely in the way the competitors' networks would be connected to the DTAG network. Again this development was foreshadowed by an Oftel decision in the UK from February 2001, which revised its original FRIACO to include a more optimal network access structure for the competition (Single Tandem Flat Rate Internet Access Call Origination).
86.   David S. Isenberg, 'Broadband Smorgasbord. Start-up launches 10-megabit to the home service on Sweden's fibre infrastructure'. Dated 1 November 1999, from the web site Isen.com, 'Intelligence at the Edge #16.' See also OECD (2001b, 39, 40) and the web site of the Stockholm utility http://www.stokab.se/.

6. Survey of internet entrepreneurship in Germany

When this research in uneven internet development was initiated in late 1997, very little was known about internet entrepreneurship in countries other than in the United States. There, entrepreneurs already had been pursuing internet opportunities for around two years.[1] In other countries, however, including Germany, remarkably little information existed on internet start-up companies, indeed, one was justified in wondering whether there were entrepreneurs pursuing internet opportunities at all. Only a handful of internet ventures had entered media awareness, and most of these were not started as internet firms and had refocused on the internet only later.[2] Only a single German company had carried out a public offering at the time of the survey which could be labelled an internet company.[3] Yet, practitioners in touch with the computer and software communities nevertheless suggested that an entrepreneurial wave associated with the internet opportunity had long been brewing in Germany. Some emphasized that German entrepreneurs had begun to address the internet opportunity as early as their US counterparts. An entrepreneurial wave seemed evident only at the end of the 1990s. At this time, the new German alternative stock exchange, the Neuer Markt, listed significant numbers of German internet ventures. The landscape seemed transformed and a revolution in internet entrepreneurship seemed under way in Germany.

Yet, the companies listed on the Neuer Markt as internet ventures were not necessarily representative of internet entrepreneurship in Germany. The stock segment was dominated by web developers and other types of consultants. Numerous ISPs had also been listed. Relatively few 'pure play' portal players or electronic commerce firms could be found on the Frankfurt exchange. One possible explanation was that web developers and ISPs had an advantage in the selection process of the financial industry because these were companies which were able to achieve relatively high revenue figures and employee numbers. To gain a more consistent picture of internet entrepreneurship in Germany, it was crucial also to have alternative data sources which were not the result of a selection process by the financial community. An important aspect of this study, therefore, is the presentation of collection of empirical data about internet venturing in

Germany. The survey presented here was carried out in Spring of 1998. This early date was useful in two respects: firstly, it pre-dated the most extreme manifestation of the stock market bubble, which was especially severe in Germany. The companies, therefore, were first generation internet ventures. Secondly, it allowed a direct comparison of German ventures with the first generation of US internet start-ups. Interestingly, this data source shows that the selection process of the Frankfurt exchange was not as distorting as one might suppose. Even in this survey from the Spring of 1998, the number of 'pure play' portal players or electronic commerce firms was very low.

The rationale for a survey, however, was not only to generate numerical data. The main reason, in fact, was to help locate entrepreneurs who could be interviewed. It was apparent that, in order to gain an understanding of the specific challenges faced by internet entrepreneurs in Germany at the time, conversations with decision-makers in a few high-profile, successful companies would not suffice. In the course of the survey, 18 founders of German internet firms were interviewed in person. Venture capitalists and persons from the academic and research community were also interviewed. This material proved invaluable in identifying the main challenges internet entrepreneurs faced in Germany at the time. It also was a crucial guide for formulating guiding concepts, which were later addressed in further interviews with internet founders in different European countries (Chapter 7).

One of the specific challenges faced while carrying out the survey was the fact that no representative list of internet firms existed which could be used as a starting point. The conventional statistical categories 'computer', 'software' or 'telecommunications' were at once too broad, because they included companies not involved in internet opportunities, and also too narrow, because they ignored internet firms focused on a diverse range of industries.[4] This forced the author to find alternative means to locate internet entrepreneurs; the path chosen was a widely marketed start-up 'contest'. This contest was conduced at a time when the internet was just beginning to gain visibility as a US phenomenon. Sufficient public interest already existed, but it was not yet subject to 'hype overdose'. For this reason, the timing was good. The survey was carried out in cooperation with a leading business publication and one of the most frequently visited web sites in Germany. It attracted significant interest and 140 firms signed up on the survey's dedicated internet site; of these, 123 met the criteria for an internet start-up. For more information about the procedure please refer to Appendix A at the back of this volume. Due to the publicity and positive response, it can be assumed, therefore, that a broad segment of internet entrepreneurs was aware of the survey and participated. A valuable pool of data was produced which is discussed in this chapter. Venture capitalists and other experts were later asked to confirm whether the data matched their current perceptions. It did. Nevertheless, due to the lack of a representative list, it was impossible to carry out the usual statistical tests for bias in the sample. The data presented here should, therefore, be viewed as complementary to the qualitative information gathered in the interviews and should not be used in isolation.

INTRODUCING THE TYPICAL GERMAN INTERNET VENTURE

The survey was comprised of data collected from 123 internet start-ups based in Germany. Of these, 23 firms were internet software companies. Examples of internet software were systems enabling electronic commerce, online publishing, knowledge management and financial transactions. The clients of these software start-ups were mostly firms offering services on the internet or building internal corporate services. An example of a software start-up was the COIN Corporate Interactive AG, a firm with 23 employees at the time, founded in Hannover in 1997. It developed internet-based corporate business process software for insurance companies and other firms involved in repetitious data processing tasks.

The most popular firm type were web development agencies, and 57 firms fit this classification. These ventures had deep knowledge of internet business, but worked primarily on a project-by-project basis for corporate clients. Companies in this group were new media agencies, which offered services such as web site design, consulting and development, and systems consultants, which carried out systems integration. Founders of web development agencies could be understood as 'evangelists' because much of their activity consisted in convincing others of the benefits of an involvement in internet and new media. Only a few adopted a high-growth path and were able to access venture capital financing.[5]

The third category was comprised of portal sites, electronic commerce ventures and business-to-business (B2B) internet exchanges, and 29 firms offered these types of internet services. They included companies involved in on-line retail services, content, services for the hotel and travel industry, information brokers and business-to-business platforms. They were the types of companies attracting media attention and very successfully raising venture capital in the United States. An example among the German survey participants was BPS, started in 1997 in Karlsruhe and at the time with 12 employees. The B2B purchasing platform connected SME fashion manufacturers to their clients, the boutiques.

The last group were 14 companies which did not fit into the previous three groups. Some of these were internet service providers (ISPs). They offered internet access for firms and individuals in a local area.

The data collected in the survey can be used to present the typical internet start-up at the time, see Figure 6.1.

THE VENTURE CAPITAL BOTTLENECK AND THE 'BALANCING ACT'

One immediate surprise in the survey was the apparently large proportion of venture capital-financed firms in Germany, 11 per cent. Although this may partially be accounted for due to the bias of the survey, the figure still stood out as an unlikely result.[6] It did not, for example, match the estimate by a German private equity research firm, Mackewicz & Partner. One of their publications at the time stated that 5 per cent of technology start-ups in Germany were successful in their search for a venture capitalist (VC). Nor did the 11 per cent figure correspond to anecdotal evidence about the difficulties of locating and convincing German VC financiers to invest in a

---

- The typical firm was 1.8 years old.
- It had 20 employees, of which six were freelance.
- It was highly likely (79%) to have been reinvesting profits to finance its growth.
- Yet, the managing founders also estimated that it would require DM 2.2 million of initial investment to jump-start high growth.
- The typical firm had a 11% chance to find a venture capital equity investor which would have provided this capital.
- It had a 5% chance of being funded through the federal Technologie-Beteiligungs-Gesellschaft (tbg).
- Had generated a turnover of DM 1 million in 1997.
- Expected a turnover of DM 3 million in 1998.
- Expected employee growth of 77% per annum.
- 52% of costs were employee costs, 15% were spent on hardware and software, 11% on telecommunications and internet access and 17% on marketing and PR.
- In the typical firm, a team of two company founders were active managing partners.

Figure 6.1   The typical German internet start-up in Spring 1998.

start-up, especially in the case of internet electronic commerce start-ups or web developers. At the time, German VCs had to act in a more risk-adverse way than their US counterparts, because the medium-term success of the alternative stock market in Frankfurt, the Neuer Markt, was not yet apparent.

In fact, the 11 per cent figure represents, more than anything else, the lack of understanding about VC financing in Germany at the time among entrepreneurs. Entrepreneurs may have thought they had venture capital financing when, in fact, they were referring to other, less supportive types of private equity finance. Some private equity firms in Germany (*Beteiligungskapitalgesellschaften*) were unable to offer the range of services, the depth of specialist know-how and breath of contacts which were associated with US-style venture capitalists.[7] For this reason, it was crucial to separate real VCs from other investor types in Germany which were mistakenly labelled VCs. The MBGs (*Mittelständische Beteiligungskapitalgesellschaften*), for example, were generally not active investors and not profit-oriented; they received only an interest rate payment return on their investment. These private equity investment funds were started in the 1970s and 1980s by business initiatives and local chambers of industry and commerce with state-level public support. The performance of the MBGs was confirmed to be under that of standard, profit-oriented venture capital firms. One research effort, furthermore, ascertained that the portfolio firms of MBGs indicated that they were dissatisfied with their investor (Kulicke and Wupperfeld, 1996, 220, 221; see also Kulicke, 1997c, 140–42). According to two different sources, there were only very few experienced and US-oriented venture capitalists in Germany at the time, and they formed a small subset of the total population of private equity investors (Wupperfeld, 1996, 248; Wupperfeld, 1997, 168; Freeman, 1998).

Indeed, from the data provided in the survey itself, there were indications that the 11 per cent figure was too high. We know, for example, that 5 per cent of all firms received financing through the Technologie-Beteiligungs-Gesellschaft (tbg). This percentage probably more accurately reflected the proportion of real VC-financed, high-growth firms in the sample (See Table 6.1). The tbg provided entrepreneurs with the possibility of raising public money only in combination with an investment by a recognized venture capitalist or a high-profile individual investor ('angel'). Like the similar Kreditanstalt für Wiederaufbau (KfW) program, the tbg co-venturing scheme actually lowered the risks for venture capital investors. Both the tbg and the KfW only worked together with venture capital firms they recognized as high-quality, profit-oriented investors. Of the firms that were supported through the tbg in combination with a recognized investor, the majority were software ventures. No web developers were financed through

Table 6.1   Forms of financing (%)

	All firms	Firms with VC financing	Firms with bank loans	Firms with tbg support
Reinvesting profits	79	43	88	33
Individuals	33	14	33	33
Bank loan	20	21	100	17
VC financing	11	100	13	83
State (*Land*) programme	8	21	17	17
Parent company	8	0	4	0
tbg support	5	36	4	100
Other	5	7	8	0
Federal program	4	21	8	17

Note: This table can also be found in Appendix A as Table A.3.

this means and very few portal and electronic commerce ventures (Appendix A, Table A.4). Venture capital was, in this early period of internet development, much more of a bottleneck in Germany than a cursory glance at the figures seems to indicate.

The most common form of growth financing for an internet start-up was by reinvesting profits, and 79 per cent of the companies included in the survey indicated that they financed their activities through what was often referred to as 'bootstrapping'. Indeed, self-financing of growth was the most common means of finance for all types of start-ups surveyed, including internet software firms and portal sites and electronic commerce start-ups and not just for web developers (see Appendix A, Table A.4). The need to generate the positive cash flow required for self-financing, however, represented a significant constraint to growth. Software companies had to carry out more project-by-project work for their clients and could not dedicate themselves to the same extent to scalable products. Web development companies were dependent upon organic growth and could not acquire other firms in their field to capture valuable know-how. Electronic commerce players, portals and other innovative internet start-ups were handicapped because they had to carry out cashflow positive activities 'on the side', such as systems integration or web development. In terms of management focus and resource allocation, this was an extremely difficult growth model to realize. The term 'mixed play' is introduced here to distinguish this growth model from that of 'pure play' US e-commerce of portal firms.

Moreover, a few German entrepreneurs preferred bootstrapping to giving up an equity stake to a venture capitalist.[8] Many software and consulting firms had in the past grown to be successful with this means of financing. The most successful German software firm, SAP, was also boot-strapped, and combined this with an early stock market listing. This pattern, bootstrapping and an early public offering without involvement by an early-stage venture capital fund, could be observed in several computer and internet companies listed on the Neuer Markt in 1998 and 1999. It reflected suspicion towards outside control in the company; a suspicion associated with the German *Mittelstand* tradition.[9] However, the survey indicated that most of the internet founders questioned did not subscribe to this view. In fact, an astounding proportion (73 per cent) of founders who embraced rapid growth also believed in the advantages of venture capital investment (Appendix A, Table A.28).

But, intentions diverged from reality in many cases. And the constraints of bootstrapping were obvious. One founder described these in the following way:

> We had to wait for one and a half years for our first pay cheques as partners. We paid our rents by working part-time for Novell. Our employees were, of course, always our first priority and we were very tight on liquidity.[10]

The survey results reflected this 'mixed play' balancing act of German internet start-ups trying to combine cashflow positive project-by-project work with their high-growth, scalable offerings. Only about 40 per cent of all selected firms generated most of their revenue (defined as 75 per cent or more) from products or scalable offerings. About one-quarter of all selected firms were complete hybrids, generating substantial income from both product as well as project work. As expected, tbg financed start-ups most closely matched the revenue streams one would expect from high-growth firms (see Table 6.2). One needs to keep in mind that the group of 30 selected firms represented the most promising high-growth category

Table 6.2   *Proportion of start-ups generating most of their sales from project work or product sales*

	All firms	% of total	tbg financed
Mostly project-by-project	10	35	0
Mostly product, scalable offerings (pure play)	12	41	3
Hybrids	7	24	1
	29	100	4

Note: The categories are defined in Appendix A, where the table appears as Table A.18.

among the survey participants. The task of web development was by nature project oriented. One clear result of the balancing act was that undercapitalized German internet start-ups could not address their specific area in the same vigour as a 'pure play' internet start-up could. Established media and telecommunications firms were not challenged by start-ups in the same way as they would have been if they had faced more 'pure-play' firms.

SLOW INTERNATIONALIZATION

A further result of the balancing act was the slow pace of internationalization of German internet start-ups in the second half of the 1990s. One of the original theses of the practitioner network thinkers, described in the introductory chapter, was that the global internet would enable small ventures to acquire and serve clients in other countries, whether businesses or consumers. Any small firm could use the network to become instantly global, ran the argument. Reality seems to have been a little different, with only a few exceptions.[11]

Among all firms surveyed, only 2 per cent of business customers were international clients and no consumers came from outside Germany (Appendix A, Table A.2). In a more detailed, second questionnaire handed only to internet software and internet electronic commerce firms, sales figures from countries outside of Germany were established. Two firms had a significant proportion of foreign sales, they derived over 90 per cent of revenues from abroad (see Table 6.3). However, most start-ups had only a

Table 6.3   Number of firms with given percentage of foreign sales

% foreign sales	Frequency	%
90–100	2	7
80–89	0	0
70–79	0	0
60–69	1	3
50–59	1	3
40–49	3	10
30–39	4	13
20–29	2	7
10–19	5	17
0–9	12	40
	30	100

Note: This table can also be found in Appendix A, as Table A.15.

small share of international revenues. The average of foreign sales was 21 per cent, the median was 10 per cent. It is important to remember here that the survey explicitly asked the most internationally active German internet firms to apply. Furthermore, the low internet penetration in the German market should have motivated firms to enter other countries more rapidly than, for example, in the United States, where the domestic internet market was already at that time relatively large. One company that targeted international markets from a early stage was the German internet software firm Intershop. But Intershop had the benefits of venture capital financing by a high-profile, internationally oriented investor; bootstrapped firms had to prepare their internationalization more carefully and had to move at a more gradual pace.

UNBALANCED DEMAND FOR INTERNET SERVICES

The two previous chapters focused on telecommunications deregulation in Germany and the laggard uptake of internet use among consumers. Business uptake was faster in Germany. As indicated in the previous chapters, some larger businesses received preferential treatment by the monopolist telecommunications operator, Deutsche Telekom. Leased line prices, which affected large business use of the internet, for example, were below those of many other countries. Evidence from management research shows that leading German firms were upgrading their computer networks as part of an effort to modernize their operations (Ruigrok et al., 1999, 52, 53). These were large German firms as well as exceptional *Mittelstand* (SME) companies. In general, internet adoption by these companies was much more rapid than among small businesses and consumers.[12] The massive costs of internet access among small firms and consumers resulted in an unbalanced uptake pattern in Germany which was highly unfavourable for internet start-ups.

As described in Chapter 2, the most advanced applications for the internet consisted in linking small businesses and consumers to each other and to larger firms in seamless business webs. It was this breakthrough which transformed the internet into a 'disruptive technology', to use a concept developed by Clayton M. Christensen (1997). In the 1980s and early 1990s, large firms had already begun to use the advantages of computer networks to exchange data among themselves. Yet, electronic data interchange (EDI) was expensive, and could not be used to link small businesses and consumers. With rapidly rising internet penetration among small firms and consumers in the United States, however, the benefits of lower transaction costs over networks could be extended, thereby creating wholly new opportunities. New ventures could exploit these opportunities first, because, in contrast to EDI efforts, large firms were not in control. Furthermore, the internet as a 'disruptive technology' linking small firms and consumers was not given full attention by large companies.

In those countries, however, where internet uptake lagged among small firms and consumers, such as Germany, the range of possible internet applications was much more limited and in many cases reduced to showcase projects. Demand for internet services was, therefore, clearly unbalanced in Germany; consumer demand was low while business demand was higher. In fact, one web development and systems integrator company founder advised internet entrepreneurs in Germany to examine advanced internet demand structures in the United States before developing their own ideas:

> To start an internet company, one should first secure DM 250 000 to have a year's worth of breathing space. Then one should head straight for the airport and catch a flight to San Francisco to collect ideas.[13]

Also for this reason, some firms such as Intershop maintained advanced technology groups in the USA while others insured transatlantic information flow through partnerships with other small firms.[14]

Unbalanced internet uptake in Germany and primitive internet demand structures were reflected in the survey results as well. The client base of internet start-ups in Germany in early 1998 consisted largely of business customers. Most of these business customers actually were technologically advanced *Mittelstand* companies. Over 70 per cent of sales to businesses were derived from the *Mittelstand*. Only a minority, 15 per cent, of internet start-ups targeted consumers (Appendix A, Table A.2). It is not wrong, therefore, to characterize the typical internet start-up in Germany in early 1998 as a firm carrying out project-by-project work for business customers while in parallel trying to experiment with new internet services. This was very different from the United States, where 604 'pure play' internet firms were financed in 1998 by venture capital to focus on specific high-growth opportunities.[15] The highest profile ventures such as Amazon.com, eBay and Yahoo! focused on where the internet was most 'disruptive': on extending the powers of the network to small firms and consumers.

TECHNOLOGY ENTHUSIASTS AND MANAGEMENT KNOW-HOW

The most common problem of new-technology based firms (NTBFs) emphasized by German-language literature was that technology know-how was not balanced with equally qualitative management know-how (Koschatzky, 1997, 1, 6; Pleschak, 1997a, 14, 15). The reason for this was that many founders started companies right out of university. In order for a NTBF to succeed, however, management know-how was considered crucial.

This observation cannot be directly confirmed with this survey of inter-net start-ups in Germany.[16] Barely any were founded right out of a science university. In fact, only one such start-up initiative was identified.[17] Several start-up initiatives, however, took shape while the founders were taking business courses at a German university. In fact, business courses were the most popular type of course founders had taken at university, followed by computer programming courses.[18] This evidence indicates that the typical internet entrepreneur in Germany was very different from the NTBF founder. NTBFs seemed to follow the traditional industrial strengths of Germany, areas such as precision tools and electronics. These were areas where the technological education system had its strengths.[19] The evidence also showed that, in general, the barriers to entry for internet ventures in the late 1990s were low in terms of know-how; very little specific techno-logical knowledge was necessary. As is discussed below, there were excep-tions to this rule, especially among software ventures developing artificial intelligence or encryption systems.

The most accurate characterization of internet founders in Germany in early 1998 was a multi-skilled person with a university, but non-science, background and with an enthusiasm for technology. The founders of the companies surveyed here counted among the very early users in Germany of consumer online networks. A significant proportion of founders, over 20 per cent, already encountered consumer network services before 1990, in this case the system of the German telecommunications operator, Btx (Appendix A, Table A.21). Very few of these early German internet entre-preneurs, however, had a strong international management background.[20]

The early founders, which could be most accurately be labelled technol-ogy enthusiasts with universal skills, need to be viewed as distinct from the programmers and engineers they hired. While the surveyed start-up com-panies are worked at 81 per cent of their potential capacity due to problems in finding personnel (Appendix A, Table A.19), this was a situation very much comparable to that in other countries, including the United States. However, loyalty among key technical personnel was better in Germany.[21]

In fact, some founders clearly indicated that availability of technical know-how was a locational advantage:

> There is no question that technical know-how is better in Germany than in the USA. The applicants are better, the quality is better. In the USA or the UK I require five engineers for the same task three carry out in Germany.[22]

Another relevant question was the existence of specialist know-how among German internet start-ups. In the late 1990s, two areas of specialist scientific knowledge found application and further development through the commercialization of the internet: software agents (classified here under 'knowledge management') and encryption systems. The first was a requirement for advanced search features across vast amounts of unstructured information and for such applications as intelligent brokers. The scientific origins of this technology lay in research in artificial intelligence, artificial life, neural networks and human–computer interaction. The best-known research programmes in this field were the Software Agents Group at MIT's Media Laboratory, the Artificial Intelligence Laboratory at the Free University of Brussels (VUB) and work carried out at the University of Cambridge. Among German internet start-ups, in this area of specialized technological know-how was under-represented when compared to a US sample (Appendix A, Table A.8, compare 'Knowledge management'). In fact, most well-known agent-technology firms were American and one, Autonomy Systems, was from the UK.

The second area of specialist knowledge, encryption systems, was necessary for confidentiality and authenticity of internet transactions, which were major requirements for conducting business and especially banking over the internet. Using these techniques, a sales contract sent over the internet could be 'signed', insuring its authenticity. Asymmetric encryption techniques, used on the internet, were pioneered in the United States in the 1970s, but research was embarked upon in numerous countries due to its affiliation with military research.

In this area, German internet firms were very well represented and seemed internationally competitive. They had ambitious strategies for international expansion. The origin of this strength could be traced to the national teletext service Btx which found its most popular expression in on-line banking applications. Most German banks offered on-line banking over Btx and several in the late 1990s began to transfer these services to the internet. Three of the companies interviewed in the course of this research, Brokat, ESD and Netlife, developed software for banks intending to offer on-line banking services over the internet. The issue of encryption, especially as an international standard, was a main issue of concern among founders of German internet start-ups (Appendix A, Table A.25).

Much effort was put into securing and extending this competitive advantage in Germany. A consensualist alliance between the banking industry and associations formed to develop the open on-line banking standard HBCI (Home Banking Computer Interface).[23] In order to promote both the use of encryption techniques as well as their development by German firms, the Federal Ministry of Education, Science, Research and Technology was instrumental in framing a multimedia and communications law in Germany, the Informations – und Kommunikationsdienste Gesetz (IuKDG). This law and its appendix relating to electronic signatures represented a framework for conducting legally binding electronic commerce. It also covered several other important areas such as responsibility over on-line content. It did not, however, address its own enforcement issues, which was a severe weakness.[24]

The comparison of the development of these two areas by German internet start-ups illustrated the concept of path dependence found within technological innovation and diffusion theory. The enthusiasm with which application of encryption technology was developed by internet start-ups could be contrasted to the difficulty in competing in an area where little research and development existed in the past, in agents technology and knowledge management systems. Apart from the specialist knowledge issues, general computer engineering know-how and management experience seemed readily available in Germany in the late 1990s. And the strong desire to embark upon a high-growth entrepreneurial experience was there.

WRONG COUNTRY, WRONG TIME

At the beginning of this chapter, the typical German internet start-up in 1998 was introduced: a 1.8 year-old company with 20 employees. The founders were seeking DM 2.2 million in venture capital. These technologically enthusiastic founders saw the opportunities of the internet and embraced rapid growth. DM 2.2 million was not a substantial amount compared to the money raised in the United States at that time.[25] Yet, it represented a lofty sum of money in a country and at a time when venture capital was just a trickle. Although the government-sponsored venture capital programmes mentioned in Chapter 4 were laudable and allowed a minimum level of activity to persist, they were not extensive enough to initiate rapid growth. The venture capital boom, which would occur in Germany later in that year fuelled by the Neuer Markt, had not reached the entrepreneurs yet. As a result, most entrepreneurs financed growth through positive cashflow.

It was also difficult for company founders to foresee that demand for internet access by consumers would shift into high gear in subsequent months. In early 1998, Germany was known for its laggard uptake among consumers, which was behind even the European average. The reasons for this have been described extensively in the two previous chapters. Those founders who expected rapid uptake in the future were nevertheless dependent upon generating income in the current market. For this reason, there were few alternatives to carrying out project work for business customers. This was highly problematic, because sophisticated internet applications at that time consisted in integrating consumers into new types of business transactions. Due to these constraints, the typical German internet start-up carried out project-by-project work to subsidize its more innovative ideas, often consumer-oriented, on the side. The game to play was a tough balancing act focused on generating cash which could be reinvested in innovative strategies. In order to realize their own ambitions, the internet founders were in the wrong country at the wrong time. They required better access to venture capital financing as well as more advanced domestic demand structures than were available in Germany in early 1998. In contrast, therefore, to the idealistic visions of network thinkers, domestic determinants did play a crucial role also for internet ventures addressing global opportunity. The most interesting finding, perhaps, of this empirical survey was that the resource allocation and strategy of German new internet ventures was considerably different from that of their US counterparts.

This survey of internet entrepreneurship in Germany was a single-country snapshot. It served to highlight the specific challenges faced by entrepreneurs. It is important now to extend the results of the data and place it in a comparative setting. The argument offered here needs to be strengthened by relating the findings back again to government policy and national institutional determinants. The conclusions arrived at in this chapter are contrasted with the experiences of other countries. In the next chapter, material from the whole period will be taken into consideration for other European countries.

NOTES

1. When referring to a date for the start of the internet boom, US commentators usually agree on the NASDAQ listing of the internet software company Netscape which occurred in August 1995. In the subsequent months after this listing dozens of companies were listed in the United States. Some of the highest profile internet companies were founded just prior to or shortly after the Netscape listing: Amazon.com was started in July 1995, eBay was founded in September 1995 and Yahoo! was transformed into a professional service during the course of 1994.
2. These were software security and encryption firms ESD Information Technology Entwicklungs GmbH (Dölzig, Leipzig), started in 1994, Utimaco Software AG (Oberursel, Frankfurt), founded 1983, and Brokat Systeme GmbH (Stuttgart), started

in 1994. Two companies focused on internet software, Intershop Communications (Burlingame and Jena), founded in 1992, and Blaxxun Interactive Group Munich, started in 1995 and supported by US venture capital. Two electronic commerce firms need also be mentioned, 1&1 Aktiengesellschaft, founded in 1988 as an online marketing service and ABC Bücherdienst GmbH, Telebuch, founded in 1991. Telebuch was later acquired by Amazon.com.

3.   The alternative stock exchange for high-growth firms, Neuer Markt, Frankfurt, was only launched in 1997 and listed (as of April 1998) seven firms belonging to one of the following industry groups: telecommunications, software, information technology and computer services. Only one of these, 1&1 Aktiengesellschaft & Co., had direct internet relevance; 1&1 was an on-line direct marketing specialist and an internet outsourcer. Intershop Communications AG, which developed internet software for electronic commerce, was listed in June 1998.

4.   One extremely valuable source of information would have been the list of companies co-financed by the Technologie-Beteiligungs-Gesellschaft (tbg), a federal programme promoting venture capital investment. To protect entrepreneurs, however, this data could only be accessed by researchers from a specific research institute. Such a list would have included almost all of the highest growth internet start-ups at the time, due to the selection process of the tbg and the popularity of the programme among venture capitalists. Recently, however, a private data source, a credit information service, has been opened for academic research (Harhoff and Steil, 1997).

5.   For more information regarding the role of the 'evangelists' in Germany and their motivations, see Waesche (1999a), as well as Waesche (2003).

6.   The survey explicitly called for leading companies in the internet arena. Venture capital firms were contacted and asked to notify their companies about the survey; therefore, it is very probable that more venture capital-financed firms participated than would have been representative of the start-up landscape as a whole.

7.   Thomas Hellmann and Manju Puri evaluated the financial strategies of a sample of around 100 Silicon Valley start-up companies. The panel data was originally collected from 1994 onwards as part of the Stanford Project on Emerging Companies (SPEC). On the basis of this and other data, Hellmann and Puri concluded that venture capital-backed firms tended to receive more funding and were more liable to change their CEO in an effort to professionalize (Hellmann and Puri, 1997). In another paper, they showed that firms following an innovator strategy were more likely to pursue venture capital financing in order to speed up their time to market. The securing of venture capital therefore seemed to be an important strategy among Silicon Valley firms racing to secure first-mover advantages (Hellmann and Puri, 1998).

8.   Interview with Netlife.

9.   The traditional German *Mittelstand* start-up model has been identified with the lone engineer intent on keeping exclusive, patriarchal control of his company until he could bequeath it to his siblings. This attitude still existed in the late 1990s and was called 'Herr im Hause' ('Master in his own house') or 'Blut, Scholle, Erbhof-Denken' ('Blood, earth, homestead mentality') (see, for example, Breuer, 1997, 326, 'Mentalitätsphänomen', Kulicke, 1997c, 130; Huhn, 1997, 86).

10.   USWeb InnoMate interview.

11.   One German firm did correspond in a textbook way to the network thinker's ideal. This company was an electronic commerce start-up selling airline tickets, TISS. The internet service compared up to 80 million airfares which were put to the disposal of its registered users. Travel Information Software Systems GmbH (TISS) was a global internet start-up company with a staff of two people based in Heilbronn, Germany. Astoundingly, only about one in ten of the bookings it referred originated in Germany; the majority were from the United States. Without a US sales office or any other physical presence on the other side of the Atlantic, TISS was responsible for referring flights with a total value of over EUR 5 million alone in the month of October 1998. But this start-up was unique in the German internet landscape. Rudi Weissmann and Dirk Trostmann started the TISS service in 1995. The founder's slogan was: 'Look big, keep

small'. This ideal was compromised later, however. In 1999, the company was venture capital financed, the founder left and expansion of the cost base was a result. TISS will be discussed again in the next chapter. Figures were provided on the TISS homepage: http://www.tiss.com/. A succinct, yet detailed article on TISS: Indra Büttner, 'Internethandel', *Econy, Business in Bewegung*, 4, December/January, 1998, 42, 43.

12. Early reports seemed to indicate that uptake among advanced small and medium-sized enterprises in Germany (the *Mittelstand*) was above the European average (European Commission DGXIII.A3, 1997, p. 26). Another source confirmed that SME uptake of information and communication technologies was higher in Germany than in other countries. The study credited trade associations, which provided information on information and communication technologies to 55 per cent of German firms (DTI, 1998, Executive Summary). These types of informational services were supplemented in 1997 by a one-time federal subsidy for SMEs for setting up an internet presence, a support scheme that was, incidentally, heavily oversubscribed. 1000 SMEs were provided with up to DM 4600 each for setting up their internet presence. Around 3000 companies applied for the subsidy administered by the 'Bundesamt für Wirtschaft', Eschborn ('Gewerbestraßen statt Gemischtwaren-Shopping', *Computerwoche*, 39, 1997, 67).

13. GFT interview.

14. The COIN Corporate Interactive partnership with Liquid Edge, New York City, for example (COIN interview).

15. In 1999, this figure grew to 1798 companies. 'Moneytree US Report Full Year and Q4 1999 Results', PricewaterhouseCoopers.

16. Nor could it be confirmed by examining the results of the first pilot programme for NTBFs, TOU. Marianne Kulicke et al. found that some entrepreneurs already had management know-how on founding and most could compensate for their deficits by learning on the job (Kulicke et al., 1993, 255).

17. They were not included in the survey because they had not founded their company by the time the data collection was completed. An interview was carried out, nevertheless (Verteilte Systeme).

18. The combination of different fields of know-how seems to have been very important for internet start-ups. Often, this was achieved by creating teams. Partners in both iXOS and Brokat emphasized the managing founder team. The teams approach was an important element in a speed management strategy (Interviews with Netlife (Claus Müller) iXOS, Brokat). In Silicon Valley, the teams approach was widespread. One survey from 1996, which examined human resource strategies, revealed that most firms were started with two founders, although there also were companies with three, four, five, six, seven, nine or even twelve founders. Among the German internet start-ups surveyed here, most firms had two founders as well, but there were fewer companies with three or four founders. The interview data on German start-ups, however, indicates the process of composing founder teams may have differed to that in Silicon Valley. The research just quoted from 1996 examined different models of employment relations. One of these models was the 'commitment model', a long-term attachment in which peer control, cultural fit and loyalty mattered. Family and friends were usually listed as key partners in the creation of the company. Among German internet start-ups, almost all founders interviewed had teamed up with friends, whereas less than 30 per cent of the Silicon Valley firms had chosen the 'commitment model'. For a short explanation of the different employment models see Baron et al. (1996a, 513). For family and friends among founding partners Baron et al. (1996b, 271).

19. This was confirmed by comparative empirical data on NTBFs in Germany, Sweden and the UK. In Germany, over half of all NTBFs were in the machine tools and precision instruments business, followed by electronics and chemicals–pharmaceuticals. Only about 3 per cent of all NTBFs were involved in computer technology. This was in strong contrast to Sweden and the UK, where electronics dominate, but where over 10 per cent of NTBFs were in computer technology (Licht and Nerlinger, 1997, 193–5).

20. Foreign founders and managers in Germany added international management experience to German teams. One example was the constellation of managers surrounding Fidelio,

a Munich-based hotel software firm which later helped spawn at least two internet firms, Serenata and NxN as well as a developer of software and hardware for the optometry industry and a call centre software firm. Fidelio was started in 1987 by an American, Keith Gruen, and two Germans, Dietmar Müller-Elmau and Dietrich von Boetticher. Vijay Sondhi, David Lehrer and Galen Bales, all of them Americans, Eric Fischer and Rick Spence, both British, and Rolf Schmiedke, Swiss, joined and left Fidelio at various stages. In 1997, Sondhi became CFO of a high-profile document management software company, iXOS. Recent immigrants to Germany have also been among internet firm founders, for example, Arvin Arora from COIN Interactive or Xuân Baldauf of Medium.Net. International experience was a very important criterion for VCs. For this reason, an experienced English software manager was placed at the helm of Hyperwave, a company specializing in intranet publishing.

21. Interviews with Netlife (Claus Müller) and Lars Heiden Jörg Füllenbach Realisationen.
22. GFT interview.
23. Positive uptake of HBCI by financial service-oriented internet start-ups was confirmed in the Brokat and ESD interviews.
24. Due to this weakness, the law could be ignored in one high-profile content responsibility case – in the case against Felix Somm carried out in Bavaria.
25. Venture capital-financed internet companies in Silicon Valley received on average US$6 million each in the fourth quarter of 1997 ('A Telling Statistic: Average Investment up 50 per cent, *San Jose Mercury News*, 14 February 1998, from the web page http://www.sjmercury.com/).

7. Varieties of internet venture development in Europe: The Swedish case

The countries of Europe provide an excellent sounding board for hypotheses of uneven internet development. This is because a direct comparison between Europe and the USA would need to take into account several country-specific variables next to telecommunications liberalization, such as taxation, legal and other conditions for entrepreneurship and equity investing. One would need to, furthermore, understand the effect of region-specific variables such as the dynamics of Silicon Valley and its venture capital community (Kenney, 2000b). A further important distinction between the United States and Europe was the size of the home market and the persisting difficulties and costs of cross-European business at the time, which were not limited to differing languages and multiple currencies. In contrast, when conditions for internet entrepreneurship are compared across the countries of Europe, significant differences existed only in terms of telecommunications liberalization and its impact on the local loop. Regarding the other country-specific and region-specific factors such as the availability of venture capital; deficits were the norm in Europe. Until the late 1990s, when the situation was transformed, European start-ups with new internet business models were in general not financed by venture capitalists. Exceptions were internet software developers and Internet Service Providers (ISPs). Furthermore, the low barriers to entry associated with the internet and its horizontal applicability meant that the usual set of national innovation criteria pertaining to the educational system did not apply.

In this chapter, learning from the German case will be extended to other European countries, to explore the 'refraction' effect in other local environments. Unfortunately, it was not possible to delve into the level of detail presented for Germany. It was also not possible to extend the quantitative survey into other countries. Nevertheless, the information available about the development of internet ventures in other countries permitted testing of the concepts derived from the German case in different environments. This comparative section was also useful to gain further understanding about the German case itself.

The country of greatest interest for the purposes of this study was Sweden. In contrast to Germany, Sweden was a European country with a high internet penetration already in 1998. In that year, 27 per cent of Swedes were internet users; this figure was roughly comparable to the proportion of internet users in the United States. Finland, although it had the highest internet penetration in the world at the time, had a very small population of 5 million and therefore was not selected. In order to adjust for the effect of country size, data on a European country roughly comparable to Germany and another roughly comparable to Sweden also was included. Although smaller than Germany in terms of population, France was useful for comparative purposes. Much was known about the development of online services in France, through the prevalence of Minitel. The French Minitel experience has already been referred to several times in this study. As a counterpart to Sweden, Holland was selected, although slightly larger in terms of population. Since it was often stated in the early days of internet development that native English-speaking populations would have a higher interest in subscribing to internet services, the United Kingdom was excluded from the group of non-English language countries under comparison here.[1]

While internet ventures throughout Europe shared a common fate of eventual oblivion, Swedish enterprise structures differed considerably. These differences were especially severe among first generation internet ventures founded in the period from 1995 to 1998. After 1998, the venture capital glut and improved conditions of internet access in the local loop eradicated most structural differences among European internet ventures. Ironically, however, it was the first generation which could have had sufficient time to grow and take advantage of the fortuitous development of the financial markets before the downturn in March 2000. The financial opportunity was especially promising for German internet ventures, which took advantage of the surprising initial success of the new Frankfurt stock exchange, started in 1997.

A disclaimer needs to be extended to the reader. With the exception of Germany, continental Europe was populated mostly by privately-held internet start-ups. Public information on quoted companies obviously was much more easily accessed, more reliable and better to compare than what was available on private firms. Many of the private companies disappeared after the turn of the decade, leaving few traces. Much of this discussion has been based on contemporary news items, analyst reports prepared by investment banks and interviews with entrepreneurs, venture capitalists, policy-makers and experts. Very little of this information was directly comparative. For this reason, a variety of different data was collected. Each of the indications alone would be insufficient, but together, they form a picture which documents internet development in Europe in the second half of the 1990s.

In the first section of this chapter, main comparative aspects of the political economy of Sweden are mentioned. By the early 1990s, both Sweden and Germany were engaged in efforts to reform their respective models. Yet, relative to other European countries, both started late. Differences between the countries existed in the path of the specific reform projects; one such difference is discussed in the third section on comparative telecommunications liberalization. In the second section of this chapter, differences in internet access will be examined in Europe in the period up to 1998. Laggard development in Germany is contrasted to high levels of access in Sweden. In the third section, explanations are supplied for differences in internet access described in the previous section. The timing and sequence of telecommunications liberalization in Sweden and Germany is discussed here. In the fourth section, the venture capital bottleneck throughout Europe is described. Other country-level factors relevant to the development of new ventures are briefly mentioned in the subsequent section. The actual development of first generation internet ventures in the two case countries, as well as in France and the Netherlands, is sketched out in section six. As has already been mentioned, only broad stroke differences are accounted for. To make comparisons possible, a classification of internet venture types is introduced. The final section before the conclusions moves forward in time to briefly discuss the rise and fall of the second generation of internet ventures, which appeared in Europe after 1998.

INSTITUTIONAL REFORM IN SWEDEN

The 1990s were a difficult decade for Europe, economically as well as socially. Of course this was, to a degree, a perception caused by the apparent success of the United States economy, especially in the second half of the 1990s, when low unemployment was combined in America with low consumer price inflation and high growth rates. The troubles in Europe were nevertheless real, and included high unemployment rates, government deficits in some countries as well as an overburdened health and social security system. Please refer to Table 7.1 for relevant details. Add to these difficulties those factors which Eurosceptics have grouped together under the term 'Eurosclerosis', manifested in inflexible labour regulations and outdated tax laws. Although all the European countries examined in this chapter shared these problems to a certain extent, they encountered the full weight of these burdens at different times.

Most European countries did very well in the 1950s and 1960s. In each

Table 7.1   Macroeconomic indicators, end 1997

	GDP (US$ Bn)	Inflation (1998)	Population (M)	Average annual growth in real GDP 1990–97 (%)	Unemployment rate (%)
USA	7783	1.6%	272	3.0	5
Germany	2321	1.0%	82	1.4	10
France	1542	0.7%	59	1.3	12
Netherlands	403	2.0%	16	2.4	6
Sweden	232	−0.1%	9	0.9	8

Source: The Economist, *Pocket World in Figures 2000*, London, 1999 (in association with Profile Books).

case, credit was given to a country-specific social and economic model. Whether these models were indeed the reason for each country's growth is subject to intense debate; for a complete analysis, one would have to also examine factors external to these domestic models such as the development of world trade. In addition, some scholars argue that growth was caused by domestic factors very different to or even contradicting the supposed model of the country in question. This point was made for Germany (see Giersch et al., 1992). In this study, a detailed critique of country-specific models cannot be carried out. As in the case of Germany, however, an understanding of the Swedish models is necessary before an analysis of the path, timing and sequence of telecommunications liberalization can be carried out.

Like Germany, Sweden is traditionally in comparative political economics seen as a corporatist county (see Katzenstein, 1985, 31, 34). Under the corporatist model, three stakeholders (government, employers and the unions) together negotiate a partial redistribution of wealth in combination with private ownership of capital. In Germany, this approach was complemented by a diffusion-oriented stance in technology policy, which emphasized small and medium-sized enterprises (SMEs) and the spread of information and new technologies to these companies (Ergas, 1987). Public resources were thus made available in smaller amounts and were tied to cooperation among firms and research organizations (Ziegler, 1997, 198). This approach complemented the skill-conscious nature of the SME *Mittelstand* (see Wengenroth, 1999, 131). While Sweden's technology policy shared traits of a diffusion-oriented model (Ergas, 1987), Sweden's technology policy, like that of France, was also marked by high defence expenditures. In addition, economic activity was concentrated among large firms, which Hans Sjögren calls a 'Schnapps glass' structure. Sjögren's glass has a wide top, thin neck and small base (Sjörgen, 1998, 159; see also Kurzer, 1993, 32). This was related to the fact that privately held wealth by the richest industrial families was relatively untouched in the Second World War due to Sweden's neutrality. This was reinforced by weak anti-trust legislation, specific aspects of shareholder laws, and tax policy (Sjögren, 1998, 167). In the early 1960s, for example, the Wallenberg family holdings employed around 13 per cent of all workers in the private sector.[2] Corporatism, therefore, operated in a different environment in Sweden compared to Germany due to the concentration of economic activity.

In Germany and Sweden, the effectiveness of their respective models deteriorated gradually from the late 1960s, leading to a crisis of the models from the late 1980s. In the words of Peter Katzenstein, the crisis began as 'a political struggle redefining the boundaries of legitimate expectations and demands in corporatist bargaining' (1985, 197). Other countries, such as France or the Netherlands, had been forced into crisis almost a decade earlier (for France, see Hall, 1986, 195–202; for the Netherlands, Visser and Hemerijck, 1997, 7). The Swedish delay was caused by the late entry of the country into the EU in 1995 and a correspondingly late dedication to tight monetary policy. In Germany, policy re-engineering was delayed due to the unforeseen unification project.

In Sweden, a particularly severe period began in the early 1990s.[3] During the previous decades, the Swedish system of direct state provision of health and other services had grown disproportionally. In the 1970s and 1980s, unemployment was kept low, but government employment rose massively. High inflation was coupled with low growth (Pettersson, 1992, 7). From 1991 to 1993, this system started to crack under its own weight; the government sector could not grow any further and unemployment shot up over 9 per cent – a rate that was previously inconceivable under the Swedish model (Sjögren, 1998, 173). Government severely curtailed its expenditures, forcing the economy into a recession. Equity values fell, and the bankruptcy rate increased dramatically. But government re-engineering was accompanied by private sector changes as well. For example, several top staff of the best-known Swedish multinationals had to lay down their jobs. Their severance payments, or 'golden parachutes' were invested into new ventures. In addition and more importantly, the managers dedicated part of their time and their network to helping the young firms. Thus, the recent shock to the country's model encouraged entrepreneurship, as in Germany (for Germany, see Chapter 4 and Lehrer, 2000, 20, 21). Many of these Swedish ventures were internet companies, responding to a strong domestic demand for internet services.

INTERNET UPTAKE IN EUROPE

In this second section, data depicting differences in internet access of selected European countries is presented. Internet access is used also as a qualitative and not only as a quantitative term. For this reason, both absolute user numbers as well as internet penetration rates per capita are included in this analysis. For the early days of internet commercialization under examination here, internet penetration rates can be used as a measure of demand sophistication. High penetration rates were crucial because many advanced internet services, especially transaction-based consumer services, only became viable after a certain proportion of total consumers were online. All new venture types which will be discussed in the sixth section of this chapter were dependent on advanced demand conditions. Early adopters, such as scientists, students and IT professionals, formed an initial base of internet users in all countries, but these were not of interest for broad marketing and sales activities. Small enterprises were also generally not among the early adopters.

The difference between absolute user numbers and internet penetration rates was most striking when comparing Germany to Sweden. In 1998, Germany's internet user base was less than three times as large as that of Sweden while Germany's total population was about ten times as large. Sweden's internet market was smaller, but much more advanced than Germany's. It had moved beyond the early adoption phase to mainstream adoption approaching one-third of the total population. The United Kingdom profited from both high absolute internet user numbers as well as a relatively high penetration (Table 7.2).

This relationship can be demonstrated in three further statistics. Table 7.3 shows the number of internet servers prepared for secure electronic commerce transactions. Sweden had a clear lead. In 1998, Germany was below the EU average for advanced web servers per capita. After the turn of the decade, Germany was catching up, while still only slightly above the EU average. In Figure 7.1, progress from 1995 to 2002 is mapped, with yet a further distinct measure of internet use, internet host penetration. This chart again shows a clear lead of Sweden over the other countries examined here throughout the period under examination.

A final statistic (Table 7.4) depicts internet advertising expenditures per internet user. In 1998, companies spent an average EUR 10 on internet advertising per user in Sweden, compared to only EUR 4 in Germany. The advertising figure is especially instructive for the purposes of this research; it reflects the vibrancy of the consumer and SME internet in the countries under examination at the time. The results for all countries with the exception of Sweden were disconcerting in the period up to 1998. Only in 1999

Table 7.2   Internet and Minitel penetration in 1998

	Est. internet users 1998 (M)	Population (M)	Penetration (%)
Finland	1.8	5.1	35
USA	79	271.8	29
Sweden	2.4	8.9	27
Netherlands	1.4	15.6	9
Germany	6.9	82.1	8
United Kingdom	5.9	58.5	10
Italy	2.6	57.4	5
France	2.5	58.5	4
France (regular Minitel users)	15	58.5	26

Sources: For sources of internet user estimates please refer to Appendix D. Due to the lack of consistent data for this early time period, several different sources were consulted and the numbers that matched most closely with the different estimates were used. The Finnish figure: Gallup Media (May 1998); Italy: Osservatorio Internet Italia (May 1998); United Kingdom: average of NOP Research Group (4.3 million in March 1998) and CNET (7.5 million in October 1998). All countries courtesy of Nua Internet Surveys (http://www.nua.net/). Population estimates were obtained from The Economist, *Pocket World in Figures 2000 Edition*, London, 1999 (in Association with Profile Books). The French Minitel user figure was quoted from OECD DSTI/ICCP/IE(97)10/FINAL (1998a, 31).

Table 7.3   Estimated absolute number of secure web servers for electronic commerce

	Sept. 1997	Aug. 1998	July 2000	Per 100.000 Inhabitants Aug. 1998	Per 100.000 Inhabitants July 2000
Finland	20	81	343	1.6	6.6
France	65	250	1 297	0.4	2.2
Germany	147	558	3 761	0.7	4.6
Sweden	53	184	811	2.1	9.2
United Kingdom	353	821	4 404	1.4	7.4
USA	7 513	16 663	65 565	6.1	24.0
Italy	88	193	795	0.3	1.4
Netherlands	75	148	541	1.0	3.4
OECD average				2.0	8.3
EU average				0.8	4.4

Source: OECD (1999a, 90); OECD (2001a, 114). OECD obtained these figures from Netcraft. Figures for 1999 were not listed.

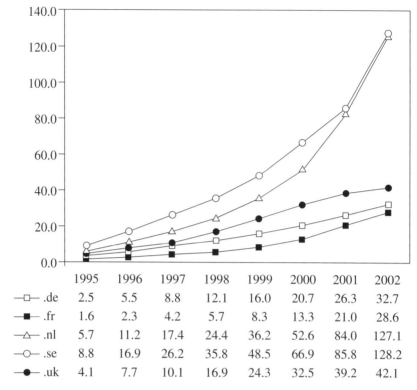

	1995	1996	1997	1998	1999	2000	2001	2002
—□— .de	2.5	5.5	8.8	12.1	16.0	20.7	26.3	32.7
—■— .fr	1.6	2.3	4.2	5.7	8.3	13.3	21.0	28.6
—△— .nl	5.7	11.2	17.4	24.4	36.2	52.6	84.0	127.1
—○— .se	8.8	16.9	26.2	35.8	48.5	66.9	85.8	128.2
—●— .uk	4.1	7.7	10.1	16.9	24.3	32.5	39.2	42.1

Notes: Hosts are computer systems connected to the internet and host counts are a measure of internet use in each country. This count did not include global top-level domain names such as .com. In many country overviews, the gTLDs were allotted to the specific countries, with the result that absolute host numbers for each country were slightly higher. Usually, this step was important only when country comparisons included the United States, due to the fact that US corporations tended to use the gTDL .com. Data is quoted from the January statistics for each year. Country population sizes were kept constant (million): Germany (.de) 82.1, France (.fr) 58.5, The Netherlands (.nl) 15.6, Sweden (.se) 8.9, United Kingdom (.uk) 58.5.

Source: Data quoted from Internet Software Consortium (http://www.isc.org/).

Figure 7.1   Country-specific top-level domain names by host count per thousand inhabitants. January 1995–January 2002

were the US levels from the year 1997 reached, in this instance, a two-year lag is visible in the data.

Advanced internet demand conditions in Sweden did not go unnoticed. Rapid internet uptake was especially attractive in combination with mobile phone usage, which was also very impressive in the Nordic countries. To

Table 7.4   Estimated internet advertising spending per internet user in Euros

	1996	1997	1998	1999
USA	5–6	9–13	22	35
Sweden	–	4	10	15
Germany	1	2	4	8
Netherlands	1	3	6	6
France	–	3–5	5–7	13

Note: Constant exchange rates were used for all four years: 1 EUR was equal to 1.1 US$, 2.0 DM, 6.6 FF, 2.2 Dfl and 8.8 SEK.

Source: Calculated from figures in Appendix D.

exploit these conditions, some US internet companies moved to Sweden. Among these were research companies, hoping to pick up on emerging consumer trends, such as Jupiter Communications (strategic internet research) and Media Metrix (internet user statistics), as well as the internet advertising network Doubleclick.[4] In most other European countries, however, internet uptake lagged – a vast proportion of the population did not have internet access in the period under consideration from 1995 to 1998.

INTERNET ACCESS PRICING AND THE TIMING OF EUROPEAN TELECOMMUNICATIONS LIBERALIZATION

The hypothesis presented here is that access prices as well as pricing composition were the main drivers of internet uptake in European countries. A crucial pricing component was the metered cost of the local phone call. The highest access prices by far in 1998 of the European countries examined here could be found in Germany, and the lowest in Sweden. In fact, Germany was the second-most expensive country in terms of access prices for consumers using the OECD access cost measure. Sweden was among the cheapest (Table 7.5). This changed after 1998.[5] For first generation internet start-ups, however, access pricing up to and including 1998, during their period of formation and growth, was crucial.

Before embarking upon a discussion of telecommunications policy as it related to the local loop, it is important to note that internet access price levels did not explain laggard internet uptake in Europe alone; they were merely one significant contributing factor. There was not in all cases a clear

Table 7.5   The most and least expensive countries for consumer internet access. OECD internet access basket 1998, in USD PPP. Charges for 20 hours internet use per month including local call telecommunications fees at discounted off-peak rates

Czech Republic	75	New Zealand	46
Germany	68	United Kingdom	46
Switzerland	67	Portugal	46
Austria	64	Spain	42
Hungary	63	Netherlands	40
Greece	60	United States	40
Luxembourg	53	Turkey	38
Japan	52	Sweden	37
Poland	51	Australia	36
Ireland	51	Italy	36
Mexico	50	Norway	35
France	48	Denmark	32
Korea	48	Iceland	31
OECD	47	Canada	31
Belgium	47	Finland	20

Source: OECD (1999a, 186). This included discount rates offered by the telecommunications operators, in France Primaliste and in Germany City Plus. For calculation details, please refer to pp. 175 to 186 of the original document.

correlation between access prices and internet penetration. Countries existed where access was pricey in an international comparison, yet where penetration rates were quite good. This point was emphasized in an early study commissioned by the EU (European Commission, 1997, 23). In an OECD survey, penetration rates and access costs have been mapped (see Figure 7.2). Some countries fit nicely on a downward sloping line, confirming a relationship between penetration and access costs. Other countries diverged strongly from the expected relationship, however. One of the best examples of divergence can be drawn from the relative positions of the Netherlands and Sweden. Access costs in those two countries were roughly similar. In fact, they were about on the same level as the USA. Yet, internet penetration in these three countries varied considerably, the two leaders being the USA and Sweden.

Next to other factors which cannot be discussed here, such as personal computer penetration rates, one significant differentiator was pricing composition. The access costs as measured by OECD only show costs for a set of hours of internet use. Further information on pricing composition is required for a more accurate assessment of the impact of local call telecom-

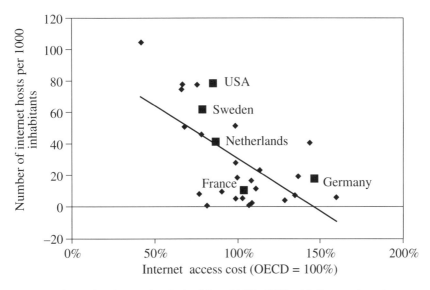

Source: Figures for 29 countries obtained from OECD, (1999a, 86) (Internet hosts in OECD countries, including gTLDs by domain registrations per 1000 inhabitants, July 1998) and page 186 (Total basket of off-peak internet access rates for 20 hours online per month, 1998). A similar chart based on similar data sources can be found in OECD (1999c, 23).

Figure 7.2   Internet cost and host density (a measure of internet penetration) in various countries, 1998

munications pricing on internet access. Although the cost of internet access in the Netherlands and Sweden in the late 1990s was roughly similar for the OECD 20-hour off-peak measure, the composition of the total price differed. In the Netherlands, the metered local call component was higher, whereas the monthly internet service provider (ISP) price was slightly lower. Internet access beyond the 20-hour period quickly became much more expensive in the Netherlands compared to Sweden, because of the metered local call pricing component (OECD, 1999a, 177, 185, 186). While an average user perhaps did not use the internet for more than 20 hours, the psychological impact of the ticking clock was discouraging.[6]

The most consumer-friendly internet pricing innovation beyond doubt was unmetered access – as offered in most of the United States and only after 1998 introduced broadly to consumers in Europe.[7] The OECD table (Table 7.5), which compared costs for 20 hours of internet access, provided an abstract measurement which did not reflect the discouraging effect of metered pricing. In fact, due to the artificial yardstick of 20 hours of internet use, the United States did not even appear as the cheapest country in the OECD list. Metered access pricing, practised in almost all European countries, penalized internet use.[8] As a result, time spent on the internet remained low (see Table 7.6; also discussion in OECD, 2001a, 98, 99). Not only consumer access, but also SME uptake was depressed through high internet access costs in Europe, as shown by a German study (quoted in Welfens and Jungmittag, 2002, 101).

Table 7.6   Hours spent online per month in 1999

USA (AOL)	30
France (Wanadoo)	10
Spain (Telefonica)	10
UK (AOL)	8
Finland	8
Germany (AOL)	7

Note: Another instructive figure available stated that Americans spent 55 minutes per day on-line compared with 17 minutes on-line per day in Europe. This figure was obtained from AOL. AOL, a popular internet and online service, was present in the US and several European markets and could therefore directly compare the effect of metered pricing on time spent on-line. Ralph Atkins, 'Interview, Andreas Schmidt, Preaching the Internet Gospel Across Europe', *Financial Times*, 27 May 1999, 13.

Source: Numbers from Noah Yasskin, Phil Dwyer, 'Free-to-Air Internet: Creating a Consumer Medium Out of a Metered Network', Jupiter Communications, March 1999, p. 5.

There was a certain irony here. On the one hand, in the United States, unmetered access was confirmed as the primary mode to charge for local calls when AT&T was split up into regional companies and a long-distance carrier. Beforehand, vicious competition between AT&T and local telephone competitors had led to a decrease in local call rates (Kenney, 2001, 9). On the other hand, the price for a local metered phone call went up significantly in Europe in the 1990s due to telecommunications liberalization. On the two sides of the Atlantic, therefore, telecommunications reform had divergent effects: in the USA, an unmetered internet access model was confirmed, while in Europe a pricey, high-cost access structure materialized. Prior to liberalization, governments on both sides of the Atlantic insured that call prices, especially local calls, were kept at acceptable levels, in the USA by capping local operator prices, in Europe through government ownership of the telecommunications operator. The overarching policy objectives were different, however. In the United States, policy addressed monopoly profits; in Europe, the social concept of telephony as a universal communications medium was appealed to. In hindsight, US policy objectives proved to be more robust while social policy goals were easily reinterpreted in many European countries. Sweden, as we will see, was an exception.[9]

Most European policy-makers allowed local call rates to rise, pointing to falling long-distance rates. Public telecommunications operators (PTOs) argued that they had offered local calls below cost in the past. The term used was 'rate rebalancing' but it was, in effect, a cosmetic measure meant to mimic competitive tariffs based on supposed cost structures. There was no competition in the local loop, however, which could have generated real competitive rates. In fact, rate rebalancing was a highly profitable exercise for the incumbent operators. Competition was expected first in the international and national call segments; it was here that the incumbent wanted to be ready for fierce price competition. Earnings generated through the local loop were used to support the incumbent in the upcoming battle and to redress balance sheets. Rate rebalancing occurred when telecommunications operators were split off from the postal service and were privatized. All this occurred before fixed-line competition was introduced. In Germany, for example, the incumbent operator was privatized in 1994, was listed on the stock market in 1996 and was exposed to fixed-line competition only in 1998. This allowed for an attractive window in which the returns on monopoly could be maximized without the responsibility previously linked to the government mandate.

Some European countries diverged from this pattern, however. The country which diverged most strongly was Finland, which never had a telecommunications monopoly and featured one of the lowest metered internet access rates in the world. Although Sweden also never had a real monopoly, its telecommunications environment was a *de facto* monopoly (see Noam, 1992). Different government institutions could run their own telecommunication services internally, but there was no market competition. Yet, competition with the state-owned PTO was allowed in 1993. The Swedish PTO, Telia, was exposed to competition with its main challenger immediately. Tele2 had already, prior to liberalization, prepared for the arrival of competition.[10] As in other countries, rate balancing occurred in Sweden as well, and local call prices were certainly raised; here also, the national operator Telia was using its ownership of the local network infrastructure to generate increased income while lowering its long-distance rates where competition was strong.[11] However, Swedish authorities realized the significance of the internet early on and implemented a transfer payment for internet access which put pressure on the PTO's local call rates.[12]

In contrast to other countries, the stock market offering of the incumbent operator was carried out late in Sweden; Telia was only listed in June 2000. The Swedish pattern of liberalization was the mirror of that in

Germany and most other European countries following the EU liberalization deadline of 1998. In Sweden, competition was introduced first, then the stock exchange listing was carried out many years later (see Table 7.7).

Policy-makers in Germany were very well aware of the significance of the local loop while liberalizing their telecommunications services. In fact, the German Telecommunications Law (TKG), passed in 1996, was very progressive. Because infrastructure competition was difficult to realize in the medium term (the incumbent retained ownership over cable TV and wireless local loop technologies (WLL) were only in development), very clear rules regarding access to the incumbent's network infrastructure were mandated.[13] Thus Germany was the first European country to allow unbundled access to the local loop upon the arrival of basic services competition.

Yet, the progressive framework did not immediately lead to increased competition in the local loop. The incumbent was initially able to delay competition through arbitrage with the regulator and with courts. The main issue of contestation was the price of unbundled access for the competition.[14] A further tactic the incumbent used were long delays of several months to connect the competition to its own network points (VATM,

Table 7.7   Key dates of telecommunications IPOs and basic services competition

	Initial Public Offering	Government share after IPO (%)	Basic services competition
Germany	1996	61	1998
France	1997	62	1998
Netherlands	1994[a]	44	1997[b]
Sweden	2000	71	1993[c]

Notes: Not to be confused with the provision of local access lines. Basic services competition dates refer to the provision of international or national telephony services over local lines offered by the incumbent. OECD, 1999a, for government shares, pages 32–3. See also detailed charts in OECD (2001a, 30–32).

[a] Royal KPN was listed in Amsterdam in June 1994. New York (October 1995), London (June 1996) and Frankfurt (July 1996) followed.

[b] Local telephony was liberalized on 01 July 97 in the Netherlands. Royal KPN (then Royal PTT Nederland) faced competition in fixed-line services by Telfort (joint venture between British Telecom and Dutch railways) as well as Enertel (Dutch power companies and cable network operators consortium). Royal PTT Nederland demerged its mail, express and logistics activities in 1998, becoming a pure telecom player, Royal KPN. The new KPN share was traded for the first time on 29 June 1999.

[c] In 1991, Tele2 AB, majority owned by Kinnevik, leased lines from the Swedish railroad to prepare to offer international telephony services, anticipating liberalization. This broke the *de facto* monopoly of Televerket (today's Telia) in public networks (Noam, 1992, 211). In 1993, the Swedish Telecom Act was passed, enabling fixed-line competition. In 1994, Tele2 offered the first national telephony services to the public.

2001, 6). Lastly, the incumbent began to offer attractive internet access rates through its own internet service provider (ISP), which competitors were unable to match because they were forced to buy local line access from the incumbent at relatively high rates.[15] By the late 1990s, the incumbent had fully understood the value of its local loop and the strategic importance of internet access. It was using its control over local loop pricing to prevent the competition from developing the internet and broadband access segments. The regulator, which had overseen impressive price declines in international and national telephony, seemed paralysed.[16] As a result, internet access rates in Germany indeed did fall after 1998, but mostly through unilateral action by the incumbent.[17]

Two main differences emerge out of a comparison between the liberalization process in Sweden compared to Germany. First, competition in Germany was delayed until 1998 while it was initiated in Sweden already in 1993. Second, even after 1998 and despite a progressive legal framework, the regulator seemed ineffective in Germany regarding the important issue of local loop competition even after 1998. Both issues were related to the fact that in Germany, as in many other European countries, policy-makers were eager to see their incumbent transform itself through a stock market listing into a global player. Efforts were therefore made not to weaken the prospective 'national champion'. Social democratic thinking which enshrined universal service and other infrastructure responsibilities of public enterprises was viewed as outdated, even among the Social Democrats themselves. It was precisely this type of thinking which persisted for longer in Sweden. A further example of this thinking was the Swedish approach to UMTS allocation, in which the state decided against expected massive windfall income generated through an auction. The conservative attitudes inadvertently resulted in more advantageous local call pricing for internet users, although the conservatism was, at the time, heavily criticized by Swedish entrepreneurs. The German state as a shareholder of a publicly listed company acted very differently from the Swedish state as a full owner of a non-listed government entity. The delays in regulatory action in Germany showed that ownership issues could transcend a progressively designed legal framework.

A further point can be made, however, pertaining to telecommunications liberalization as an aspect of national innovation policy in the New Economy. In addition to enjoying the initially high valuation of its shareholdings in the listed former PTO, policy-makers subscribing to the vision of a 'national champion' may actually have believed that they were promoting national innovation. They emphasized the research capabilities of the incumbent operator and also their demand-side effect on backward supplier linkages. In the scope of this vision, however, innovation was limited to the telecommunication sector itself. The implicit assumption made was that a single company actively competing on a global scale exerts more beneficial backward innovation linkages than fragmented, domestic competitors can. This simplistic view, inspired by mature export industries such as the automotive industry, was not challenged.[18] While the telecommunications industry was large – in Germany in 1999, for example, 226 000 people were employed in the EUR 48 billion industry (Welfens and Jungmittag, 2002, 35) – a broader view of the impact of telecommunications reform would have needed to take into consideration other forward-linked New Economy service sectors which included the internet ventures discussed here.

In Germany, the timing of reform was a compromise solution between the desire of creating a 'national champion' and a less naive view embracing competition and emphasizing infrastructure aspects. From 1996 to 1998, Deutsche Telekom was to maximize its returns. Competition and its effect on pricing was suppressed. Competition was similarly repressed in the German cable TV network. The political economists Welfens and Jungmittag heavily criticized German policy-makers for their missing awareness of issues and basic economic findings (2002, 12, 13).

Lessons can be drawn from this material. Local loop pricing varied considerably in Europe and resulted in different internet access rates. In all countries, pricing was influenced by telecommunications policy inadvertently; that is, policies were originally devised for different reasons completely unrelated to internet uptake.[19] Policy-makers were not aware of the importance of local call rates for internet uptake in the mid-1990s; in fact, many were not aware of the importance of the internet at all. They had underestimated the effect of the internet was having as a 'disruptive technology'. However, in some countries, a policy compromise between a tempting but highly contentious vision of a global player and domestic infrastructure considerations was consciously made. This compromise was made in terms of timing: a delay in the start of competition, a delay of the sale of the cable TV network by the incumbent and a delay of effective regulatory action regarding the local loop.

THE EUROPEAN VENTURE CAPITAL BOTTLENECK

Historically in Europe, start-ups in knowledge-intensive service industries such as software and biotechnology, and especially the types of internet ventures described here, had severe problems in securing adequate growth financing. In contrast to the United States, so-called true venture capital (VC) focused on early-stage technology start-ups was underdeveloped in all European countries – including the United Kingdom, which boasted a sizeable venture capital industry but which emphasized later-stage, less risky investments. Europe financed its growth mostly through bank loans, an instrument suitable for 'old' industries with significant capital stock and slow depreciation. The venture capital bottleneck, which existed until the late 1990s, influenced the entrepreneur's ability to succeed at home and abroad.

Europe tried hard to establish a true venture capital industry. In the 1970s and 1980s, indigenous venture capital funding appeared in Europe but disappeared again. An early ill portent were the problems encountered by the most innovative VC firm pioneering pan-European investments in the late 1970s, European Enterprises Development SA (EED) (Coutarelli, 1977, vi). EED was founded in France as early as 1964 (Lorenz, 1985, 156). The main reason for the decline of the industry was the lack of what venture capitalists call an attractive exit option, a strong, growth-oriented technology stock market. A risk-embracing venture capital industry can only be sustained with such a public capital market – this exit opportunity allows high returns to offset losses in a VC's portfolio.

Witnessing the decline of the industry, private as well as public initiatives attempted to break up the venture capital bottleneck in Europe. A private initiative was launched by the European Venture Capital Association (EVCA), which was founded with the objective of promoting venture capital in Europe. EVCA sought to tackle the problem head-on, in conjunction with venture capital groups Capricorn Venture Partners and Apax, and started an alternative, growth-oriented stock market modelled on NASDAQ in the USA. EASDAQ was opened in Brussels in 1996. EASDAQ has had some success and has provided venture capitalists with a new exit opportunity. Yet its progress as a pan-European growth exchange was hampered by the lack of an EU-wide regulatory framework for securities.[20] A further reason for its slow development may have been that European investment behaviour was still largely national in orientation, even among institutional investors. The significance of home nation investment inclination was demonstrated by the temporary success of the Frankfurt exchange Neuer Markt.

From its founding in 1997 up to its peak in 1999, EASDAQ was overshadowed by a newcomer, the Neuer Markt, based in Frankfurt. Whereas Brussels had a small impact, the Neuer Markt improved the situation for venture capitalists considerably, mostly in Germany but also in other European countries. The liquidity of the Neuer Markt was much higher than that of EASDAQ or any other growth exchange in Europe, such as Nouveau Marché. The companies listed there achieved valuations which were significant and comparable to those at NASDAQ. In fact, Neuer Markt had the largest market capitalization of all the exchanges in the confederation of European growth markets, Euro.NM. Even before the peak, in 1999 (see Table 7.8), the Frankfurt-based exchange made up 81 per cent of Euro.NM, while Nouveau Marché contributed 13 per cent and Amsterdam's Nieuwe Markt NMAX only 5 per cent.[21]

Table 7.8   Number of new listings on Europe's growth exchanges, January to October 1999

Neuer Markt, Frankfurt	86
AIM, London	35
Nouveau Marché, Paris	20
EASDAQ	10
Nieuwe Markt, Amsterdam	1

Source: 'Flaute an den Wachstumsmärkten, Seit Juli kein Börsengang bei Euro.NM-Partnern des Neuen Marktes', *Süddeutsche Zeitung*, 7 October 1999.

Salvation came late, however. The impact of the Neuer Markt on the investment behaviour of venture capitalists in Germany was only felt from 1998 onwards, because it took time before the Frankfurt-based exchange could prove its robustness and build liquidity. The impact of the market beyond Germany was delayed even further as European VCs not based in Germany learned how they could approach a placement there. Because of the delayed effect of the Neuer Markt on venture capital investments, the first generation of internet start-ups in Germany generally did not profit from the new inflow of venture capital. The second generation, launched after 1998, initially did, but experienced the effects of the subsequent downturn very soon afterwards. In effect, private funding for internet ventures dried up before most of these second generation companies could list on public markets. German venture capitalists had a dangerous proportion of their funds tied up in second generation internet ventures when the downturn came.[22]

The success of the Neuer Markt and the struggle of EASDAQ demonstrated the crucial role of a tightly integrated, domestic capital market. To some, EASDAQ represented an idealistic European dream whose time had not yet come. The story of the two markets also represented a problem to those who expounded the rise of global, unfettered, 'casino' capitalism. While top US investment banks backed EASDAQ and channelled funds into it, companies listed there were arguably regarded as 'orphan stocks' because they were not backed by any domestic financial community.[23] Instead, local funds were poured into the Neuer Markt, coming in large part from the domestic retail sector, composed of private shareholders. The rise of the Neuer Markt was actually accompanied by a powerful, popular movement embracing private shareholding in Germany.[24] From 1997 to 2000, the number of Germans who invested in stocks directly or through funds had almost doubled to more than 11 million.[25] One of the executives at the German exchange joked: 'Entire families that used to watch the soaps on TV in the evening are tuning to Bloomberg TV or the German equivalent.'[26]

Other reasons frequently mentioned for the initial success of the Neuer Markt seem less crucial than the shift in investment behaviour: A focus on technology and media companies, a certain degree of transparency including company disclosure rules, an advanced computer-based trading platform available in several countries as well as an 'adoption' policy specifying that at least two investment banks need to pledge market-making responsibility to each listed company.[27] According to *Institutional Investor*: 'The Neuer Markt . . . was part of a single-minded and highly organized initiative aimed at building up the German financial services industry, which included far-reaching changes in security and bankruptcy laws.'[28] Yet, despite these efforts, after the global downturn of technology stocks and after severe cases of fraud were uncovered, the rules of the Neuer Markt were questioned and revised.[29]

Venture capitalists in Germany and other European countries operating in the period up to 1998 had no way of knowing that new exchanges, led by the Neuer Markt, would soon enter a boom period. As a result, European venture capitalists made investment decisions that were far more risk-adverse than their colleagues in the USA. The best indication of this was the proportion of early-stage investments (Table 7.9). Without significant early-stage activity, the innovation potential of new technology ventures is limited. After 1998, when the proportion of venture capital invested in early stage companies stagnated or declined slightly in the United States, it shot up in many European countries as a late response to internet euphoria and the Neuer Markt. Only two countries had consistently significant early-stage investments before 1998, the Netherlands and Germany. The relatively large proportions invested in early-stage firms in these two countries reflected the success of high quality public programmes specifically targeting early-stage ventures. In France, a similar set of programmes existed, but they were less efficient and targeted technology investments narrowly; internet innovations such as the types listed here would not have been eligible (Interview, Simoncini, 6 November 1999).

The main innovation by government authorities consisted of integrating know-how of the private venture capital industry into the funding process, in 'co-venturing' schemes. Thus, government invested side-by-side with a venture capitalist. Alternatively, refinancing programmes also existed.

Table 7.9   *Early-stage venture capital investments by amount of investment compared with total venture capital investments (%)*

	1996	1997	1998	1999	2000
USA	N/A	32	34	27	28
Germany	13	15	24	32	35
Netherlands	16	20	16	20	19
France	11	7	15	19	22
Sweden	1	1	12	19	10
United Kingdom	2	3	2	2	12

Sources: Source for the US figures: PricewaterhouseCoopers, 'MoneyTree Survey Full Year 2000 and Q1 2001 Results', (for annual figures from 1998 to 2000, p. 8). See also: 'MoneyTree US Report Full Year and Q4 1999 Results', 'MoneyTree Current Quarter Highlights / Q4 '98' and 'National Venture Capital Survey, Results for Fourth Quarter 1997'. European data from: EVCA, *Yearbook 1998, Yearbook 1999, Yearbook 2000* and *Yearbook 2001.*

Here, VCs were provided with unsecured loans or guarantees, with a similar effect of lower early-stage risk. In Germany, the tbg offered a co-venturing programme and the KfW provided refinancing for financiers.

Government programmes in France, Germany and the Netherlands made an important contribution to the venture capital industry in each country. The programmes saved the venture capital industry from extinction in the 1990s, until the effect of the alternative stock exchanges kicked in, which occurred in parallel to an increasing public market appetite for internet stocks. The fact that they kept early-stage technology investment activity alive is visible in the proportions of early-stage investments, shown in Table 7.9. Yet, the absolute amounts invested until 1998 were minimal. This is shown in Table 7.10, where total technology investment levels are compared; these figures include later-stage investing. While early-stage investing was kept alive, therefore, liquidity was extremely low and was able to benefit only an extremely small amount of companies.

The bottleneck was broken only with the impact of stock market euphoria from 1998 onwards. It is argued here that the break-up of the VC bottleneck came too late for first generation internet ventures. While funding was available for early-stage ventures before 1998, it was invested in a small number of lower-risk software and biotechnology investments. In Germany, the only internet ventures financed by local VCs in that period were software developers such as Intershop or Brokat. It is important to note, however, that low-scale early-stage investing activity was important to insure that a human capital base of a precious few VCs were active in

Table 7.10   Venture capital investments in technology (Euro million)

	1996	1997	1998	1999	2000
Sweden	22	69	110	443	595
Germany	182	331	664	1347	2516
USA	8876	11434	15790	42074	79567
France	232	242	485	1242	2644
United Kingdom	636	1165	1820	2381	4407
Netherlands	147	172	243	657	727

Notes: In the PricewaterhouseCoopers survey 'MoneyTree Survey Full-Year 2000 and Q1 2001 Results' the historic annual figures for US technology venture capital investments were heavily revised due to the incorporation of new data sources. Although material from previous surveys was available to the author, only the figures listed in the year 2000 report were used. Previous figures in US$ from PricewaterhouseCoopers, 'MoneyTree Current Quarter Highlights / Q4 '98' and 'MoneyTree US Report Full Year and Q4 1999 Results' were: 1996, 5.5 billion; 1997, 8.3 billion; 1998, 10.8 billion; 1999, 32.4 billion. These figures were again slightly, but not substantially, different from the US figures listed in the PricewaterhouseCoopers, 'Money for Growth, The European Technology Investment Report 1998', as well as other, earlier PricewaterhouseCoopers sources. Please refer to the internet site http://www.pwcmoneytree.com/. European data from: EVCA, *Yearbook 1998, Yearbook 1999, Yearbook 2000* and *Yearbook 2001*. Technology investments in Europe were defined as the sum of investments in the following sectors: 'communications,' 'computer-related,' 'other electronics-related,' 'biotechnology' and 'medical/health-related.' Please note that the category 'high-tech investment,' which appeared in recent years for many EVCA countries, was not used for reasons of comparability. In Europe, historically, only a low proportion of investments was made in high-technology companies. This is why a sectoral approach was necessary. The US data used here, however, included non-technology investments. Constant exchange rates were used for all years. The depreciation of the Euro against the US dollar was, therefore, not accounted for: 1 EUR equals 1.1 $US, 2.0 DM, 6.6 FF, 2.2 Dfl, €0.7 and 8.8 SEK. In the case of Germany, France and the Netherlands, investments appeared in Euro after 1999 in the EVCA statistics; in these cases, the EVCA Euro figures were used and currency conversions were not made.

Germany and the Netherlands to react to the new opportunity. This was the real benefit of the government programmes.[30]

During the boom period, however, the government programmes lost their purpose, especially in Germany, the home of the Neuer Markt. Then, the amount invested in early-stage companies greatly exceeded the capacity of human capital. Companies led by inexperienced entrepreneurs were funded by inexperienced venture capitals; most of them had narrow consulting or investment banking backgrounds.[31] Nevertheless, government programmes were still available to mitigate the risk of venture capital firms; a further reason for overinvestment in early-stage ventures after 1998. In terms of early-stage funding, the two periods before and after 1998 could not have been more different in Europe – especially in Germany.

In Sweden, government support programmes oriented towards high-growth companies similar to those in France, Germany and the Netherlands were only recently initiated; older government programmes were too slow and unfocused in their execution and high-potential internet entrepreneurs did not take advantage of them.[32] As a consequence, the technology-focused and early-stage venture capital industry had a much harder time surviving in Sweden. Adverse circumstances existed despite the fact that Sweden was one of the earliest adopters of the venture capital concept in Europe in the 1970s. Yet, the venture capital industry did not really disappear; it moved abroad and changed its approach. Funds were invested privately instead of in institutional venture capital funds. We will delve into this issue later. It suffices at this moment to point out that fund investments by the Swedish venture capital industry were considerably lower than in the rest of Europe, although subject to impressive growth from a very low starting point.

INSTITUTIONAL REFORM IN OTHER POLICY AREAS

Obviously, there were other policy areas which affected entrepreneurs in the internet field. One such policy area was electronic commerce legislation. Yet here, even the country that by the late 1990s moved ahead the most rapidly in enacting new legislation, Germany, only began to provide some very basic pointers. In addition, the importance of electronic legislation for the initial years of internet commerce was exaggerated by commentators at the time. The market grew despite an inconsistent legal framework. Then, there were creative and useful government initiatives, such as Sweden's tax regulation change that allowed employers to provide computers for employees at home.[33] Diverse activities such as the Swedish one were found in all countries. In 1998, France set aside FF 6 billion for a broad set of measures, from education to 'paperless government'.[34]

Yet, these diverse initiatives distracted from the fact that more could have been done to promote entrepreneurship in general. Taxation issues and regulatory measures affecting entrepreneurs were not glamorous 'cyberissues', but were more important. Here, however, all European countries had their share of problems (see especially Cowie, 1999, 31–8). Even the business climate in the Netherlands, a country which prided itself in having moved the furthest in increasing flexibility and reducing regulatory obstacles in the 1990s, was, according to one entrepreneur: 'Absolutely start-up unfriendly' (Interview, de Hoop, 26 October 1999). In none of the countries reviewed here did entrepreneurs feel that taxation and labour regulation was favourable. Of course, it would be astounding to find any country on earth where entrepreneurs are content with taxation and regulation issues. In Europe, however, the taxation of options was especially unclear and muddled; some policy-makers did not seem to understand options taxation and why it was an important issue. In the Netherlands, for example, options were taxed when they were granted, based on an estimate of the future (phantom) value a company may have. This may have been fine for established firms, which could more or less accurately predict future earnings, but for start-ups it presented headaches. Some companies had to provide their employees with loans to pay the taxes (Interview, de Boer, 14 October 1999). In Sweden, companies granting options had to move in a legal grey area in order to insure that the options were not taxed as income. 'In Sweden, we live by the Eleventh Commandment: Don't get caught', commented one internet entrepreneur. In fact, many of the Swedish electronic commerce start-ups moved their official headquarters out of Sweden or were not set up there in the first place – citing the difficulty with taxation rules as applied to share options.[35] In France and Germany, options taxation seemed to be a little clearer, although uncertainty remained in this key area also in these countries. Entrepreneurs in Germany and the Netherlands were in the recent past blessed with a removal of capital gains taxation (with holdings below 25 per cent in the case of Germany and 5 per cent in the case of the Netherlands). Yet here also, statements by policy-makers were creating new uncertainty by the end of the decade. From an entrepreneur's perspective, capital gains tax reduced his power to invest as a private 'angel' investor in new ventures or to start new businesses. Capital gains tax, therefore, could be regarded as a tax on future start-up activity, as United States experience in the 1980s shows.[36] Labour regulation also was the object of severe criticism by entrepreneurs, who were running risky start-up businesses and were, therefore, uncertain of their long-term ability to retain employees. Yet, all countries made it difficult to lay off employees once fully hired.[37]

Public statements encouraging entrepreneurship in Europe were common but they were rarely underscored with policy in those areas where entrepreneurs would feel real benefits, such as in options taxation and capital gains taxation. No country examined here moved much beyond public statements.[38]

DEVELOPMENT OF INTERNET VENTURES IN EUROPE

In this third section, the development of first generation internet ventures from Germany, Sweden and other European countries will be described and compared. The fact that significant structural differences existed between German and Swedish internet ventures can be attributed to differences in the timing of telecommunications liberalization and the impact of this timing on the local loop. Other factors pertaining to the development of the internet included the availability of venture capital. Yet, this was low throughout Europe. In Sweden, even less risk financing was available than in countries with high-quality government programmes supporting early-stage technology investments such as Germany and the Netherlands. To account for country size and the possibility that the small home market drove Swedish start-ups to internationalize faster, the experience of the Netherlands is also considered in this section.

Unfortunately, no directly comparative data existed on the structures of German and Swedish internet ventures. However, broad stroke indicators for basic structural differences existed. They related to differences in terms of international organization as well as revenue model. Since a wide variety of different types of internet business models abounded, it is important for comparative purposes to begin by classifying the types which will be discussed in this section. The emphasis will be on new categories of business models associated with the commercialization of the internet, and not on software companies which developed internet-specific software.[39] These companies (examples were Intershop or Brokat), were financed by the small European venture capital industry extant in some countries even before 1998. Also not included in this analysis are internet service providers and other data networking companies. These enterprises were direct competitors to services offered by the incumbent telecommunications operator and were in the direct scope of telecommunications regulation.

The new categories of internet business models to be examined here are web developers, electronic commerce firms and portal ventures. Web developers were consultants working on a project basis for established clients, mostly by helping them in creating their internet presence. Hundreds of web developers were founded in Europe; they were by far the most popular type of internet company. They did not require large up-front investments and could finance their growth through earnings. Yet, the largest web developers and the most ambitious internationalizers among them had aggressive financing requirements. The fastest-growing web developers also were dependent upon advanced internet demand structures, just like other internet ventures. Only by realizing sophisticated, transaction-based internet projects for their clients could they generate income levels which would sustain rapid growth. The rapid growth period of the web developers ended with the demise of the New Economy. Web developers were severely affected by the reduction of IT budgets at the start of the new decade. The fastest-growing American web developer, USWeb, later renamed

MarchFirst, filed for bankruptcy in April 2001. One surviving US firm, Scient Corporation, merged with another publicly quoted competitor, iXL Enterprises, to avoid being delisted from NASDAQ.

Electronic commerce firms were those enterprises that sought to sell products and services to consumers over the internet. The survivors of this type of internet venture, not being dependent on the IT budgets of large companies, did a little better after the demise of the New Economy. One US survivor was Amazon.com; a further survivor was the consumer trading exchange eBay. Like web developers, these companies depended on a broad consumer base and advanced penetration rates. Unlike web developers, however, whose costs were mostly composed of salaries for consultants, electronic commerce firms required advanced IT systems and, if they were 'e-tailers', logistics operations. Internet retail was a scale business characterized by high fixed costs.[40] An experienced European venture capitalist estimated that the cost for e-commerce technology for three country presences in the late 1990s usually exceeded US$4 million.[41] In the year 2000, Amazon.com, for example, spent 10 per cent of its net sales, or US$269 million, on technology and content for its US and foreign internet sites.[42] In addition to market sophistication, therefore, market size was crucial. European ecommerce ventures were at a disadvantage here compared with their US competitors. Many electronic commerce firms which did not survive into the new decade failed because of the cost and challenges of their IT and logistics systems. Nevertheless, some US ventures and even some European companies managed to overcome these challenges and build the scale necessary to be successful.

The final category to be discussed here are portal ventures. The revenue model of portal sites was originally based on advertising; after the turn of the decade, they increasingly generated subscription income from high-end web services as well as transaction-based income through electronic commerce. As for the previous types of ventures, advanced penetration rates were crucial for portal ventures; advertisers would only be interested if they could expect to reach a certain minimum proportion of their potential customers through the medium. The US independent survivor here was Yahoo!. Due to the reduction of internet advertising spending, the revenues of Yahoo! were actually smaller in 2001 than in 2000 (see Table 7.11). Unlike the other types of ventures listed above, the success of independent portal ventures were strongly challenged by competitors dominant software markets or ISP markets. In the United States, Microsoft was able to achieve a top portal position (see Table 7.10) due to its dominance on the PC desktop; this relationship was explored in the Microsoft trials. In Europe, again due to the impact of telecommunications regulation, ex-PTOs offered popular ISP services. Like software developers, ISPs could, to a certain extent, influence the internet starting-page a consumer used.

Table 7.11   The largest independent web development companies in four European countries plus USA, end 1999.

Country	Firm	Employees	Financing	International presence
USA	USWeb/ CKS	4000	IPO (NASDAQ, December 1997)	USA (37), Canada, France, Belgium, Germany (2), Luxembourg (2), The Netherlands, Norway, Sweden, Switzerland (2), United Kingdom
Germany	iXL	1700	IPO (NASDAQ, June 1999)	USA (15), UK, Germany (2), Spain
	I-D Media AG	240	IPO (Neuer Markt, June 1999)	USA, Germany (5), UK
	Kabel New Media	230	IPO (Neuer Markt, June 1999)	Germany (3)
France	Cythere	75	Private	France, USA
	Pictoris	55	Minority investment by US-based company Agency.com (July 1999)	France
Netherlands	NetlinQ	100	Private	The Netherlands (4), USA, Germany (January 2000)
	Lost Boys	200	Private	The Netherlands, Spain
Sweden	Icon Medialab	850	IPO (Stockholm Stock Exchange O-List; SBI listing on June 1998)	USA (2), Sweden, Finland, Denmark, Norway, Germany, France, UK, The Netherlands, Belgium, Spain (2), Italy, Malaysia
	Cell Network	480	Cell Network AB resulted out of a merger between the listed company Linné Group AB, the Cell Consulting Group and Norway's New Media Science ASA. The merger was announced in May 1999. Linné IPO (Stockholm Stock Exchange O-List)	Sweden (2), Norway, Denmark, France

216

Notes: It is important to note that the leading German web development firm by employees (390) and international locations (USA, Germany (4), France, UK, Switzerland (2), Austria) was Pixelpark. Pixelpark, however, was majority-owned by Bertelsmann. Negotiations to acquire the first 50 per cent took place at the end of 1995. For an early history of web development companies in Germany, see Waesche, 1999a. In October of 1999, Pixelpark carried out an IPO on the Neuer Markt, with 60 per cent of the public entity still owned by Bertelsmann Multimedia GmbH and 20 per cent by the co-founder Paulus Neef. Pixelpark, Press release (from the web site http://www.pixelpark.de/), 'Pixelpark-Aktien erstmals am Neuen Markt notiert; Emissionspreis bei 15 EURO pro Aktie', 4 October 1999. The Swedish web development firm Spray Network is not on the list because it was acquired by New York-based Razorfish. As a result, Spray Ventures had a 33 per cent stake in Razorfish. 'Spray to Compete Online With Yahoo, AOL in Europe,' *Reuter Economic News*, 9 September 1999. Compare this table to an earlier version including only US and Sweden-based firms as well as Pixelpark from late 1998 in Waesche (1999b).

Source: Information from company sources published on their web sites (http://www.usweb.com/, http://www.ixl.com/, http://www.idmedia.de/, http://www.kabel.de/, http://www.cythere.com/, http://www.pictoris.com/, http://www.cellnetwork.se/, http://www.lostboys.nl/), accessed in December 1999. Icon Medialab, Press release, 'Icon Medialab Acquires Nicholson NY, A Leading US Internet Services Firm', 22 November 1999 (from http://www.iconmedialab.se/); Cell Network AB Press release, 'General meeting of the Linné Group approves merger between Cell and NMS', 26 August 1999 (from the investor information site http://www.huginonline.se/). Thanks also to Marc Simoncini (France), Roel de Hoop (Netherlands), Adriaan Meij (Netherlands) and Niels Valkering (Netherlands) for very helpful advice. Source on Cythere: e-mail from Christophe Tricaud, Cythere, 3 December 1999. Source on NetlinQ: Jacob van Duijn, 3 December 1999 (e-mail).

The types of ventures discussed here faced different conditions for success. Despite the obvious fact that they may still be acquired or go out of business, the most successful US companies of each category managed to build an impressive international network and, by the turn of the decade, began to generate profits. The last of the electronic commerce and portal companies mentioned above to reach profitability, Amazon. com, generated positive net income in the fourth quarter of 2001.[43] The pure forms of business models which allowed the new ventures to focus their resources on rapid growth were abandoned after the turn of the decade as consolidation set in.

For internet entrepreneurship, the period from 1995 to 1998 was crucial. During this time span, the first generation of US ventures began their vigorous expansion and were listed on the NASDAQ stock exchange.[44] 1995 was the Year of Internet. It was the year of the stock market listing of Netscape as well as Bill Gates's internal Pearl Harbour Day declaration that Netscape's dominance of the internet would be challenged by Microsoft.[45] It is crucial to emphasize that the fastest European entrepreneurs responded to the internet opportunity not much later than their US competitors.[46] Some of these managed to carry out a stock market listing before the financial downturn. For example, the Swedish web developer Icon Medialab listed in Stockholm in June 1998. It had already begun its international expansion in 1996, the year of its founding.[47] Most start-ups from European countries other than Sweden, however, in this early period focused on their home market and only begun internationalizing after 1998.

The leading German web development companies were all publicly quoted in 1999. Nevertheless, although they grew rapidly, their progress in terms of internationalization was disappointing compared with the top players in the USA and Sweden. Also, their employee count did not match that of their US and Swedish competitors. In the home market, German web developers seemed to have been established firmly and initially proved themselves next to tough competition from the advertising and consulting sectors. Although French web development companies boasted very strong technical skills, their growth and pace of internationalization were also not strong compared to US and Swedish competition. In contrast to Germany, where most top-tier web development firms were listed on the stock exchange, some of the best-known French web developers remained private or were acquired. As in Germany and France, the top Dutch web development agencies built an excellent pool of technical know-how, but essentially remained national players. Two of the top web developers, Twinspark Interactive People and CyberConsult, were acquired by international web development firms in Autumn 1999.[48]

The contrast between Sweden and the Netherlands was instructive.[49] Both were small countries, yet the consumer demand structure for internet services was more sophisticated in Sweden than in the Netherlands. A strong lead in internationalization was taken in Sweden by the largest web development companies, Icon Medialab, Spray Network, Linné Group (later Cell Network) and Framtidsfabriken. Icon Medialab and Cell Network were listed on the Stockholm Stock Exchange. Icon Medialab and Spray Network established a strong presence in most major European internet markets as well as in Asia. The initial lead of the Swedish web developers *vis-à-vis* the European competition is clear from Table 7.10 above. The table shows the level of development at the end of 1999, some months before the market downturn. From 2000 onwards, Swedish players encountered problems because, despite their originally organic growth strategies, they had over-extended themselves and their revenues could not cover the significant costs they were incurring.[50] Icon Medialab merged in early 2002 with the independent Dutch web developer Lost Boys, which was well financed despite the downturn. With Cell and Framtidsfabriken, now called Framfab, still surviving, there is a possibility that at least one Swedish web development firm will persevere as an independent entity with a significant international agency network.

What was remarkable, however, was how the Swedish players got so far with relatively little capital compared to their US counterparts. American web developers combined strong venture capital backing and cheap capital from NASDAQ to acquire European start-up companies. Swedish web developers, by contrast, initially moved abroad through organic growth and complemented this with minor acquisitions. Icon Medialab's shopping spree was an exception and it began to intensify only during 1999.[51]

Although Swedish entrepreneurs liked to praise the advantages of organic growth and frequently pointed out the dangers of acquisition-only growth,[52] organic growth was not a choice, but rather a necessity. Icon Medialab and Cell Network were listed on the Stockholm Stock Exchange, yet the capital they had managed to raise through this insignificant exchange was not comparable to what they would have generated through an IPO on the Frankfurt Neuer Markt. For this reason, many Swedish players had considered listing on the rival German exchange.[53] Funds provided by the venture capital industry for internet ventures were almost non-existent in Sweden in the years leading up to 1998. Instead, private investors placed their own money into start-ups. At the time, the Swedish venture capitalist Pär-Jörgen Pärson of Cell Ventures put it succinctly: 'Swedish start-ups have less cash than their US counterparts because they are funded by angel investors. But what they do receive is smart capital in terms of network and access of people. This investment network has allowed

Swedish firms to move much further, much faster, with less cash than others' (Interview, 2 December 1999). However, the funding capacity of the angel investors was limited.[54] Government support schemes for promoting venture capital were only in development in the late 1990s, most notable was the reorientation of Swedish pension funds into venture capital.[55]

The web development firms discussed here essentially all had the same revenue model focused on generating consulting income from project work. Differences existed among their growth strategies and international organization. International expansion was related, among other factors, to the demand structures web development firms faced in their home markets. Advanced demand structures enabled higher income levels from more sophisticated projects. They also provided a credible consulting experience base and IT skill set which could be sold to clients in other countries which were not as developed as the home country.

Electronic commerce firms differed not just in their growth strategies and international organization, but also in the purity of their revenue models. Countries with lagging internet access only in exceptional cases were able to sustain revenue models based exclusively on electronic commerce. Ventures in these countries had to combine consumer-oriented electronic commerce activity with consulting work, such as systems integration or web development. The same applied to portal ventures. Thus, one broadstroke firm-level structural difference examined in this chapter next to international expansion is a 'pure play' versus a 'mixed play' revenue model (see Table 7.11). Running a 'mixed play' company was difficult due to the complexities of resource allocation. These companies worked simultaneously for both business clients as well as consumers. There were relatively few 'mixed play' companies in markets with underdeveloped internet access. Yet, 'pure play' electronic commerce ventures, while they existed in these markets as well, were even rarer. There were further tell-tale signs for an underdeveloped e-commerce market among new ventures. Many addressed a particular industry, such as tourism or the career market.

The exceptional, independent 'pure play' electronic commerce firms in underdeveloped countries tended from a very early point in time in their company development to concentrate on international customers. Essentially, they were forced to seek more advanced markets. They became distinguished examples of companies innovating in the electronic trade of services across borders. A frequent drawback to their strategy was its niche approach. Also, those companies pioneered pure services on the internet which did not require logistical operations. Two examples of exceptional 'pure plays' in Germany were TISS AG, later known under its brand name Flights.com, and Jobs & Adverts AG, later renamed Jobpilot AG. Both ventures were founded in 1995. They both successfully raised venture capital after the break-up of the venture capital bottleneck, in 1999 and 1998 respectively.[56] TISS, an internet airline ticketing intermediary, began to focus immediately after founding on the US market, almost completely ignoring its German home market in the early years. Jobs & Adverts established its first international subsidiary in Thailand in July 1997 and then opened up 18 further subsidiaries in Europe by the year 2000. Only then did it list on the Neuer Markt.[57] Yet, the fate of both was uncertain. While Jobpilot managed to generate relatively impressive revenues, its addressable market was small. An offer was made for the acquisition of Jobpilot AG in early 2002 by the Swiss time-share firm Adecco SA.[58] The most successful German 'pure play' venture, the internet broker Consors (founded 1994 as a telephone brokerage) was not an entirely independent entity, but was initially supported and majority-owned by a small German private bank founded in 1828.[59] ricardo.de AG and other well-known 'pure play' internet ventures from Germany were founded in 1998 and later and therefore were actually second generation ventures. Of these, only ricardo.de managed to list on the stock exchange before the financial markets downturn.

Exceptions aside, a typical German first generation electronic commerce firm was i:FAO. i:FAO was listed on the Neuer Markt in 1999 and classified as a high-growth electronic commerce stock. In fact, i:FAO was founded in 1977 as a travel service company for enterprises. It only in 1996 began to develop software to support corporate travel booking processes. Later, it added internet functionality and began to address the consumer market. In 1998, it generated 88 per cent of its sales through corporate travel services. In the year 2000, the year i:FAO spun off its service business, the division still generated about a third of total revenues.[60] At the time of its listing in January 1999, therefore, it was essentially an 'old economy' consulting firm focused on a niche segment. A further example was the holding fluxx.com AG. The oldest fluxx.com entity was founded in 1986 as a design studio. Two of the original design studio founders went on to start a multimedia agency in 1992 and a developer of internet entertainment applications, EIP Entertaining Interactive Productions GmbH, in 1997. By the time of its listing on the Frankfurt exchange in 1999, fluxx.com AG consolidated marketing and web development services for corporations with an internet gambling offer for consumers. In 1999, the holding still generated 92 per cent of its turnover with services, the rest through its e-commerce internet gambling activities.[61] Other examples existed in the portal segment, the best-known 'mixed play' portal from Germany being Web.de.[62] A Swedish 'mixed play' portal also existed. The portal Spray was started by the web developer with the same name.[63] (For a summary of company structures see Table 7.12.)

Table 7.12 *Prevalent structures of leading electronic commerce ventures in different countries up to 1998*

	Structure	International activity	Growth strategy	Financing	Demand structures
USA	'Pure play'	High	Acquisition	Venture capital	Advanced
Sweden	'Pure play'	High	Organic	'Angel' investors	Advanced
Germany	'Mixed play'	Low	Organic	Cash flow	Lagging

Table 7.13 *Internationalization of Swedish 'pure play' electronic commerce start-ups, end 1999*

Name	Focus	Headquarters	Founded	International presence
Boxman	Music retail	London	1997	Sweden, Norway, Denmark, Finland, France, UK, Germany, the Netherlands
Boo.com	Fashion, sports retail	London	1998	Sweden, UK, France, Germany, Finland, Denmark
EPO.com	Financial services	Stockholm	1998	Sweden, UK
Letsbuyit.com	Group buying	Amsterdam	Jan. 1999	Sweden, Norway, Denmark, Finland, Germany, UK, Switzerland, Austria
Dressmart AB	Fashion	Stockholm	1999	Sweden, UK, Netherlands, Finland, Norway, Denmark

Source: Information from the web sites of the companies, accessed in December 1999. Also: 'Ghost in the Machine; Will Boo.com Be Able to Meld What's Hot in Athletic Footwear Across Continents?' *Footwear News*, 2 August 1999.

In Sweden from 1995 to 1998, 'mixed play' firms existed, but a significant number of 'pure plays' were established as well.[64] The number of 'pure plays' emerging out of Sweden was unique for Europe (see Table 7.13). The only other country with significant 'pure plays' among first generation ventures was the United Kingdom. The United Kingdom was an example of an internet market which was both relatively large as well as relatively advanced. The large home market allowed for better economies of scale while demand sophistication of the home market promoted international competitiveness (see Tables 7.1, 7.2 and 7.3). UK 'pure plays' included the auction site QXL ricardo plc as well as the travel service Lastminute.com. Both companies were listed in London and in the year 2000 acquired some of the strongest continental ventures in their business, the German auction-eer ricardo.de and the French Minitel travel service Degriftour. Degriftour had been highly successful as a Minitel service and had successfully managed the transition to the internet.[65] Internationalization of both UK 'pure plays' was rapid. Lastminute.com, for example, launched sites in France, Germany and Sweden in September, October and December 1999. Lastminute.com's business model of matching travel suppliers and consu-mers did not require inventory.

Swedish examples of 'pure play' e-commerce ventures did not survive long; they were short-lived 'fireflies before the storm'.[66] From a timing per-spective, the Swedish 'pure plays' listed here were founded just early enough to have had an opportunity for a stock market listing, as Letsbuyit proved on the Frankfurt exchange. However, their pan-European ambitions were challenging and costly to implement in terms of IT and logistics systems. They did not have a large enough home market to sustain their activities. In most cases, these challenges were fatal. Ironically, some of the more domestically oriented, 'mixed play' e-commerce competitors from Germany carried out an IPO in time and would manage to hang on a lot longer as niche players with low market capitalizations.

In 2001, the most promising and one of the earliest internationally active Swedish e-commerce ventures, the music 'e-tailer' Boxman, went bank-rupt.[67] One of its founders explained later:

> Some of the new electronic commerce ventures created by Swedish entrepren-eurs such as Letsbuyit, started by one of the Icon Medialab founders, or Dressmart, which I helped initiate after leaving Boxman, had experimental busi-ness models. The small margins of Letsbuyit were not sustainable and Dressmart's online tailoring service was simply not accepted by consumers. In contrast, Boxman was a proven, well-known offering accepted and actively used by close to one million internet shoppers from many European countries. However, Boxman management had made a technology decision which turned out to be detrimental to the company. It was too costly and did not work. Boxman would have managed a successful IPO in London in time before the downturn had it not been for the dysfunctional technology, which resulted in dropping sales numbers just before the IPO deadline (Interview, Ahlvarsson, 12 February 2002).

The type of indigenous independent internet venture which fared least well in Europe was the portal player. The only exception was in France. The popularity of Minitel presented start-ups with a unique opportunity not available in other European countries. Due to Minitel, established French media and telecommunications companies responded more slowly to the internet than their competition in other countries. The internet only fully came into French public consciousness in the Summer of 1999, according to the founder and chief executive of iFrance, Marc Simoncini (Interview, 6 November 1999).[68] Swedish portal start-ups, in contrast, met considerable resistance by a number of powerful, established media and telecommunications companies.[69] As shown in Table 7.14, established players had an easy time in Europe building consumer internet brands. This applied especially to telecommunications operators, who, through their successful ISP activities, could influence the start page presented to consumers logging into the internet. The German former PTO, for example, served 37 per cent of all German internet subscribers through its ISP. The Swedish ex-PTO served 30 per cent of Swedish internet subscribers (OECD, 2001a, 111).

The three different types of ventures fared very differently in the countries examined here. The most successful players on a global scale were the Swedish web development firms. They could use the advanced demand conditions in their home market to their full advantage. Although they were also dependent on external financing, their requirements were initially not as substantial as those of electronic commerce firms. More importantly, their fixed costs were lower so that they could adapt better to new, lean times through lay-offs. German web developers, while offered excellent financing opportunities through the Neuer Markt, failed to keep improving their know-how base in terms of strategic consulting expertise and IT integration skills (Waesche, 2003). This was a result of laggard demand conditions in their home market. German web developers also were slow in terms of their international expansion.

Electronic commerce firms failed throughout Europe. The high fixed costs associated with electronic commerce were a severe drawback for European entrepreneurs. Single European internet markets, with the exception of Germany and the UK perhaps, were not large enough to enable the significant economies of scale required to achieve break-even. And in Germany, the large home market was not as attractive as it appeared due to its low penetration rates. The on-line bookseller Amazon.com acquired in Germany was older than Amazon.com itself, yet far less advanced in terms of its IT. Other German firms attempted to address the electronic commerce opportunity 'on the side' in 'mixed play' structures. Profiting from advanced demand conditions at home, numerous Swedish players were far more experimental with creative new businesses models in 'pure play' companies, but here also, the complexities of European electronic commerce led to failure.

Table 7.14   Most popular web properties in Autumn 1999 with independent local new ventures marked in bold

USA	Germany	France	Netherlands	Sweden
AOL Network	FOCUS Online	Voila – Wanadoo (France Telecom)	World Online (WOI)	MSN/ Hotmail
Yahoo!	DINO-Online	Yahoo France	Lycos	Passagen Natverk
Microsoft Sites	Infoseek	**MultiMania**	Ilse	Tele2
Lycos	**Consors Brokers World**	**Caramail**	World Access / Planet Internet	Microsoft
Go Network	RTL Online	AOL France (Cegetel)	Royal KPN	AOL
Excite@Home	ProSieben Online	AltaVista	Publieke Omroepen	Yahoo!
Amazon	AOL Homepage	**Chez.com**	Startpagina.NL	Telenordia
Time Warner Online	Spiegel Online	Les Echos	IDG	Altavista
RealSite Portfolio	Coupe	**iFrance**	VNU	Telia
Altavista Sites	RZ-Online	Club Internet (Lagadere)	De Telegraaf	Aftonbladet
eBay	DSF SportsWorld	Excite	Microsoft Nederland	Torget
Go2Net Network	DM-Online	MSN	Veronica	**Spray**
LookSmart	Süddeutsche Zeitung Online	**Nomade**	Nederlandse Spoorwegen	Lycos Network
Bluemountainarts.com	Fun Online	Lycos	PCM Uitgevers	Modern Times Group
ZDNet Sites	Com! Online	Infonie	Versatel Telecom	TV4

Sources: Most sources measured the popularity of consolidated marketing 'internet properties', not individual sites. Focus Online in Germany, for example, included different web sites such as the *Focus* magazine's web page as well as the GMX site, which was an internet start-up offering e-mail and messaging services. Sources: USA: Media Metrix (can be found on http://www.mediametrix.com/), data from the month of September. Germany: IVW Online Medien Reichweiten (can be found on http://www.pz-online.de/), data from the month of September, France: Le Journal du Net quoting figures by Benchmark Group (http://www.journaldunet.com/), data from the month of August, accessed on 25 September 1999, Netherlands: Multiscope (e-mail Stefan Pauls to author, 5 October 1999), data from the month of August, Sweden: Sifo Interactive Media/Media Metrix (e-mail Mikael Ohlsson, Research Manager, to author, 18 October 1999), data from the month of September. These sources all used different measurement techniques. It can be assumed that the German IVW figures were both inaccurate as well as not representative. Instead of measuring unique visitors to a site using user tracking techniques (such as Media Metrix in USA and in Sweden), IVW measured visits based on server-side software measurements. There was no way to distinguish unique visitors, this caused distortions between transaction-oriented sites that were frequently visited to check e-mail or make auction bids. Furthermore, many top sites refused to participate by not installing the required software. These included the independent internet start-up Web.de the American players Yahoo! and Excite, and Deutsche Telekom's T-Online, the top portal in Germany. Special thanks go to Frederic Madre for guiding me through the French internet scene.

Portal ventures also failed in Europe. Media players managed to leverage their brands extremely well and telecommunications firms pushed their portals through their ISP offerings. The only exception was France; here, Minitel was a distraction for established players. This observation runs counter to the commonplace opinion that the Minitel hindered internet development in France. In the rest of Europe, those independent portals which managed to survive were not able to build an international presence.

The exclusively domestic focus of many German, French and Dutch players, however, made them attractive acquisition candidates for US internationalizers. Several promising ventures, such as the German firms Lava, InnoMate, ABC Bücherdienst Telebuch, Alando.de and Ricardo were acquired by the US players iXL, USWeb, Amazon.com, eBay and the British start-up QXL. Others, such as Web.de, i:Fao and Fluxx, managed to survive well into the new decade on the funds raised during their IPO on the Neuer Markt. Measured by a number of indicators, such as revenues and the number of employees, they remained insignificant players in the internet sector. The Frankfurt stock exchange provided these 'mixed play' ventures with a chance for survival other European internet start-ups did not have. The winners of the so-called 'internet era' at the end of the 1990s seem to have been a very small number of surviving first generation American new ventures which managed to establish themselves internationally and secured sufficient funding to reach break-even before the capital market downturn. Also in Europe, they occupied leading positions, sharing the market with the established European media and telecommunications companies. Boston Consulting Group estimated in February 2000 that it was ten times more likely that a US internet company makes a sale in Europe than the other way around (quoted in Welfens and Jungmittag, 2002, 55). Please refer to the table of surviving ventures in early 2002 (Table 7.15).

THE FATE OF THE 'SECOND GENERATION'

After 1998, across Europe, significant changes pertaining to the conditions for internet entrepreneurship were under way. While fixed-line telecommunications competition begun in January 1998, improvement in local loop pricing and customer response was a slow development lasting years. Yet steady improvement, in addition to the massive rise of mobile phone use, engulfed many European countries and made the Swedish home market with its advanced demand structures appear less unique.

While telecommunications liberalization resulted in steadily improving internet access, the most significant change in Europe after 1998 was surely the break-up of the venture capital bottleneck. An unprecedented venture

Table 7.15 Examples of surviving, independent internet companies, early 2002

Country of origin	Company	Capitalization (US$ million)	Employees	Full Year Net Sales (US$ million)	International presence
Web developers					
USA	Scient (merger iXL and Scient completed Nov. 2001)	60	1600	659.5 (2000) (Pro forma combined iXL and Scient sales)	USA, UK, France (affiliate), Japan (affiliate) (other offices were closed or sold)
Sweden	Framtidsfabriken AB (Framfab)	35	630	146.7 (2000) 66.7 (2001)	Denmark, France, Germany, Netherlands, Sweden, UK
Sweden	Cell Network AB	49	1769	149.9 (2000)	Denmark, Estonia, Finland, Germany, Italy, Norway, Sweden, UK, Malaysia
Sweden/ Netherlands	Icon Medialab (merger Icon Medialab and Lost Boys N.V. completed Jan. 2002)	28	1500	162.7 (2000)	The Netherlands, Spain, Switzerland, Germany, Belgium, Denmark, Germany, Sweden, Finland, Portugal, UK, Italy, Norway, France, Austria, USA, Hong Kong, Australia, China, Singapore
E-commerce					
USA	Amazon.com	3 777	7800	2 762 (2000) 3 122 (2001)	USA, Germany, France, Japan
USA	eBay	16 557	1927	431.4 (2000) 748.8 (2001)	USA, Germany, UK, Australia, Japan, Canada, France, Austria, Italy, South Korea
UK	Lastminute.com	74	307	5.4 (2000) 26.5 (2001)	UK, France, Germany, Sweden, Australia (jv), South Africa (jv), Italy, Spain (jv), The Netherlands
UK	QXL Ricardo	22	383	9.9 (2000) 21.7 (2001)	UK, Belgium, Germany, Spain, Finland, France, Italy, The Netherlands, Norway, Poland, Sweden, Switzerland

227

Table 7.15 (continued)

Country of origin	Company	Capitalization (USD million)	Employees	Full Year Net Sales (US$ million)	International presence
Germany	Consors Discount-Broker (under sale)	497	1346	294.9 (2000)	Germany, France, Spain, Switzerland, Italy
Germany	Jobpilot (under sale to Adecco)	57	165 (Germany only)	29.5 (2000) 39.8 (2001)	Austria, Belgium, Czech Republic, Denmark, France, Germany, Hungary, Italy, The Netherlands. Norway, Poland, Spain, Switzerland, UK
Portals USA	Yahoo!	10 937	3 259	1 110 (2000) 717.4 (2001)	USA, Argentina, Australia, Brazil, Canada, Denmark, France, Germany, Hong Kong, India, Italy, Japan, South Korea, Mexico, Norway, Singapore, Spain, Sweden, Taiwan, UK
Germany	Web.de	140	230	10.5 (2000)	Germany

Sources: Data collected on 20 January 2002 from the websites of NASDAQ, Stockholmsbörsen, London Stock Exchange, Deutsche Börse as well as from company web sites. Except: Data for Jobpilot, collected on 3 February 2002 from Deutsche Börse, Cell Network, collected on 13 February 2002 from Stockholmsbörsen and Framfab, collected on 14 February 2002 from Stockholmsbörsen. Additional information on 2001 sales from the Amazon.com press release: 'Amazon.com Announces 4th Quarter Profit. Exceeds sales and profit objectives. Lower prices for customers drove sales and profits', Seattle, 22 January 2002. Exchange rates used were: EUR/US$ 0.88, SEK/US$ 0.10, GBP/US$ 1.44. Information on revenues of Lastminute.com quoted from the 'Annual Review and Summary Financial Statement 2001' of the company for the year ending 30 September 2001. 2001 revenues as well as recent employee figures for Framtidsfabriken AB were quoted from 'Year-end Report January–December 2001. Framfab reports profit for Q4 2001'. Independent ventures were not majority-owned by an incumbent telecommunications or media company at the time.

capital glut ensued in response to the worldwide financial internet bubble.[70] Financial overheating was especially strong in Germany, where the temporary success of the Neuer Markt became a further domestic factor influencing venture capital investments.

As a response to the overheating stock market and the venture capital glut, a host of new electronic commerce start-ups, portal sites and other types of internet ventures appeared after 1998 all across Europe. A 'Top 100' table of European internet start-ups from August 2000 listed several start-ups from different European countries, with a significant number headquartered in Germany, but also several from France and Sweden (see Table 7.16). Although the relevant founding dates were not available, most firms, except for TISS, Degriftour, EPO.com and Boxman, were founded only in 1999. In contrast to their predecessors, the majority of second generation European internet start-ups were venture capital-financed. Furthermore, all were 'pure play' ventures. Europeans followed the models provided by US ventures. Entrepreneurs and financiers could point to improving internet penetration rates in Europe, which were approaching one-third of the population.[71] Finally, second generation companies were much more fervent and rapid internationalizers than their predecessors. It

Table 7.16   Company headquarter locations in Bathwick Group e-League of Top 100 European internet ventures, August 2000

	Start-ups in 'Top 100'	Company names
Germany	14	Tiss.com, goindustry.com, dooyoo.de, ciao.com, 12snap.com, elabseurope.com, surplex.com, webmiles.com, efoodmanager.com, vitago.com, glomedix.com, censio.de, webvertising.de, beautynet.de
France	9	degriftour.fr, kelkoo.com, omniticket.com, finance-net.com, allocine.fr , proXchange.com, doubletrade.com, wineandco.com, femmeonline.fr
Sweden	5	epo.com, boxman.com, funplanet.com, citikey.com, wapshealth.com
Netherlands	0	

Sources: These were the results of the second e-League table. It incorporated feedback from the first Bathwick Group e-League table published in the *Sunday Times* on 2 July 2000 and was therefore more accurate than the first table. The table still showed a strong tendency to favouring UK firms; in fact, in the second table, 62 companies from England were named. However, it was one of the few comparative sources on internet start ups across Europe. Published under http://www.bathwick.com/, accessed on 30 August 2000. Bathwick Group was a consulting and research firm.

was this generation which entered public awareness in Europe and came to represent the 'internet hype'.

In August 2000, these second generation ventures were all very young, private companies, however. Most of them were still vulnerable and dependent upon ongoing venture capital financing. Most disappeared in the course of capital markets downturn in the years 2000 and 2001.

CONCLUSION

European development provides a useful comparison allowing one to better understand internet entrepreneurship in the United States. While practitioners at the time were aware of the significance of country-level variables such as internet access, how these variables affected the new ventures themselves was not apparent. Although their business concepts were similar or even identical copies, European internet ventures were different from leading ventures in the US. Alternative company structures, such as the 'mixed play' start-up, appeared in Europe in response to underdeveloped internet access. It is, therefore, not sufficient to view the difference between Europe and the US in terms of a two-year lag, as many practitioners did.[72] Although country-level variables such as internet access eventually converged after a time lag, the first generation enterprises themselves remained distinct, preserving unevenness in development. European internet development was presented by distinguishing between two different generations of internet ventures. The whole institutional landscape, including enterprises as well as regulatory bodies, had to be taken into account for an accurate cross-national comparison.

This chapter also described the course of recent telecommunications liberalization in Europe. In fact, the much observed timing differences between the US and Europe were a result of telecommunications reform. The trade-off between policy designed to strengthen a single major player, on the one hand, and infrastructure policy committed to national innovation in a variety of sectors, on the other hand, was made through the timing of reform. The incumbent was granted a preparatory period between the stock market listing and the start of fixed-line competition. The possibility for infrastructure competition through cable TV was minimized. Policy-makers did not believe a delay would be problematic, because they perceived changes in global competitive conditions and the birth of a New Economy in terms of a continuous, steady evolution. The timing of liberalization implied that a strong 'global champion' could be created out of a privatized state enterprise first. Then, new venture activity would be released as a second step enabled through a progressive legal framework outlining extensive unbundling possibilities.

Yet, this delay had an adverse impact on first generation internet ventures in Europe. First generation ventures were forced to adopt structurally to weaker demand conditions caused by prohibitive local telecommunications prices. A unique global window of opportunity provided by the commercialization of the internet was thereby missed.

NOTES

1. In reality, national differences in English-language skills actually did not seem to have a significant influence on internet development. Local languages dominated the internet in Europe, even in the early days of the internet's commercialization. In 1997, the largest proportion of all websites (42 per cent) in the EU were in the native tongue only and originated in non English-speaking countries (European Commission, 1997, 28, 29).
2. Wealthy families and the institutional investment vehicles controlled by them were closely interwoven into the financial and industrial world. These families were the Wallenbergs, Söderbergs, Bonniers and others. Petersson calls them 'owners' and discusses their 'inherited network' (Pettersson, 1992, 179, 181, 183). The Wallenberg figure is quoted from Kurzer (1993, 128).
3. Paulette Kurzer emphasizes this delay in her book on political and economic change in Europe (1993, viii).
4. Jupiter Communications, press release, 'Jupiter Communications Acquires Swedish-based Intelligence AB, a Leading Scandinavian Research Company,' New York, 5 August 1999. In 1999, Jupiter's research network included offices in London, San Francisco, Stockholm, and Sydney. Media Metrix, press release, 'Swedish Web User Habits Similar to US Users, Media Metrix Releases The Top 50 Swedish Web Sites at Home and at Work, First Available Internet Audience Ratings Outside the US Provided by Media Metrix and its Partner SIFO Interactive in Sweden', New York, 1 June 1999. Through a partnership, Doubleclick extended its advertising network's reach into Sweden before its IPO in February 1998; at that time, it had offices in Australia, Canada and the United Kingdom and partnerships in other countries as well. In Europe, Doubleclick was present only in Sweden, the United Kingdom and Spain. After the IPO, the international presence was expanded aggressively into many further countries. Filing of Doubleclick Inc. with US Securities and Exchange Commission (http://www.sec.gov/), S-1, 16 December 1997, as well as Doubleclick web site.
5. Using the same access price measure, Germany had fallen to below the OECD average by late 2000 and was only the 15th most expensive OECD country. But even in late 2000, access prices in Germany stood a little above the EU average in terms of US$ PPP. OECD (2001a, 190). In September 2000, 20 hours of internet access at discounted off-peak rates including telecommunications fees in Germany amounted to US$ PPP 34. Sweden stood at 24.14, the United States at 21.43. The OECD average was calculated to be US$ PPP 34.19, the EU average was 32.03.
6. Pricing innovations and user-friendly pricing were crucial for technology uptake also in other instances. A further example is the massive boost given to mobile telephony services in the late 1990s in the United Kingdom, when prepaid phone packages were introduced. 'Im britischen Mobilfunk sind Vorauszahler der Wachstumsmotor', *Frankfurter Allgemeine Zeitung*, 3 November 1999, 28.
7. The Minitel experience also is instructive here. In the mid-1990s, Minitel reached an astounding penetration of about 26 per cent, which made the Minitel the most successful Teletex service, with numbers able to match those of internet penetration in the most advanced countries (see Table 7.1). But Minitel reached a peak in 1994 and subsequently usage call volume started to decline. The main reason cited was high costs – especially

the fact that usage of services was charged by the time spent on-line. According to OECD, this metered charging system discouraged use and proved to be a disincentive stunting further development (OECD, 1998a, 19–23).

8. Several newspaper articles pointed to the adverse effects of metered pricing. For example: Paul Taylor, 'Telephone tariffs put net take-off on hold', *Financial Times*, 27 October 1999, 16; 'Schlagaustausch online', *Frankfurter Allgemeine Zeitung*, 27 August 1999, 22. AOL Europe, Hamburg, in 1999, commissioned a study at the University of Potsdam of the economic effects which potentially would be achieved through the introduction of a flat-rate, unmetered access tariff in Germany. The research institute concluded that 100 000 to 400 000 jobs would be created due to greater internet uptake encouraged by a flat rate (Welfens and Jungmittag, 1999). This finding was reviewed again in Welfens and Jungmittag (2002, 102–21).

9. Although competition was introduced to US long-distance telephony, local calls were still constrained in a tightly monitored monopoly structure, with regional 'Baby Bells' having to offer affordable local call pricing packages. Even after 1996, with the passing of a new Telecommunications Act, local carriers needed to demonstrate the existence of local competition before they could begin to act as fully independent companies. In essence, US policy did not budge, even when the local carriers applied significant pressure on the federal telecommunications authority, loudly objecting to the fact that they were subsidizing the growth of the internet.

10. Tele2 was the creation of the Swedish industrial holding Kinnevik, which under the leadership of the grandson of one of the co-founders, Jan Hugo Stenbeck, aggressively and consistently formed companies competing against Swedish monopolies, including in radio and television. The official history of Industriförvaltnings AB Kinnevik, posted on its website, reads: 'The second half of the 1980s is characterized by the aggressive formation of new companies and hard battles against Sweden's telecommunications, radio and TV monopolies', http://www.kinnevik.se/ accessed on 12 February 2002. See also Noam (1992, 210).

11. Furthermore, network infrastructure competition for internet access was difficult to realize in Sweden. The incumbent was allowed to retain control over the cable TV network, as in many other European countries. Ethernet LANs to the home, or so-called 'property networks' were an alternative local loop network innovation pioneered in Sweden later by a broadband competitor, Bredbandsbolaget (B2). See: OECD (2001b, 39, 40).

12. Telia owned over 90 per cent of the local loop in Sweden. An interconnection fee transfer was triggered when access calls were placed from local lines owned by the incumbent operator to the dial-in nodes of competitors. The success of competitive internet access offerings, especially that of Tele2, created a situation in the years 1997 and 1998 in which Telia was a net payer for internet access calls. As a result, Telia was forced to lower its local call rates (Interview, Billinger, 21 December 1999).

13. For a statement regarding alternative infrastructures such as WLL, power line or cable TV, see Monopolkommission (2001, 62, 123, 124).

14. The incumbent intended to impose a price of unbundled access for the competition which was higher than the monthly subscription fee the incumbent charged its own consumers. This made the introduction of attractive offers difficult for the competition (Monopolkommission, 2001, 39, 121–3, 152).

15. A flat-rate internet offer by the incumbent made in 2000 was attacked as a 'dumping price' and withdrawn a year later, only to be again offered as a broadband service (see Welfens and Jungmittag, 2002, 32, 64, 69).

16. Only in 2002, for example, did it implement an enforcement mechanism so it could charge the incumbent fees when it delayed the connection of competitors to its network. 'Telekom soll bei Verzug Entschädigung zahlen', *Süddeutsche Zeitung*, 13 February 2002, 21.

17. After rising continually, the ISP market share of the competition in terms of internet connection minutes fell in the first quarter of 2001 from 28 per cent to 25 per cent (Monopolkommission, 2001, 51). After four years of competition, the former monopolist still fully controlled over 97 per cent of all access lines (VATM, 2001, 14).

18. Regarding the policy trade-off between the research capabilities of a global telecommu-

nications champion and domestic infrastructural concerns, Welfens and Jungmittag made an interesting proposal (2002, 131). National incumbents should have been broken up throughout Europe and allowed to reshape along European lines, thereby allowing for the formation of large global players, yet without the adverse effect of the dominance of old monopolists in single national markets. However, the controversy surrounding retention national control (for example, in the proposed merger between the German and Italian incumbents), showed that policy-making was still national in orientation and not as European as would have been necessary for the implementation of the Welfens and Jungmittag proposal.

19. Thanks to Sam Paltridge, OECD Secretariat, for clearly making this point to me in an e-mail exchange.

20. See an excellent article about the advantages of an EU-wide framework, which, however, could benefit EASDAQ as much as it could boost the cross-border activities of Frankfurt's Neuer Markt: 'No SECs Please, we're European, European Financial Regulation, Regulatory Muddle is Impeding Europe's Progress Towards its Goal of a Single Market in Financial Services', *The Economist*, 21 August 1999.

21. One French VC exclaimed: 'The Nouveau Marché is terrible. There is no liquidity, only a few really good companies are listed there. EASDAQ also is in bad shape. Top French companies go for NASDAQ.' The Euro.NM market capitalization percentages from: 'Europe's New Markets Flourish Despite Turbulence and Euro', *European Venture Capital Journal, Source Express*, 1 January 1999.

22. 'Teueres Abenteuer. Wagniskapital: Der Absturz vieler Internet-Unternehmen verdirbt den Fonds die Renditen', *Manager Magazin*, May 2001, 27, 30.

23. Paul Lerbinger, Managing Director of Investment Banking Division, Deutsche Bank, stated in a roundtable discussion: 'EASDAQ will find it very hard to expand to become the hi-tech stock exchange of Europe. Most of the stocks listed there are in danger of becoming orphan stocks because they do not have a natural home market.' From: 'The New World of German Equity', *ABI-Inform, Euroweek International Equity Review Supplement*, May 1999.

24. Hans Peter Roemer, Managing Director at Dekia Kapitalanlage, one of the largest German mutual fund companies stated in early 1999: 'At the end of last year we had 1.7 Million accounts held by private investors. In the first four months of this year that figure rose by half a million, or by almost 30 per cent. This is not just happening at Dekia. You see the same trend in every large German mutual fund company.' He also declared: 'Since the Deutsche Telekom flotation, German investors have become more aware of the need to save for their retirement through equities.' From: 'The New World of German Equity', *ABI-Inform, Euroweek International Equity Review Supplement*, May 1999.

25. 'Aktienfonds ziehen Millionen neuer Anleger an', *Handelsblatt*, 2 August 2000, 1.

26. 'The Neuer Markt's Wild Ride', *Predicasts PROMT, Institutional Investor International Edition*, 1 April 1999.

27. 'A German Coup: European Stockmarkets', *The Economist*, 9 January 1999.

28. 'The Neuer Markt's Wild Ride', *Predicasts PROMT, Institutional Investor International Edition*, 1 April 1999.

29. Alfred Kueppers, 'Neuer Markt Endures Growing Pains As Need for Market Regulation Rises', *Wall Street Journal*, 1 August 2001.

30. See Professor John Freeman's study of venture capital in Germany, Freeman (1998).

31. Waldemar Janz, a very experienced German venture capital manager who worked for many years for TVM before starting his own fund, believed that the human capital base in Germany would realistically allow about 120 early-stage investments annually, funded with DM 1.2 billion. See: Niko Waesche, 'Venture World. Wir sinken tiefer', *Financial Times Deutschland*, 6 September 2001, 33. For a brief article about VC experience in Germany, see: Niko Waesche, 'Venture World. Ganz neu im Club', *Financial Times Deutschland*, 2 August 2001, 30.

32. Interviews with venture capitalists confirmed this: Pärson (2 December 1999) and Spangberg (17 November 1999). For an overview of Swedish programmes see OECD (1998b, 148, 149).

33. On Sweden's regulatory initiative, see the mention in: Nicholas George, 'Chilly Regions of North Warm to the Net', *Financial Times*, 13 October 1999, 16.
34. 'Address by Prime Minister Lionel Jospin at the 20th Summer Forum on Communication', Service d'information du gouvernement (SIG), 26 August 1999, Hourtin (can be found on http://www.internet.gouv.fr/, accessed on 19 September 1999).
35. English abstract of Swedish article (World Reporter). 'Linne and Spray Remain in Sweden, Linne och Spray stannar i Sverige', *Dagens Industri*, 20 September 1999.
36. Cowie describes succinctly the US experience. Capital gains tax was raised in 1969 and lowered again in 1979. Private equity commitments rose substantially as a result of the reduction (1999, 32, 33).
37. It is useful to recall that the entrepreneur's perception of policy in these areas was based on the situation in the United States. Although US tax policy is much clearer and labour regulation in many aspects more flexible, Europe as a whole enjoyed an advantage to the US, which many entrepreneurs pointed out as well. Employee loyalty seemed to have been stronger in Europe; this was especially important given the dearth of knowledge workers with IT skills at the time. In a way, this compensated for some of the problems entrepreneurs encountered in Europe – one of the reasons for extensive options programmes in the USA was to improve employee loyalty. Obviously, options programmes also motivated employees and European entrepreneurs were eager to make use of them.
38. For France, see OECD (1999b, 18, 19).
39. It is important to note, however, that the most important and most inspiring company at the beginning of internet commercialization was Netscape, the internet software company which was listed on NASDAQ in August 1995.
40. Although basic 'brochureware' web sites required very little know-how, advanced electronic commerce systems in the late 1990s still were complex to develop and maintain. 'Out of the box' software, developed by internet software companies such as Intershop and others, was often not stable and needed to be tightly integrated into the specific company's process and logistics.
41. Pierre Morin, Partner at the London office of the US venture capital firm GRP Partners, stated: 'At the end of the 1990s, full-fledged electronic commerce systems were still extremely difficult to build and complex to maintain. This was especially true for pan-European initiatives. For an IT system covering three different countries, a start-up would have to face costs of at least four million USD and would require a minimum of six to seven months of development time to be fully operational' (e-mail, 14 February 2002).
42. Amazon.com, '2000 Annual Report', p. 23.
43. Amazon.com turned a profit in the fourth quarter 2001 for the first time since being founded nearly seven years earlier. For that quarter, Amazon.com reported net income of US$ 5.1 million on sales that exceeded US$ 1 billion. Press release: 'Amazon.com Announces 4th Quarter Profit. Exceeds sales and profit objectives. Lower prices for customers drove sales and profits', Seattle, 22 January 2002.
44. The search service and portal site Yahoo! launched in Germany, France and the United Kingdom during 1996, in Sweden, Australia, Singapore, Korea, Denmark and Norway during 1997 and Italy, Hong Kong and Spain in 1998. See Filing of Yahoo Inc. with US Securities and Exchange Commission (http://www.sec.gov/), 8-K/A, 12 November 1999. Yahoo! could have remained content with focusing exclusively on the largest internet marketplace, the US – especially since competition in the United States was vigorous and encompassed established players from media, telecommunications and retail industries as well as well-funded start-up companies. Yet, US internet ventures developed innovative services for their advanced home market, which they launched abroad as demand improved elsewhere. US start-ups also profited from funding opportunities handed to them by angel investors, venture capitalists and growth-focused public capital markets. Yahoo!, however, was the most successful early internationalizer among US internet start-ups. Yahoo! also boasted a for US ventures unusual expansion strategy, which was mostly organic with relatively few acquisitions.
45. David Bank discusses the Microsoft strategy respective to the internet in his book, based

on internal Microsoft correspondence (2001, for Pearl Harbour Day, see p. 61). 'The Internet Tidal Wave' memo by Bill Gates from May 1995 is mentioned by Martin Kenney. Kenney also describes the timing of internet development in the United States (2001, 20–22).

46. In a survey of 30 German internet start-ups carried out by the author jointly with the business publication *Manager Magazin* in early 1998, exactly half were founded in the years 1994, 1995 or 1996.

47. Icon Medialab was founded in March 1996 and opened its first international office in Madrid in August the same year, as well as in San Francisco in December. In 1997, Icon Medialab opened offices in London, Kuala Lumpur, Copenhagen and Tampere (Finland). In May 1997, Icon Medialab hired its 100th employee. From: 'Four friends founded Icon Medialab in March 1996', on the website of Icon Medialab, http://www.iconmedialab.se/default/about_us/history/1997.html, accessed on 27 November 1999.

48. Agency.com, press release, 'Agency.com Announces Acquisition of Leading Dutch Interactive Firm', 2 August 1999 (from the corporate web site http://www.agency.com/); CyberConsult, Press release, 'Icon Medialab International neemt CyberConsult over "E-vikings landen in Nederland"' 27 September 1999 (from http://www.iconmedia-lab.nl/). Thanks to Roel de Hoop of Hot-orange.com for the pointers.

49. My understanding of the Swedish internet space was boosted considerably through numerous interesting discussions with Johan Jörgensen, former editor of an IT magazine and Chief Operating Officer of the internet start-up Municel.

50. For web developers worldwide, the most threatening development after the year 2000 next to the disappearance of easy funding was the reduction of IT expenditures by large corporations. For a review of the fate of web developers in Germany, see: 'Internetberater werden Übernahmeziele. International Großkonzerne bemühen sich um Unternehmen wie Kabel New Media oder GFT Technologies', *Financial Times Deutschland*, 16 May 2001, 4.

51. These include the small Cologne-based shop Killakanu (September 1998), Dutch agency CyberConsult (September 1999) and the New York interactive consultant Nicholson NY (November 1999).

52. A Swedish entrepreneur, Ola Ahlvarsson, celebrated the organic growth strategy, referring to Boxman and Dressmart: 'In the music industry, it has been clear for a long time that you can't just create hits by throwing millions of marketing dollars at a certain band. You need to create a convincing story that consumers and journalists just can't pass by. Once you manage to do this, roll it out in as many countries as possible' (Interview, 18 October 1999).

53. See: 'Sweden's Icon Medialab prepares for foreign IPO', *Reuter News Service*, 22 September 1999.

54. An informal network of 'angel' investors with a high-calibre background was very supportive of the Swedish internet start-up scene. The former top executive of Scandinavian Airlines, Jan Carlzon, was one of the initial backers of many start-ups including Boxman. It was characteristic of the Swedish start-up scene that one of the best-known Swedish venture capitalists at the time, Kjell Spangberg, invested his own private money out of San Francisco without being associated with a fund (Interview, Spangberg, 17 November 1999). What was furthermore unique about Sweden was the survival of powerful, wealthy families, such as the Wallenbergs and its Investor Group. Investor AB backed Spray's pan-European portal initiative with a substantial amount of funding, approximately US$ 62 million. 'Spray to Compete Online With Yahoo, AOL in Europe', *Reuter Economic News*, 9 September 1999. An important characteristic of all of these backers was the strong personal support they offered, opening doors and adding instant legitimacy to an entrepreneur. Although the backing of Investor Group in Spray's portal project was large even by US standards, the sums invested by informal investors, mostly private persons, were often paltry. The initial investment in Icon Medialab by a former media executive was reputed to have been SEK 250000 (EUR 28 000) for 10 per cent of the company.

55. 'Sweden Allows Pension Funds More Freedom', *Financial Times*, 25 June 1999.
56. TISS AG was financed in 1999 by a venture capital consortium composed of Goldman Sachs, Star Ventures, T-Venture and the public fund tbg. The successful founder, Rudi Weissmann, who managed to build up the company with an impressively low cost base and only three employees, left the company, however. Jobs & Adverts was financed in 1998 through the corporate venture capital arm of 1&1, the German online marketing company and ISP, now United Internet AG.
57. Information from the IPO documentation of Jobs & Adverts AG (Verkaufsprospekt, dated 4 April 2000).
58. Cordula Eubel, 'Adecco schnappt sich Internet-Jobbörse', *Financial Times Deutschland*, 7 February 2002, 6.
59. Consors Discount-Broker AG encountered great difficulties surviving after the stock market downturn and the decline of 'online broker' euphoria. For a while, Consors was extremely successful among German internet brokerage companies, in a market space hotly contested by spin-offs from established players such as Deutsche Bank, Commerzbank and HypoVereinsbank (Direkt Anlage Bank). Consors was founded as a telephone direct broker in 1994, it offered its services over T-Online in 1995 and over the internet from November 1996. Consors was started by 25-year-old Karl Matthäus Schmidt, who came from a German private banking family. The Hof- and Nuremberg-based family-owned SchmidtBank KGaA initially gave support to the new venture. It also owned a majority share of the discount broker (the family was forced to sell its own majority stake in SchmidtBank in November 2001). The internationalization pace of Consors lagged behind that of US or Swedish electronic commerce ventures. The international expansion of Consors occurred only after its stock market listing on the Frankfurt Neuer Markt in April 1999. Consors in July 1999 acquired Axfin SA, an online stockbroker in France, in October 1999 it established itself in Switzerland and in December 1999 acquired a majority stake of a Spanish online broker SIAGA, S.V.B. S.A. Yet, Consors was one of the fastest internationalizers among German independent internet ventures. Most other electronic commerce players, even among listed companies, were even slower to internationalize or focused exclusively on German-speaking neighbours. Consors Discout-Broker AG, Press release, 'Consors erwirbt Mehrheitsbeteiligung an Axfin, Paris', 5 July 1999; Consors Schweiz AG, press release, 'Der günstigste Discount-Broker der Schweiz heißt Consors Schweiz', 1 October 1999; Consors Discount-Broker AG, 'Consors übernimmt führenden spanischen Online-Broker', 10 December 1999.
60. i:FAO, 'Internet Travel Solutions 1999 Annual Report', page 34. The market capitalization of iFAO in February 2002 on the Frankfurt Neuer Markt was EUR 9.9 million (in June 2000: Euro 147.4 million). Its 2001 sales were EUR 3.4 million, having spun off its non-software business segments (2000 revenue: EUR 7.2 million). For the breakdown of services in the year 2000, see i:FAO, 'Internet Travel Solutions 2001 Annual Report', p. 53.
61. In 2000, 77 per cent of revenues were generated through services. Total net revenues were DM 17.7 million in 1999 and DM 33.1 million in 2000. flux.com AG, 'Geschäftsbericht 2000', p. 44. For further information on the history of the group, see: flux.com AG 'Verkaufsprospekt', 24 September 1999.
62. Web.de was launched and for a long time run by Cinetic Medientechnik GmbH, a German systems integrator. Web.de was spun off and listed on the Neuer Markt. Throngs of smaller portals were in the late 1990s still run 'on the side'. For more examples of 'mixed play' German companies which financed their internet start-up businesses through other cash-flow generating activities on the side, see: Niko Waesche, 'Tough Balancing Act for German Internet Start-ups', *Tornado-Insider.com Magazine*, 2, May 1999, 24, 25. The article from 1999, however, mentioned examples of 'pure play' electronic commerce firms, which actually were further examples of 'mixed play' approaches, such as i:FAO and Fluxx.com. Still other 'pure play' portal firms, such as another popular German portal, DINO-Online, were run on an extremely tight budget and were later acquired.

63. Spray Services was in January 1999 acquired by the US web development firm Razorfish. The Spray portal was acquired by Lycos Europe in September 2000. Press release, Lycos Europe, 'Lycos Europe acquires Spray Network for 674 Million Euro in shares and extends its leadership position in Europe', 21 September 2001.
64. Swedish entrepreneurs also formally founded 'pure plays' outside of their home country to avoid dysfunctional options taxation. The Swedish home market remained an important test market for these companies.
65. In 1998, growth in Degriftour's sales was attributable to the internet and not any more to the development of Minitel. In December 1998, 400000 clients visited Degriftour's Minitel site and already 300000 had visited the internet web site. English abstract of French article, 'Degriftour's Web Site is Successful, Chez Degriftour, le Web Supplante le Minitel', *Globalbase, Informatique*, 22 January 1999.
66. In May 2000, the first of them, Boo.com, had already gone bankrupt. Due to the large sums of money invested in it, its unbridled ambitions and its early bankruptcy, Boo.com became a symbol of the excesses of the internet bubble in Europe. Dressmart went bankrupt in July/August 2000. Letsbuyit.com, after a delayed listing on the Neuer Markt, had to lay off about a fifth of its employees in August 2000 and subsequently hovered near bankruptcy for months. The financial services venture EPO.com was acquired in early 2001 by a UK venture, EO plc. See: 'Letsbuyit.com', *Financial Times Deutschland*, 31 August 2000, 15. 'Fireflies before the storm' was a phrase used by IBM CEO Lou Gerstner in 1999 to collectively describe new internet ventures. 'Face value. Follow that. Will Sam Palmisano, IBM's new boss, be a worthy successor to Lou Gerstner?' *The Economist*, 8 February 2002, 60. The founder of boo.com commemorated the fate of his company in a book, appropriately named *boo hoo* (Malmsten, et al., 2001).
67. The Swedish internet music retailer Boxman managed to start internationalization early enough in the internet adoption cycle to profit from internet uptake in Europe. Founded in December 1997, Boxman employed 120 people by December 1999. By that time, it managed to establish itself as a recognized consumer brand in the Scandinavian countries as well as in France, the United Kingdom, Germany and the Netherlands. In September 1999, Boxman signed a major cross-promotion deal with the music television channel MTV. Boxman developed innovative international business models; it built a centralized warehouse in the Netherlands linked to its internet ordering system. In Scandinavia, Boxman secured 4–5 per cent of total compact disc retail sales; this figure included sales via traditional retail outlets. In 1999, between 3000 and 5000 orders were placed each day over the international Boxman web sites. Interview with Tony Salter, CEO, Boxman AB, 03 December 1999. Please refer also to the analyst report by Morgan Stanley Dean Witter, Equity Research Europe, 'The European Internet Report', June 1999, p. 189. Further: Interview with Ola Ahlvarsson, CEO, Result Ventures Knowledge, 18 October 1999. Also: Kimberley A. Strassel, 'Using an Old-Fashioned Approach, Boxman Becomes Big Hit in Europe', *Wall Street Journal*, 8 July 1999. See also: English abstract of Swedish article (World Reporter). 'Boxman Records Huge Losses, Boxman gor brakforlust', *Finanstidningen*, 18 September 1999. In the article, the sales of the company were cited to be SEK 77 million (approximately EUR 9 million) in the first half of 1999 with losses of SEK 188 million (EUR 21 million). The article continued to state that Boxman raised a total of SEK 400 million (EUR 45 million) in venture capital.
68. French portal start-ups did very well, by combining search services with public forums ('communities'). There were a significant number of independent portal players among the top 15 web sites in France, including the VC-backed firms MultiMania and iFrance. Again, however, like most European portals, French portal ventures did not internationalize much. Only one of the leaders mentioned here, iFrance, was a fast internationalizer and by 1999 had expanded into French-speaking Canada, the Benelux countries and Switzerland. The competing portal service MultiMania in 1999 did not yet have an international business. 'MultiMania concludes capital increase, preparing for bourse listing', *Reuter Textline, Les Echos*, 7 October 1999. French electronic commerce firms also were slow internationalizers. While a few electronic commerce players such as Chateauonline moved into neighbouring markets UK and Germany, most French firms focused on

France, or, when they internationalized, they started with French-speaking countries or Italy and Spain. The Goldman Sachs-financed iBazar Group, which included the iBazar auction site as well as the online hosting site Chez.com and was later acquired by eBay, was present in France, Italy and Spain in 1999. 'Goldman Sachs funds invests in iBazar e-commerce site', *Reuter Textline*, *Les Echos*, 6 October 1999. On Chateauonline see Morgan Stanley Dean Witter, Equity Research Europe, 'The European Internet Report', June 1999, 190. German internet start-ups in the portal business were on the whole not successful. The space was dominated by telecommunications and media companies. DINO-Online (AIS Axon Internet Services GmbH) was an independent start-up but was acquired in January 1999 by the telecommunications operator MobilCom AG. As in Germany, the top 15 portal sites in Holland in 1999 were dominated by telecommunications and media companies which quickly moved into the portal space.

69. Next to the telcos Telia, Tele2 (owned the ISP Swipnet) and Telenordia (Algonet), the Norwegian publishing group Schibsted was particularly strong in the Swedish internet through its stakes in Aftonbladet. Passagen was the Swedish portal of Scandinavia Online (SOL), an internet company co-owned by Telia, Norwegian telco Telenor and Schibsted. Swedish Post's PostNet owned the portal site Torget.
70. The term internet bubble was first widely publicized by Perkins and Perkins (1999).
71. In Autumn 2001, 31 per cent of all Germans were reported to have internet access in their homes. Quoted in RegTP (2001).
72. One of Bruno Giussani's now classic 'Eurobytes' columns written for the internet edition of the *New York Times* focused on this debate. In retrospect, Giussani underestimated the strength of US internet entrants in Europe. Bruno Giussani, 'Eurobytes. Europe's Internet Lag: An American Fabrication?' *New York Times on the Web*, 14 September 1999.

8. Conclusion: The timing of policy reform and internet entrepreneurship in Europe

From its launch in 1997, the Frankfurt technology stock exchange Neuer Markt developed spectacularly. Many Europeans thought that a new era of entrepreneurship had dawned. Following the severe downturn in the Spring of 2000, however, the search for blame began. Investment banks, which had carried out the initial public offerings (IPOs), were faulted for a lack of research and unreasonably high initial enterprise valuations.[1] Several fund analysts, previously the stars of the Neuer Markt, were fired. The Frankfurt exchange itself was criticized for its lax standards. Venture capitalists were blamed for financing 'me too' concepts and pushing entrepreneurs too early into a stock market listing. Finally, the entrepreneurs themselves were faulted for their gold digger's mentality. Insider dealing investigations and other reported criminal activities by the management of listed companies confirmed these suspicions. The Frankfurt 'nightmare' exchange, as it came to be known,[2] went through the most exaggerated cycle of the European exchanges. As a result, the reaction to the internet bubble was stronger in Germany than in other European countries. Elsewhere, however, the search for blame was also focused on the financial players and the entrepreneurs themselves.

Although this search for blame revealed some weaknesses of the financial system in Europe and the inexperience of participants within this system, important aspects of the downturn were not the subject of public commentary. Underlying policy determinants were not cited as having contributed to weak domestic entrepreneurship. Moreover, the downturn in the technology stock markets was not limited to Germany or Europe alone. The development was global and was led by the US technology exchange NASDAQ. For contemporary observers, the complex knot of domestic and global determinants seemed difficult to unravel. Even regarding the Frankfurt exchange itself, public commentary did not present the full picture. Although the rules of the Neuer Markt were tightened in the aftermath of the downturn, they were already stricter and more transparent than those of other European exchanges.[3]

In the Introduction to this volume, the question was raised to what extent the wave of internet entrepreneurship in the late 1990s in Europe should be seen as part of a global development and to what extent it was specific to Europe. In order to effectively be able to explore the impact of global opportunity *vis-à-vis* country-specific determinants, a framework called 'refraction' was presented. Refraction measures the extent to which domestic determinants impact upon the commercial opportunities presented by global technological shifts. The method chosen was that of a detailed, single country study, supported by comparative evidence from other European countries.

REFRACTION REVISITED

The refraction framework assumes the parallel existence of two opposing interpretations of technological change. Scholars examining technological change and economic history have closely linked innovation to social shifts in a specific localized environment. Although many changes are incremental and evolutionary in nature, some are seismic shifts occurring within short phases of 'punctuated equilibrium'. Yet, these seismic shifts are always accompanied by localized social changes. Alternatively, network thinkers have understood recent changes wrought by the proliferation of the internet as a worldwide, disruptive shift clearly emerging out of the techno-economic sphere. It was seen as overriding local societal variations and eradicating differences.

It is helpful to make a brief detour and mention two writers who have had a strong influence on recent theorizing, Max Weber and Joseph Schumpeter. Although Weber and the younger Schumpeter cooperated on some projects, and tried to answer some of the same questions, their focus differed. It was a fundamental issue, which will appear in different guises when summarizing and drawing conclusions from this study. This difference has also been emphasized by several authors in an issue of the journal *Industrial and Corporate Change* dedicated to these two canonical thinkers (Hamilton, 1996; Galambos, 1996). Weber tried to unite economics, history and sociology. He saw change as multi-causal, emanating from different parts of the greater, interwoven institutional setting. Thus, different institutions, including firms, changed jointly, moved by broad trends. Technology was not a specific, isolated issue of concern. In his early writings (1934), Schumpeter acknowledged the greater institutional setting as well, but narrowed in on economic actors more so than Weber did. He tended to focus on technological change and entrepreneurship. His understanding of change was 'endogenous', or contained within the economic system (Rosenberg, 1994). Despite his pessimism about a world he viewed as becoming increasingly bureaucratized, Schumpeter believed the primary strength of the capitalist system lay in its encouragement of constant, entrepreneurial change.

Network thinkers perceived technology as the driver in a global shift towards greater equality and an erosion of differences. Kevin Kelly's approach was to summarize network thinking, thus the three basic trends he highlighted in the beginning of his book *New Rules for the New Economy* provide a good overview (1998). According to Kelly, the three most important aspects of the New Economy were that it was global, interlinked and intangible. These factors are related to the three characteristics of internet opportunity emphasized in this study: the internet's internationality, its horizontal applicability and the low barriers to entry. Kelly perceived his factors together to be responsible for a decentralized, egalitarian force of upheaval, which was in the process of breaking up the 'Old Economy'. What was happening was that, for the first time, 'we are connecting everything to everything' (p. 12). This was why the internet was perceived as being significantly different from the worldwide corporate electronic networks which had existed for three decades. It was precisely because small firms and individuals were being integrated into the global network that real, lasting changes were occurring. The previous mainframe and client/server eras did not allow this ubiquitous integration. The beneficiaries of this networked vision were the people and also the small firms whose success was enabled by the global network. Accordingly, most old-style organizations, including governments, would not be able to cope with these changes and they would see their influence decline. In their place, the network would bring about new institutions, which were not dependent upon centralized, geographically founded means of control. New types of firms and new types of government would operate according to principles of performance and voluntarism.

The market mechanism as a means of insuring equal opportunity was grafted onto the 1960s anti-establishment vision of network thinking. In fact, the network would behave very much like a free market, with an ongoing selection process in operation. The economic sphere was privileged. In this context it is worthwhile to re-read Esther Dyson's explanation: 'How I Got the Story and Learned to Love Markets' in her book *Release 2.1* (1998).

Although the two different sets of ideas concerning technological change described above, institutionalist analysis and network thinking, really did seem to come from different worlds, both provided answers to our central question: 'Who was in the driver's seat?' It was not that one set of thinkers pointed to one actor and the other to another; the very basis of their analysis was different – as was the difference between Weber's and Schumpeter's approaches to change. Whereas the historically guided institutionalist work

described first had as its essential unit institutions in a geographically defin-
able entity, sometimes a nation, sometimes a smaller or larger regional unit,
this was not the case with the network thinkers. In fact, the very purpose of
institutionalist analysis was to ask why some regions did very well and
others didn't. Since firms were seen as part of a larger political, social and
economic institutional landscape, these authors looked for combinations of
factors encouraging or stifling growth. Institutionalist work would have
difficulties explaining rapid global shifts. This was the strength of network
thinking, which distanced itself from geographically defined entities.
Network thinkers looked for types of actors, which would be successful in
a networked, global market environment, such as small, fast ventures, self-
employed knowledge workers and new, non-governmental global move-
ments and organizations. They juxtaposed these to geographically based,
old entities, which would not be able to keep up the fast pace, such as
domestic governments. In most cases, network thinking did not reach the
depth of Schumpeter's analysis, which explored the causes of change, questioned them and arrived at an endogenous change model based on long-
term waves. Most network thinkers simply thought of technological change
as deterministic and external. While the weaknesses of network thinking
are recognized here, the aim of this book is to see what insight could be
derived from network thinking regarding the global internet opportunity
for entrepreneurs.

Readers knowledgeable of the institutionally guided literature from Max
Weber to Douglass North and David S. Landes can easily downplay the
once fashionable topic of writing about the network economy and its lack
of rigour. This is not the issue here. These same writers acknowledge the
importance of profound technological changes occurring occasionally in
history in combination with strong social shifts. Apparent contemporary
changes in technology may signal a global socio-economic shift in progress;
this possibility needs to be taken seriously by scholarship. Some sociologists, especially urban sociologists, critics of postmodernity as well as of
globalization, have analysed current technological developments to
uncover possible parallel social currents. The sociologists discussed in this
study included Manuel Castells (1996), Saskia Sassen (1996) and David
Harvey (1990). Yet these sociologists also understood that, despite a digital
network and marketplace accessible all over the world, those firms which
managed to innovate, to create the most value and to grow faster were
located only in a few specific locations. Innovation did not seem to be
equally pronounced everywhere.

To answer the guiding question pitting localized, institutional structures
against global technology, the study was divided into two parts. The first,
comprising Chapters 2 and 3, focused on global change. It asked what

underlying international trends could have spawned perceptions of networked change. It examined the internet in terms of its technological design as well as the global demand and supply of internet services. A global elite of pioneer users was identified. The impact of international policy-making was also considered. In effect, Part I tried to show what was real about the global virtual economy. The second part focused on domestic institutions and turned the question around: What aspects of the network economy were 'hype?' This study focused on one 'old-style' entity, a single domestic economy, Germany, with its government and its firms, as well as a 'new-style' player, the internet venture. In doing so, it contrasted two changing entities: the new activities initiated by ventures and the multi-causal reform of domestic institutions. The challenge was to understand the impact of domestic institutions which were being modernized simultaneously with the appearance of new ventures. The argument was then extended to Europe as a whole; diversity within the European environment allowed further insight into of the impact of domestic institutions.

SUMMARY OF PART I – GLOBAL OPPORTUNITY

No single, early event symbolized the entrepreneurial wave which would be unleashed by the internet more than the initial public offering of the internet software company Netscape on NASDAQ on 9 August 1995. The start-up was financed by aggressive venture capital partners. Its vision combined idealism and self-serving business sense: transform the internet into a horizontal and global consumer network. Its initial advantage was an internet designed to accommodate newcomers through its low barriers to entry.

For a long time, electronic networks had been put to use in corporate environments. Since the 1970s, multinational manufacturers as well as financial services used global electronic networks to coordinate their business processes. But installing and maintaining these mainframe-based or client/server-based networks was very expensive and, importantly, the investment was borne exclusively by the participating parties. The internet turned the top-down cost structure on its head; numerous parties shared the costs of the decentralized network. The internet featured an 'end-to-end' design, meaning that intelligence was located at the periphery and not in the centre. This was important because the decentralized technology of the internet provided a point of easy entry for a vast range of new enterprises which challenged established players. These technological design characteristics associated with the internet were crucial preconditions for horizontality and internationality.

Horizontality inspired and enabled a broad range of new, sophisticated services. By integrating the consumer into seamless business webs (Tapscott, et al., 2000), business processes in numerous industries from manufacturing to warehousing, distribution and finally consumption could be carried out digitally. Company-only networks were opened up and extended to other companies and consumers. One of the first types of start-ups to target the opportunities described here were indeed software companies such as Netscape. But others thrived initially as well: internet service providers (ISPs) were perceived as a threat to telecommunications carriers; web development firms competed against consultants and portals challenged media conglomerates. Then there were the throngs of different electronic commerce service companies in diverse business areas from retail to financial services. From 1995 onwards, a first wave of new ventures in the USA strove to become first-movers in this vast array of different service segments. These entrepreneurial firms had an important stake in the sophistication of internet services; they helped create the ubiquitous marketplace by evangelically demonstrating the potential value of their newly created and still imperfect offerings.

Next to horizontality, internationality was a crucial aspect of the internet opportunity. The fastest-growing among the US internet ventures almost immediately began to internationalize and set up a presence in different country markets. In Europe, they confronted indigenous start-ups as well as established firms. Most indigenous ventures had not internationalized in a similar manner to their US brethren; they were domestic in orientation and some represented attractive acquisition candidates. The supply side represented by these internet ventures needs to be viewed jointly with the demand side, however. Due to the increasingly global nature of specific service businesses such as banking and consulting as well as multinational industrial enterprises, a small, elite segment of the worldwide population desired personal access to an international data network. The emergence of this 'international society' needs to be seen in conjunction with the appearance of transnational enterprises as well as international and US domestic government policy. US government was especially instrumental in enabling the rise of unregulated data networks, a domestic move with global implications.

Not all shifts in the global economy associated with the internet were breathtaking and new, however. Parts of our understanding were plainly wrong. The global network economy itself was not new. And governments did not forfeit as much control over the world network flows as was claimed in the late 1990s. Even global financial flows could be controlled. The problem seemed to be instead that subtle policy instruments were not sufficiently explored. The role of government policy on both an international and a domestic level was crucial for the development of the internet.

SUMMARY OF PART II – NATIONAL POLITICAL ECONOMY

In the second part, the study departed from the global network revolution to examine the development of the internet in a specific, domestic environment. The reason for this downshift in geographic scale was the following: a detailed examination of internet firms in their home environment would reveal to what extent these firms were dependent on domestic institutions. The objective of the study was to explain uneven development in internet entrepreneurship despite a unique, global innovation opportunity and a strong worldwide entrepreneurial response. The data presented in this study showed that, as in the US, the first generation entrepreneurial response in Europe pre-dated the subsequent glut in venture capital and the euphoria on the stock markets. A perceived global innovation opportunity certainly existed, which was separate from the financial markets response. Yet, the entrepreneurial response was refracted nationally by the Achilles' heel of internet development, the local telecommunications loop. While telecommunications was liberalized across Europe in the 1990s, it was the precise impact on the local loop which was of importance.

Europe provided an excellent sounding board for hypotheses of uneven internet development. This was because a direct comparison between Europe and the USA would have needed to take into account several country-specific variables next to telecommunications liberalization, such as taxation, legal and other conditions for entrepreneurship and equity investing. Furthermore, one would need to understand the effect of region-specific variables such as the dynamics of Silicon Valley and its venture capital community (Kenney, 2000b). A further important distinction between the United States and Europe was the size of the home market and the persisting difficulties and costs of cross-European business at the time, which were not limited to differing languages and multiple currencies.

In contrast to the complexities involved in the US–European discussion, when historic conditions for internet entrepreneurship are compared across the countries of Europe, significant differences existed only in terms of the timing of telecommunications liberalization and its impact on the local loop. Regarding the other country-specific and region-specific factors such as the availability of venture capital, deficits were the norm in Europe. Until the late 1990s, when the situation was transformed, European start-ups with new internet business models were in general not financed by venture capitalists. Exceptions were internet software developers and internet service providers (ISPs). Furthermore, the international nature of the internet, its horizontal applicability and the low barriers to entry meant that the classic set of national innovation criteria pertaining to the educational system were not as fundamental as in other innovation opportunities. Experience gained by experimentation in environments characterized by sophisticated internet demand structures was more important for enterprise know-how resources. After the turn of the century, barriers to entry associated with the internet rose again, increasing the know-how requirements for competition (Waesche, 2003).

While internet ventures throughout Europe shared a common fate of eventual oblivion, their enterprise structures differed considerably. These differences were especially severe among first generation internet ventures founded in the period from 1995 to 1998. After 1998, the venture capital glut and improved conditions of internet access in the local loop eradicated most structural differences among European internet ventures. Ironically, however, it was the first generation which could have had sufficient time to grow and take advantage of the fortuitous development of the financial markets before the downturn in March 2000. The financial opportunity was especially promising for German internet ventures, which could take advantage of the surprising initial success of the new Frankfurt stock exchange, launched in 1997.

Much has been written elsewhere about global institutional convergence, yet timing differences seem to have led, in this example, to a persistence of institutional path dependence and variety. In this example, institutional variety was retained on the firm level itself, despite the fact that institutional reform may have resulted in a convergence of the regulatory framework and, as a consequence, a convergence of country-level variables. While policy-makers during the mid-1990s were not aware of the significance of the internet and the appearance of new internet business models, they were responding to what they perceived to be a new era of global competition. The 1990s were an interesting decade in which different policy approaches to New Economy competition were tested by national governments. Some of these approaches were described in Chapter 4.

This study also described the course of recent telecommunications liberalization in Europe. In fact, the timing differences between the US and Europe were a result of telecommunications reform. One the one hand, the former public telecommunications operator was to be listed on the stock market and converted into a 'national champion' with significant research budgets and reach into international markets. The short-term attraction of the state as a stock market shareholder also was tempting. On the other hand, a highly competitive telecommunications infrastructure was seen to have a major impact on sector growth as well as forward linkages to other New Economy sectors.

As shown in Chapter 5, in Germany and some other European countries, the trade-off between policy designed to strengthen a single major player and infrastructure policy committed to national innovation in a variety of sectors was made through the timing of reform. The incumbent was granted a preparatory period between the stock market listing and the start of basic telephony services competition. The possibility for infrastructure competition through cable TV was minimized. German policy-makers did not believe a delay would be problematic, because they perceived changes in global competitive conditions and the birth of a New Economy in terms of a continuous, steady evolution. The timing of liberalization implied that a strong 'global champion' could be created out of a privatized state enterprise first. Then, new venture activity would be released as a second step enabled through a progressive legal framework mandating extensive unbundling possibilities.

Yet, this delay had an adverse impact on first generation internet ventures in Europe. These ventures were forced to adapt structurally to weaker demand conditions caused by prohibitive local telecommunications prices. A unique global window of opportunity provided by the commercialization of the internet was thereby missed. Historians of innovation have long been aware that innovation does not have to be a continuous, steady process, but instead can occur in discontinuous periods of 'punctuated equilibrium' (Mokyr, 2000, 69–72).

COMPARING INNOVATIVE ACTIVITY

There was no such thing as a global internet venture. Instead, there were American, European and other ventures. Also, the structures of start-up companies within Europe differed, thanks to variations in the timing of telecommunications reform. That the strategy and resources of internet ventures were different from one country to the next was one of the most important findings of the project and was presented in Chapters 6 and 7.

In order to investigate geographic particularity in the 'network age', this study explored the influence of two vital determinants of start-up activity: internet demand and the availability of venture capital (VC). In the United States, sophisticated demand approaching ubiquity as well as a long-established venture capital industry could both be associated with the wave of entrepreneurial activity on the internet. Both factors together helped bring about the 'model' internet start-up. It had the following three characteristics. Firstly, the company was a 'pure play' start-up focusing all of its resources on a very specific area and catering to sophisticated demand for internet services. Secondly, the firm could run negative cash flow over a number of years; private and public investors supported its vigorous growth strategy. Thirdly, its growth was international and was in part achieved through acquisition. Obviously, there existed US internet start-ups which did not match the above 'pure play' model and were not VC-financed. They were, in fact, the majority of firms. But the commercialization of the internet was strongly influenced by those firms which did correspond to this model.

Germany and other European countries were home to the 'mixed play' company. Firstly, the European start-up was more of a general service firm, combining project-specific consulting, web development or systems integration services for clients with 'pure' offerings on the internet. Project-specific services therefore supported the 'pure' work. Secondly, very few companies were venture capital-financed from 1996 to 1998. Those firms that enjoyed the advantages of venture capital financing in the internet arena were firms which were more traditional software companies, such as Blaxxun, Intershop or Brokat. The traditional means of industrial financing in Europe and in Germany in particular, bank credits, were not extended liberally to knowledge-intensive industries lacking securities, such as the internet entrepreneurs. 'Bootstrapped' growth mostly was organic. Acquisitions were few in number. Venture capital in Germany only really took off after 1998, when public market appetite for internet investments grew and the success of the Neuer Markt became evident. Thirdly, international expansion was cautious; only after 1998 did it become more vigorous. European internet ventures were preoccupied with their domestic market.

Yet, despite these traits, which could be found not only in Germany but also across other countries in Europe, national distinctions existed. Particularly interesting was a subset of Swedish internet ventures, which shared some of the above European characteristics, but in the period from 1995 to 1998 started to internationalize and grow rapidly. While Swedish first generation companies faced a funding gap, they benefited from advanced internet demand structures. These Swedish start-ups, such as web developer Icon Medialab or electronic commerce firm Boxman, initially compensated for the lack of a thriving, technology and early-stage oriented venture capital industry by drawing upon active, private 'angel' investors and by embracing a lower-cost organic growth strategy. Advanced home demand, a result of early telecommunications liberalization, however, transformed Sweden into a hotbed for internet innovation. The start-ups rapidly developed advanced consumer-oriented services, which were then exported to other countries. The small size of the Swedish economy was not a barrier to development. Yet, it was also not a lone facilitator, as is often argued; the Netherlands is also a small economy, but its internet demand initially was less sophisticated. Internet start-ups in Holland were more domestic in orientation. However, after an initial phase of European expansion, the capital-constrained Swedish ventures encountered strong obstacles to securing their position and creating sustainable companies.

In this study, we have carried out a broad sweep from a global internet opportunity to domestic telecommunications policy and institutional path dependency to demand structures and have arrived at innovation, firm structure and resource allocation. The detailed investigations of German and Swedish ventures in this study revealed that entrepreneurial firms did not respond to global opportunities directly, but instead to a domestically refracted version of these opportunities. Refraction was influenced by the country-specific institutional environment. After 1998, institutional change had made itself felt in factors influencing internet entrepreneurship, including significantly lower access prices and a growing volume of venture capital. This came late. A second generation of German internet start-ups which profited from these improved home conditions appeared from 1998; they were born into an environment already cluttered with first generation internet start-ups, established players and US entrants. The second generation had to face the consequences of stock market downturn in 2000 while they were still very young. As a consequence, they did not have favourable growth opportunities either, despite institutional reform and changes in fundamental conditions for entrepreneurship in Germany.

POLICY TIMING AND UNEVEN DEVELOPMENT

The global innovation opportunity spawned by the commercialization of the internet was discussed in the first part of the study. In the second part, which was dedicated to the German case study, it was shown that German entrepreneurs responded to the internet opportunity at roughly the same time as in other countries, including the US and Sweden. While the internet did have this discontinuous, cross-border effect, the first generation German internet start-up was unlike its US or Swedish counterparts. German entrepreneurs followed a 'mixed-play' approach, which focused largely as a services firm on the IT needs of established, domestic corporations in the internet era. The first generation German internet start-up was not able to directly focus on the three innovative, unique aspects of the internet opportunity: its internationality, its horizontal ubiquity among small companies and consumers, and its low barriers to entry. Nevertheless, the entrepreneurial response in Germany was amplified through the successful and rapid launch of the Neuer Markt, the alternative technology stock exchange. Due to the Neuer Markt, Germany appeared the most entrepreneurial country in Europe during the internet stock bubble, while the underlying reality of the entrepreneurial response was lacking vigour.

With the downturn of the market, this became apparent. The entrepreneurial response in Germany therefore can be seen to exhibit continuities with the weak path of IT development in Germany.

A series of factors can be listed to explain why Germany missed this 'leapfrogging' opportunity. As discussed in Chapter 6, one important factor surely was know-how and the structure of expert networks, which included entrepreneurs, the research community, venture capitalists and investment bankers. These experts attempted to emulate the Silicon Valley model of innovation but were challenged by their own inexperience. They also had to face persevering traditional German innovation models in which the entrepreneur carries more personal risk as well as retaining more control. Yet these were less severe in the first phase of internet commercialization marked by low barriers to entry. Furthermore, attitudes to entrepreneurship had begun to change, as was shown by the survey presented in Chapter 6. This change was linked to rising insecurity, which was spreading through the German economic model; incidentally, the situation was very similar in Sweden.

After 1998, fixed-line liberalization in Germany led to improved internet demand structures. In parallel, innovation in the capital markets made itself felt in Germany. Yet, shifts in these two specific determinants had only limited impact on first generation internet ventures. Their resources and strategies were to a large degree aligned with the older conditions. Therefore, despite the fact that convergence with US conditions had occurred, the timing of changes was crucial. As a result, when one examines the development of the internet, Germany remained distinct from the United States. Established media and telecommunications companies had a better position in Germany *vis-à-vis* internet newcomers than their counterparts in the United States.

The thinking put forward here thus far could lead one to think that convergence, an adjustment of one's home political economy to American conditions, is a key to creating global business advantage. American conditions have been regarded largely as 'hands-off' government. Yet it would be more correct to characterize US policy as purposely asymmetric, strict telecommunications regulation offset by unregulation of data networks. The simplification resulting out of a bipolar classification of policy into 'hands-off' and 'hands-on' is not very useful.

If one seeks to orient one's economy to current American conditions one implicitly assumes that technology is static. Innovation activity is intimately linked to domestic demand structures, which, in the case of the internet, were associated with the Achilles' heel of local loop telecommunications regulation. It is difficult to predict, however, what aspects of domestic demand will turn out to be crucial in the future. Technology waves, especially major disruptions, are difficult to forecast, as we have seen. Policy-makers in Europe had not been aware of the particular importance of the local loop. As Hayek pointed out, government does not have a sufficient basis of knowledge to be able to rationally intervene on behalf of a specific technology. The market mechanism alone distinguishes effectively between rival technologies.

Finally, there existed severe institutional challenges in convergence. Europe was historically characterized by a public telecommunications infrastructure. Therefore, privatization was a crucial milestone pursued as an end in itself. The liberalization challenge was addressed as a step-by-step process. Privatization and the stock market listing were carried out before the introduction of competition in basic services. This sequence led to a situation which was detrimental for the development of internet entrepreneurship in Europe, as the German case showed.

In Sweden, however, the sequence took place in reverse; competition was allowed to build up in basic telephony services before the stock market listing of the formerly public telecommunications operator. Historically, Sweden shared some of the institutional traits of Germany, as discussed in Chapter 7. Despite the fact that policy-makers faced specific institutional hurdles and that innovation activity is intrinsically difficult to predict, policy-makers with objectives other than the introduction of competition and the reduction of telecommunications prices were able to capture the liberalization process in some European countries. Financial interests of national government and 'national champion' notions were able to influence the path of liberalization. Share ownership by government as practiced in Germany seemed retrospectively to have been more damaging than direct ownership, as practiced in Sweden, which carried with it a higher level of public responsibility.

Neither enlightened 'Information Society' policy, nor the glamorous, yet naive, notion of a 'national champion' were beneficial for internet entrepreneurship in Europe. Instead, the lesser tasks seemed significant: a clear awareness of objectives, a setting of the rules of the road, a reduction of particularist policies and an emphasis on vibrant competition. These aspects of the classic liberal approach were not in itself foreign to in the context of German policy-making. German *Ordoliberal* writers, influential in the period right after the Second World War, preferred framework rules enforcing competition; experimental process intervention was shunned (Sally, 1998, 108–9; see also Eucken, 1990). But although Ordoliberalism had its home in Germany, the country was exposed to 'the reality of daily mercantilism' (Starbatty, 1999, 170–1).

The emphasis on enterprise competition should also be extended to include the competition of rival technological standards. A recent OECD survey of competition in broadband internet access identified the simultaneous existence of rival technologies as a prime reason for the success of some countries in establishing an early lead in broadband penetration (OECD, 2001b). Competition between rival technologies was actively shunned in the development of the German research data network. European policy support for ISO/OSI, the favourite standard of the public European telecommunications operators, delayed internet adoption in Europe. The cable TV network in Germany was purposely suppressed; it would later be extremely difficult and expensive to build up this alternative technology for internet access. In contrast, in the United Kingdom, the 'Siamese' approach to combining coaxial TV cable with telephone copper pairs was already initiated in the late 1980s.[4]

Active government technology policy advocating single-standard adoption has often been praised when discussing GSM, the European telecommunications standard. Indeed, the scale benefits of European GSM were apparent to large, pan-European operators and especially for the equipment manufacturers. Yet, the GSM standard was introduced in parallel with successful, early liberalization and pro-competitive policy in the mobile telephony segment. Furthermore, the GSM standard was in competition with older, analogue mobile technologies. By mentioning GSM as an example, we are being sympathetic to European technology policy. Large-scale standard setting in Europe has also failed by missing the needs of the market; this is not surprising, since market needs are notoriously difficult to forecast. The diffusion of technology standards always needs to be viewed in conjunction with the associated business models. Limitations on standards may have an effect to limit experimentation with diverse business models. The technology of analogue switched telephony networks, for example, favoured metered pricing schemes, just as packet-based data networks did not require this prohibitive pricing method. While government can intervene in favour of a single technological standard, it could alternatively choose to encourage rivalry between technologies.

What was not discussed in this study was the extent to which internet entrepreneurs made a sustained impact on economic development in different countries. The 'Old Economy' will reap the benefits of business webs and the 'real time economy' (Litan and Rivlin, 2001). The few surviving internet companies which developed an international presence did not by themselves form a new sector of the economy, but have been absorbed by other sectors, such as retail, financial services, media and marketing or information technology. It was, however, the entrepreneurs who through their evangelical activity initiated change and helped promote demand for new services. Wal-Mart improved its distribution by learning from Amazon.com. While the internet venture Ventro itself did not end up running an internet procurement exchange for large and small players in the pharmaceutical industry, as it originally intended, it ended up supplying its software to enterprises intending to further integrate their supply chains with external small firms. There were numerous more examples, also outside of the US. The absorption of the achievements of entrepreneurs was described by Schumpeter. What will need to be examined elsewhere, with the added benefit of further hindsight, is the impact of uneven development of internet entrepreneurship on industry competitiveness in different countries. One could predict that, while global convergence seems to be particularly strong during waves of innovation opportunity, variety has a tendency to reinstate itself. In the case studied here, the timing of convergence itself was one mechanism contributing to variety.

NOTES

1. 'Aufstieg und Fall des Neuen Marktes: Die Rolle der Emissionsbanken. Auf dem Friedhof der Kuscheltiere', *Financial Times Deutschland*, 15 March 2001, 21.
2. A book by the founder of a web development company describes his experience of a listing on the 'nightmare' exchange (Lindenberg, 2002).
3. 'New Rules Aim to Clarify Neuer Markt dealings', *Financial Times*, 21 December 2000, 17.
4. See the overview article: Stephen Pritchard, 'Rival technology threatens the status of cable services', *Financial Times* Telecoms Supplement, page III, 20 March 2002.

Appendix A: Procedure and results of the globalstartup survey

As stated in Chapter 6, in early 1998, a representative list of internet start-ups in Germany was not available. Nor had the press identified internet companies beyond a small handful of high-profile firms. For this reason, firms had to identify themselves by responding to a publicity campaign. The response rate was boosted by the participation of the monthly business publication *manager magazin*. The magazine announced that it would publish an article on a selection of start-up case studies in Autumn 1998 drawn from the pool of survey participants.[1] The editors of *manager magazin* as well as 'Spiegel Online,' the web publication of *Der Spiegel*, are thanked here for their indispensable and very kind cooperation.

An important factor which had to be taken into consideration was that entrepreneurs in the first months of their start-up phase have very limited spare time. In order to speed up the registration process, a web site was set up which allowed on-line registration (under http://www.global-startup.com/ and http://www.smallfirm.org/). The initial questionnaire was comprised of a brief set of basic questions. These were specifically devised to be filled out by entrepreneurs: questions on possibly confidential data such as sales figures were avoided. A selection of these internet start-ups were identified as potential high-growth companies. These entrepreneurs were asked to spend additional time on a second questionnaire. They were personally contacted by the author who assured them that he would respect their confidentiality concerns. The second questionnaire was designed to generate numerical data not contained in the first, such as sales figures. In addition, many of the founding managers of these selected companies were interviewed in person by the author to generate qualitative data for the project.

For the reasons just outlined, the design of the study had to address issues usually not present in other empirical surveys. The lack of a representative list of internet start-ups was the most important issue. The results must, on the one hand, be viewed as tentative and useful mainly for the generation of leads and key concepts, for an initial taxonomy and for the identification interview partners. On the other hand, the good timing of the survey at the beginning of increasing public interest in Germany for the internet start-up phenomenon resulted in a good awareness and a high number of responses. Contemporary experts, such as German venture capitalists, believed that the pool of responding firms was indeed representative. The numbers generated reflected their own observations at the time.

PROCEDURE

1. Publicity Campaign

Publicity efforts began in mid-January 1998. Firms could sign up on the globalstartup.com and smallfirm.org web sites until 15 March 1998.

Several internet start-ups as well as venture capital (VC) firms were contacted directly via e-mail. VC investment managers were asked to identify the internet companies they had invested in.

Posts were placed in two internet newsletters. One was the official mailing list of dmmv, the German multimedia association. The 'dmmv E-Flash,' was subscribed to by 360 member firms. The post appeared on 6 February 1998. The other was a marketing mailing list, which was promoted by the multimedia marketing trade journal 'Horizont.net'. The 'Netmarketing-Digest' had 1800 subscribers when the post appeared on 29 January 1998.

An announcement of the study was made on 'Spiegel Online' (http://www.spiegel.de/). The announcement ran from 15 February until 15 March 1998 under the business section of the home page. According to the 'Informationsgemeinschaft zur Feststellung der Verbreitung von Werbeträgern e.V.' (IVW, http://www.ivw.de/) the site had 688015 visits in January 1998 and was among the most frequently visited German-language content sites.

An announcement was made on p. 36 in the March 1998 print issue of *manager magazin*, which was released on 20 February. At the time, *manager magazin* had a readership exceeding 500000 according to IVW.

2. Signing Up

The following restrictions were announced:

- The firm has to have its headquarters in Germany.
- The firm should not be older than two years or must have redefined its business strategy in the last two years.
- The firm needs to have an international focus.
- Products or services of the firm should have a direct connection with the internet or other online services.

The firms were free to interpret these criteria themselves and fill out a questionnaire of 28 questions.

3.   First sample (*n* = 123) of internet start-ups

A total of 140 entries were collected. Eleven entries were excluded from further analysis because the firms were in their sixth year of existence or older (founded before 1994; they could not be considered firms in a start-up or seed phase). Two entries were excluded because they were not firms; both were projects at universities. One New York-based LLC and one Delaware corporation were removed; there were two double entries; 123 firms remained.

The ventures were then classified according to a taxonomy: 22 business areas and four groups ('web developers;' 'software;' 'portals sites, electronic commerce start-ups and business-to-business exchanges;' and 'others') were defined. The classification was carried out on the basis of an evaluation of the returned survey as well as information found on the web sites of the firms.

4.   Second sample (*n* = 30) of internationally active or potentially internationally active internet start-ups

Of the firms that had signed up, 52 firms belonged to business groups that seemed especially promising for international expansion ('software,' and 'portal sites, electronic commerce start-ups and business-to-business exchanges'). These were further analysed according to the level of their international activity or potential international activity. This was again based on the survey answers as well as the firm's web sites. Twenty-eight start-ups were selected for an informal interview and a second questionnaire. Three firms from other business groups that none the less were potentially high growth were added to this sample.

The founding managers of 18 firms were informally interviewed in person. Two founding managers were interviewed in their offices and the rest during the computer trade fair CeBIT '98 in Hannover. Thirteen were contacted over the phone. The founding managers of the selected firms were asked to fill out a second survey, which required more detailed and sensitive information than the first questionnaire. All agreed to fill out this second questionnaire on an anonymous basis, meaning that the results would only appear in aggregate form. The second survey was sent out by e-mail in April and returned by 30 founding managers. One founding manager failed to return the second survey due to time constraints.

This procedure insured that two separate survey results could be analysed, one with a sample of 123 respondents and a second, more detailed survey, with a sample of 30 respondents (the names of the 30 selected firms are listed at the end of this Appendix). In addition, 18 personal interviews with founding managers were carried out.

FIRM TAXONOMY DETAILS

Before analysis, the firms were classified according to their primary business area. Business areas were grouped into potentially international, high growth segments ('software' and 'portal sites, electronic commerce start-ups and business-to-business exchanges') as well as generally project-oriented start-ups with a national or regional focus, the web developers. Firms with a software and a portal focus were related in that, much of the time, internet software enabled internet portal sites and electronic commerce companies to conduct their business.

The classification by business area was central to the study. Of course, overlaps were possible. Some firms were placed into one area, although they could conceivably belong to another area as well.

Note: in calculations where absolute numbers of international and domestic clients as well as turnover approximations were used, one electronic commerce start-up had to be excluded because the number of its consumers exceeded the totals of all other firms together. This caused strong distortions especially in comparisons between software and service start-ups.

The different start-up types

a)   Web developers, $n = 57$
These firms worked primarily on a project-by-project basis. They were systems consultants or new media agencies. Their revenue came from assisting other firms in realizing their internet presence or an internet-supported business model. In the mid-'90s, entrepreneurs involved in this business described themselves as 'evangelists' because they saw it as their task to convince their clients and also consumers of the benefits of internet activity (see Waesche, 1999a).

New media agencies Companies that specialized in the design and development of internet sites and other digital media. They often had marketing know-how and co-operated with systems consultants in realizing projects for their clients.

Systems consultants   Companies that developed custom software configurations for clients and carried out systems integration. Usually this involved database technology.

Consultants, training   Companies that trained business users in use of the internet or consulted firms on all aspects of internet business.

TV/ internet studios   Firms that carried out video productions for use as streaming video over the internet.

3D   New media agencies that concentrated on 3D productions for the internet.

b)   Software start-ups, *n* = 23
Internet software firms with a high product standardization potential.

E-commerce software   Standardized or semi-standardized software that facilitated electronic commerce. E-commerce was defined as the sale of digital or non-digital products over the internet. E-commerce software often involved software for database-driven product catalogues and transaction components such as a virtual shopping basket. Firms partnered with financial software firms and financial service institutions. Clients were retailers.

Publishing systems   Standardized or semi-standardized software to control the process of publishing either solely on internets and intranets or also on other platforms such as CD-ROM or print catalogues. The ability to publish on other platforms was referred to as 'cross-media'. Publishing large internet sites or handling intranets with several sites was very complex task. This software tried to solve some of the problems associated with this task. Clients thus could be publishing houses or corporations with intranets.

Knowledge management   Software that attempted to solve the problem frequently referred to as 'information overload'. This type of software could be very simple or very complex, ranging from personal browser-based web-search tools to on-line information analysis systems for sales force databases. Information filters, autonomous agents and customer profiling and addressing were all part of this category. A wide variety of different clients were possible including consumers and corporates in the service sector.

Financial software/encryption   Software that managed transactions over the internet improved security. Could be used to insure that data could not be used by third parties or to insure that a given document transferred over the internet was actually from a given party and authentic. Clients could be financial institutions or internet retailers.

E-Business (Business processes)   Internet software that supported business processes, either work-flow processes common to service corporations such as insurance companies and airlines, or production or sale processes including warehouse management systems. Software often needed to integrate with SAP or legacy systems and thus had a strong middleware component. Clients could be all types of firms, service or manufacturing.

E-Business (Communication)   Internet software for firms that aimed to improve internal and external communications. E-mail, fax and internet conference system software all belonged to this genre.

c)   Portal sites, electronic commerce start-ups and business-to-business exchanges (forthwith: 'Portal sites'), *n* = 29
Internet start-ups with a high growth potential offering content, retail or exchange services to consumers or business clients.

Sale of products   This group included both the so-called 'e-tailers' which targeted consumers as well as procurement specialists, focusing on businesses. Competition by price, sometimes also by dynamic prices, was combined with branding and community approach.

Content   All types of content developed for publishing on the internet targeting consumers as well as businesses. Revenue could come from different sources: internet advertising through banners, sponsorship by a firm or subscription fees.

Hotel, travel   The consulting group Datamonitor (http://www.datamonitor.com/) identified the travel industry as the internet industry with the highest proportion of total on-line sales (in a release of 28 April 1998). In this survey, the travel area included not only the sale of travel services but also the development of online application services for hotels, such as booking systems hosted by the start-up.

Brokers   Internet-based services that provided bidding services or classified ads for their clients.

Extranets   Extranets were networks linking two or more firms. The use of the term has since become unpopular and was replaced by 'business-to-business exchanges' (B2B). Neither of the two terms was very precise and could refer to a wide array of different data network services connecting separate firms, including transfer of pricing information and/or warehousing information for supply chain optimization. It could also just refer to internal company news content being shared among different firms. Extranets were the successors to electronic data interchange (EDI). Relative to EDI, extranets were be cheaper to install and maintain, thus new combinations of businesses could be linked. EDI would have in the past been much too expensive, for example, for electronically linking small retail outlets with a manufacturer.

Community, chats   Chat-based communities were usually consumer communities. Their purpose was entertainment. Revenue from hosting a chat community came from internet advertising or, again, from sponsorship. The obstacles to building a successful revenue model were similar to those for content services.

Entertainment   As is the case with hotels and travel, firms in this business area catered to both business clients and consumers. This category included firms specialized in providing application services for businesses which enabled game design. Alternatively, they provided internet entertainment experiences for consumers directly.

Marketing, ad services   This referred to centralized services for internet advertising. Service firms hosted advertising networks, which allowed what were usually small firms to participate in group advertising initiatives.

d)   Others, *n* = 14:
Businesses that could not be placed into one of the above groups.

Provider, internet outsourcer   Firms that specialized in providing access to the internet or in hosting sites. This was a pioneering industry for the internet. By 1998, consolidation had already set in worldwide.

Hardware for internet access   Any equipment that was required for accessing the internet (such as modems).

Telecommunication services, networks   Telecommunication services such as software for locating the cheapest telecom provider. Telecommunications networking and telecommunications infrastructure.

MAIN SURVEY RESULTS

1. The average German internet firm that participated in the survey was 1.8 years old and employed 20 people.

The total number of employees of all firms together: 2422. Mean total employment was 19.7.

Table A.1   Breakdown of employees

	Mean	% of total	Median
Contract	11	54	5
Free	6	31	4
Abroad	3	15	0

36 per cent of all firms were incorporated as Personengesellschaften, 59 per cent as GmbH and 6 per cent as AG.

2. Discounting international employment, the potential high-growth firms that were selected for the second, detailed questionnaire had more aggressive financial strategies than the general group.

Table A.2   Key characteristics of the original sample and the 30 selected firms

	Original sample	Selected firms
Number of firms	$n = 123$	$n = 30$
Average age (years)	1.8	1.7
Total employees/firm	19.7	17.6
International employees/firm	3.0	1.9
% int. employees	15%	11%
% int. partnerships	16%	22%
% int. business clients	2%	13%
% int. consumers	0%	3%
% consumer firms of total	15%	7%
Likelihood of VC financing	11%	30%
Likelihood of tbg support	4%	13%
Likelihood of federal support	4%	7%
Likelihood of state support	8%	7%
Likelihood of bank loan	20%	20%
% are Personengesellschaften	36%	27%

3.   The most popular form of financing an internet firm was by reinvesting profits. This was followed by investment by individuals (angels or founders), bank loans and venture capital.

At first glance, venture capital seemed a relatively significant form of financing for internet firms in Germany. It was the fourth-most popular financing option with 11 per cent of all firms being VC-financed. Instead of 'VC-financed', a more appropriate term for this group of firms, however, would have been 'private equity-financed'. In Germany, at the time, the range of services, which should have been available through an active venture capital investor, were not yet well understood. Entrepreneurs thought they were recipients of venture capital investments, when, in fact, they were not. The two terms 'private equity' and 'venture capital' were sometimes used interchangeably (instead of understanding venture capital as an early-stage, technology-oriented and active type of private equity investor).

Furthermore, the survey design contained a bias towards venture capital-backed firms. High profile venture capital investors had been contacted and their portfolio firms were asked to participate.

tbg-backed companies automatically required an individual or an active VC firm as a co-investor. Due to the selection process of the tbg, these companies better matched the criteria, which one would have associated with high-growth, VC-financed firms. For example, the proportion of firms which generated profits available for reinvesting was low. Furthermore, the proportion of 'pure play' companies was higher and project-by-project work lower (see Tables A.17, A.18). However, only 5 per cent of all companies in the sample were tbg-financed and the majority of these were software start-ups.

Table A.3   Forms of financing (%)

	All firms	Firms with VC	Firms with bank loans	Firms with tbg support	Selected firms for second survey
Reinvesting profits	79	43	88	33	70
Individuals	33	14	33	33	23
Bank loan	20	21	100	17	20
VC	11	100	13	83	30
State (*Land*) programme	8	21	17	17	17
Parent company	8	0	4	0	3
tbg	5	36	4	100	13
Other	5	7	8	0	3
Federal programme	4	21	8	17	7

Table A.4   Financial strategies of different business areas (%)

	All firms	Web developers	Software	Portal
Individuals	33	33	30	31
Reinvesting profits	79	86	70	79
VC	11	4	17	21
Bank	20	23	22	14
tbg	5	0	17	7
Federal programme	4	2	9	0
State programme	8	7	4	7
Parent company	8	7	4	7
Other	5	7	0	3

Note: Most firms used more than one different type of financing.

4.   The largest employers were internet service providers and software start-ups. Portal sites, electronic commerce start-ups and business-to-business exchanges were among the smallest employers.

Table A.5   Business areas and employment

	Number of firms in sample	Number of employees	Employees/ firm (rounded)
New media agencies	33	555	17
Systems consultants	15	267	18
Sale of products	6	57	10
E-commerce software	8	356	45
Publishing systems	7	113	16
Content	6	40	7
Hotel, travel	3	15	5
Brokers	4	68	17
Consultants, training	5	40	8
Provider, outsourcer	9	458	51
Knowledge management	2	40	20
Hardware for access	1	20	20
Telecom. services, networks	4	35	9
TV/internet	2	31	16
Extranets, EDI	4	52	13
3D	2	14	7
Community, chat	2	38	19
Financial software/ encryption	1	41	41
E-business (Business processes)	4	125	31
Entertainment, games	3	33	11
Marketing, ad service	1	18	18
E-business (Communication)	1	6	6
	123	2422	20

Table A.6   The largest average employers (mean total employment/firm)

Provider, outsourcer	51
E-commerce software	45
Financial services/ encryption	41
E-business (business processes)	31

Table A.7   The smallest average employers (mean total employment/firm)

Hotel, travel	5
E-Business (Communication)	6
3D	7
Content	7

5.   The most popular business areas for German internet software start-ups were electronic commerce software, publishing systems and business processes. Internet portal start-ups focused on the sale of products ('e-tailers' and procurement specialists), content, information brokerage and extranets ('B2B').

In the United States, firms emphasized roughly the same areas with the exception that knowledge management software was a much more frequent and electronic commerce software a less frequent business focus than in Germany.

Table A.8   Frequencies of software and service start-ups by business area

	Frequency	% of start-ups	Frequency (US sample)	% of start-ups (US sample)
Software start-ups				
E-commerce software	8	15	5	7
Publishing systems	7	13	11	16
Knowledge management	2	4	18	26
Financial software/ encryption	1	2	0	0
E-business (Business processes)	4	8	16	23
E-business (Communication)	1	2	4	6
Portal sites and electronic commerce start-ups				
Sale of products	6	12	0	0
Content	6	12	7	10
Hotel, travel	3	6	1	1
Brokers	4	8	1	1
Extranets, EDI	4	8	1	1
Community, chat	2	4	5	7
Entertainment, games	3	6	0	0
Marketing, ad service	1	2	1	1
Total	52	100	70	100

Note: US data was obtained from Upside Media Inc.'s 'Upside's 1998 Hot 100 Private Companies' which was found on http://www.upside.com/. The report was dated 30 March 1998. Since the companies were categorized differently, the profile of each US firm was evaluated and the company placed into one of the business area groupings above. Firms from areas which were not relevant to this survey, such as semiconductor equipment, were not included. Included were firms from the following: e-commerce, online content, net infrastructure, enterprise software and business automation. The Upside survey was similar to globalstartup in that the companies nominated themselves. One difference in the table above is important, however: the Upside list included only selected firms; this particular globalstartup list included all software and service start-ups that participated. The Upside list therefore already reflected the selection process of the editors and industry experts.

6.   Business area alone did not seem to influence the level of international activity of a firm. Software start-ups were internationally active to a greater degree when measured by the numbers of employees abroad. Web developers and portal sites cultivated international partnerships to compensate for their lack of offices in countries outside of Germany.

Table A.9   Business areas and proportion of international activity (%)

	All firms (n = 123)	Web developers (n = 57)	Software (n = 23)	Portal (n = 29)
% int. employment	15	7	22	16
% int. partnerships	16	19	19	12
% int. business clients	2	13	4	23
% int. consumers	0	12	N/A	5

7.   Overall, growth expectations were good among those internet firms selected for the second survey. The firms expected to grow in sales by over 200 per cent and in employees by over 60 per cent in 1998. Software start-ups expected to generate DM 5.2 million in sales; portal sites, electronic commerce start-ups and business-to-business exchanges around DM 1.2 million. The growth expectations of portal sites, however, lagged behind those of software firms considerably.

Table A.10   Expected turnover and current employee growth (DM millions)

	All selected firms	Software	Portal
1997 turnover	1.00	1.26	0.74
1998 expected turnover	3.00	5.17	1.24
Sales growth	200%	310%	68%
Current employees (rounded)	17	24	11
Growth in employees/year	77%	103%	61%

Note: Due to the fact that many firms were founded in 1997 or 1998, only 18 respondents gave turnover figures for 1997. For 1998 expected turnover, 28 firms responded.

8.   Estimated total start-up capital required by the selected internet firms to reach break-even ranged between DM 14 000 and DM 12 500 000. The average start-up capital required by a software firm was DM 2.8 million and for a portal site DM 1.3 million. These requirements seemed low compared to those of US internet firms and reflected the greater reliance in Germany on business models with early profit expectations.

Table A.11 Start-up capital required by selected internet firms (DM)

Mean	2 171 172
Median	1 000 000
Maximum	12 500 000
Minimum	14 000
Standard deviation (sample)	2 826 348

Note: $n = 29$, one firm did not respond to this question.

On average, the selected firms estimated months to break-even as 21 months. The median was quite close to this figure, 19. Minimum was 6 months, maximum 42 months.

Table A.12 Mean start-up capital required in DM millions and months to break-even by internet firm type

	Start-up capital	Months to break-even
Software	2.8	24
Portal	1.3	19

9. Because portal sites, electronic commerce start-ups and business-to-business exchanges offered their services over the internet, their hardware and software as well as telecommunication and provider costs were substantial. Telecommunication and provider costs of internet software start-ups were much lower because they still sold software as a shrink-wrapped product and generally only conducted market research and software support over the internet.

Table A.13 Mean distribution of costs (%)

	All selected firms	Software	Portal
Employees	52	57	47
Hard- and software	15	12	19
Telecommunication and provider	11	7	15
Marketing, PR and advertising	17	19	15
Other	5	6	3
	100	100	100

10. tbg financed companies were internationally more active than the average selected software company but about equally active to portal sites.

However, these figures have been influenced by the fact that high international sales were achieved by a small number of very active companies. Most start-ups in Germany were not internationally active.

Table A.14   Geographic distribution of sales %

	All selected firms	Software	Portal	tbg financed companies
Germany	79	90	66	67
Rest of Europe	12	5	20	24
Rest of world	9	5	15	9
	100	100	100	100

The median for all selected firms was 90 per cent sales in Germany, 10 per cent total foreign sales. Eleven of the selected firms, however, had a significant proportion of total foreign sales, between 30 per cent and 90 per cent.

Table A.15   Number of firms with given percentage of foreign sales

% foreign sales	Frequency	%
90–100	2	7
80–89	0	0
70–79	0	0
60–69	1	3
50–59	1	3
40–49	3	10
30–39	4	13
20–29	2	7
10–19	5	17
0–9	12	40
	30	100

11.   Software as well as portal sites, electronic commerce start-ups and business-to-business exchanges all concentrated mainly on the US market for future expansion. Aside from this US focus, however, portal firms were geographically more diversified and were interested also in the Asian market.

Table A.16   Importance of different international markets: percentage of firms in group that answered affirmatively

	Software	Portal
'The USA is an important market.'	85	79
'An office in the USA is necessary.'	54	50
'Eastern Europe is an important market.'	38	50
'Asia is an important market.'	54	71

12.   On average, a large proportion of sales by both software as well as portal sites was derived from project-by-project work. Software start-ups were especially dependent on project-by-project income. About one fourth of all selected firms were hybrid companies generating revenue through both significant project sales as well as significant product work. Only about 40 per cent of the selected firms were 'pure play' firms focused on generating sales mostly from products or scalable offerings.

Table A.17   Break-up of revenue sources from project work or products by internet firm type (%)

	Software	Portal	tbg-financed
Project-by-project	62	43	30
Product, scalable offerings	38	57	70

Table A.18   Proportion of start-ups generating most of their sales from project work or product sales

	All firms	% of total	tbg financed
Mostly project-by-project	10	35	0
Mostly product, scalable offerings (pure play)	12	41	3
Hybrids	7	24	1
	29	100	4

Note: 'Mostly project-by-project' was defined as project revenues of 75 per cent or above, 'Mostly product, scalable offerings' as product or scalable service sales of 75 per cent or above. The two consumer start-ups were included in this latter category. One firm did not respond to this question.

13.   The 30 selected firms together had 134 job openings. German software start-ups in particular were working significantly under capacity.

Table A.19   Percentage current working capacity

	All selected firms	Software	Portal
Mean	81	78	86

14.   Most German internet firms had two active managing directors who were also the founders of the firm. There still were a significant number of start-ups with a single founding manager.

Table A.20   Number of active founding managers

Number of active managers	Frequency in sample	% of total
1	10	33
2	14	47
3	5	17
4	1	3
5	0	0
	30	100

The average number of active founding managers was 1.90 over all firms, 2.00 for software start-ups and 1.86 for portal start-ups.

These results can be compared with those of the Stanford Project on Emerging Companies (SPEC). In 1996, 160 start-ups of the Bay Area were examined. The most common number of founders also was two, but there were firms with three, four, five, six, seven, nine and twelve founders. The mean was therefore higher: 2.81 (http://www-gsb.stanford.edu/research/programs/SPEC/).

15.   Founding managers of internet portal sites and electronic commerce start-ups generally had encountered commercial online networks earlier than their counterparts at software start-ups. One reason may have been the slightly higher average age of service founding managers.

Table A.21   When did managing directors first encounter commercial value-added networks? (Number of affirmative indications. Multiple answers possible.)

		All selected firms	Software	Portal
1977–90	Btx	8	2	6
1991–94	On-line services	19	9	9
1995–	Internet	9	5	2

The mean age of all founding managers was 33 at the founding of their firm. The founding managers of software start-ups were on the average 31 at the founding of their firm; portal entrepreneurs were 34.

16.   Most founding managers of the selected internet firms completed a university programme. The number of founding managers who studied in a computer science-related programme was matched by those who elected a business-related programme.

Table A.22   Types of university or vocational college courses completed by founding managers

	All firms	Software	Portal
Business courses	19	11	7
Computer courses	15	10	5
Other courses	12	2	7

Table A.23. Other career experiences listed by founding managers

	All firms	Software	Portal
Uncompleted university/vocational college	4	4	0
Programming experience	15	8	6
Started a company before	12	6	4
Employee at SME	15	7	7
Employee at MNE	14	5	9
Self-employment	19	8	10

17.   Those founding managers who recommended a public funding programme were matched almost exactly by those who advised against all programmes. DtA, KfW and state (*Land*) programmes were in equally high regard by those who recommended public funding.

Table A.24   Number of entries from selected firms, which recommended
public funding in Germany

	All selected firms
Can recommend	13
Cannot recommend	12
No comment	5

Table A.25   Recommended public funding programmes

	All selected firms[a]
DtA tbg	5
DtA Existenzgründer	1
KfW	5
State[b]	5

Notes:
[a] Multiple selections of different programmes possible.
[b] Named were: Land Baden-Württemberg, MFG Medien – und Filmges. Baden Württemberg, Sächsische Entwicklungsges. für Telematik mbH, Mittelstandsförderung Sachsen and Bayern Kapital.

18.   The German multimedia law (IuKDG) of 1997 did not seem very relevant to German internet firms at the time, but the deregulation of the telecommunications market did.

Table A.26   Number of affirmative responses to the question whether the
given issue affects the firm today (%)

	All selected firms
'Is the IuKDG relevant to your business today?'	53
'Is the deregulation of telecommunications relevant to your business today?'	70
'Are German provisions regarding data security relevant to your business today?'	60

19.   The managing founders of 77 per cent of all selected firms believed the internet required international laws and controls, especially laws relating to digital signatures and encryption.

Table A.27   Demand for international laws and controls regulating the internet (percentage of all selected firms)

	All firms	Software	Portal
Value added tax	20	15	29
Copyrights	57	46	64
Trust centers for digital signatures and encryption	63	62	71
Political or social undesirable content	0	0	0

Note: Multiple selections possible, this is why the percentages did not add up to 77 per cent. 77 per cent was the proportion of all firms that believed international laws were necessary. The percentages should be read in the following way: 20 per cent of all firms in the selected group indicated that value added tax regulation was necessary. Not: 20 per cent of the 77 per cent who believed laws were necessary.

20.   The objective of most selected German internet firms was rapid growth, and most of these firms believed this objective could only be achieved with venture capital and a later IPO. Portal sites, electronic commerce start-ups and business-to-business exchanges were, however, less inclined towards venture capital than software start-ups.

Table A.28   Percentage of affirmative answers on questions regarding growth objective and financing

	All selected firms	Software	Portal
Is rapid growth your objective?	87	92	86
If so, do you believe rapid growth can only be achieved with venture capital and a possible later IPO?	73	83	67
Do you think your financing options have improved through the launch of the Neue Markt at the German Stock Exchange and the better access of venture capital in Germany?	79	85	79

Note: Only firms that answered the previous question affirmatively.

21.   German internet start-ups were generally involved in strategic partnerships with other small and medium-sized enterprises (SMEs) and those with business clients generated most of their income from SMEs as well.

Table A.29   Break-up of revenue sources by client firm type (consumer firms did not answer this question) (%)

	All selected firms	Software	Portal
Multinational enterprise (MNE) clients	29	29	24
Small and medium-sized (SME) clients	71	71	76
Total	100	100	100

Whereas the mean break-up between MNE and SME clients was 29 per cent/71 per cent, the median break-up was 20 per cent/80 per cent.

Of the 30 selected firms , there were five with no MNE sales and one with no SME sales. 18 firms were relatively independent of MNE sales, with a proportion of MNE sales from 0 per cent to 30 per cent. Only three generated substantial sales proportions from MNEs, between 70 per cent 100 per cent. Seven firms generated significant sales to MNEs, between 31 per cent and 69 per cent.

Table A.30   Percentage of affirmative answers on questions regarding partnerships

	All selected firms	Software	Portal
Are you in a strategic partnership with a large firm/ MNE?	50	69	43
Are you in a strategic partnership with SMEs?	83	85	79

22.   American software companies involved in the internet business were the most popular MNE partners of German internet start-ups, followed by Deutsche Telekom and Siemens Nixdorf.

Table A.31   Existing strategic alliances with major corporations

	All selected firms
Deutsche Telekom	3
Siemens Nixdorf Informationssysteme	3
SAP	1
A German universal bank (Bayerische Hypo- und Vereinsbank, Commerzbank, Deutsche Bank, Dresdner Bank)	2

Table A.31   (continued)

	All selected firms
German public TV station (ARD, ZDF)	1
German private TV station (RTL, SAT1, PRO7)	1
Java/ NC alliance (SUN, Netscape, Oracle)	4
Microsoft	5
Others	7

23.   Distribution partnerships were the most frequent type of partnership for software start-ups. Portal sites, electronic commerce start-ups and business-to-business exchanges were not as active in partnering; some engaged in distribution, marketing and technology partnerships.

Table A.32   Likelihood of selecting a given partnership (%)

	All firms	Web developers	All selected firms	Software	Portals
Distribution	46	42	46	61	34
Marketing	46	49	40	43	38
Consulting	25	32	13	17	10
Technology	54	63	42	48	38
Outsourcing	13	14	8	9	7
Financial	12	9	12	22	3
Product development	28	30	23	26	21
Other	22	26	17	13	21

24.   Among the sample of 123 firms, the greatest likelihood for an internet firm's location was southern Bavaria (postal codes 80000–89999). The most important cluster for international activity was the greater Munich area (postal codes 80000–83999 and 85000–85999). When firms with above-average international activity were isolated, one-fifth of these were located in the greater Munich area.

Table A.33   Frequency of firms with given postal code

Postal code	Sample cities in area	All selected firms	All firms (% of total)	Above average international activity index[a]	Above average int. activity index (%)
0–9999	Halle, Leipzig, Dresden	3	2	1	4
10000–19999	Berlin, Schwerin, Rostock	7	6	1	4
20000–29999	Hamburg, Bremen, Lübeck	17	14	3	11
30000–39999	Hannover, Kassel, Fulda	11	9	4	14
40000–49999	Düsseldorf, Essen, Osnabrück	14	11	1	4
50000–59999	Mainz, Bonn, Köln	11	9	3	11
60000–69999	Frankfurt am Main, Wiesbaden, Heidelberg	18	15	0	0
70000–79999	Stuttgart, Karlsruhe, Konstanz	14	11	5	18
80000–89999[b]	Munich, Ingolstadt, Ulm	21	17	7	25
90000–99999	Passau, Würzburg, Erfurt	7	6	3	11

Notes:
[a] The mean of a firm's percentage of international partnerships and clients/consumers. If this mean was above 13 per cent the firm was considered an internationally active firm. 13 per cent was the mean of all firms where $n = 123$.
[b] 17 firms were located in the greater Munich area, carrying the postal codes 80000–83999 and 85000–85999. The area formed a triangle with the vertices at Garmisch-Patenkirchen, Rosenheim and Ingolstadt. Seventeen companies corresponded to 14 per cent of the total. Six scored above average on the international activity index. This meant that 21 per cent of the firms with above-average international activity were located in the greater Munich area.

The 14 venture capital-supported firms were found in 12 different cities. The only city that occured more than once was Munich. Four VC-supported firms were located in greater Munich area. Thus, about one-quarter of all VC-supported firms were located in the Munich area.

THIRTY SELECTED GERMAN INTERNET START-UPS

Table A.34 Software start-ups

#	Name	Year	Employees	City	Product/service description	Partners/clients
E-commerce systems						
1.	Shopmaker GmbH Deutschland Electronic Commerce Solutions http://www.shopmaker.de	97	23	Limburg	Software for internet-shops. Interfaced with SAP, Sage KAK, Oracle. SQL database system.	GEN (US Telecom.), GEFM (Deutsche Bank subsidiary), Schöpflin (fashion direct retailer), Sage KAK, SAP
2.	USWeb InnoMate http://www.innomate.de	94	25	Düsseldorf	Internet integrator with modular solutions for internet shopping and product databases.	Deutsche Telekom, Oracle, IBM, Compuserve
Publishing solutions						
3.	Hyperwave http://www.hyperwave.com	97	39	Munich	Web-based knowledge management/ intranet development platform which combined web document and web content managment into an integrated and scalable system.	Motorola, Siemens, Lufthansa, Deutsche Bank
4.	Systembureau GmbH http://www.systemfabrik.de	96	14	Düsseldorf	Publishing system for internet and intranets.	Bauboden Bank

Table A.34 (continued)

#	Name	Year	Employees	City	Product/service description	Partners/clients
5.	HFR Heiden Fuellenbach Realisationen http://www.hfr.de	94	12	Düsseldorf	Project management and software solutions for cross-media-publishing and marketing needs. Combined internet, CD-Rom and print product catalogues. Close developmental partnership with Munich-based software company.	AIWA Deutschland GmbH, 3M/ Imation, various German publishers
6.	2CK http://www.2ck.com	94	35	Munich	Publishing system for use in intranets.	
7.	SAC ProMedia http://sac.promedia.de	96	7	Regensburg	Cross-media publishing system. CD-ROMs in internet-standard which could be updated.	
E-business software (business processes)						
8.	Coin Corporate Interactive AG http://www.coin.de	97	23	Hannover	Internet-based system for workflow. Software solutions avaliable for publishers, insurance firms and other service corporations.	Hannoverische Lebensversicherung
9.	Eway http://www.eway.de	96	5	Melle	Web-based applications for the sales force. Web-based calendar.	
10.	ONEstone http://www.one stone.de			Paderborn	Workflow systems integrated with the groupware platforms LotusNotes and MS-Exchange.	CSC Ploenzke, GIS Langhagen, Dialog Switzerland
11.	i-net software http://www.inetsoft ware.de	96	13	Berlin	Software for running a computer help desk over an intranet.	Microsoft, GSW Berlin (Gemeinnützige Wohnungsbauges.)

Financial software/encryption

12.	NetLife http://www.netlife.de	96	51	Hamburg	On-line banking and E-Commerce solutions (SET). Subsidiary in Singapore, sales offices in New York and Vienna.	Drei-Banken-EDV Austria, Postbank AG, dvg Hannover (large German IT supplier)

E-business (communication)

13.	MSG Media Service http://www.media-service-group.com	97	10	Oldenburg	Developed a virtual web-based office for 'mobile professionals' called www.smartmessage.de. Another product was IntraSoft, an email workflow system for corporate feedback management. In addition, carried out project-based implementation services.	EWE (local electricity provider), Milagros USA, Hong Kong (Textiles and glasses), mezzo.net, Spain

Table A.35   Portal sites and electronic commerce start-ups

#	Name	Year	Employees	City	Product/service description	Partners/clients
Sale of products ('e-tailers' and business-to-business procurement specialists)						
1.	Friedrich Ingredients http://gewuerz.de and http://www.ingre dients.de	98	4	Konstanz	Sale of food ingredients over the web. Managing founder had long export experience. Targeted Asia, South America and Eastern Europe.	
Content						
2.	Localglobal http://localglobal.de	97	17	Stuttgart	Web-based content for SME exporters. Virtual trade fairs, calendar, articles. Editors based in Milano, Beijing and Poznan.	Deutsche Messe AG
3.	PropackExpo GmbH http://www.propack expo.de	97	3	Karlsruhe	A virtual trade fair including products, manufacturers, news and developments in the fields of processing and packaging technologies. Target group were the pharmaceutical, chemical, food and cosmetics industries.	Tellux GmbH
4.	OSM GmbH http://www.online test.de	97	4	Gleichen	Compiled consumer information which could be sold to portal sites. Database technology centrally held information separate from the layout, which could be adjusted to the hosting site. Content on computer products and software was sold to 51 German language sites.	Horizont, Chip, T-Online, Hoppenstedt, Wer liefert Was?, Weka Verlag, Bertelsmann

Hotel, travel

5.	Serenata http://www. serenata.de	96	10	Munich	Online reservation service for hotels that included software 'middleware' to link different front desk systems.	Hilton, Hyatt, Sheraton, Steigenberger, Intercontinental and others.
6.	Tiss http://www.tiss.com	95	3	Heilbronn	Internet-based flight ticket service run through an international network of independent travel agencies.	Travelocity, unnamed German media corporation

Extranet services/EDI/B2B exchanges

7.	BPS http://www.bps.de	97	12	Karlsruhe	Ran a business-to-business (B2B) procurement platform for the fashion industry that linked producers with retailers in Germany and Europe.	Lee Cooper (UK jeans manufacturer), 14 German SMEs in the textile industry
8.	Virtualheaven http://undercover. virtualheaven.de:8080	97	9	Cologne	Extranet for SME publishers. On the system, international licensing offers could be announced to members.	
9.	n:media http://www.nmedia.de	98	15	Düsseldorf	B2B exchange linking manufacturers of PR articles and retailers using hybrid CD-ROM technologies. European focus with more than 50% foreign customers and a planned office in London.	

Entertainment, games

10.	NxN http://www.nxn.net	97	9	Munich	Tools software to design computer games. The software allowed the design process to take place in a distributed environment by using the internet. The firm also hosted tool environments for game developers.	Unnamed major games and multimedia companies

Table A.35 (continued)

#	Name	Year	Employees	City	Product/service description	Partners/clients
11.	Entertaining Interactive Productions (EIP) http://www.eip.de	97	18	Altenholz	Produced on-line and off-line entertainment applications. Launched a popular German lottery service on the internet (http://www.jaxx.de/).	SAT.1 TV
	Community/chat					
12.	Medium.net http://www.medium.net	98	2	Leipzig	Modular software for communities on the internet. Chat software was already being sold and a popular chat site was being hosted. Managing founders were 16 and 17 years old.	UNICUM (Internet service for students), AIESEC, Wirtschaftsmesse Wien, Radio Bremen
13.	21TORR http://21torr.com	94	36	Reutlingen	Ran a German-language internet community with more than 140 000 participants. Users averaged 60 minutes per session. Banner advertising was avoided as a revenue stream, instead, companies could host events, promotions and chat channels. Managing founders called this approach 'soft sponsoring.' Expansion into Austria and Switzerland was planned. Partnership in France.	Levi's, ZDF, Havas, Hewlett-Packard
	Brokers					
14.	Up2Day Telekommunikation http://www.kostenlos.de	96	14	Duisburg	Hosted one of the most popular German-language classifieds service offers. Currently was developing a pay-for-view and search system for a major German publisher.	Unnamed major German publisher

Table A.36 Others

#	Name	Year	Employees	City	Product/service description	Partners/clients
New media agencies						
1.	FORK Unstable Media http://www.fork.de	96	12	Hamburg	New media agency with two American and one German managing founders. Planned expansion to New York.	Beiersdorf, B&D Verlag, Kabel New Media
Consultants, training						
2.	InnoVatio Verlags AG/Netz-Informations-Analyse http://www.netz-analysen.de	97	8	Leipzig	Carried out on-line research for clients. Included regular reports as well as programmed alert mechanisms. Co-operations being formed with Ostavia, Berne, Dover and Vancouver.	Hoechst, Mercedes-Benz, Nestlé
Hardware for access						
3.	Tixi.com http://Tixi.com	96	20	Berlin	Development of the Tixi-box, which was an autonomous modem-device that was able to receive emails from the provider and store them without the computer being on. Targets were SMEs that needed to answer e-mail requests but did not want to invest in an expensive router infrastructure.	

NOTES

1. Helene Laube, Jochen Rieker, 'Neue deutsche Welle' and 'Shooting Stars', *Manager Magazin*, October 1998, 208–31.

Appendix B: Interviews

INTERVIEWS WITH REPRESENTATIVES OF PRIVATE ENTERPRISE

1&1 Internet GmbH (Eigendorfer Straße 57, 56410 Montabaur)
20 March 1998, 11:00–12:00
CeBIT, Hannover, Halle 6
With Anastasia Antoniadou, Dipl.-Betriebswirt (FH)

1&1 Multimedia Service GmbH (Multimedia-Internet-Park, Gebäude 71, 66482 Zweibrücken)
20 March 1998, 12:00–12:30
CeBIT, Hannover, Halle 6
With Frank Ufer, Consultant

2CK Gesellschaft für DV-Dienstleistungen mbH (Kirchtruderinger Straße 22, 81829 München)
21 March 1998, 13:00–14:00
CeBIT, Hannover, Tagungscentrum Messe (TCM)
With Christian Koch, Dipl.-Infom. (FH), Managing Director, and Christoph Köberle, Dipl.-Infom. (FH), Managing Director

21Torr (Christophstraße 31, 72760 Reutlingen)
19 March 1998, 16:00–17:00
Halle 1, CeBIT, Hannover
With Martin Cserba, Managing Director, Marketing and Sales

Atlas Venture
16 July 1997, 09:00–10:30
Office of Atlas Venture, Steinstraße 70, 81667 München
With Ingo Johannsen, Partner

Blome + Partner Managementberatung für Vertrieb + EDV (Werner-von-Siemens-Straße 19, 49124 Georgsmarienhütte)
20 March 1998, 14:00–15:00

Tagungscentrum Messe (TCM), CeBIT, Hannover
With Frank F. Blome, Managing Director

BPS Online-Bestellsysteme GmbH (Greschbachstraße 3B, 76229 Karlsruhe)
23 March 1998, 13:00–14:00
CeBIT, Hannover, Halle 1
With Diana Schulirsch, Dipl.-Wi.-Ingenieur, Project Head, Member of Management

Brokat Informationssysteme GmbH (Industriestraße 3, 70565 Stuttgart)
22 March 1998, 17:00–18:00
CeBIT, Halle 18, Hannover
With Dr Boris Anderer, Managing Partner

Callisto Germany.net GmbH (Stresemannallee 30, 60586 Frankfurt am Main)
13 July 1999, 11:00–12:00
Interview in company offices
With Stefan Kühler, Presse- und Öffentlichkeitsarbeit

COIN Corporate Interactive AG (Göttinger Chaussee 115, 30459 Hannover)
23 March 1998, 12:00–13:00
CeBIT, Hannover, Halle 1
With Arvin Arora, Member of the Executive Board, and Hartmut Poppinga, Head of Marketing

DeTeCSM (Pfnorstraße 1, 64293 Darmstadt)
9 July 1999, 12:00–14:30
Interview in company offices
With Dr Hartmut Wittig, Dir. Corp. Strategy

ESD Information Technology Entwicklungs GmbH (Ringstraße 33, 04430 Dölzig/ Leipzig)
12 April 1998, 10:00–11:15
At London Office, 35A Smith Street, London SW3 4EP
With Rembert von Meysenbug, Head Multimedia Division (based in Leipzig), and Nicolas J. Ziegler, Representative UK

GFT Informationssysteme Gmbh & Co. KG (Leopoldstraße 1, 78112 St. Georgen)

19 March 1998, 13:00–14:00
CeBIT, Hannover, Halle 3
Gespräch mit Ulrich Dietz, Dipl.-Ing. (FH) Managing Partner

Hyperwave Information Management GmbH (Stefan-George-Ring 19, 81929 München)
21 March 1998, 10:00–11:00
CeBIT, Hannover, Halle 6
With Georg Thamer, Head of Sales and Marketing

i-net Software GmbH (Friedrichstraße 231, 10969 Berlin)
24 March 1998, 11:00–12:00
CeBIT, Hannover, Halle 2
With Torsten Klose, Dipl.-Ing., Managing Director

iNETiative Venture Capital Neue Medien GmbH & Co. KG
16 March 1998, 12:00–13.30
Office of iNETiative, Kaistraße 14, 40221 Düsseldorf
With Mirko Jovanovski, Investment Manager, iNETiative, Niklas Mahrdt, iNETiative and Oliver Gardey, Smedvig Capital, London

iNETiative Venture Capital Neue Medien GmbH & Co. KG
16 April 1998, 17:15–19.30
Office of iNETiative, Kaistraße 14, 40221 Düsseldorf
With Mirko Jovanovski, Investment Manager, and Niklas Mahrdt

Intershop Communications
20 February 1998, 18:30–19:50
Office of Intershop Communications (UK) Ltd., Hygeia Building, 66 College Road, Harrow, Middlesex, HA1 1FD
With Wilfried Beeck, Managing Director Europe and Nicole Fischer, Director of Strategic Alliances, Europe (both based in Hamburg)

iXOS Software AG (Technopark Neukeferloh, Bretonischer Ring 12, 85630 Grasbrun/ München)
19 March 1998, 11:00–12:00
CeBIT, Hannover, Halle 2
With Eberhard Färber, Dipl.-Kfm., Speaker of the Executive Board

Lars Heiden Jörg Füllenbach Realisationen (HFR)
4 March 1998, 18:00–19:30
Office of HFR, Gerresheimer Straße 22–24, 40211 Düsseldorf
With Lars Heiden and Jörg Füllenbach, Founding Managers

Living Systems AG (Roggenbachstrasse 1, 78050 VS-Villingen)
18 April 1999, 20:00–20:30
Interview in Queen's Arms pub, Queen's Gate Mews, London SW7
With Kurt Kammerer, Vorstand Consulting

local global, Magazin für Außenwirtschaft (Rotebühlstraße 154, 70197
Stuttgart)
19 March 1998, 14:00 -15:00
TCM (Tagungszentrum Messe), CeBIT, Hannover
With Hans Gäng, Publisher

Lucent   Technologies   Business   Communications   Systems   &
Microelectronics GmbH (Bramfelder Straße 121, 22305 Hamburg)
Lucent Technologies Network Systems GmbH (In der Raste 26, 53129
Bonn)
24 March 1998, 14:00–15:00
CeBIT, Hannover, Halle 16
With Michael Grün, Manager Business Management, Business
Communications Systems (based in Hamburg) and Harald Kettenbach,
Public Relations Manager, Corporate Communications (based in Bonn)

Medium.net (Dinterstraße 13, 04157 Leipzig)
22 March 1998, 13:00–14:00
CeBIT, Hannover, Halle 22
With Xuân Baldauf und David Uhlmann, Founders

Microsoft GmbH (Edisonstraße 1, 85716 Unterschleißheim)
24 March 1998, 10:00–11:00
CeBIT, Hannover, Halle 2
With Thomas Baumgärtner, Press Liaison Internet & Tools

MobilCom Aktiengesellschaft (Postfach 520, 24753 Rendsburg –
Büdelsdorf)
13 September 1999, 09:00–09:20
Telephone interview
With Stefan Arlt, Press Speaker

Nacamar Data Communications GmbH (Robert-Bosch-Straße 32, 63303
Dreieich)
12 July 1999, 10:00–11:00
Interview in company offices
With Michael Wirsik, Marketing Manager

Netlife Internet Consulting und Software GmbH (Elbberg 1, 22767 Hamburg)
23 March 1998, 14:30–15:00
CeBIT, Hannover, Halle 18
With Claus Müller, Managing Partner

Netlife Internet Consulting und Software GmbH (Elbberg 1, 22767 Hamburg)
23 March 1998, 14:00–14:30
CeBIT, Hannover, Halle 18
With Andreas Schlichtmann, Head of Marketing

NETCOLOGNE Gesellschaft für Telekommunikation mbH (Maarwegcenter, Maarweg 163, 50825 Köln Braunsfeld)
30 April 1999, 09:00–09:30
Telephone interview London–Cologne
With Werner Hanf, Managing Director

NetPartners Venture Capital, Milano
14 April 1998, 17:45–18:15
Telephone London/ Milano
With Michelle Appendino, Managing Partner

ONEstone Information Technologies GmbH (Riemekestraße 160, 33106 Paderborn)
24 March 1998, 12:00–13:00
CeBIT, Hannover, Halle 2
With Oliver Heinz, Managing Director

Online Marketing und Vertriebs GmbH (Im Dörmke 8, 37130 Gleichen/ Klein Lengden)
20 March 1998, 15:00–16:00
CeBIT, Hannover, Halle 6
With Hartmut Stöpler, Managing Director

ShopMaker GmbH Landesvertretung Deutschland (Justus-Staudt-Straße 2, D 65555 Limburg)
19 March 1998, 09:30–10:30
CeBIT, Hannover, Halle 6
With Dr. rer. oec. Luigi Carlo De Micco, Founding Manager

Tixi.Com GmbH (Karmeliter Weg 114, 13465 Berlin Frohnau)
23 March 1998, 9:15–10:00
CeBIT, Hannover, Halle 6
With Simon Verdenhalven, Sales and Marketing

TTM Investor GmbH (Ermekeilstraße 46, 53113 Bonn)
19 February 2002, 18:00–18:30
Telephone interview with Dr. Bernd Jäger

TPS Labs AG (Balanstraße 49, 81541 München)
27 February 1998, 09:00–10:30
Regents Park Marriot, 128 King Henry's Road, London NW3 3ST
With Michael Wenglein, Sales and Marketing Analyst and Marc Philipp
Gösswein, Sales and Marketing Analyst (both based in Munich)

TVM Techno Venture Management GmbH & Co. KG
16 July 1997, 15:00–16:00
Office of TVM Techno Venture Management, Tölzer Straße 12A, 82031
Grünwald
With Peter Kaleschke, Managing Partner

USWeb InnoMate
16 June 1998, 10:00–12:00
Office of USWeb InnoMate, Hallbergstraße 28, 40239 Düsseldorf
With Oliver Höck, Managing Director, Birgit Merz, Marketing, and
Jochen Rieker, Redakteur, *Manager Magazin*

USWeb InnoMate (Hallbergstraße 28, 40239 Düsseldorf)
24 March 1998, 13:00–14:00
CeBIT, Hannover, Halle 18
With Kai Petersen, Dipl.-Informatiker, Managing Director

Verteilte Systeme, Universität Stuttgart, Institut für Parallele und Verteilte
Hochleistungsrechner (IPVR) (Breitwiesenstraße 20–22, 750565 Stuttgart)
20 March 1998, 13:00–14:00
CeBIT Hannover, Halle 22
With Dipl.-Inform. Hartmut Benz

Webplanet Corporation (Ostring 7e, 85630 Grasbrun)
23 March 1998, 18:00–19:00
CeBIT, Hannover, Tagungscentrum Messe (TCM)
With Dieter E. Hesse, CEO and President

INTERVIEWS WITH PARLIAMENTARIANS, THEIR STAFF, GOVERNMENT OFFICIALS AND REPRESENTATIVES OF PRIVATE OR PUBLIC INSTITUTIONS

Arne Börnsen, Director Telecom, A.T. Kearney GmbH, Düsseldorf
Former Vizepräsident, Regulierungsbehörde für Telekommunikation und Post (RegTP), Tulpenfeld 4, 53113 Bonn
19 February 2002, 15:00–16:00
Café in Munich, Pacellistraße

Georg M. Bröhl, Ministerialrat, Medienrecht
Dr Alexander Tettenborn, Oberregierungsrat, Medienrecht
Anton-Josef Cremer, Referent, Medienrecht
10 May 1999, 15:00–15:50
Bundesministerium für Wirtschaft und Technologie, Haus VI, Villemombler Straße 76, 53123 Bonn

Dr Manuel Kiper, former MdB (Bündnis 90/ Die Grünen)
31 May 1999, 9:30–9:45
Via telephone London–Oldenburg

Dr Marianne Kulicke, Deputy Head, Department Innovation Services and Regional Development, Gerhard Samulat, Public Relations with Jochen Rieker, Editor, *Manager Magazin*
Fraunhofer-Institut für Systemtechnik und Innovationsforschung (ISI) (Institute Systems and Innovation Research)
24 June 1998, 10:30–12:00
Fraunhofer-Institut für Systemtechnik und Innovationsforschung (ISI), Breslauer Straße 48, 76139 Karlsruhe

Kilian Lenard, Speaker
European Net Economy Forum (ENEF), Kurfürstendamm 132a, 10711 Berlin
15 August 1999, 9:00–9:15
Via telephone Munich–Berlin

Dr Hans-Peter Lorenzen, Ministerialrat, Unterabteilungsleiter 6A
Kathrin Meyer, Referat 6A 5
11 May 1999, 10:30–11:30 Uhr
Bundesministerium für Wirtschaft und Technologie, Haus VI, Villemombler Straße 76, 53123 Bonn

Harald Lux, Consultant and freelance journalist
Nettraffic.de ISP Watch, Heinen & Lux GbR (Sandkaule 5–7, 53111 Bonn)
10 July 1999, 11:30–14:30
Summer lunch in a restaurant on the Rhine

Dr Martin Mayer (Siegertsbrunn) MdB (CSU)
23 April 1999, 13:00–13:30
Via telephone London–Bonn

Dr Michael Meister, MdB (CDU)
22 March 1999, 15:00–16:00
Bundeshaus, 53113 Bonn

Siegmar Mosdorf, Parlamentarischer Staatssekretär, MdB (SPD)
Andreas Schaal, Persönlicher Referent des Parlamentarischen
Staatssekretärs
Kathrin Meyer, Referat 6A 5
10 May 1999, 13:00–13:45
Bundesministerium für Wirtschaft und Technologie, Villemombler Straße
76, 53123 Bonn

Lutz Reulecke, Medienpolitischer Mitarbeiter (FDP)
25 March 1999, 17:15–18:15
Bundeshaus, 53113 Bonn

Jörg Tauss, MdB (SPD)
25 March 1999, 16:15–17:00
Bundeshaus, 53113 Bonn

VATM, Verband der Anbieter von Telekommunikations- und
Mehrwertdiensten e.V. (Oberländer Ufer 180–182, 50968 Köln)
14 July 1999, 15:00–16:00
Interview in offices of the association
With Jürgen Grützner, Stellvertretender Geschäftsführer, and Eva-Maria
Schreiter, Referentin für Presse- und Öffentlichkeitsarbeit

INTERNATIONAL INTERVIEW PARTNERS

Ola Ahlvarsson, CEO
Result Ventures Knowledge (Peter Myndes Backe 12, 118 46 Stockholm,
Sweden)

18 October 1999, 12:00–12:45
Telephone interview

Ola Ahlvarsson, CEO
Result (Grevture Gatan 18, 114 86 Stockholm, Sweden)
12 February 2002, 18:00–18:30
Telephone interview

Nils Gunnar Billinger, Head
Post and Telecommunications Authority (P.O. 5398, 10249 Stockholm, Sweden)
21 December 1999, 11:00–11:30
Telephone interview

Klaas de Boer, Former Investment Director
Vannenberg Group in Putten, Netherlands (now independent start-up consultant living in London, W8)
14 October 1999, 11:15–11:45
Telephone interview

Benoit Grossmann, Partner
Viventures Partners SA, (Tour Séquïa 1, Place Carpeaux, 92915 Paris La Défense, France)
8 October 1999, 18:00–18:30
Telephone interview

Roel de Hoop, Founder
Hot-Orange.com, (Stephensonstraat 19, 1097, Amsterdam, The Netherlands)
26 October 1999
E-mail interview

Johan Jörgensen, COO
Municel (c/o Result Venture Knowledge, Peter Myndes Backe 12, 118 46 Stockholm, Sweden)
11 October 1999, 11:00–11:30
Telephone interview

Pierre Morin, Partner
GRP (Europe) Ltd. (139 Piccadilly, London W1J 7NU, UK)
14 February 2002
E-mail exchange

Pär-Jörgen Pärson, CEO
Cell Ventures AB (Hightechbuilding 111, 101 52 Stockholm, Sweden)
2 December 1999, 15:45–16:15
Telephone interview

Tony Salter, CEO
Boxman AB (Innovation Centre, 68 Milton Park, Abingdon, Oxon OX14
4RX, UK)
3 December 1999, 11:00–11:15
Telephone interview

Marc Simoncini, PDG
Opsion Innovacion/ iFrance (Boulogne Billancourt 92100, France)
6 November 1999
E-mail interview

Kjell Spangberg
Swedish private investor living in San Francisco
17 November 1999, 17:00–17:30
Telephone interview

Appendix C: Selected financial figures for international telecommunications operators

Table C.1 Selected financial figures for international telecommunications companies, 1998[a]

	Net revenue US$ million	Net income (loss) US$ million	Net income as percentage of net revenue	Shareholder equity US$ million	Return on equity (on the basis of net income) (%)	Year-end share price US$	Number of shares issued (million)	Basic earnings (loss) per share	Market capitalization US$ million
European telecommunications operators									
Deutsche Telekom (DT)	39126	2493	6.3	27853	9.0	31	2743	0.91	85582
France Télécom (FTE)	27359	2553	9.3	18860	13.5	70	1025	2.49	71750
Mannesmann	21142	699	3.3	7060	9.9	109	390	1.79	42666
Royal KPN N.V.	8926	763	8.5	6565	11.6	47	473	1.61	22373
Telia Group	6381	559	8.8	3438	16.3				
US telecommunications operators									
AT&T (T)	53223	6398	12	25522	25.0	76	1784	3.59	135227
Sprint Corporation[b]	17134	[c]853	5.0	12448	6.9	95	431	1.98	40945
US telecommunications/cable entrants									
MCI WorldCom (WCOM)	17678	[c]−2571	–	45003	–	72	1274	−2.02	91728
Qwest Communications (QWST)	2243	−844	–	4238	–	25	278	−3.02	6975

IXC Comminications (IIXC)	668	c−221	—	—	35	36	−6.15	1 260
Level 3 Communications (LVLT)	392	d−128	2165	—	42	302	−0.43	12 684
@Home Network (ATHM)	48	−144.18	494	—	40	114.24	−1.26	4 560

Notes:

a Based on Annual Reports. Share prices were not always contained in the Annual Reports. In these cases, year-end share prices were approximated from stock exchange data. Exchange rates used were 1.76 DM per US$ (Deutsche Telekom), 1.11 US$ per 1 Euro (Mannesmann, Royal KPN and France Télécom) and 8.03 SEK (Swedish Krona) per 1 US$ (Telia).

b Sprint Corporation acquired 100 per cent ownership of the wireless operator PCS and split its stock into Sprint FON and Sprint PCS. These figures represented the combined group.

c These figures were recalculated to be applicable to common shareholders.

d This income figure was based on operating income.

Table C.2   Market capitalization of selected firms as of 25.08.99

Ticker	Share price in US$	Number of shares (million)	Market capitalization US$ million
DT	43	2994	128742
FTE	78	1025	79950
T	48	3196	153408
WCOM	80	1861	148880
FON	45	868	39060
QWST	29	746	21634
IIXC	36	37	1332
LVLT	63	340	21420
ATHM	42	368	15456

Notes:
In addition: Mannesmann had a capitalization of US$ 63 836 million and Royal KPN of US$ 22 933 million. As with the original table, a uniform exchange rate of 1.11 US$ = 1 EUR was used.
For ticker symbols, please refer to Table C.1 in this Appendix.

Table C.3   Market capitalization as multiples of net revenues, 1998 and market capitalization growth of selected telecommunications and cable companies[a]

	Market cap multiple 1998	Growth of market cap December 1998 to August 1999 (%)
European operators		
Deutsche Telekom	2.19	+50
France Télécom	2.63	+11
Mannesmann	2.02	+50
Royal KPN	2.51	+3
US telecommunications operators		
AT&T	2.54	+13
Sprint	2.39	−5[b]
US telecom and cable entrants		
MCI WorldCom	5.19	+62
Qwest	3.11	+210
IXC	1.89	+6
Level 3	32.36	+69
@Home	95.00	+239

Notes:
[a]   Please refer to Table C.1 of this Appendix for details on the figures. Market capitalization multiples were market capitalization in US$ at year-end 1998 divided by net income for 1998 in US$. Growth in market capitalization was relative to values as of 25 August 1999.
[b]   Due to a stock split into Sprint FON and Sprint PCS.

Appendix D: Internet advertising expenditures and the number of internet users by country

Table D.1   Internet advertising expenditures and users

		1996	1997	1998	1999
USA	Spend	US$ 267 M (IAB/ Coopers & Lybrand); US$ 236 M (Cowles/ Simba)	US$ 907 M (IAB/ Coopers & Lybrand); US$ 597 M (Cowles/ Simba)	US$ 1 920 M (IAB/ PWC)	US$ 4 620 M (IAB/ PWC)
	Users	40 M (FIND/SVP)[a]	62 M (Intelligest)	79 M (CommerceNet/ Nielsen)	119 M (Nielsen// NetRatings)
Germany	Spend	DM 6 M (G+J EMS)	DM 24 M (G+J EMS)	DM 50 M (G+J EMS); US$ 27 M (Prognos, ZAW)	DM 150 M (G+J, EMS); US$ 82 M (Prognos)
	Users	2.8 M (Computer Industry Almanac)	5.5 M (IDC)	6.9 M (G+J EMS)	9.9 M (G+J EMS, 4th Wave)
France	Spend	–	US$ 6.7 M (Havas); FF 30 M (IAB France/ PWC)	US$ 13.5 M (Havas); FF 80 M (France Pub); FF 113 M (IAB France/ PWC)	FF 516 M (IAB France/ PWC)
	Users[b]	0.8 M (Computer Industry Almanac)	1.3 M (Computer Industry Almanac)	2.5 M (Mediangles)	6.2 M (Mediangels)

Netherlands	Spend	US$ 1 M (Jupiter)	Dfl 6 M (Media Plaza)	Dfl 18 M (Media Plaza)	Dfl 30 M (Media Plaza)
	Users	0.7 M (Computer Industry Almanac)	1.0 M (Computer Industry Almanac)	1.4 M (Computer Industry Almanac)	2.3 M (Pro Active)
Sweden	Spend	–	SEK 61 M (IRM)	SEK 207 (IRM)	SEK 408 M (IRM)
	Users	1.1 M (Computer Industry Almanac)	1.8 M (Computer Industry Almanac)	2.4 M (Sifo Interactive Media)	3.2 M (Sifo Interactive Media)

Notes:

a Early internet user figures were generally very inaccurate in all countries, because they were often not based on representative surveys, but on internet host counts (it was impossible to accurately say how many internet users accessed a given host computer). The added difficulty faced here was that often only one figure in each country was available for a whole year, and the month these numbers were estimated were not uniform. Given the rapid growth of the internet, it could make a great difference whether indicators from the beginning or the end of the year were taken. The early US data actually was released early in the next year instead of the year indicated. To obtain the figures used in this table, several different sources were consulted and the numbers that matched most closely with the different estimates were used.

b Did not include Minitel users.

Sources: Advertising expenditure estimates were obtained from the following sources on the internet: Internet Advertising Bureau (http://www.iab.net/), Cowles/ Simba Information (http://www.simbanet.com/), Nielsen// NetRatings (http://www.nielsen-netratings.com/), G + J Electronic Media Service (http://www.ems.guj.de/), Media Plaza (http://www.mediaplaza.nl/), IRM Institutet för Reklam & Mediestatistik (http://www.irm-media.se/). Internet user numbers were compiled from different sources by Nua Ltd. Online Relationship Management, 'How many online?' Dublin and could be accessed on http://www.nua.net/. To complement these figures, Computer Industry Almanac estimates were used, these were quoted in Morgan Stanley Dean Witter, 1999, 248–0. The following web sites were also consulted: Nielsen// NetRatings (http://www.nielsen-netratings.com/). Sifo interactive Media (http://www.sifointeractive.com/). For French statistics, see also http://www.journaldunet.com/.

Bibliography

Abelshauser, Werner (1983), *Wirtschaftsgeschichte der Bundesrepublik Deutschland 1945–1980* (Frankfurt am Main: Suhrkamp Verlag).

Abelshauser, Werner (1984), 'The First-Post Liberal Nation: Stages in the Development of Modern Corporatism in Germany', *European History Quarterly*, 14: 3, July, 285–318.

Abelshauser, Werner (2001), 'Markt und Staat. Deutsche Wirtschaftspolitik im langen 20. Jahrhundert', in Spree (2001).

Ackroyd, S. (1995), 'On the Structure and Dynamics of Some Small, UK-Based Information Technology Firms', *Journal of Management Studies*, 32:2, March.

Adam, Marie-Christine and Farber André (1994), *Le financement de l'innovation technologue. Théorie économique et expérience européenne* (Paris: Presses Universitaires De France).

Albach, Horst and Knieps, Günter (1997), *Kosten und Preise in wettbewerblichen Ortsnetzen* (Baden-Baden: Nomos).

Allen, John (1992), 'Post-Industrialism and Post-Fordism', in Hall et al. (1992).

Altinger, Laura and Enders, Alice (1996), 'The Scope and Depth of GATS Commitments', *World Economy*, 19:3, May, 307–32.

Arthur, W. Brian (1989), 'Competing Technologies, Increasing Returns and Lock-In by Historical Events', *Economic Journal*, 99, March, 116–31.

Ash, A. et al. (1994), 'Editorial: Forum for Heterodox International Political Economy', *Review of International Political Economy*, 1:1, Spring.

Baker, P. (1996), 'Spatial Outcomes of Capital Restructuring: "New Industrial Spaces" as a Symptom of Crisis, Not Solution', *Review of Political Economy*, 8:3, July.

Baldwin, Robert, Scott, Colin and Hood, Christopher (1998), *A Reader on Regulation* (Oxford: Oxford University Press).

Bane, P. William, Bradley, Stephen P. and Collis, David J. (1998), 'The Converging Worlds of Telecommunications, Computing and Entertainment', in Bradley and Nolan (1998).

Bank, David (2001), *Breaking Windows. How Bill Gates Fumbled the Future of Microsoft* (New York: Free Press).

Bannock, G. and Albach, H. (1991), *Small Business Policy in Europe: Britain, Germany and the European Commission* (Worchester).

Barbrook, Richard and Cameron, Andy (1995), 'The Californian Ideology', *Mute*, 3, Autumn.

Baron, James N., Burton, Diane and Hannan, Michael T. (1996a), 'Inertia and Change in the Early Years: Employment Relations in Young, High Technology Firms', *Industrial and Corporate Change*, 503–35.

Baron, James N., Burton, Diane and Hannan, Michael T. (1996b), 'The Road Taken: Origins and Evolution of Employment Systems in Emerging Companies', *Industrial and Corporate Change*, 239–75.

Bartlett, Christopher A. and Ghoshal Sumantra (1995), *Transnational Management. Text, Cases and Readings in Cross-Border Managment*, 2nd edition (Chicago, IL: Irwin).

Beck, Ulrich (1986), *Risikogesellschaft. Auf dem Weg in eine andere Moderne* (Frankfurt am Main: Suhrkamp Verlag).

Berger, Georg and Nerlinger, Eric (1997), 'Regionale Verteilung von Unternehmensgründungen in der Informationstechnik: Empirische Ergebnisse für Westdeutschland', in Harhoff (1997).

Berger, Suzanne and Dore, Ronald (1996), *National Diversity and Global Capitalism* (Ithaca, NY: Cornell University Press).

Berghahn, Volker (1985), *Unternehmer und Politik in der Bundesrepublik* (Frankfurt am Main: Suhrkamp Verlag).

Berners-Lee, Tim with Fischetti, Mark (1999), *Weaving the Web. The Past, Present and Future of the World Wide Web by its Inventor* (London: Orion Business Books).

Bhagwati, Jagdish N. (1984), 'Splintering and Disembodiment of Services and Developing Nations', *World Economy*, 7:2 June, 133–44.

Bhagwati, Jagdish and Hirsch, Mathias (eds) (1998), *The Uruguay Round and Beyond. Essays in Honour of Arthur Dunkel* (Berlin: Springer).

Blumenthal, Marjory S. and Clark, David D. (2001), 'Rethinking the Design of the Internet: The End-to-End Arguments Vs. The Brave New World', in Compaine and Greenstein (2001).

BMBF – Bundesministerium für Bildung, Wissenschaft, Forschung und Technologie (1996), *Bundesbericht Forschung* (Bonner Universitäts-Bonn: Buchdruckerei).

BMBF – Bundesministerium für Bildung, Wissenschaft, Forschung und Technologie (1997), *Informations- und Kommunikationsdienste-Gesetz-Umsetzung und Evaluierung- Chancen für Wirtschaft, Erwartungen an Verwaltung und Gesetzgebung- Dokumentation der Fachveranstaltung des BMBF vom 8. Dezember 1997* (Bonn: BMBF).

BMBF and BMWi – Bundesministerium für Bildung, Wissenschaft, Forschung und Technologie and Bundesministerium für Wirtschaft (ed.) (1998), *Innovationsförderung für kleine und mittlere Unternehmen* (Bergheim: Druckpunkt Offset).

BMWi – Bundesministerium für Wirtschaft (1997), 'Informationsgesellschaft in Deutschland. Daten und Fakten im internationalen Vergleich. Zwischenbericht der Prognos AG zum Benchmarking-Projekt. Nr. 428.'

Borch, O.J. and Arthur, M.B. (1995), 'Strategic Networks Among Small Firms: Implications for Strategic Reseach Methodology', *Journal of Management Studies*, 32:4, July.

Borrus, Michael and Zysman, John (1997), 'Globalization with Borders: The Rise of Wintelism as the Future of Global Competition', *Industry and Innovation*, 4:2, December 1997.

Boyd-Barrett, Oliver (1989), 'Multinational News Agencies', in Enderwick (1989).

Bradley, Stephen P. and Nolan, Richard L. (eds) (1998), *Sense and Respond. Capturing Value in the Network Era* (Boston, MA: Harvard Business School Press).

Breuer, Rolf-E. (1997), 'Venture Capital – Besseres Umfeld ist notwendig', *Die Bank*, June.

Brose, Eric Dorn (1993), *The Politics of Technological Change in Prussia. Out of the Shadow of Antiquity 1809–1848* (Princeton, NJ: Princeton University Press).

Buchheim, Christoph (1990), *Die Wiedereingliederung Westdeutschlands in die Weltwirtschaft 1945–1958* (München: R. Oldenbourg Verlag).

Bude, Heinz and Schleissing, Stephan (eds) (1997), *Junge Eliten. Selbständigkeit als Beruf* (Stuttgart: W. Kohlhammer).

Burgel, Oliver, Murray, Gordon, Fier, Andreas, Licht, Georg and Nerlinger, Eric (1998), 'The Internationalization of British and German Start-up Companies in High-Technology Industries.'

Cannon, Robert (2001), 'Where Internet Service Providers and Telephone Companies Compete: A Guide to the Computer Inquiries, Enhanced Service Providers and Information Service Providers', in Compaine and Greenstein (2001).

Carnoy, M., Castells, M., Cohen, S.S. and Cardoso, F.H. (1993), *The New Global Economy of the Information Age; Reflections on our Changing World* (PA: Pennsylvania State University Press).

Cash jr., J.I., McFarlan, F.W., McKenney, J.L. (1992), *Corporate Information Systems Management. The Issues Facing Senior Executives* (Homewood, IL: Irwin).

Caspar, Steven, Lehrer, Mark and Soskice, David (1998), 'Can High-Technology Industries Prosper in Germany? Institutional Frameworks and the Evolution of the German Software and Biotechnology Industries', *Industry and Innovation* 6:1, 5–24.

Castells, Manuel (1996), *The Information Age: Economy, Society and Culture. Volume I. The Rise of the Network Society* (Oxford: Blackwell).

Castells, Manuel (1997), *The Information Age: Economy, Society and Culture. Volume II. The Power of Identity* (Oxford: Blackwell).

Castells, Manuel and Hall, Peter (1994), *Technopoles of the World. The Making of 21st Century Industrial Complexes* (London: Routledge).

Cave, Martin and Waverman, Len (1998), 'Introduction. The Future of International Settlements', *Telecommunications Policy*, 22:11, 883–98.

Ceruzzi, Paul E. (1998), *A History of Modern Computing* (Cambridge, MA: MIT Press).

Cerny, Philip G. (1996), 'International Finance and the Erosion of State Policy Capacity', in Gummett (1996).

Chandler, Alfred D. Jr. and Cortada James W. (eds.) (2000a), *A Nation Transformed by Information* (Oxford: Oxford University Press).

Chandler, Alfred D. Jr. and Cortada James W. (2000b), 'The Information Age. Continuities and Differences' in Chandler and Cortada (2000a).

Charles, David and Howells, Jeremy (1992), *Technology Transfer in Europe. Public and Private Networks* (London: Belhaven Press).

Christensen, Clayton M. (1997), *The Innovator's Dilemma. When New Technologies Cause Great Firms to Fail* (Boston, MA: Harvard Business School Press).

Clemens, Clay (1994), 'The Chancellor as Manager: Helmut Kohl, the CDU and Governance in Germany', *West European Politics*, 17:4, October, 28–51.

Clinton, William and Gore Jr., Albert (1997), 'A Framework for Global Electronic Commerce' July.

Cohen, Stephen S. and Zysman, John S. (1987), *Manufacturing Matters: The Myth of the Post-Industrial Economy* (New York:Basic Books).

Cohen, Stephen S. and Fields, Gary (1999), 'Social Capital and Capital Gains in Silicon Valley', *California Management Review*, 41:2, Winter, 108–30.

Cohen, Stephen S., DeLong, J. Bradford and Zysman, John (2000), 'Tools for Thought: What is New and Important About the 'E-conomy', BRIE Working Paper #138, manuscript dated 27 February.

Compaine, Benjamin M. and Greenstein, Shane (eds) (2001), *Communications Policy in Transition. The Internet and Beyond* (Cambridge, MA: MIT Press).

Cooke, Philip (1997), 'Regions in a Global Market: the Experiences of Wales and Baden-Württemberg', *Review of International Political Economy*, 4:2, Summer.

Council on Foreign Relations (ed.) (1994), *Competitiveness. An International Economics Reader. A Foreign Affairs Reader* (New York).

Coutarelli, Spiro A. (1977), *Venture Capital in Europe* (New York: Praeger Publishers).

Cowie, Harry (1999), *Venture Capital in Europe* (London: Federal Trust for Education and Research).

Cox, R.W. (1987), *Production, Power and World Order; Social Forces in the Marking of History* (New York: Columbia University Press).

Coyle, Diane (1997), *The Weightless World. Strategies for Managing the Digital Economy* (Oxford: Capstone).

Cross, John, Earl, Michael J., Sampler, Jeffrey L. (1998), 'Transformation of the IT function at British Petroleum', Manuscript dated 20 August, London Business School, Sussex Place.

Curran, J., Stanworth, J. and Watkins, D. (eds) (1986), *The Survival of the Small Firm; Employment, Growth, Technology and Politics*, Volume 2 (Aldershot: Gower).

Currie, Wendy (1995), *Management Strategy for IT: An International Perspective* (London: Pitman).

Cusumano, Michael A. and Yoffie, David B. (1998), *Competing on Internet Time. Lessons from Netscape in Its Battle with Microsoft* (New York: Free Press).

Czada, Roland (1994), 'Konjunkturen des Korporatismus: Zur Geschichte eines Paradigmenwechsels in der Verbändeforschung', in Streeck (1994).

Daniels, P.W. (1985), *Service Industry. A Geographical Appraisal* (London: Methuen).

Darbishire, Owen (1995), 'Switching Systems: Technological Change, Competition and Privatization', *Industrielle Beziehungen*, 2: 2, 156–79.

Dasgupta, Partha and Stoneman, Paul (eds) (1987), *Economic Policy and Technological Performance* (Cambridge: Cambridge University Press).

Davidson, James Dale, Rees-Mogg, William (1997), *The Sovereign Individual. The Coming Economic Revolution and How to Survive and Prosper in It* (London: Macmillan).

Davies, Andrew (1996), 'Innovation in Large Technical Systems: The Case of Telecommunications', *Industrial and Corporate Change*, 5:4, 1143–80.

DeLong, J. Bradford (2000), 'Macroeconomic Implications of the "New Economy"', *Wirtschaftspolitische Blätter*, 47:4, 476–9.

DeLong, J. Bradford (2001), 'Do we have a "New" Macroeconomy?' manuscript dated March from http://www.j-bradford-delong.net/.

Dery, Mark (1996), *Escape Velocity. Cyberculture at the End of the Century* (London: Hodder & Stoughton).

Dery, Mark (1999), *The Pyrotechnic Insanitarium. American Culture on the Brink* (New York: Grove Press).

Dicken, Peter (1992), *Global Shift, The Internationalization of Economic Activity*, 2nd edition (London: Paul Chapman).

Dolowitz, D. and Marsh, D. (1996), 'Who Learns What from Whom: A Review of the Policy Transfer Literature', *Political Studies*, 44.

Donges, Juergen B. (1995), *Deutschland in der Weltwirtschaft. Dynamik sichern, Herausforderungen bewältigen* (Mannheim: B.I.-Taschenbuchverlag).

Donges, Juergen B. (1998), 'Die Wirtschaftspolitik im Spannungsverhältnis von Regulierung und Deregulierung', *ORDO. Jahrbuch für die Ordnung von Wirtschaft und Gesellschaft*, 48, 201–15.

Dornbusch, Rudi (2000), *Keys to Prosperity. Free Markets, Sound Money and a Bit of Luck* (Cambridge, MA: MIT Press).

DTI – Department of Trade and Industry, United Kingdom (1987), *The Economic Effects of Value-Added and Data Services*, Vanguard Government and Industry Initiative.

DTI – Department of Trade and Industry, United Kingdom (1998), 'Moving into the Information Age. An international benchmarking study. Commissioned from Spectrum Strategy Consultants'.

Dunning, John H. (1993a), *The Globalization of Business. The Challenge of the 1990s* (London: Routledge).

Dunning, John H. (1993b), *Multinational Enterprises and the Global Economy* (Reading: Addison-Wesley).

Dunning, John H. (ed.) (1997), *Governments, Globalization and International Business* (Oxford: Oxford University Press).

Duysters, G. and Hagedoorn, J. (1995), 'Strategic Groups and Inter-Firm Networks in International High-Tech Industries', *Journal of Management Studies*, 32:3, May.

Dyson, Esther (1998), *Release 2.1 A Design for Living in the Digital Age* (London: Penguin Group).

Dyson, Kenneth (ed.) (1992), *The Politics of German Regulation* (Aldershot: Dartmouth).

Dyson, Kenneth and Humphreys, Peter (eds) (1990), *The Political Economy of Communications. International and European Dimensions* (London: Routledge).

Dyson, Kenneth and Humphreys, Peter with Negrine, Ralph and Simon, Jean-Paul (eds) (1988), *Broadcasting and New Media Policies in Western Europe. A Comparative Study of Technological Change and Public Policy* (London: Routledge).

The Economist Newspaper (1996), *Going Digital. How New Technology is Changing our Lives* (London: Profile Books).

Eggertsson, Thráinn (1990), *Economic Behavior and Institutions* (Cambridge: Cambridge University Press).

EITO – European Information Technology Observatory – European Economic Interest Grouping (1999), *European Information Technology Observatory 1999*, Frankfurt am Main.

Electronic Commerce Advisory Council (1998), 'If I'm so Empowered, Why do I Need You? Defining Government's Role in Internet Electronic Commerce', State of California, November (http://www.e-commerce. ca.gov/).

Enderwick, Peter (ed.) (1989), *Multinational Service Firms* (London: Routledge).

Engel, Christoph (2001), 'The Path to Competition for Telecommunications in Germany', in Sidak et al. (2001).

Engel-Flechsig, Stefan, Maennel, Frithjof A. and Tettenborn, Alexander (1998), *Neue gesetzliche Rahmenbedingungen für Multimedia. Die Regelungen des IuKDG und des MDStV* (Heidelberg: Verlag Recht und Wirtschaft).

Enquete-Kommission (1998), *Schlußbericht der Enquete-Kommission Zukunft der Medien in Wirtschaft und Gesellschaft – Deutschlands Weg in die Informationsgesellschaft* (Deutscher Bundestag, Drucksache 13/11004, 22 June).

Ergas, Henry (1987), 'Does Technology Policy Matter?', in Guile and Brooks (1987).

Ergas, Henry (1987), 'The importance of technology policy', in Dasgupta and Stoneman (1987).

Ergas, Henry and Pogorel, Gerard (1994), 'Multilateral cooperation in International Telecommunications: Sources and Prospects', in Noam and Pogorel (1994).

Eucken, Walter (1990), *Grundsätze der Wirtschaftspolitik* (Tübingen: J.C.B. Mohr).

European Commission Communication (1997-157 final), 'A European Initiative in Electronic Commerce', 15 April.

European Commission Communication (1998-586 final), 'Proposal for a European Parliament and Council Directive on Certain Legal Aspects of Electronic Commerce in the Internal Market', 18 November.

European Commission, DGXIII (1994), *The Internet and the European Information Industry* Information Market Observatory IMO, IMO Working Paper 94/ 3, Final, September (Luxembourg).

European Commission DGXIII.A3 – Telecommunication Infrastructures (1997), 'Evolution of the Internet and the WWW in Europe' (Final Report by Databank Consulting, IDATE, TNO) October, Study GI 2.2/96 – Contract N. 45532.

EVCA – European Venture Capital Association (1997), *Yearbook 1997* (Zaventem).

EVCA – European Venture Capital Association (1998), *Yearbook 1998* (Zavantem).

EVCA – European Venture Capital Association (1999), *Yearbook 1999* (Zavantem).

EVCA – European Venture Capital Association (2000), *Yearbook 2000* (Zavantem).

EVCA – European Venture Capital Association (2001), *Yearbook 2001* (Zavantem).

Featherstone, Mike (ed.) (1990), *Global Culture. Nationalism, Globalization and Modernity* (London: Sage).

Featherstone, Mike (1991), *Consumer Culture and Postmodernism* (London: Sage).

Feketekuty, Geza (1998), 'Trade in Services – Bringing Services into the Multilateral Trading System', in Bhagwati and Hirsch (1998).

Foley, Bernard J. (ed.) (1998) European Economics since the Second World War (Elgar).

Foss, N. J. (1996), 'Research in Strategy, Economics and Michael Porter', *Journal of Management Studies*, 33:1, January.

Freeman, Christopher (1988), 'Introduction to Small Countries Facing Technological Revolution', in: Freeman and Lundvall (1988).

Freeman, Christopher and Lundvall, Bengt-Åke (eds) (1988), *Small Countries Facing the Technological Revolution* (London: Pinter Publishers).

Freeman, Christopher, Sharp, Margaret and Walker, William (1991), *Technology and the Future of Europe: Global Competition and the Environment in the 1990s* (London: Pinter Publishers).

Freeman, Christopher and Soete, Luc (1997), *The Economics of Industrial Innovation. Third Edition* (Cambridge, MA: MIT Press).

Freeman, John (1998), 'Venture Capital and Growth Businesses in Germany', dated 3 November 1998, University of California, Manuscript.

Fremdling, Rainer (1975), *Eisenbahnen und deutsches Wirtschaftswachstum 1840–1879. Ein Beitrag zur Entwicklungstheorie und zur Theorie der Infrastruktur* (Dortmund: Gesellschaft für Westfälische Wirtschaftsgeschichte e.V.).

Freytag, Andreas and Jäger, Bernd (1996), 'Der künftige Ordnungsrahmen des deutschen Telekommunikationsmarktes. Anmerkungen vor dem Hintergrund des Telekommunikationsgesetzes', *ORDO. Jahrbuch für die Ordnung von Wirtschaft und Gesellschaft*, 47, 215–39.

Frieden, Jeffry A. (1991), 'Invested Interests: The Politics of National Economic Policies in a World of Global Finance,' *International Organization*, 45:4, Autumn.

Galambos, Louis (1996), 'End of the Century Reflections on Weber and Schumpeter – With Karl Marx Lurking in the Background', in *Industrial and Corporate Change*, 5:3.

Gamble, A. (1995), 'The New Political Economy', *Political Studies*, 43, 516–30.

Gandal, Neil (2001), 'Sorting out the Search Engine Market', in Compaine and Greenstein (2001).

Garnham, Nicholas (2000), *Emancipation, the Media and Modernity. Arguments about the Media and Social Theory* (Oxford: Oxford University Press).

Garrett, Geoffrey and Lange, Peter (1996), 'Internationalization, Institutions and Political Change', in Keohane and Milner (1996).

Gereffi, Gary and Korzeniewicz, Miguel (eds) (1994), *Commodity Chains and Global Capitalism* (Westport, CT: Praeger).

Gerpott, Torsten J. (1998), *Wettbewerbsstrategien im Telekommunikationsmarkt* (3., überarbeitete und erweiterte Auflage) (Stuttgart: Schäffer-Poeschel).

Gerschenkron, Alexander (1962), *Economic Backwardness in Historical Perspective. A Book of Essays* (Cambridge, MA).

Giersch, Herbert, Paqué, Karl-Heinz and Schmieding Holger (1992), *The Fading Miracle. Four Decades of Market Economy in Germany* (Cambridge: Cambridge University Press).

Gilder, G. (1989), *Microcosm – The Quantum Revolution in Economics and Technology* (New York: Simon & Schuster).

Gilder, George (1993), 'The Death of Telephony', *The Economist*, 11 September.

Gilder, George (2000), *Telecosm. How Infinite Bandwidth Will Revolutionise Our World* (New York: Free Press).

Gilpin, Robert (2001), *Global Political Economy. Understanding the International Economic Order* (Princeton, NJ: Princeton University Press).

Glotz, Peter (2001), *Ron Sommer. Der Weg der Telekom* (Hamburg: Hoffmann und Campe).

Goffee, R. and Scase, R. (eds) (1987), *Entrepreneurship in Europe: The Social Processes* (London: Croom Helm).

Goodmann, S.E., Press, L.I., Ruth, S.R. and Rutkowski, A.M. (1994), 'The Global Diffusion of the Internet: Patterns and Problems', *Communications of the ACM*, August, 37:8.

Gross, Johannes (1995), *Begründung der Berliner Republik* (Stuttgart: Deutsche Verlags-Anstalt).

Guile, Bruce R. and Brooks, Harvey (eds) (1987), *Technology and Global Industry. Companies and Nations in the World Economy* (Washington, DC: National Academy Press).

Gummett, Philip (ed.) (1996), *Globalization and Public Policy* (Cheltenham: Edward Elgar).

Hagström, Peter (1991), *The 'Wired' MNC. The Role of Information Systems for Structural Change in Complex Organizations* (Stockholm: Akademisk Auhandling).

Hall, Peter A. (1986), *Governing the Economy: The Politics of State Intervention in Britain and France* (Oxford).

Hall, S., Held, D. and McGrew, T. (eds) (1992), *Modernity and its Futures* (Cambridge: Polity).

Hamilton, Gary G. (1996), 'The Quest for a Unified Economics,' *Industrial and Corporate Change*, Volume 5, Number 3.

Harhoff, Dietmar (ed.) (1997), *Unternehmensgründungen – Empirische Analysen für die alten und neuen Bundesländer* (Baden-Baden: Nomos).

Harhoff, Dietmar and Steil, Fabian (1997), 'Die ZEW-Gründungspanels – Konzeptionelle Überlegungen und Analysepotential', in Harhoff, (1997).

Harm, C. (1992), *The Financing of Small Firms in Germany*, Policy Research Working Papers, Financial Policy and Systems, Country Economics Department, World Bank, WPS 899, May.

Harmon, Steve (1999), *Zero Gravity. Riding Venture Capital from High-Tech Start-up to Breakout IPO* (Princeton, NJ: Bloomberg Press).

Harrison, Bennet (1994), *Lean and Mean. The Changing Landscape of Corporate Power in the Age of Flexibility* (New York: Basic Books).

Harvey, David (1990), *The Condition of Postmodernity. An Enquiry into the Origins of Cultural Change* (Oxford: Blackwell).

Haskins, G. with Gibb, A. and Hubert, T. (eds) (1986), *A Guide to Small Firm Assistance in Europe*, European Association for National Productivity Centers (Aldershot: Gower).

Helleiner, Eric (1998), 'Electronic Money: A Challenge to the Sovereign State?' *Journal of International Affairs*, 51:2, Spring.

Hellmann, Thomas F. and Puri, Manju (1997), 'The Professionalization of Start-up Firms by Venture Capital: Empirical Evidence on CEO Turnover, Growth and Exit' (Preliminary draft).

Hellmann, Thomas F. and Puri, Manju (1998), 'The Interaction between Product Market and Financing Strategy' (Preliminary draft).

Henzler, Herbert A. and Späth, Lothar (1997), *Countdown für Deutschland. Start in eine neue Zeit?* (München: Wilhelm Goldmann Verlag).

Herdzina, Klaus (1993), *Wettbewerbspolitik*, 4. Auflage (Stuttgart: Gustav Fischer Verlag).

Hill, C.W.L. and Deeds, D.L. (1996), 'The Importance of Industry Structure for the Determination of Firm Profitability: A Neo-Austrian Perspective', *Journal of Management Studies*, 33:4, July.

Hills, Jill (1986), Deregulating Telecoms. Competition and Control in the United States, Japan and Britain (London: Frances Pinter).

Hirst, Paul and Thompson, Grahame (1996), *Globalization in Question. The International Economy and the Possibilities of Governance* (Cambridge: Polity Press).

Hodgson, G. M. (1994a), *Economics and Evolution: Bringing Life Back into Economics* (Cambridge: Polity Press).

Hodgson, G. M. (1994b), 'Some Remarks on "Economic Imperialism" and International Political Economy', *Review of International Political Economy*, 1:1, Spring.

Hodgson, G.M. (1996), 'Varieties of Capitalism and Varieties of Economic Theory', *Review of International Political Economy*, 3:3, Autumn.

Hoffmann-Riem, Wolfgang (1990), 'New Media in West Germany: The Politics of Legitimation', in Dyson and Humphreys (1990).

Hornschild, K. and Meyer-Krahmer, F. (1992), *Evaluation of Economic Effects: Relevance and Impacts of EC-Programmes Promoting Industrial R&D With Special Emphasis on Small and Medium Sized Enterprises.* Pilot Methodological Study, Commission of the European Communities, Luxembourg, Directorate-General Telecommunications, Information Industries and Innovation, March.

Huhn, Wolfgang (1997), 'Gründung lernen', in Bude and Schleissing (eds) (1997).

Humphreys, Peter et al. (1988), 'New Media Policy Dilemmas in West Germany: From ideological Polarisation to Regional Economic Competition', in Dyson and Humphreys (1988).

Humphreys, Peter (1992), 'The Politics of Regulatory Reform in German Telecommunications', in Dyson (1992).

Humphreys, Peter (1994), *Media and Media Policy in Germany. The Press and Broadcasting since 1945*, 2nd Edition (Oxford: Berg Publishers).

Humphreys, Peter and Simpson, Seamus (1996), 'European Telecommunications and Globalization', in Gummett (1996).

IMRG – Interactive Media in Retail Group (1998), 'Electronic Commerce in Europe. An Action Plan for the Marketplace', www.imrg.org, July.

Inayatullah, Naeem (1997), 'Theories of Spontaneous Disorder', *Review of International Political Economy*, 4:2, Summer.

Isenberg, David S. (1997), 'Rise of the Stupid Network. Why the Intelligent Network was once a Good Idea, but isn't Anymore.' Manuscript dated 4 June also on http://www.computertelephony.com/ct/att.html).

Isenberg, David S. (1998a), 'The "Stupid Network" approach to innovation', *Communications Week International*, Issue 201, 16 March.

Isenberg, David S. (1998b), 'Backlash against the Stupid Network,' *CommunicationsWeek International*, Issue 211, 21 September.

Jagger, Nick and Miles, Ian (1991), 'New Telematic Services in Europe', in Freeman et al. (1991).

Jarke, Matthias (ed.) (1986), *Managers, Micros and Mainframes. Integrating Systems for End-Users* (Chichester: John Wiley & Sons).

Jomer, Per (1998), 'Why Stupid Networks Need a Little Intelligence', *CommunicationsWeek International*, Issue 208, 20 July.

Junne, Gerd (1989), 'Competitiveness and the Impact of Change: Applications of "High Technologies"', in Katzenstein (1989).

Kassim, Hussein and Menon, Anand (eds) (1996), *The European Union and National Industrial Policy* (London: Routledge).

Katz, Michael J. and Shapiro, Carl (1996), 'Technology Adoption in the Presence of Network Externalities', *Journal of Political Economy*, 94:4, 822–41.

Katzenstein, Peter J. (ed.) (1978), *Between Power and Plenty. Foreign Economic Policies of Advanced Industrial States* (Madison, WI: University of Wisconsin Press).

Katzenstein, Peter J. (1985), *Small States in World Markets. Industrial Policy in Europe* (Ithaca: Cornell University Press).

Katzenstein, Peter J. (ed.) (1989), *Industry and Politics in West Germany. Toward the Third Republic* (Ithaca, NY: Cornell University Press).

Katzenstein, Peter J., Keohane, Robert O. and Krasner, Stephen D. (eds) (1999a), *Exploration and Contestation in the Study of World Politics* (Cambridge, MA: MIT Press).

Katzenstein, Peter J., Keohane, Robert O. and Krasner, Stephen D. (1999b), '*International Organization* and the Study of World Politics', in Katzenstein et al. (1999a).

Kay, J. (1993a), *Foundations of Corporate Success* (Oxford: Oxford University Press).

Kay, J. (1993b), 'Keeping up with the Market', *The Economist*, 11 September.

Kelly, Kevin (1994), *Out of Control; The New Biology of Machines* (London: Fourth Estate).

Kelly, Kevin (1998), *New Rules for the New Economy, 10 Radical Strategies for a Connected World* (New York: Viking Penguin).

Kenney, Martin (2000a), 'Note on Venture Capital', BRIE Working Paper 142, E-conomy Project Working Paper 17.

Kenney, Martin (ed.) (2000b), *Understanding Silicon Valley. The Anatomy of an Entrepreneurial Region* (Stanford, CA: Stanford University Press).

Kenney, Martin (2001), 'The Growth and Development of the Internet in the United States', BRIE Working Paper 145, prepared for a forthcoming book edited by Bruce Kogut.

Keohane, Robert O. and Milner, Helen V. (eds) (1996), *Internationalization and Domestic Politics* (Cambridge: Cambridge University Press).

Kerber, W. (1993), 'Rights, Innovation and Evolution. The Distributional Effects of Different Rights to Innovate', *Review of Political Economy*, 5:4.

King, Anthony (1990), 'Architecture, Capital and the Globalization of Culture', in Featherstone (1990).

Klandt, H. (1987), 'Trends in Small Business Start-Up in Germany', in Goffee and Scase (1987).

Kleinert, Hubert and Mosdorf, Siegmar (1998), *Die Renaissance der Politik* (Berlin: Wolf Jobst Siedler Verlag).

Koschatzky, Knut (ed.) (1997a), *Technology-Based Firms in the Innovation Process. Management, Financing and Regional Networks* (Heidelberg: Physica-Verlag).

Koschatzky, Knut (1997b), 'Technology-Based Firms in the Innovation Process: Object of Theory and Research', in Koschatzky (1997a).

Knudsen, Jette Steen (1998), 'Breaking with Tradition: Liberalization of Service Trade in the EU', (Manuscript of paper prepared for delivery at the 1998 Annual Meeting of the American Political Science Association, 3–6 September).

Krasner, S.D. (1994), 'International Political Economy: Abiding Discord', *Review of International Political Economy*, 1:1, Spring.

Kreile, Michael (1978), 'West Germany: The Dynamics of Expansion', in Katzenstein (1978).

Krugman, P. (1996), *Pop Internationalism* (Cambridge, MA: MIT Press).

Kruse, Hans, Yurcik, William and Lessig, Lawrence (2001), 'The InterNAT: Policy Implications of the Internet Architecture Debate', in Compaine and Greenstein (2001).

Kubicek, Herbert (1998), 'Von der Angebots- zur Nachfrageförderung. Die Medien- und Kommunikationspolitik in und nach der Ära Kohl', *Blätter für deutsche und international Politik*, 9, September, 1093–1104.

Kulicke, Marianne (1997a), 'The Importance of Consulting in the German Federal Pilot Schemes for New Technology-Based Firms', in Koschatzky (1997a).

Kulicke, Marianne (1997b), 'The Promotion of New Technology-Based Firms in Germany', in Koschatzky (1997a).

Kulicke, Marianne (1997c), 'The Financing of New Technology-Based Firms', in Koschatzky (1997a).

Kulicke, Marianne et al (1993), *Chancen und Risiken junger Technologieunternehmen. Ergebnisse des Modellversuchs 'Förderung technologieorientierter Unternehmensgründungen'* (Heidelberg: Physica-Verlag).

Kulicke, Marianne and Wupperfeld, Udo (1996), *Beteiligungskapital für junge Technologieunternehmen. Ergebnisse eines Modellversuchs* (Heidelberg: Physica-Verlag).

Kurzer, Paulette (1993), *Business and Banking. Political Change and Economic Interdependence in Western Europe* (Ithaca: Cornell University Press).

Küster, Georg H. (1974), 'Germany', in Vernon (1974).

Landes, David S. (1969), *The Unbound Prometheus: Technological Change and Industrial Development in Western Europe from 1750 to the Present* (Cambridge: Cambridge University Press).

Lash, S. and Urry, J. (1994), *Economies of Sign and Space* (London: Sage Publications).

Lauder, G. and Westall, A. (n.d.) *Small Firms On-Line,* Commission on Public Policy and British Business, Issue Paper No. 6.

Laurence, Henry (1996), 'Regulatory Competition and the Politics of Financial Market Reform in Britain and Japan', *Governance: An International Journal of Policy and Administration*, 9:3, July, 311–41.

Leggewie, Claus (1997), 'What's Next? Junge Eliten in den USA', in Bude and Schleissing (1997).

Leggewie, Claus and Maar, Christa (eds) (1998), *Internet Politik. Von der Zuschauer- zur Beteiligungsdemokratie* (Köln: Bollmann Verlag).

Lehmbruch, Gerhard (1992), 'The Institutional Framework of German Regulation', in Dyson (1992).

Lehrer, Mark (2000), 'Has Germany Finally Fixed its High-tech Problem? The Recent Boom in German Technology-based Entrepreneurship', *California Management Review*, Summer.

Leiner, Barry M., Cerf, Vinton G., Clark, David D., Kahn, Robert E., Kleinrock, Leonard, Lynch, Daniel C., Postel, Jon, Roberts, Larry G. and Wolff, Stephen (1998), 'A Brief History of the Internet, Version 3.1, Dated: 20 February 98' (The manuscript can be accessed under http://info.isoc.org/internet/history/brief.html).

Leopold, Günter and Frommann, Holger (1998), *Eigenkapital für den Mittelstand. Venture Capital im In- und Ausland* (München: C.H. Beck).

Lessat, Vera, Hemer, Joachim, Eckerle, Tobias H., Licht, Georg and Kulicke, Marianne (1999), *Beteiligungskapital und technologieorientierte Unternehmensgründungen. Markt – Finanzierung – Rahmenbedingungen* (Wiesbaden: Gabler).

Lessig, Lawrence (1999), *Code, and Other Laws of Cyberspace* (New York: Basic Books).

Lessig, Lawrence (2001), *The Future of Ideas. The Fate of the Commons in a Connected World* (New York: Random House).

Licht, Georg, Hemer, Joachim and Kulicke, Marianne (1998), *Beteiligungskapital und technologieorientierte Existenzgründungen. Gutachten für das Bundesministerium für Wirtschaft und Technologie. Referat VI A5. Kurzfassung*, manuscript prepared by the Fraunhofer Institut für Systemtechnik und Innovationsforschung FhG-ISI and the Zentrum für Europäische Wirtschaftsforschung ZEW, Karlsruhe and Mannheim, December 1998.

Licht, Georg and Nerlinger, Eric (1997), 'Junge innovative Unternehmen in Europa: Ein internationaler Vergleich', in Harhoff (1997).

Licht, Georg and Nerlinger, Eric (1998), 'New Technology-based Firms in Germany: A Survey of Recent Evidence', *Research Policy*, 26, 1005–22.

Lindenberg, Andreas (2002), *Albtraum Neuer Markt. Eine brisante Internetstory vom Aufstieg und Fall eines Zukunftsunternehmens*, (München: FinanzBuch Verlag).

Litan, Robert E. and Rivlin, Alice M. (2001), *Beyond the Dot.coms. The Economic Promise of the Internet* (Washington, D.C.: Brookings Institution Press).

Lorenz, Tony (1985), *Venture Capital Today. A Guide to the Venture Capital Market in the United Kingdom* (Cambridge: Woodhead – Faulkner).

Lütz, Susanne (1996), 'The Revival of the Nation State? Stock Exchange Regulation in an Era of Internationalized Financial Markets', Max Planck Institute for the Study of Societies, December, manuscript (available on Columbia International Affairs Online: http://www.ciaonet. org/).

Lux, Harald (1995), *Der Internet-Markt in Deutschland. Provider und Dienstleister* (Heidelberg: dpunkt).

Lux, Harald and Heinen, Irene (1997), *Der Internet-Markt in Deutschland. Provider und Dienstleister. Erweiterte und aktualisierte Auflage* (Heidelberg: dpunkt).

Lux, Harald and Heinen, Irene (1999), 'Nettraffic.de. ISP watch – Businessreport Internet-Markt in Deutschland', Mimeograph (Heinen & Lux GbR).

MacDougall, Patricia P. (1989), 'International Versus Domestic Entrepreneurship: New Venture Strategic Behavior and Industry Structure', *Journal of Business Venturing*, 4, 387–400.

MacDougall, Patricia P. and Oviatt, Benjamin M. (1996), 'New Venture Internationalization, Strategic Change, and Performance: A Follow-up Study,' *Journal of Business Venturing*, 11, 23–40.

Mackewicz & Partner Management Consultants (N.D.), 'Venture Capital und Corporate Venture Capital vor dem Hintergrund notwendiger Finanzierungsalternativen für innovative Existenzgründungen und junge Technologieunternehmen' (München).

MacKie-Mason, Jeffrey K. and Varian Hal R. (1998), 'Economic FAQs About the Internet', in McKnight and Bailey (1998).

MacMillan, I.C., Kulow, D.M. and Khoylian, R. (1988), 'Venture Capitalists' Involvement in their Investments: Extent and Performance', *Journal of Business Venturing*, 4, 123–137.

Magaziner, Ira C. (1998), 'The Framework for Global Electronic Commerce: A Policy Perspective' (Interview) *Journal of International Affairs*, 51:2, Spring.

Maier, Charles S. (1975), *Recasting Bourgeois Europe. Stabilisation in France, Germany and Italy in the Decade after World War I* (Princeton, NJ: Princeton University Press).

Majone, G. (1998), 'The Rise of the Regulatory State in Europe', in Baldwin et al. (1998).

Malmsten, Ernst, Portanger, Erik and Drazin, Charles (2001), *boo hoo. A Dot.com Story from Concept to Catastrophe* (London: Random House Business Books).

Mason, Robin (1998), 'Internet Telephony and the International Accounting Rate System', *Telecommunications Policy*, 22:11, 931–44.

Mathews, Jessica T. (1997), 'Power Shift', *Foreign Affairs*, 76:1, January/February.

Mayntz, Renate (1980), 'Executive Leadership in Germany: Dispersion of Power or "Kanzlerdemokratie?"', in Rose and Suleiman (1980).

Mayntz, Renate and Derlien, Hans-Ulrich (1989), 'Party Patronage and Politicisation of the West German Administrative Elite 1970–1987 – Toward Hybridization?', *Governance: An International Journal of Policy and Administration*, 2:4, October, 384–404.

McKenna, Regis (1997), *Real Time. Preparing for the Age of the Never Satisfied Consumer* (Boston, MA: Harvard Business School Press).

McKnight, Lee W. and Bailey, Joseph P. (eds) (1998), *Internet Economics* (Cambridge, MA: MIT Press).

Milner, Helen V. (1997), *Interests, Institutions and Information. Domestic Politics and International Relations* (Princeton, NJ: Princeton University Press).

Milner, Helen V. and Keohane, Robert O. (1996), 'Internationalization and Domestic Politics: An Introduction' and 'A Conclusion', in Keohane and Milner (1996).

Milward, Alan S. (1984), *The Reconstruction of Western Europe 1945–1951* (Berkeley, CA: University of California Press).

Mokyr, Joel (1990), *The Lever of Riches. Technological Creativity and Economic Progress* (Oxford: Oxford University Press).

Mokyr, Joel (2000), 'Innovation and its Enemies: The Economic and Political Roots of Technological Inertia', in Olson and Kähkönen (2000).

Monopolkommission (2001), 'Wettbewerbsentwicklung bei Telekommunikation und Post: Unsicherheit und Stillstand. Sondergutachten der Monopolkommission gemäß § 81 Abs. 3 Telekommunikationsgesetz und §44 Postgesetz,' Report, Bonn, December.

Morgan Stanley Dean Witter Equity Research Europe (1999), 'The European Internet Report. Déjà Vu? Internet Usage Ramped Quickly in the US . . . Now It's Happening in Europe' (Manuscript, June 1999).

Morton, Michael S. Scott (ed.) (1991), *The Corporation of the 1990s.*

Information Technology and Organizational Transformation (Oxford: Oxford University Press).

Mowery, David (1995), 'The Practice of Technology Policy', in Stoneman (1995).

Mowery, David C. and Nelson, Richard R. (eds) (1999a), *Sources of Industrial Leadership. Studies of Seven Industries* (Cambridge: Cambridge University Press).

Mowery, David C. and Nelson, Richard R. (1999b), 'Introduction' and 'Explaining Industrial Leadership', in Mowery and Nelson (1999).

Mueller, Milton L. (1998), 'The Battle over Internet Domain Names', *Telecommunications Policy*, 22:2, 89–107.

Müller, Markus (2001), Reconstructing the New Regulatory State in Germany: Telecommunications, Broadcasting and Banking', *German Politics*, 10:3, December, 37–64.

Mullineux, A. (1994), *Small and Medium-Sized Enterprise (SME) Financing in the UK: Lessons from Germany* (London: Chameleon Press).

Negroponte, Nicholas (1995), *Being Digital* (New York: Alfred A. Knopf).

Nelson, Richard R. (ed.) (1993), *National Innovation Systems. A Comparative Analysis* (Oxford: Oxford University Press).

Nelson, Richard R. and Romer, P.M. (1996), 'Science, Economic Growth and Public Policy', in Smith and Barfield (1996).

Nelson, Richard R. and Rosenberg, Nathan (1993), 'Technical Innovation and National Systems', in Nelson (1993).

Nelson, Richard R. and Winter, S.G. (1982), *An Evolutionary Theory of Economic Change* (Cambridge, MA).

Neuman, W. Russell, McKnight, Lee and Solomon, Richard Jay (1997), *The Gordian Knot. Political Gridlock on the Information Highway* (Cambridge, MA: MIT Press).

Newhouse, John (1997), 'Europe's Rising Regionalism', *Foreign Affairs*, 76:1, January/February.

Noam, Eli M. (1992), *Telecommunications in Europe* (Oxford: Oxford University Press).

Noam, Eli M. (1994), 'Is Telecommunications Liberalization an Expansionary Process?', in Noam and Pogorel (1994).

Noam, Eli M. and Pogorel, Gerard (eds) (1994), *Asymmetric Deregulation: The Dynamics of Telecommunications Policy in Europe and the United States* (Norwood: Ablex Publishing Company).

Nörr, Knut Wolfgang and Starbatty, Joachim (1999), *Soll und Haben – 50 Jahre Soziale Marktwirtschaft* (Stuttgart: Lucius & Lucius).

North, Douglass C. (1966), *The Economic Growth of the United States. 1790–1860* (New York: W.W. Norton).

North, Douglass C. (1990), *Institutions, Institutional Change and Economic Performance* (Cambridge: Cambridge University Press).

Odaka, Konosuke and Sawai, Minoru (1999) *Small Firms, Large Concerns. The Development of Small Business in Comparative Perspective* (Oxford: Oxford University Press).

OECD – Organization for Economic Cooperation and Development (1996a), 'Internet Access Pricing in the OECD, 96-73b'.

OECD – Organization for Economic Cooperation and Development (1996b), 'Current Status of Communication Infrastructure Regulation Cable Television'.

OECD – Organization for Economic Cooperation and Development (1997a), 'Government Venture Capital for Technology-Based Firms, 97–201'.

OECD – Organization for Economic Cooperation and Development (1997b), 'Technology Incubators: Nurturing Small Firms, 97–202'.

OECD – Organization for Economic Cooperation and Development (1998a), 'France's Experience with the Minitel: Lessons for Electronic Commerce over the Internet, DST/ICCP/TISP(97)10/FINAL'.

OECD – Organization for Economic Cooperation and Development (1998b), *Economic Surveys: Sweden* (Paris: OECD).

OECD – Organization for Economic Cooperation and Development (1998c), *Economic Surveys: Netherlands* (Paris: OECD).

OECD – Organization for Economic Cooperation and Development (1998d), *OECD Economic Surveys: Germany* (Paris: OECD).

OECD – Organization for Economic Cooperation and Development (1999a), *Communications Outlook* (Paris: OECD).

OECD – Organization for Economic Cooperation and Development (1999b), *Economic Surveys: France* (Paris: OECD).

OECD – Organization for Economic Cooperation and Development (1999c), *Science, Technology and Industry Scoreboard, Benchmarking Knowledge-based Economies* (Paris: OECD).

OECD – Organization for Economic Cooperation and Development (1999d), *Economic Surveys: Sweden* (Paris: OECD).

OECD – Organization for Economic Cooperation and Development (2001a), *Communications Outlook* (Paris: OECD).

OECD – Organization for Economic Cooperations and Development (2001b), *The Development of Broadband Access in OECD Countries* (Paris: OECD).

Ohmae, Kenichi (1994), *The Borderless World. Power and Strategy in the Global Marketplace* (London: HarperCollins Publishers).

Olson, Mancur (2000), *Power and Prosperity. Outgrowing Communist and Capitalist Dictatorships* (New York: Basic Books).

Olson, Mancur and Kähkönen, Satu (eds) (2000), *A Not-So-Dismal Science. A Broader View of Economies and Societies* (Oxford: Oxford University Press).

Oxman, Jason (1999), 'The FCC and the Unregulation of the Internet', Office of Plans and Policy, Federal Communications Commission, Washington DC, OPP Working Paper No. 31, July.

Paterna, Mischa (1996), *Globalisierung der Telekommunikationsmärkte – Internationaliserungsstrategie der Netzbetreiber am Beispiel der Deutschen Telekom AG.* Dissertation der Universität St Gallen (Hallstadt: Rosch-Buch).

Pauly, Louis W. and Reich, Simon (1997), 'National Structures and Multinational Corporate Behavior: Enduring Differences in the Age of Globalization,' *International Organization*, 51, 1, Winter.

Penrose, E.T. (1966), *The Theory of the Growth of the Firm* (Oxford).

Perkins, Anthony B. and Perkins, Michael C. (1999), *The Internet Bubble, Inside the Overvalued World of High-Tech Stocks – And What You Need to Know to Avoid the Coming Shakeout* (New York: HarperCollins Publishers).

Peterson, John (1996), 'Research and Development Policy', in Kassim and Menon (1996).

Pettersson, Lars (1992) 'Sweden', in Dyker (1992).

Pleschak, Franz (1997a), 'Development Problems of Small Technology-Based Firms and Ways of Overcoming Them', in Koschatzky (1997a).

Pleschak, Franz (1997b), 'Technology and Incubator Centres as an Instrument of Regional Economic Promotion', in Koschatzky (1997a).

Porter, Michael E. (1990), *The Competitive Advantage of Nations* (London: Macmillan).

Porter, Michael E. (2001), 'Strategy and the Internet', *Harvard Business Review*, March, 63–78.

Posner, Dirk (1996), *Early Stage Finanzierungen. Spannungsfeld zwischen Gründern, Investoren und staatlichen Rahmenbedingungen* (Wiesbaden: Gabler).

Pospischil, Rudolf (1993), 'Reorganization of European Telecommunications. The Cases of British Telecom, France Télécom and Deutsche Telekom', *Telecommunications Policy*, November, 603–21.

Pospischil, Rudolf (1998), 'Fast Internet', *Telecommunications Policy*, 22:9, 745–55.

Putnam, Robert D. with Leonardi, Robert and Nanetti, Raffaella Y. (1993), *Making Democracy Work: Civic Traditions in Northern Italy* (Princeton, NJ: Princeton University Press).

Quah, Danny Tyson (1997), 'The Weightless Economy: Nintendo and Heavy Metal', *CEP's CentrePiece*, 2:1, February, 25–7.

Quah, Danny Tyson (1998), 'Devise and Conquer', *Information Strategy* (*The Economist Group*), May, 18–21.

Rabach, Eileen and Kim, Eun Mee (1994), 'Where is the Chain in Commodity Chains? The Service Sector Nexus', in Gereffi and Korzeniewicz (1994).

Raymond, Eric S. (1999), *The Cathedral and the Bazaar, Musings on Linux and Open Source by an Accidental Revolutionary* (Sebastopol, California: O'Reilly).

Reich, Robert B. (1991), *The Work of Nations. Preparing Ourselves for 21st Century Capitalism* (London: Simon & Schuster).

Reid, Robert H. (1997), *Architects of the Web. 1,000 Days that Built the Future of Business* (New York: John Wiley & Sons).

RegTP – Regulierungsbehörde für Telekommunikation und Post (1999a), *Jahresbericht 1998*, Bonn: Referat für Presse und Öffentlichkeitsarbeit.

RegTP – Regulierungsbehörde für Telekommunikation und Post (1999b), *Telekommunikations- und Postmarkt im Jahre 1999, Stand: 30. Juni 1999*, Bonn: Referat für Presse und Öffentlichkeitsarbeit.

RegTP – Regulierungsbehörde für Telekommunikation und Post (2000), *Halbjahresbericht 2000*, Bonn: Referat für Presse und Öffentlichkeitsarbeit.

RegTP – Regulierungsbehörde für Telekommunikation und Post (2001), *Jahresbericht 2001*, Bonn: Pressestelle.

Robertson, Roland (1992), *Globalization. Social Theory and Global Culture* (London: Sage).

Robischon, Tobias (1999), *Telekommunikationspolitik im deutschen Einigungsprozess. Steuerung und Eigendynamik sektoraler Transformation* (Frankfurt am Main: Campus Verlag).

Rose, Richard and Suleiman, Ezra N. (eds) (1980), *Presidents and Prime Ministers* (Washington, DC: American Enterprise Institute for Public Policy Research).

Rosen, Sherwin (1981), 'The Economics of Superstars', *The American Economic Review*, December, 845–58.

Rosenau, James N. (1990), *Turbulence in World Politics. A Theory of Change and Continuity* (Brighton: Harvester Wheatsheaf).

Rosenberg, Nathan (1982), *Inside the Black Box* (Cambridge: Cambridge University Press).

Rosenberg, Nathan (1994), 'Joseph Schumpeter: Radical Economist', in Shinoya and Perlman (1994).

Rosenbloom, Richard S. and Spencer, William J. (eds) (1996), *Engines of Innovation. US Industrial Research at the End of an Era* (Boston, MA: Harvard Business School Press).

Rothwell, R. (1986), 'The Role of Small Firms in Technological Innovation', in Curran et al. 1986.

Rothwell, R. and Zegveld, W. (1982), *Innovation and the Small and Medium Sized Firm; Their Role in Employment and in Economic Change* (London).

Ruigrok, Winfried, Pettigrew, Andrew, Peck, Simon and Whittington (1999), 'Corporate Restructuring and New Forms of Organizing: Evidence from Europe', *Management International Review*, 39:2, Special issue, 41–64.

Sachverständigenrat zur Begutachtung der gesamtwirtschaftlichen Entwicklung (1997), *Jahresgutachten 1997/98. Wachstum, Beschäftigung, Währungsunion- Orientierungen für die Zukunft*, Deutscher Bundestag, Drucksache 13/ 9090.

Sachverständigenrat zur Begutachtung der gesamtwirtschaftlichen Entwicklung (1998), *Jahresgutachten 1998/99. Vor weitreichenden Entscheidungen*, Deutscher Bundestag, Drucksache 14/73, 20 November.

Sally, Razeen (1994), 'Multinational Enterprises, Political Economy and Institutional Theory: Domestic Embeddedness in the Context of Internationalization', *Review of International Political Economy*, 1:1, Spring.

Sally, Razeen (1995), *States and Firms; Multinational Enterprises in Institutional Competition* (London: Routledge).

Sally, Razeen (1998), *Classical Liberalism and International Economic Order. Studies in Theory and Intellectual History* (London: Routledge).

Samuelson, Pamela (1998), 'Foreword', *Berkeley Technology Law Journal*, 13:3, Autumn

Sassen, Saskia (1996), *Losing Control? Sovereignty in an Age of Globalization* (New York: Columbia University Press).

Sassen, Saskia (1998), *Globalization and its Discontents* (New York: New Press).

Sassen, Saskia (2000), *Cities in a World Economy, Second Edition* (London: Pine Forge Press).

Saxenian, AnnaLee (1994), *Regional Advantage. Culture and Competition in Silicon Valley and Route 128* (Cambridge, MA: Harvard University Press).

Scharpf, Fritz W. (1994), 'Community and Autonomy: Multi-Level Policy Making in the European Union', *Journal of European Public Policy* 1:2, Autumn, 219–42.

Schefold, Bertram (1994), *Wirtschaftsstile. Band 1: Studien zum Verhältnis von Ökonomie und Kultur* (Frankfurt am Main: Fischer).

Schefold, Bertram (1995), *Wirtschaftsstile. Band 2: Studien zur ökonomischen Theorie und zur Zukunft der Technik* (Frankfurt am Main: Fischer).

Schendel, D. (1996a), 'Editor's Introduction to the 1996 Summer Special Issue: Evolutionary Perspectives on Strategy', *Strategic Management Journal*, 17, Summer Special Issue.

Schendel, D. (1996b), ' Editor's Introduction to the 1996 Winter Special Issue: Knowledge and the Firm', *Strategic Management Journal*, 17, Winter Special Issue.

Schiller, Robert J. (2000), *Irrational Exuberance* (Princeton, NJ: Princeton University Press).

Schmidt, Susanne K. (1998), 'Commission Activism: Subsuming Telecommunications and Electricity under European Competition Law', *Journal of European Public Policy*, 5:1, 169–84.

Schmidt, Susanne K. (1991), 'Taking the Long Road to Liberalization. Telecommunications Reform in the Federal Republic of Germany', *Telecommunications Policy*, June, 209–22.

Schneider, Volker (1989), *Technikentwicklung zwischen Politik und Markt: Der Fall Bildschirmtext* (Frankfurt am Main: Campus Verlag).

Schneider, Volker (1997), 'Evolution im Cyberspace: Die Anpassung nationaler Bildschirmtext-Systeme an das Internet', in Werle and Lang (1997).

Schneider, Volker (1999), *Staat und technische Kommunikation. Die politische Entwicklung der Telekommunikation in den USA, Japan, Großbritannien, Deutschland, Frankreich und Italien* (Opladen: Westdeutscher Verlag).

Schumpeter, Joseph A. (1934), *The Theory of Economic Development; An Inquiry Into Profits, Capital, Credit, Interest and the Business Cycle* (Cambridge, MA).

Schumpeter, Joseph A. (1975), *Capitalism, Socialism and Democracy* (New York: Harper Colophon).

Schulz, Günther (1999), *Geschäft mit Wort und Meinung. Medienunternehmer seit dem 18. Jahrhundert. Büdinger Forschungen zur Sozialgeschichte* (München: Harald Boldt Verlag im R. Oldenbourg Verlag).

Shapiro, Carl and Varian, Hal R. (1999), *Information Rules. A Strategic Guide to the Network Economy* (Boston, MA: Harvard Business School Press).

Shinoya, Yuichi and Perlman, Mark (eds) (1994), *Schumpeter in the History of Ideas* (Ann Arbor, MI: University of Michigan Press).

Shonfield, Andrew (1969), *Modern Capitalism. The Changing Balance of Public and Private Power* (London: Oxford University Press).

Sidak, J. Gregory, Engel, Christoph and Knieps, Günter (eds) (2001), *Competition and Regulation in Telecommunications. Examining Germany and America* (Dordrecht: Kluwer).

Singh, J.P. (1999), *Leapfrogging Development? The Political Economy of Telecommunications Restructuring* (Albany, NY: State University of New York Press).

Sjögren, Hans (1998) 'Scandinavia' in Foley (1998).

Smith, Gordon (1976), 'West Germany and the Politics of Centrality,' *Government and Opposition*, 11:4, 387–407.

Smith, L.R. and Barfield, C.E. (eds) (1996), *Science, Economic Growth and Public Policy* (Washington, DC).

Sobel, Andrew C. (1994), *Domestic Choices, International Markets. Dismantling National Barriers and Liberalizing Securities Markets* (Ann Arbor, MI: The University of Michigan Press).

Soete, Luc and Kamp, Karin (n.d.), 'The Bit Tax: Taxing Value in the Emerging Information Society', MERIT, University of Maastricht, manuscript (http://meritbbs.unimaas.nl/cybertax/cybertax.html).

de Sola Pool, Ithiel (1983), *Technologies of Freedom* (Cambridge, MA: Belknap Press of Harvard University Press).

Sontheimer, Kurt and Bleek, Wilhelm (1998), *Grundzüge des politischen Systems in Deutschland* (Völlig überarbeitete Neuausgabe) (München: Piper Verlag).

Spree, Reinhard (ed.) (2001), *Geschichte der deutschen Wirtschaft im 20. Jahrhundert* (München: C. H. Beck).

Starbatty, Joachim (1999), 'Strukturpolitik im Konzept der Sozialen Marktwirtschaft?', in Nörr and Starbatty (1999).

Steier, L. and Greenwood, R. (1995), 'Venture Capitalist Relationships in the Deal Structuring and Post-Investment Stages of New Firm Creation', *Journal of Management Studies*, 32:3, May.

Steinmo, S., Thelen, K. and Longstreth, F. (1992), *Structuring Politics; Historical Institutionalism in Comparative Analysis* (Cambridge: Cambridge University Press).

Stolper, Wolfgang F. (1994), *Joseph Alois Schumpeter. The Public Life of a Private Man* (Princeton, NJ: Princeton University Press).

Stoneman, Paul (ed.) (1995), *Handbook of the Economics of Innovation and Technological Change* (Oxford: Blackwell).

Stopford, John M. (1997), 'Implications for National Governments', in Dunning (1997).

Stopford, John M., Strange, Susan and Henley, John S. (1991), *Rival States, Rival Firms. Competition for World Market Shares* (Cambridge: Cambridge University Press).

Storey, D.J. and Tether, B.S. (1998a), 'New Technology-Based Firms in the European Union: An Introduction', *Research Policy* 26, 933–46.

Storey, D.J. and Tether, B.S. (1998b), 'Public policy measures to support new technology-based firms in the European Union', *Research Policy*, 26, 1037–57.

Strange, Susan (1988), *States and Markets* (London: Pinter).

Strange, Susan (1994), 'Wake up, Krasner! The World Has Changed', *Review of International Political Economy*, 1:2, Summer.

Strange, Susan (1997), 'An International Political Economy Perspective', in Dunning (1997).

Streeck, Wolfgang (ed.) (1994), *Staat und Verbände* (*Politische Vierteljahresschrift*, 35. Jahrgang, Sonderheft 25) (Opladen: Westdeutscher Verlag).

Swire, Peter P. and Litan, Robert E. (1998), *None of Your Business. World Data Flows, Electronic Commerce and the European Privacy Directive* (Washington, DC: Brookings Institution Press).

Tapscott, Don (1996), *The Digital Economy. Promise and Peril in the Age of Networked Intelligence* (New York: McGraw-Hill).

Tapscott, Don, Ticoll, David and Lowy, Alex (2000), *Digital Capital. Harnessing the Power of Business Webs* (Boston, MA:Harvard Business School Press).

tbg – Technologie-Beteiligungs-Gesellschaft mbH der Deutschen Ausgleichsbank (1997), 'Junge High-Tech Unternehmen auf Erfolgskurs. Ergebnisse einer tbg-Umfrage', Pamphlet dated November.

tbg – Technologie-Beteiligungs-Gesellschaft mbH der Deutschen Ausgleichsbank (n.d., ca. 1997), 'Technologie und Beteiligungen. Eine Bilanz der tbg'.

Thatcher, Mark (1996), 'The European Community and High Technology: The Importance of the National and International Context', in Kassim and Menon (1996).

Thatcher, Mark (1999), *The Politics of Telecommunications. National Institutions, Convergence and Change in Britain and France* (Oxford: Oxford University Press).

Thimm, Alfred (1992), *America's Stake in European Telecommunication Policies* (Westport, CT: Quorum Books).

Thomas, Frank (1995), *Telefonieren in Deutschland. Organisatorische, technische und räumliche Entwicklung eines großtechnischen Systems* (Frankfurt am Main: Campus).

Thurow, Lester C. (2000), *Building Wealth. The New Rules for Individuals, Companies and Nations in a Knowledge-Based Economy* (New York: HarperBusiness).

Timmons, J.A. and Bygrave, W.D. (1986), Venture Capital's Role in Financing Innovation for Economic Growth', *Journal of Business Venturing*, 1, 161–76.

Trischler, Helmuth and vom Bruch, Rüdiger (1999), *Forschung für den Markt. Geschichte der Fraunhofer-Gesellschaft* (München: C.H. Beck).

Turner, Louis and Hodges, Michael (1991), *Global Shakeout. World Market Competition – The Challenges for Business and Government* (London: Century Business).

Tüselmann, Heinz-Josef (1998), 'Standort Deutschland: German Foreign

Investment – Exodus of German Industry and Export of Jobs?' *Journal of World Business*, 33:3.

UNCTAD Division on Transnational Corporations and Investment, United Nations Conference on Trade and Development (1995), *World Investment Report 1995. Transnational Corporations and Competitiveness* (New York: United Nations).

US Department of Commerce (1998), *The Emerging Digital Economy* (Springfield: National Technical Information Services).

US Government Working Group on Electronic Commerce (1998), 'First Annual Report', November.

VATM – Verband der Anbieter von Telekommunikations- und Mehrwertdiensten e.V. (2001), 'Jahresbericht. Überblick über die Entwicklung im deutschen Telekommunikationsmarkt im Jahre 2001', Annual Report, Cologne, December.

Vernon, Raymond (ed.) (1974), *Big Business and the State. Changing Relations in Western Europe* (Cambridge, MA: Harvard University Press).

Visser, Jelle and Hemerijck, Anton (1997), *A Dutch Miracle, Job Growth, Welfare Reform and Corporatism in the Netherlands* (Amsterdam: Amsterdam University Press).

Vogel, David (1995), *Trading Up. Consumer and Environmental Regulation in a Global Economy* (Cambridge, MA: Harvard University Press).

Vogel, Steven K. (1996), *Freer Markets, More Rules. Regulatory Reform in Advanced Industrial Countries* (Ithaca, NY: Cornell University Press).

Vogelsang, Ingo (1996), 'Studie des VTM "Kosten des Ortsnetzes" erstellt durch Prof. Ingo Vogelsang, Mai 1996'.

Waesche, Niko (1999a), 'Missionare und Evangelisten. Unternehmer der online-Medien 1991–1995', in Schulz (1999).

Waesche, Niko (1999b), 'Die Chancen der Neuen. Das Internet und die Formierung eines Dienstleistungssektors in Deutschland 1995–1998', *Jahrbuch für Wirtschaftsgeschichte*, 1, 185–206.

Waesche, Niko (2003) 'Rational Exuberance. Wirtschaftsgeschichtliche Kommentare zu Finanzeuphorie und Gründeroptimismus während der New Economy', excerpts of the paper can be found in: Zerdick, et al. (2003).

Wallerstein, I. (1979), *The Capitalist World Economy* (Cambridge).

Waters, Malcolm (1995), *Globalization* (London: Routledge).

Webber, D. (1994), 'The Decline and Resurgence of the "German Model"; The Treuhandanstalt and Privatization Politics in East Germany', *Journal of European Public Policy*, 1:2.

Wengenroth, Ulrich (1999), 'Small Scale Business in Germany. The Flexible Element of Economic Growth' in Odaka and Sawai (1999).

Welfens, Paul J.J. and Graack, Cornelius (1996), *Telekommunikationswirt-schaft. Deregulierung, Privatisierung und Internationalisierung* (Berlin: Springer-Verlag).

Welfens, Paul J.J. and Jungmittag, Andre (1999), 'Auswirkungen einer Internet-Flat-Rate auf Wachstum und Beschäftigung in Deutschland', EIIW-Discussion Paper 75, Potsdam, 6 December.

Welfens, Paul J. J. and Jungmittag, Andre (2002), *Internet, Telekomliberali-sierung und Wirtschaftswachstum. 10 Gebote für ein digitales Wirtschaftswunder* (Berlin: Springer-Verlag).

Welzk, Stefan (1998), 'Dichtung und Wahrheit in der Reformdebatte. Zur Steuerbelastung deutscher Kapitalgesellschaften und ihren Gestaltungsmöglichkeiten', *Blätter für deutsche und international Politik*, 9, September, 1080–92.

Werle, Raymund and Lang, Christa (eds) (1997), *Modell Internet? Entwicklungsperspektiven neuer Kommunikationsnetze* (Frankfurt am Main: Campus).

Wigand, R., Picot, A. and Reichwald, R. (1997), *Information, Organization and Management. Expanding Markets and Corporate Boundaries* (Chichester: John Wiley & Sons).

Williamson, Oliver E. and Winter, Sidney G. (1992), *The Nature of the Firm: Origins, Evolution and Development* (Oxford: Oxford University Press).

Wilson, Rob and Dissanayake, Wimal (ed.) (1996), *Global – Local. Cultural Production and the Transnational Imaginary* (Durham).

Winston, Brian (1998), *Media Technology and Society. A History: From the Telegraph to the Internet* (London: Routledge).

Wischermann, C. (1992), *Preußischer Staat und westfälische Unternehmer zwischen Spätmerkantilismus und Liberalismus* (Köln: Böhlau).

Wischermann, C. (1993), 'Der Property- Rights- Ansatz und die "neue" Wirtschaftsgeschichte', *Geschichte und Gesellschaft*, 19, 239–58.

Wupperfeld, Udo (1996), *Management und Rahmenbedingungen von Beteiligungsgesellschaften auf dem deutschen Seed-Capital Markt* (Peter Lang: Frankfurt am Main).

Wupperfeld, Udo (1997), 'The Venture Capital Market in Germany', in Koschatzky (1997a).

Yoffie, David B. and Cusumano, Michael A. (1999), 'Judo Strategy. The Competitive Dynamics of Internet Time', *Harvard Business Review*, January – February, 71–81.

Zerdick, Axel et al. (1999), *Die Internet-Ökonomie. Strategien für die digi-tale Wirtschaft* (European Communication Council Report) (Berlin: Springer-Verlag).

Zerdick, Axel, Picot, Arnold, Schrape, Klaus, Silverstone, Roger,

Burgelmann, Jean-Claude, Feldmann, Valerie, Heger, Dominik and Wolff, Caroline (2003) e-Merging Media. Digitalisierung der Medienwirtschaft (Springer Verlag: Berlin).

Ziegler, J. Nicholas (1997), *Governing Ideas. Strategies for Innovation in France and Germany* (Ithaca, NY: Cornell University Press).

Zorn, Werner (1998), 'Verfehlte Entwicklung. Telekommunikationspolitik in Deutschland', in Leggewie and Maar (1998).

Zysman, John (1983), *Governments, Markets and Growth; Financial Systems and the Politics of Industrial Change* (Ithaca, NY: Cornell University Press).

Index

Titles of publications appear in *italics*.

Abelhauser, W. 103, 104, 128
access costs *see* costs, internet access
Ahlvarsson, O. 235
Amazon.com 45, 48

bilateral flows and US internet
    dominance 53–5
bit tax 71–2
bootstrapping, Germany 179–80
Börnsen, A. 111, 157
Borrus, M. 79
Boxman 223
Btx 105–6, 123, 152–3
business-to-business (B2B) exchanges
    176

cable TV, Germany 148–51
California Effect 83, 84
capital gains taxation 213
Cartel Law, Germany 102–3
Casino Capitalism 35
Castells, M. 7, 8, 35, 43
Chandler, A.D. 46
Christensen, C. 45, 137, 182
city carriers, telecommunications
    investment 160–61
Clement, W. 112–13
Clinton administration, and internet
    development 64–5
Cohen, S.S. 22
Communications Outlook 141
competition
  policy 84
  telecommunications 137–9, 202–6,
    250–52
    Deutsche Telekom 155–8
    see also liberalization
computer networks *see* data networks
consumers, integration into network
    42–3

corporate taxes, Germany 100
corporatism 103–4
Cortada, J.W. 46
cost challenge, telecommunications
    137–9
costs, internet access 139–44
  and demand 44
  Deutsche Telekom 162–3
  and distance insensitivity 66–8
  Europe 199–203
  Germany 134–6
  T-Online 153–5
customized ordering 43
Cusumano, M.A. 6

data networks 34–40
  international regulation 63–8
  see also internet
data protection, Europe 74–5
debt, Deutsche Telekom 142–3
decentralization of innovation 7–8
DECT 110–11
Delaware Effect 82
demand for internet services
  Germany 182–3
  transnational 41–5
deregulation, telecommunications see
    liberalization,
    telecommunications
Dery, M. 9
Deutsche Telekom AG (DTAG) 26
  and cable TV 148–51
  and competition 137–9, 155–8,
    162–4
  debt 142–3
  and internet access 133–44, 151–5,
    162–4
  and liberalization 107–13
  network infrastructure 144–8
Deutsches Forschungsnetz (DFN) 106–7

Dicken, P. 39
digital mobile telephony standard
    (GSM) 78
digital signatures 76–7
    law, Germany 114
distance insensitivity, internet 63–8
Dittberner, K.-H. 141
domain name system (DNS) 81
Donges, J. 106
Dwyer, P. 166
Dyson, E. 5, 7
Dyson, K. 102, 115

E*TRADE 48
EASDAQ 207–8
EDI (electronic data interchange) 42
EED (European Enterprises
    Development SA) 207
electronic commerce
    firms 48, 215, 220–23, 224
    regulation 80–85
electronic data interchange (EDI) 42
embeddedness 17
encryption legislation, US 75
encryption system skills, Germany
    185–6
enterprise resource planning (ERP)
    36
entrepreneurship 45–51
    Europe 3–4, 23–5
    Germany 22–3, 174–87
equity investment support, Germany
    118–9
Ergas, H. 23, 88
Erhard, L. 102, 104
Eucken, W. 126
Europe
    data protection 74–5
    internet access pricing 199–206
    internet demand 196–9
    internet ventures 191–2, 196–9,
        213–31
    venture capital funding 206–12
    see also individual countries
European Enterprises Development
    SA (EED) 207
European Venture Capital Association
    (EVCA) 207
evolutionary change 15
evolutionary economics 13

FDI *see* foreign direct investment
Fields, G. 22
finance *see* funding
financial controls, internet 72
financial industry, networks 35–6
financial services, regulation 83
foreign direct investment (FDI)
    Germany 101
    and globalization 37–8
*Framework for Global Electronic
    Commerce, A* 64–5, 71
France
    online network 39, 192
    portal ventures 223–4, 226
    web developers 218
Freer Markets, More Rules 83
Freytag, A. 111–12
funding, internet ventures 49–51,
    206–12
    Germany 118–21, 177–81

German Development Bank 118–19,
    122
Germany
    digital signatures legislation 77,
        114–15
    economy 95–101
    electronic commerce firms 220–21,
        224
    internet entrepreneurship 3–4, 22–3,
        24–5, 174–87, 249–50
    internet uptake 182–3, 196
    internet ventures 213–26
    multimedia legislation 113–18, 122–3
    policy-making 101–4
    research network 106–7
    telecommunications liberalization
        107–13, 123–4, 204–6
    venture capital 118–21, 207–11
    videotex system 105–6, 123
    web developers 218, 224
Gerpott, T.J. 140, 145
Gilder, G. 5, 9
Giussani, B. 238
globalisation, effect on individual 43–4
Glotz, P. 145
Google 56
Gore, A. 65
government policy
    Germany 122–4

innovation support, Germany 118–21
internet development 19–20, 64–5,
133–5
technology, Germany 105–7
telecommunications 96–7, 107–13
see also legislation, regulation
Greenspan, A. 24, 27
GSM digital mobile telephony
standard 78, 252

Haaren, K. van 112–13
Hagström, P. 57–8
Hall, P. 11
Harvey, D. 8, 60
Helleiner, E. 88–9
Hellman, T. 188
Hills, J. 68
Hirst, P. 39
historical institutionalism 11
Hodgson, G. 10, 11, 15
horizontality of internet 243–4
Humphreys, P. 109, 125

income taxes, Germany 100
industrial cluster-based theory 13–14
industry, network-based services 36
Information and Communication
Services Act, Germany 113–18,
122
infrastructure, network, Germany
144–8, 163–4
innovation
centres 7–8
policy, Germany 97–8
Silicon Valley 22
small firms 21–2, 79–81
see also entrepreneurship
Innovator's Dilemma, The 137
institutional reform, Sweden 193–5
institutionalist theory 10–16, 240–42
intellectual property rights 75–6
international networks regulation
66–8
international political economy (IPE)
17–18
International Telecommunications
Union (ITU) 66
internationalization
German internet start-ups 181–2
internet 33–4, 244

internet
access costs *see* costs, internet access
business models 214–26
domain name system (DNS) 81
entrepreneurship *see*
entrepreneurship
software companies, Germany 176
standards 85–6
subsidy, USA 69–70
tariffs 71–4
technology 1–2, 40–41
see also telecommunications
and telecommunications policy
133–64
unregulation 63–87
uptake
Europe 196–9
Germany 182–3
USA dominance 52–6, 68–70
ventures
Europe 213–30
Germany 174–87
and regulation 63–4, 79–81
investment
internet ventures
Europe 206–12, 226, 229
Germany 177–81
USA 46, 49–51
network infrastructure 67, 158–62
see also venture capital investment
ISDN, Germany 146–8
Isenberg, D. 58–9
ITU (International
Telecommunications Union) 66

Jäger, B. 111–12
Janz, W. 233
Jobpilot AG (Jobs and Adverts AG)
220–21
Jungmittag, A. 2

Katzenstein, P. 102, 195
Kelly, K. 6, 7, 8, 15, 241
Kenney, M. 47
KfW (Kreditanstalt für Wiederaufbau)
118–19, 121, 122
knowledge management skills,
Germany 185
knowledge workers 43
Kohl, H. 102

Kreditanstalt für Wiederaufbau (KfW)
    118–19, 121, 122
Kühler, S. 153

Laurence, H. 83
leased lines 67
legislation, Germany 101–4
    multimedia 97, 113–18, 122
Lerbinger, P. 233
Lessig, L. 10, 40
liberalization, telecommunications
    Germany 107–13, 123–4, 204–6
    and internet pricing 202–3
    and internet ventures 2–3, 230–31
    Sweden 203–4, 205–6
    see also competition
Litan, R. 73, 79, 82
local loop, and internet development
    2–3
    Germany 110–11, 134–5, 163
Lux, H. 145, 146, 154
Lycos 48

Mackie-Mason, J.K. 165
Magaziner, I.C. 71, 73
Maier, C.S. 103
Majone, G. 84
management skills, German internet
    entrepreneurs 184
Mannesmann AG, telecommunications
    investment 159–60
Mannesmann Arcor 162
market capitalisation,
    telecommunications companies
    160
Mayer, M. 110–12
Meister, M. 114
Milner, H. 12, 19
Minitel 39, 223–4, 226
mixed play portals 221–2, 248
MobilCom 161–2
mobile telephony standards 78
Mokyr, J. 13
Morin, P. 234
Möschel, W. 124, 161
Mosdorf, S. 113, 135
Mowery, D.C. 18
Müller, M. 112
Müller, W. 112
multilateral flows, internet 52–3

Multimedia Law, Germany 97, 113–18,
    122

Nation Transformed by Information, A.
    46
national carriers, telecommunications
    investment 159–60
national online networks 39–40
Negroponte, N. 163
Nelson, R.R. 13, 18
Netherlands
    taxation and entrepreneurs 212–13
    web developers 218–19
network
    effects 7
    externalities 51
    thinking 5–7, 9–10, 14–16, 241–2
networks
    development 34–40
    infrastructure, Deutsche Telekom
        144–8
    international regulation 66–8
Neuer Markt 207–9, 239
New Rules for the New Economy 241
Noam, E. 71, 84
North, D.C. 11, 12

Ohmae, K. 44
Olson, M. 11, 12
open but owned systems 79
open technology, internet 40–41
options taxation 213

packet switched networks 137–8
penetration, internet 49
Pogorel, G. 88
policy convergence 87
policy-making 19–22
    Germany 101–4
political economy, and internet
    development 245–7
polyarchy 19
portal sites 48, 215
    Europe 223–4, 226
    Germany 176
Porter, M.E. 13–14, 49
pricing, internet *see* costs, internet
    access
private equity finance, Germany
    178

public telecommunication operators
(PTOs) 20–21
punctuated equilibria 13
pure play electronic commerce firms
220–23, 247–8
Puri, M. 188

Quah, D.T. 7, 55–6

rational choice institutionalism 11
Rechtsstaat 102
and multimedia legislation 113–18
refraction 17–18, 95–6, 240–43
RegTP 107–8, 155–7
regulation
electronic commerce 80–85
and innovation 79–81
international networks 66–8
and internet 70–76
regulator, German telecommunications
107–8, 155–7
Reich, R. 43
Request for Comments (RFC) 40
research network, Germany 106–7
resource-based innovation research 13
Reulecke, L. 117–18
Riesenhuber, H. 107, 122
Rise of the Regulatory State in Europe,
The 84
Roemer, H.P. 233
Rosenau, J.N. 43
Rule of Law, Germany *see* Rechtsstaat

Sally, R. 17
SAP 36–7
Sassen, S. 8, 89
Scharpf, F. 115
Schiller, K. 102
Schneider, V. 105
Schumpeter, J. 15, 240
Schwarz-Schilling, C. 109
Scott Morten, M.S. 60
second-generation companies 226–30
sectoral innovations systems research
13
self-regulation, US 73–4
Silicon Valley 3, 22
Sjörgen, H. 195
SKF, computer network use 36
skills, German internet ventures 184–6

small and medium sized enterprises
(SMEs)
funding, Germany 118–21
innovation capacity 21–2
and regulation 79–81
Sobel, A. 83
social programmes, impact on German
economy 98–101
sociology
and globalization 6
and internet use 43–4
Soete, L. 71
software agent skills, Germany 185
Sommer, R. 140, 158
standards, technological 76–9, 85–6
GSM 78, 252
see also regulation
Starbatty, J. 106
start-up firms *see* internet ventures
Stopford, J.M. 44
Strange, S. 35, 44
stupid networks 41
subsidy financing 119
subsidy, US internet 69–70
superstar economics 55–6
supply, internet services 45–51
Sweden
economy 194–5
electronic commerce firms 221–3
internet penetration 196–9
internet ventures 192, 213–26,
248–9
portal ventures 224
taxation 212–13
telecommunications liberalization
203–4, 205–6
venture capital 212
web developers 218–20, 224
Swire, P. 73, 79, 82
symbolic analysts 43

tariffs, internet 71–4
Tauss, J. 72, 135
taxation 100, 212–13
technological standards 76–9, 251–2
Technologie-Beteiligungs-Gesellschaft
(tbg) 118–19, 122
technology policy, Sweden 194–5
technology skills, German internet
ventures 184–6

telecommunications
  cost challenge 137–9
  costs 66–7
  Germany 95–8, 107–13
    see also Deutsche Telekom
  infrastructure investment 158–62
  liberalization *see* liberalization,
    telecommunications
  networks, regulation 66–8
  policy and internet development
    64–5
  standards 78, 252
  start-ups, investment 161
  subsidy, US, and internet 69–70
Thatcher, M. 87
The Future of Ideas 40
Thimm, A. 77
Thompson, G. 39
TISS (Travel Information Software
  Systems) 43, 188–9, 220–21
T-Online 151–5 *see also* Btx
trade unregulation and internet
  development 64
trademark law 81
transnational demand for internet
  services 41–5
Tüselmann, H.-J. 125

UK *see* United Kingdom
UMTS 78
unbundling 134–5, 157–8
Ungerer, H. 150
unification, impact on German
  economy 98–101
United Kingdom
  cable TV 148–9
  pure play ventures 222–3
United States
  digital signatures legislation 77
  encryption legislation 75
  government role in internet
    development 63–5

intellectual property rights 75–6
internet dominance 52–6, 68–70
internet entrepreneurship 24
internet subsidy 69–70
unmetered access 201–2
venture capital funding 49–51
unmetered access 201–2
unregulation, internet 63–87
US *see* United States

Varian, H.R. 165
venture capital investment
  Europe 206–12, 226, 229
  Germany 118–21, 177–81
  USA 46, 49–51
videotex, Germany 105–6, 123,
  152–3
Vogel, D. 83, 84
Vogel, S. 83, 129

web development companies 47–8
  Europe 214–15, 218–20, 224
  Germany 176
Weber, M. 15, 240
Welfens, P.J.J. 2
Winter, S.G. 13
wireless local loop *see* local loop
Witte Commission 109
Wolf, D. 135
World Wide Web 34
WorldCom 138
WTO and internet regulation 80

Yahoo! 48
Yoffie, D.B. 6

Zerdick, A. 117
Ziegler, J.N. 126
Zorn, W. 106, 107
Zuschussfinanzierung (subsidy
  financing) 119
Zysman, J. 79